The Book of the
A4 PACIFICS

By
Peter J Coster

IRWELL PRESS

First published in the United Kingdom in 2005
and reprinted in 2008
by Irwell Press Limited, 59A, High Street, Clophill,
Bedfordshire MK45 4BE
01525 861888
www.irwellpress.co.uk
Printed by Konway Press

CONTENTS

PREFACE

APPENDICES:

SILVER KING with the southbound 'Flying Scotsman' crossing the Royal Border Bridge on May 11th 1938. It is likely that through running had just started, in which case the use of this particular engine was out of the ordinary. The coaching stock is in excellent condition; presumably it is the 1928 set, as the new train was introduced later in the year. The photographer's vantage point is intriguing, since Berwick's advance starter is only 200 yards ahead. The A4 has her original A4 corridor tender No.5591.

PREFACE

As a very small boy I can remember a little of my first railway book. It had a title something like *The Boy's Book of Trains* and, like my contemporaries, I would pore over the pages of British, European and Transatlantic trains, becoming almost word perfect. One illustration stood out, which I later learnt was staged by the LNER Publicity Department at Waterworks Sidings at Wood Green, which I have seen repeated many times since. It showed three A4s, each at the head of a rake of coaching stock, in echelon, with towering exhausts, with an A3 farthest away from the main line, accelerating away. It was a fine photograph, dating back to the days when public relations and publicity were very much in their infancy, as I was. It left a small boy impressed but bewildered. It was a very impressive sight, but if the A4 was the best of the LNER's express locomotives, why wasn't it called an A1? Didn't A1 mean the best, the absolutely top quality?

So began a gentle dilemma that has been lifelong. Which looked better, the magnificent A3, the culmination of the conventional steam locomotive, or the streamlined A4, the LNER's sports model, exciting, shrouded in plate, the achiever of marvellous feats of speed. It is a question that I still have to answer, as many others have as well. The Gresley Society Trust, when it placed the commemorative plaque at Edinburgh Waverley, spoke on it of fine engineering and beauty of line. One without the other is incomplete. Sir Nigel Gresley achieved it with both his A3 and his A4, which is why both are celebrated on the plaque.

It is the A4 which we study in this book, thirty-five remarkable locomotives which brought with them the concept of a high speed express train for the first time. The A4 is one of the greatest locomotive designs of the steam age, and it was certainly one of the fastest. The A4 was built originally to haul special passenger trains that were scheduled to travel at speeds far higher than the vast majority in Britain at that time. It is the grandfather of the High Speed Train. It was completely master of the task for which it was built, it was as economical in both fuel and cost as any other design and none in the UK was better. Well maintained, it was reliable in performance pre-war, and powered the streamlined and other principal services successfully. After the war, with a changed maintenance environment, a number of modifications were needed before the pre-war standard of reliability was regained, if not exceeded in the 'Indian Summer' of steam on the East Coast main line. Included in this account is the experimental high pressure locomotive No.10000, which when rebuilt looked and performed like an A4. In a number of minor ways the W1 influenced the A4 design and when rebuilt included features intended for the future development of the design.

There are other favourites from the steam age which compete for our attention of course, notably Sir William Stanier's magnificent 'Princess Coronation' Pacifics, the ultimate development of the Churchward four cylinder express locomotive. They were some 10% or so more powerful than the double Kylchap A4s, but in terms of fuel consumption, if handled skilfully, marginally less economical. Then there was Arthur Peppercorn's A2 and then his A1, developing the Gresley Pacific as he saw it in the post-war years. Much earnest discussion and partisan argument has been aired, but the real pleasure comes from having a diversity of magnificence in these powerful and speedy locomotives. But when arguments cease and it comes to economy in construction, repair and operation, the A4 yielded only to its derivative, the Peppercorn A1, as was demonstrated by the figures revealed by the LNER and its successor, and later by the costing system introduced by BR.

Of course trains had travelled at high speeds before, notably the GWR's 'Cheltenham Flyer', but the A4s were introduced to haul three 'streamlined' trains, trains of a new era. Not only the locomotives, but also the rolling stock, the timetable and the staff were all part of an entity. Even the on-train literature was bespoke, all part of the project. If the appearance of the locomotive and her train were not revolutionary enough, the astonishing début of SILVER LINK on September 27th 1935 ensured that the name of Sir Nigel Gresley, as he became, was forever synonymous with his A4s, his high-speed locomotives.

The A4 was not without its critics however. My friend the late Eric Neve, a contemporary of the time of steam supremacy and an expert on all things GNR and LNER, rose early to see the new creation in September 1935 on its first outing. His reaction was one of astonishment at seeing the first fully streamlined express locomotive in Britain, but also a slight sense of dismay, rather than displeasure, at the radical departure from the handsome and balanced appearance of the traditional steam locomotive. His dilemma is one which we all share to some extent or another.

The LNER's 'Coronation', for just over two short years, was the hardest turn of duty for an express steam locomotive in Britain. Gresley had set a very exacting task. It was not simply speed for the sake of it, but consistent hard running, yes at high speed, but critically, uphill as well as down. The record of economy and reliability of the A4s was good. For those of us who came to know them later, their exploits before the war bordered on the fantastic compared with the monotony of post-war austerity. But within a few years we saw the brilliance return on the post-war services, notably the non-stop 'Elizabethan', 'Flying Scotsman', 'Tees-Tyne Pullman' and 'the 'Talisman' services. The quality of performance with the Non-stop', especially, stands alongside the pre-war exploits. When many of us, later, travelled behind an A4 it was immediately obvious that for all the outward appearances, underneath was a fine locomotive, powerful, and one that had a tremendous turn of speed. And it was undeniably a Gresley express locomotive.

When Gresley built the A4, his aim was a fast and economical locomotive, and he succeeded magnificently. As they were known at Kings Cross, the 'Blue 'Uns' could always fly, from that incredible debut of SILVER LINK on September 27th, the epic sprint by MALLARD and on still further to the final years of steam traction. For those of us of a certain age, as the A4 on an up express passed Stoke box or Eryholme Junction there was a mounting excitement and exhilaration of the prospect of 20 miles or more of high speed. We were not usually disappointed, especially in the days that preceded the use of continuously welded rail (CWR), as the exciting sound of the railjoints steadily rose with the speed. Often there was the impatience with speed limits as one felt that the speed could have been higher. Then there was the frustration as either signal checks or the civil engineer's speed limits intervened to spoil what might have been a glorious sprint. As down trains accelerated away from Langley troughs, the similar sensations occurred, but then with a silent prayer added that the Hitchin signalmen were doing their stuff!

To stand on Essendine platform and watch them racing down the hill towards Peterborough was an awesome sight: to see them working hard at speed with a big train at such places as Northallerton or Sandy was exhilarating, a spectacle not easily forgotten. But to ride on one at full throttle was unforgettable. There was no more exhilarating place on this earth than on the footplate of an A4 at full speed, as the vibration of the gauges and controls gradually subsided into a smooth roar, broken only by the sound of the fireman's shovel. The engine somehow seemed ready to go faster and faster. When put to it, they rarely disappointed. The journey's end always came far too soon. From its humble beginnings at the hands of such as Stephenson and Trevithick, the steam locomotive had developed to a sophisticated high-speed machine, but the noise of the footplate at speed always hinted at its ancestry with the sounds of firing coal and boiling water.

On the East Coast, it was the A4s that did great things, and for that they hold an unique place in our affections. It is why there are six preserved, four in Britain and two in North America. It is a great pity that the first one built, SILVER LINK, with so many achievements in high speed to her name, was not kept. Second only to MALLARD for obvious reasons, SILVER LINK was scrapped by a mercenary British Railways Board wholly bereft of a sense of history and achievement, determined to economise and eradicate the history of the past in favour of the then anonymous, underpowered, unreliable and ephemeral new traction. Since then the industry has

made great strides in the efficiency of operation, of course, but it is a thousand pities that the transition could not have been made with sensitivity and generosity rather than a fanatical determination to bury the past.

The risk in writing a retrospective account such as this is the tendency to romanticise. Although the history of the A4s involved higher speeds, and their capacity for speed was enjoyed by railwaymen and enthusiasts alike, for much of the time they were one of the two principal express locomotives working East Coast main line services efficiently, economically but unspectacularly. I have added comments from a general management perspective, since the context in which the A4s worked is important, and the influence of other departments' responsibilities on running is discussed.

But when we lay down our memories of the past and look at railway development in the later 20th century, we must acknowledge that the change from steam to diesel and electric traction has made an enormous and beneficial impact on the railway industry. The East Coast main line has continued the cult of excellence that Gresley inherited from Ivatt, refined and improved, moving from steam traction to the power of the Deltic diesels, which took express performance to a far higher level. Then they in turn were superseded by the heirs to the pre-war streamliners, the High Speed

Trains, later replicated in electric traction. Not only did the replacement of steam by diesels and electrics make the railway a cleaner, safer and more civilised place of work, but the Deltics raised the speeds of the East Coast services to a level unattainable by the existing steam traction. I remember in the mid-1960s the Deltic-hauled 'Aberdonian' topping Stoke bank at 82 mph, exactly the same speed as Bill Hoole in May 1959 but with, also exactly, twice the load. Realistically, but sadly, I had to accept that SEAGULL, MALLARD, or SILVER LINK in all their glory had now been outclassed.

So, apart from MALLARD at the national Railway Museum, we have SIR NIGEL GRESLEY owned by the A4 Preservation Society Trust and currently under general overhaul, UNION OF SOUTH AFRICA, owned by John Cameron, and BITTERN, being restored at the Mid-Hants Railway. With this four go DWIGHT D. EISENHOWER in America and DOMINION OF CANADA in Canada, preserved by museum authorities. We thank all concerned for their investment of money and hard work, and wish them every success. We are lucky to have these engines to remind us of one of the great steam designs, and a streamlined one as well.

But it would not be right to remember the locomotives without thoughts for the men that made them run, the drivers, the firemen, the fitters and cleaners. One should not

The two A4s of the 'West Riding Limited' together at Kings Cross, GOLDEN SHUTTLE and GOLDEN FLEECE.

QUICKSILVER pulls away from old platform 6 at Kings Cross probably with the 'Silver Jubilee', in the days of short trousers and long woollen socks. The date lies between 1936 and May 1938. The platforms had not yet been extended, and the extensions outside the train shed were still timber. (H.N. James)

forget the engineers and managers who designed, built and oversaw the running of the A4s as well. All this was achieved in conditions that were often Dickensian, dirty and potentially dangerous. The LNER was not a wealthy company that could afford to invest in its depots and workshops. As this account makes clear, their contribution was crucial. The men 'on the ground' were largely taught by their seniors or just self-taught by personal observation, men who worked hard in Spartan and often dangerous conditions, often at times when they should rightly have been asleep. At times they were required, with no training or preparation, to handle strange engines or familiar engines over strange roads, or to travel at speeds far greater than normal, always maintaining a high standard of safe operation. One thinks of men such as Alf Pibworth, Tom Dron, Joe Duddington, Bill Sparshatt, and Arthur Taylor pre-war, and Jim Swan, Bill Stevenson, Ted Hailstone and Bill Hoole post-war along with their firemen and their lesser known colleagues who handled these express locomotives, to our interest, our delight and now for our fond recollection.

Inevitably this book carries forward the story which was started with *The Book of the A3 Pacifics*, and is best read with it. I have, however, repeated parts of that story that apply here, so that the book itself is a free-standing account. There is an enormous wealth of information on the A4s published and available, and I acknowledge that I have drawn freely upon it. Indeed it would be impossible to write about the class without duplicating something published elsewhere. Information has been gathered from the official records held at Kew, Edinburgh (where a record of every run of the 'Coronation' is held) and the NRM at York. As with the history of the A1 and A3 Pacifics, the principal sources of reference are the RCTS LNER *Locomotive Survey*, the *Registers* of the late W.B. Yeadon, the book *The East Coast Pacifics at Work* by P.N. Townend and numerous articles in *The Gresley Observer*. In addition the performances referred to are from the relevant articles by C.J. Allen and O.S. Nock in *The Railway Magazine* and *Trains Illustrated*, together with various other books dealing with the subject.

I have great pleasure in acknowledging the help of many friends over the years in my knowledge of the A4s, and in particular I would like to thank Peter Townend, MIMechE, formerly Shedmaster at Kings Cross, and George Carpenter, C.Eng, MIMechE. Both are eminent locomotive engineers with a long and close association with Gresley's locomotives, with detailed knowledge and experience of the A4s, and I am very grateful for their recollections and advice. I must also thank Gordon Pettitt, holder of many senior positions with British Railways, and, briefly, fireman to Bill Hoole in his apprentice days, for the use of his records of steam days. Also Dr Geoffrey Hughes, who has studied both the LNER and Sir Nigel himself and his family, Malcolm Crawley, senior locomotive engineer, Chairman

of the Gresley Society Trust and Doncastrian, Melvyn Haigh, Education Officer of the Sir Nigel Gresley Preservation Trust, and my old friend Canon Brian Bailey who has provided information and photographs from his Arthur Cawston bequest. I am grateful also to M.B. Thomas of the former Eastern Region of BR, who was the member of the PR&PO's staff saddled with the task of answering my many queries long ago.

I am also in the debt of the late Messrs. Willie Yeadon, Eric Neve, Ken Hoole and Leslie Burley. The first is well known as I have acknowledged before, the amazing and indefatigable Registrar of all things LNER and the Pacifics in particular. Eric was a great expert on all things LNER, particularly pertaining to the old GNR, and was the focus for the many enthusiasts and professional railwaymen who took a keen interest in the system at the southern end. In my youth he was a kind and wise friend from whom I learnt much about the industry I had joined. Ken was his counterpart for the North Eastern. The late Leslie Burley was also a great enthusiast and one who kept in touch with Eric. He was a precise and accurate man by nature who knew a considerable number of railwaymen and enthusiasts pre-war, including many of the senior drivers at Kings Cross. It is thanks to Leslie that so much is known about the streamlined services that complements the official records, and they have been an indispensable source of information and confirmation of facts in this account.

I set out to use previously unpublished photographs, but some used elsewhere have been added to illustrate a particular point, or because they were too good to leave out. Many come from Barry Hoper of the Transport Treasury, but I am also grateful to Initial Photographics, Geoff Goslin, Vice-President of the Gresley Society Trust who keeps the photographic archive, and my friend John Aylard. I hope that readers will find this a fitting tribute to the achievements of dedicated and expert men who did great things many years ago.

Peter J. Coster
Pendoggett,
Cornwall.

QUICKSILVER on the up 'Flying Scotsman' coming through Doncaster. The absence of numbers on the front suggests that 1935-6 is the likeliest date. The tender by this time was A4 corridor No.5589. (The Transport Treasury)

CHAPTER ONE
Progress Towards Higher Speeds

The locomotive development of the Great Northern Railway had progressed under the stewardship of Henry Ivatt and then his successor, Nigel Gresley, to 1922, when in the late evening in the life of the GNR, Gresley produced his first Pacific, No.1470 GREAT NORTHERN. It was the first of a number of great technological forward leaps with which Gresley astonished the railway industry and its followers. GREAT NORTHERN was a large and impressive locomotive not just in appearance but in operation, too. As Gresley became the CME of the new company, the LNER, it is not surprising that the new designs usually had the Doncaster 'look', although some latitude was allowed. He continued to build pre-Grouping designs as well as his own, and one of Gresley's achievements that is rarely mentioned is his success in keeping no less than six very disparate workshops and drawing offices reasonably content and preventing open dissent between them!

For the background to the A4 Pacific, one has to go back to 1922 and the emergence of No.1470 GREAT NORTHERN. Gresley had considered a number of options for a more powerful express passenger locomotive, and had concluded that three cylinders, all driving on to the second coupled axle, with external Walschaerts valve gear, was the best. He had solved the problem of the middle cylinder valve operation with his unique conjugated valve gear arrangement, driving the valve off the two external valve gears through horizontal levers. The arrangement had been used on 127 Prussian Railway 4-6-0s of 1914, but with a different layout similar to that envisaged in Holcroft's 1909 patent.

We can, however, sharpen the focus down to early 1927 when two apparently quite separate developments were under way. The first occurred when Nigel Gresley had decided to assess the importance of boiler pressure after the virtuoso display by the Great Western's 'Castle' class in 1925. The second was in France. In 1927 Gresley, with his assistant, Bulleid, had met André Chapelon at Paxmans, the British concessionaires for Lentz poppet valve gear, at their Colchester works and a very fruitful friendship developed with M. Chapelon and M. Lancrenon, CME of the Nord Railway in France. Chapelon, Locomotive Development Engineer with the Paris-Orléans Railway, was about to rebuild a 1913 compound Pacific with remarkable results.

The 1925 Exchanges had confirmed in the mind of Gresley's Locomotive Technical Assistant, Bert Spencer, the need to improve the valve design of the A1s. There were many times when the Drawing Office played a vital role and the senior men there and in Gresley's London office played an important but rarely acknowledged part in development of design. Bert Spencer was one such, Teddy Windle was another. I feel that the contribution to Gresley's work by Bert Spencer has never really been acknowledged. Perhaps he was not a leader, but he was an analytical thinker and an invaluable assistant. He was a man who understood locomotive design well, had a sharp mind and understood as clearly as his CME – if at times a little more so – the way in which development should move forward. He was a kind and gentle colleague who was very much a Doncaster and Gresley man. In 1947 his important role was acknowledged when he presented a classic paper to the Institution of Locomotive Engineers, 'The Development of Locomotive Design at Doncaster 1923-1947', with Arthur Peppercorn's support and encouragement. At a time when one needed care and respect in tackling one's seniors, his tenacity in discreetly pressing Gresley, until he

SILVER FOX with the down 'Coronation' after 1937 in garter blue livery. The location is not given but is probably near Retford.

yielded, was never clearer than in the case of the redesign of the A1 valve gear. It was Spencer's design that was used on all LNER Pacifics. In 1920 Gresley had already used long travel valves, $6^5/_8$ ins, in his K3 2-6-0 successfully, but at higher speeds the supporting frame cross-member for the main pivot of the 2:1 valve gear was not sufficiently rigid, resulting in over-travel. He drew back from using the K3 valve setting in his A1, preferring to wait until a more rigid support had been proved. At the time the A1 was kept within coupled axle load weight limits with difficulty, and modifications invariably added rather than subtracted weight. Anything likely to increase engine weight would not have been good news! There seemed to be no immediate hurry to do so, which is probably what disappointed Spencer. As CME, Gresley had, in addition to the responsibility of staying within his budget, many preoccupations arising from the newly formed LNER, but he was sometimes slow to accept and apply small improvements that would have made life easier in service.

The story of the valve gear development, together with the equally important improvement afforded by the use of multiple narrow piston rings, was dealt with more fully in *The Book of the A3 Pacifics*. Gresley had also decided to establish the extent to which higher boiler pressure had contributed to the performance of the Castle. Previously he had been reluctant to increase boiler pressure, believing that it would lead to heavier scaling, but improved water treatment had begun to remove the problem. He had authorised the construction of five 220 psi boilers with enlarged superheaters, three going on NE Area A1s. The other two went to Southern Area engines, No.4480 ENTERPRISE retaining 20 ins cylinders, and No.2544 LEMBERG of Doncaster, which had her cylinders lined down to 18¼ ins to give approximate parity with the tractive effort of the A1s. Had the axle load limit remained at 20 tons, the heavier 220 psi boiler could not have been used, but the CCE must have been aware of the impending report of the Bridge Stress Committee, and agreed to the heavier conversions. In 1929 the Bridge Stress Committee had reported in favour of three and four cylinder engines, and the weight limit had been raised generally on the East Coast main line. Significantly, though, it was not agreed on the Doncaster-Leeds section, due to continuing concern at the capacity of the Calder Viaduct at Wakefield.

Two of the North Eastern Area engines, HARVESTER and SHOTOVER, were sent to Haymarket Depot at Edinburgh in May 1928 to work the non-stop 'Flying Scotsman'. The five 220 psi engines were reclassified 'A3', with subdivisions covering the variations initially, but later these were dropped. Testing was carried out to establish the benefit or otherwise of higher boiler pressures, but curiously, No.2544 was only tested against a standard 180 psi A1, No.4473 SOLARIO, and ENTERPRISE was excluded from testing altogether. After a short sojourn at Carlisle, No.4480 ENTERPRISE remained in the south with No.2544 LEMBERG.

The tests had revealed what we would have suspected, that at moderate power outputs, the dimensions of the locomotives were too close to make any significant difference in coal and water consumption. Boiler pressure was a matter of indifference in this case. Indeed one could argue that the tests showed that a move to higher boiler pressure had no advantage, as the controversial mechanical engineer W.A. Tuplin argued. Contrariwise one could claim that there was no cost penalty in going for the higher pressure either, apart from that of slightly thicker boiler plates. Gresley was concerned that the maintenance costs for the 220 psi boilers might show a significant increase, but in fact the higher pressure boilers showed a very slight saving over a long period. This conclusion was influenced by a number of factors, not least the increasing sophistication of water treatment advocated by T. Henry Turner, the LNER's Chemist. The friction losses due to relatively inadequate steam passages and sharp bends on the A1 steam circuit would have been proportionally higher in the A3 with its higher boiler pressure, since the front end layout was the same. However, the steam flow to the A3 cylinders in the form of superheated steam at higher pressure possessed much greater potential energy, and the new or rebuilt engines had a greater reserve of power. The A1s had shown that in certain circumstances with heavier trains, greater power was required.

It was clear that No.2544 did not lack power either, despite a lower tractive effort, and was an exceptionally fast engine. She was a Doncaster loco and in the hands of her regular top link driver, Charlie Molson, she was a common sight on the so-called 'Breakfast Flyer', the fast early morning Leeds-Kings Cross express. Speeds up to 97 mph had been reached down Stoke Bank with the Pacific. So whilst the trials had not shown any significant advantage in raising boiler pressure itself, No.2544 had shown that with a higher boiler pressure, the cylinders could be reduced without significantly detracting from the engine's ability to move a heavy load. A better balance had also been achieved between valve and cylinder diameters, which was important in terms of steam flow. Gresley, having settled his mind, produced ten A3s, and turned his thoughts to his high pressure four cylinder compound, No.10000. Later, a further 17 A3s were built, making 27 in all.

In France the Paris-Orléans Railway had ordered a large number of four cylinder compound Pacifics from 1907 onwards from the manufacturer Societé Alsacienne, at Belfort, and other builders. The first were Class 4500, and in fact No.4501 was the first European Pacific. She was a four cylinder compound with 6ft 0¾ins coupled wheels and a remarkably high boiler pressure of 16 hectopièze, 232psi. The first 70 engines were not superheated. Then in 1909 a 6ft 4¾ins superheated version of the 4500 class was produced, numbered as the 3500 class. One might speculate as to whether 4ins made very much difference to performance in practice. In tests between 1908 and 1911, it was established that the maximum indicated power output of a 3500 Pacific was 2,156 HP at 62mph. This was a much higher figure than anything comparable in Britain at the time, yet the French authorities were concerned that by pro rata comparison with their compound Atlantics, the Pacifics were under-performing quite seriously. The P-O Atlantics were similar to Nos.103/4 that ran on the GWR, No.102 being equivalent to the slightly smaller Nord Atlantic. Theoretical calculation based on comparative dimensions indicated that the maximum power output of the Pacifics ought to be nearer 2,860 IHP.

After France recovered from the First World War the problem remained, and from 1926 a team including the Locomotive Development Engineer, M. André Chapelon, was remitted by the CME, Maurice Lacoin, to deal with the problem. After a considerable period of investigation and experiment, Chapelon received permission to rebuild one engine, and chose the worst steaming locomotive, No.3566, known ironically to the crews as 'Le Choléra'. In November 1929, No.3566 emerged rebuilt and, on test, developed 3,000 IHP. The power output had been increased by 50%, the steaming problem had gone, and the fuel consumption was reduced by 15-25%. The results of rebuilding were little short of miraculous. It had astonished those locomotive engineers in Europe and America with open minds, and overnight their best designs hitherto had been relegated to second place or lower.

Clearly there were important lessons to be learnt.

André Chapelon was a brilliant engineer and a determined one too. He saw all too clearly the shortcomings of many designs in failing to heed the simple laws of motion and physics, especially relating to combustion and the use of hot steam. He had enlarged and straightened the steam passages, provided a much more efficient draughting system and used poppet instead of piston valves, all to reduce throttling losses and pressure drop. In addition to these changes there were several others, but the general effect achieved by Chapelon was an easement of the passage of energy from the fireman's shovel to the chimney, generally referred to as internal streamlining. In place of a locomotive that nobody wished to work on, No.3566 was a free-steaming 3000 IHP flyer.

In passing, it seems strange that Chapelon was one of the few locomotive engineers to bring the theory of physics and thermodynamics to bear on locomotive design, and not allowing convenience and practicality to deflect his attention away from the objective. His designs were developed later to the point where his 4-8-0s, at full power, were developing over 4,000 IHP, and a peak of 4,320 IHP was recorded on test. In terms of IHP/sq.ft of grate area, that is 108 IHP/sq.ft. In Britain the highest achieved was approximately 75 IHP/sq.ft, the IHP value being calculated rather than measured. One would have

thought that British engineers would have reached the same conclusion, but generally not, at least at the senior level where such decisions were made. The fundamental principles learnt at college were blurred by other considerations. Any comparison between British and French railway practice needs to take account of different systems and attitudes. One very significant difference was that the French railways, like those of other European countries, trained their footplate and maintenance staffs to a higher technical level, and could therefore rely on a more informed approach to more sophisticated equipment. They chose to investigate design developments more rigorously than in the UK, and then use those findings in new designs. In the UK, development was subsumed into the general process of design, and forward progress was generally sound but occasionally opportunities were wasted. The CME was personally involved in design even if only laying down the basic parameters, and as indicated earlier it was a time when few cared to argue with their senior, at least publicly. Moreover, heads of engineering departments were considerably older and generally less flexible than in more recent years, and with their wide responsibilities, it was understandable that basic engineering principles were occasionally overlooked. It was fortunate for the LNER that their CME team consisted of men of the calibre not only of Gresley and

Bulleid, but also of Bert Spencer, Teddy Windle, and Robert Thom and in the Drawing Offices.

So, by 1932 Gresley had these events to shape his future ideas. Whilst on the subject of compounding, it is appropriate that mention should be made here more fully of the experiment that was in progress at that time. The genesis of No.10000 is explained in great detail in Gresley's classic paper, 'High Pressure Locomotives' to the Institution of Mechanical Engineers in 1930, and Part 6C of the RCTS *Locomotive Survey*, and it is therefore only necessary to touch on the more important aspects of the locomotive's history. The decision to build a high pressure compound was Gresley's, and as no authority was issued for its construction, its cost must have fallen on Gresley's budget for development, no doubt with agreement principally from Andrew McCosh, Chairman of the Locomotive Committee, and Sir Ralph Wedgwood, the Chief General Manager.

The coal consumption of many express locomotives was quite heavy as the loads hauled were relatively large. That of the A1 Pacifics in the first few years of their operation with the original valve gear, taking their greater haulage capacity into account, was still heavier than Gresley would have liked, and Gresley was looking for a reduction in fuel costs. The use of very high steam pressure was widely thought to offer possibilities of economy. To obtain the full advantage from high

GANNET arriving at Kings Cross. The engine looks fairly new and I would plump for 1938. The A4 has its original non-corridor tender No.5675.

3

boiler pressure it was necessary to use compounding, however, to cope with the greater degree of expansion required. A number of experimental locomotives were built as part of the search for greater efficiency and reliability, but all were destined to fail, some quickly and some, with a modicum of success, still failed to supplant the simple and effective Stephensonian model.

Gresley was aware that Churchward had experimented with compounding, but had concluded that his way forward was with his own efficient simple expansion machines. In France one could be sure of a high standard of enginemanship and maintenance, necessary prerequisites for the successful operation of compounds. In the early 1920s the Delaware & Hudson Railroad in America had applied very high pressure compounding – 350 and 500 psi – very successfully insofar as design and coal train performance were concerned, but much higher maintenance costs coupled with altered railway operational considerations led to its abandonment.

No doubt the operation of considerable numbers of compounds in France encouraged Gresley to explore the possibilities for himself. In the matter of high pressure, he consulted Messrs. Yarrow & Co, famous Clydeside marine engineers. The latter were at that time courting the railway companies in order to expand their business. There does not appear to have been very much awareness on the part of Yarrow of the nature of the industry that they were trying to cultivate. The outcome was a consultancy with Yarrow to design and build a boiler capable of 500 psi suitable for locomotive service. The latter figure became 450 psi subsequently. It had to be a marine type water-tube boiler, since there was no experience in the UK railway industry of anything more than half that pressure. The use of higher boiler pressures would have required much closer staying, which would have restricted water circulation. The American 500 psi high pressure compound 2-8-0s and 4-8-0s referred to earlier had water tube fireboxes and firetube boilers.

The outcome was the famous marine type water tube boiler working at 450 psi, with three drums, roughly resembling a rib cage, and totally unlike any other locomotive boiler in existence. The boiler design grew larger during its development and the dimensions changed repeatedly in order to remain within the structure gauge and meet railway operational requirements. Gresley's Assistant CME, Arthur Stamer, with his Darlington drawing office, was clearly having a trying time with

experts in marine boiler work, other experts in theoretical design, compounding, and aerodynamics. They had a struggle reconciling the high-pressure boiler design with the chassis and, more importantly, the rolling stock gauge. The marine boiler was a very large structure by railway standards, and mounting one on an express locomotive chassis was extremely difficult. Yarrows were famously quoted, in response to receiving another set of alterations, as remarking that the only thing that was now left unchanged was the title block on the drawing!

What had started conceptually as a Pacific that could be compared with the simple expansion A1 and its later form as an A3 was no longer capable of accommodating the water tube boiler without alteration. Gresley was forced to lengthen the frames and accept an additional carrying axle at the rear. A change to a rear bogie would have precipitated a considerable amount of redesign. As the design featured the successful Cortazzi rear carrying radial axle there would be difficulties with excessive lateral play in adding a second behind the first. A simpler answer was a Bissel truck added with the pivot bearing attached low at the rear of the frames, and the drag box was extended over the truck, making the design a 4-6-2-2 strictly speaking. As it was, the rear of the boiler came well into the cab, farther than in the usual Gresley cab. Gresley was almost at the point of being forced into a 4-8-2 to create enough room for the boiler to be mounted conventionally. The thought that the high pressure drum was a few feet from their heads no doubt focussed the minds and attentions of the footplate staff!

The boiler cladding was necessarily quite different from a conventional locomotive, and it was this feature that attracted as much attention as anything else. As 'streamlining' was the fashion of the day, it was widely regarded as the first streamlined railway locomotive in the UK, which ironically was no part of the experiment. A cylindrical smokebox of considerable length was provided originally, with the Darlington door secured by a wheel fastening. This was replaced by fabricated smokebox the contour of which was dictated by both the shape of the water tube boiler and the need to achieve effective smoke deflection. At the rear there was a firegrate with 85% of the grate area of an A1/A3 Pacific; the air to the firebed was drawn in through intakes at each side of the smokebox door, and preheated in passing through the 'tunnel' between the outer and inner boiler casings. The locomotive was fitted

with a steam reverser and electric lighting.

The four cylinder compounding system used was designed with the assistance of the eminent engineer, Professor W.E. Dalby. While it might have been possible to place all four cylinders in line, *en batterie* as with the P-L-M compounds and indeed with a number of Raven designs, Gresley departed from his preferred unified or concentrated drive, using divided drive as in the De Glehn layout for many compound designs. Obviously with a steam pressure nearly double the highest used hitherto, the steam flows were reduced, and the volume of the high-pressure (HP) cylinders were reduced correspondingly to avoid excessively large piston thrusts. The HP cylinders were 12 ins in diameter, and the LP was 20 ins, all four having the standard 26 ins strokes. There was some talk of using Lentz poppet valves, but conventional long travel, long lap piston valves were ultimately preferred, and a similar design of exhaust to the A1s and A3s. The intermediate receiver was between the HP cylinders in the same casting, and the engine was a Du Bousquet-De Glehn compound. The former engineer introduced the system on the Nord Railway that enabled the locomotive to be started as a four cylinder simple expansion locomotive, and then changed to compound working. If necessary the intermediate receiver could be reinforced with live steam at reduced pressure. The divided drive layout of the four cylinders was introduced by De Glehn.

After nearly five years' development, the engine was completed at Darlington in October 1929, turned out in a startling grey livery. Indeed startling was something of an understatement. After a lengthy period of testing and familiarisation, No.10000 went into service at Gateshead depot. The engine worked alongside the Pacifics, and seemed capable, on her day, of emulating their performance. She worked the 'Queen of Scots' Pullman and the Leeds-Glasgow express later to be named the 'North Briton', but frequently needed attention. As ever, new design features entailed dealing with teething troubles, and the locomotive took longer in works visits, waiting for adaptation and modification. This process was aggravated by financial stringency during the recession.

No.10000 was known as the 'Hush-hush' due to the secrecy that surrounded its design and construction. The boiler was in fact a superbly designed and manufactured product, but mounting it on a rail chassis created considerable problems not experienced in the

The 'Hush-hush', No.10000, pauses at Grantham with an up express. A remarkable locomotive, and apparently in good condition without leaks and well cleaned. Quite how much the driver could see round such bulk would have been a problem in daily operation, but there were worse problems to overcome in its original condition. The tender was A3 type corridor No.5484. The date is 1930. One can see very clearly that the engine and tender were designed and built 76 miles apart! (Cawston Bequest, Canon Brian C. Bailey Collection)

marine or industrial environment. The inner boiler cladding tended to leak both air and heat, through ovalised rivet holes after a period in service. This could have been overcome by welding, a technique that was not widely used in railway engineering in the early 1930s. As a result the preheated air supply was short circuited and the vacuum inside the boiler and the effectiveness of the draughting were reduced. The latter was giving cause for concern in any case, and in retrospect it was optimistic in the extreme to expect the A1/A3 draughting arrangement to operate on the water tube boiler of the compound. Nor was that all, for the novel design of steam reverser gave trouble, and the smoke deflection arrangement at the front needed modification as well. Although the engine worked the 'Flying Scotsman' as a non-stop service as well as in winter, together with most of the diagrams of the Gateshead Pacifics, it was often out

The W1 No.10000 working a test train south of Grantham, and she seems to have a good load behind the Darlington dynamometer coach. The date is February 13th 1930. Tender No.5484. (Cawston Bequest, Canon Brian C. Bailey Collection)

of service, and could not be considered as a reliable alternative to the A1s and A3s.

The association of compounding with very high boiler pressure on No.10000 did not produce the reliability and economy that was hoped for. The work of the A1 and A3 Pacifics with long valve travel on the other hand was excellent: a little later, in 1935, Gateshead's Bob Knight recovered 25 out of 26 minutes late start with the new A3 FIRDAUSSI on 450 tons south of Newcastle. Meanwhile Gresley had to think about the design of a powerful locomotive that the Scottish Area had requested for the Edinburgh-Aberdeen route, and a mixed traffic locomotive for fast heavy freight and relief passenger work. Having evaluated the use of high pressure and compounding he decided against using it, but Chapelon's use of smooth, straight, adequate steam passages allied to a powerful exhaust design made sense to him in considering these new designs.

A few years earlier, the railways of Europe and America were beginning to venture into higher speeds, and the GWR had made much of Brunel's superbly laid main line between Paddington and Swindon with the 'Cheltenham Flyer'. A light semi-fast train as far as Swindon, normally, it had been timed to run briskly to Paddington. It offered the perfect opportunity for the GWR to demonstrate the ability of the 'Castles' to maintain high speed. The timing was progressively reduced at the turn of the thirties, until in September 1932 the train was

required to run to Paddington in 65 minutes, an average of 71.4mph start to stop. In America there were a number of claims for the achievement of high speeds or high power outputs, some fanciful, but with modern steam and diesel railcars more high and sustained speeds were being recorded and verified.

Driver Bill Sparshatt, a name destined to figure prominently in the history of the LNER in the 1930s, entered the Kings Cross top link in July 1931 from the Pullman 1A link in place of Driver Ben Glasgow. It had been decided to investigate the potential for acceleration of services, and in December 1931, Sparshatt, known to be a hard runner when he was in the lower links, brought Ivatt Atlantic No.3295 up from Peterborough with 285 tons in 71 minutes 10 seconds, 67 minutes net. Then on December 10th, with A1 No.2547 DONCASTER he brought the time down to 66 minutes 10 seconds with an exhilarating 92 mph at Barnet with a net time of 62 minutes. The 7.50 ex-Leeds 'Breakfast Flyer' was one of the most important services run by the LNER, worked by Doncaster depot, and non-stop from Grantham to London. On December 16th Driver Watson of Doncaster, with his regular engine A3 No.2743 FELSTEAD, ran from Grantham to Kings Cross in 92 minutes 42 seconds, reaching 90mph at Essendine and Oakleigh Park.

There was a general level of concern in the commercial and operating departments of the LNER that schedules were too slow at the turn of the 1930s. In particular the

lethargy of the Anglo-Scottish schedules was highlighted by the schedule of the non-stop 'Flying Scotsman' which was required to spin out very slow section times that in theory were comfortably within the scope of a 4-4-0. This was due to the agreement with the LMSR that the companies would not compete for business by reducing schedules below 8¼ hours. This was terminated by mutual consent in 1932. The experiments in faster running in 1931 preceded the tightening of schedules generally on May 2nd, 1932. The 'Flying Scotsman' schedule was cut by 25 minutes stopping and 45 minutes non-stop. The morning up 7.50 Leeds express 'The Breakfast Flyer' was a major revenue earner for the LNER. The timing of the Grantham-Kings Cross section was reduced to 100 minutes, an average start to stop of 63.3mph, which was taxing when the loading rose from 9 coaches to 13, 4-500 tons. This had become one of the hardest duties in the UK at the time. Yet Charlie Molson and LEMBERG with a full load, still beat the schedule by three minutes!

Events were, however, moving quickly, with a number of manufacturers building experimental and speculative prototypes in Europe and America. By the early 1930s the new diesel electric railcars in America had got a firm foothold and there were some 700 in service there, mainly on shorter stopping services. In France and Germany railcars of various sorts were setting new records for high-speed travel. Lightweight vehicles on rubber tyred

Doncaster's new double Kylchap A4 MALLARD; the location is not known, but it's probably Carr Loco. The tender is A4 non-corridor No.5642.

wheels were on trial in a number of countries. In Germany the railway system had been subject to a general speed limit of 100 kph, but a new generation of railcars had raised that substantially. An experimental propeller-driven railcar, powered by BMW petrol engines, the Kruckenberg, had run between Hamburg and Berlin at 99.5 mph, with a maximum of 124 mph. This was a unique experiment, but internal combustion was a coming force in the railway world. Mechanical engineers in the railway industry strove to harness the heavy oil engine, with all its advantages, for rail traction.

The LNER's May 1932 accelerations had almost immediately been countered by events elsewhere. The GWR deliberately chose to reassert its seniority a month later with a carefully planned series of high-speed runs laid on for the benefit of the technical press on June 6th 1932. With the road ahead cleared, as some seven years earlier for CALDICOT CASTLE, TREGENNA CASTLE brought the 195 tons 'Cheltenham Flyer' into Paddington in 56 minutes 47 seconds, a start to stop average speed of 81.6mph. The GWR had, in Brunel's main line, an almost perfect piece of track on which to run at high speed, and it made the most of it, brilliantly. It was a tremendous run, and was destined never to be beaten by steam. This was followed by the recording party returning to Swindon behind MANORBIER CASTLE on another lightweight express in 60 minutes 1 second, 77.3 mph start-to-stop. Then they were swept back to London behind DUDLEY CASTLE, again with a short train, in 66 minutes 33 seconds, 69.7 mph. As C.J. Allen may well have said, a tour de force indeed – and no doubt a publicity triumph as well! One might consider the pros and cons compared with what was to come from Doncaster, but it should be remembered that by that time the GWR, with its Castle 4-6-0 and Brunel's main line, established both the fastest steam schedule and fastest start-to-stop steam run in the British Isles. In retrospect it would have been very interesting to see later what SILVER LINK or one of her double Kylchap sisters would have achieved on such a road in the right hands.

In Europe, Germany in particular, in the spring of 1932 the Deutsche Reichsbahn's express diesel railcar *Der Fliegende Hamburger* commenced trial running and attracted a great deal of attention. The name no doubt seemed logical at the time, but half a century later it would have been comic to the point of incredulity, like some other names

in railway history. Language moves on. It was destined to become one of the most famous railcar designs of all. It was a two-car articulated diesel-electric unit built for the DR and powered by two 12-cylinder Maybach GO engines, newly designed with a maximum speed of 103 mph. The GO type was I believe a four-stroke engine, operated at 1,500 RPM, and developed 410 HP. From the parameters the engine appears to have been fairly small, comparable in size to the larger underfloor engines of the DMU fleet of British Railways, but obviously run at higher speeds to produce more power. The rotational speed was very high for a four-stroke engine of the 1930s, and it was not until the much bigger and heavier Ventura engine was introduced in the HST in the 1970s that such engine speeds were achieved in Britain.

On May 15th 1933 it entered regular service running between Berlin and Hamburg, 178 miles, at an average speed of 77.4mph. Approximately 80% of the route was graded at less than 1 in 1000, and much straighter and even flatter than the East Coast route. The unit was described as a railcar, which it was, but the description had misleading light railway/branch line connotations in this country. The German unit was a high-speed express train, albeit with only two coaches but of continental length and rolling stock gauge. After its successful introduction, 13 more units were built, enabling the diesel-electric service to be extended to the other major German cities. Some, such as the 'Fliegende Kölner' were three coach sets. In France, three coach sets with similar power equipment were introduced on the Nord Railway in 1934, and Bugatti petrol railcars were introduced between Le Havre, Deauville and Paris. The notable feature of these vehicles was the aerodynamic effect of the wedge-shaped ends.

Gresley, in the spring of 1934, drew the attention of the Chief General Manager and the directors of the LNER to the new service. We know that Gresley visited the Continent several times a year. He was a member of the Technical Committee of the International Union of Railways (UIC) and was well acquainted with current practice there. The Chairman, William Whitelaw, and the Chief General Manager, Sir Ralph Wedgwood, did not want the LNER to be left behind, and the Board agreed on June 29th to further investigation. The story of the genesis of high-speed rail travel has been related generally as a preface to the story of the development of the A4. The latter is of course the main focus, and therefore the credit tends to be handed to Gresley. Certainly he

was the central figure in bringing the whole project to a successful conclusion, but the role of his senior, Sir Ralph Wedgwood, should not be undervalued.

In September 1934 a party led by Gresley visited Germany and the works of the builder, Maybach Motorenbau. An extremely important contract such as this would have been dealt with by Gresley himself, authorised by Wedgwood, advised by his top assistants, and the preliminary enquiries were a vital first stage. He would certainly have met the senior staff and inspected the works and their products before committing the LNER further. Gresley had been authorised, if satisfied technically, to seek a quotation from the German manufacturers for a diesel unit capable of working a service from London to Leeds and Newcastle, two of the LNER's prime passenger services. The manufacturer's tender required an appreciation of the characteristics of the East Coast main line and its traffic, for it was a much harder proposition than the Berlin-Hamburg main line. The latter was largely straight and flat with very few speed restrictions and, as mentioned previously, a very different proposition altogether.

When it was received the proposal was somewhat disappointing. The 115 tons three coach unit envisaged would have only seated 140 passengers in somewhat Spartan conditions, and its estimated journey time to Leeds was 165 minutes. The time to Newcastle was 4 hours 15½ mins down and 4 hours 17 mins up, not a sufficiently large acceleration to attract passengers to a premium service. One suspects that the installed power of the German unit was adequate for 80-90mph on level or near-level track but there was little reserve of power at that speed, and certainly none to maintain that speed on significantly more adverse gradients. It was reported that the LNER Board was disappointed, and it was distinctly apprehensive of the effect on revenue. The reaction of North Country passengers in particular to the prospect of a cold buffet instead of a hot square meal was viewed with apprehension. Not for the last time did railway management respect the sanctity of the Great British Breakfast, and rightly so!

Maybach sought to improve the schedule with two more powerful turbo-charged engines of 600BHP, but at the time turbo-charging was a very new method of improving the power output of a diesel engine, and no examples were in revenue-earning service. It was unknown territory. It was not until 1936 that the improved engine entered service as the prime mover for four three-car units. Germany has a number of important routes that are laid on flat country, and within a few years the high-speed railcar had developed to the point where the now four car Fliegende Kölner was booked to cover the 109.6 miles from Hanover to Hamm at 82.2 mph, for example. Since then the turbo-charged diesel engine has moved on to conquer the world as a prime mover. Gresley decided against the offer, fatefully. His decision was viewed subsequently by G.F. (Gerry) Fiennes, one of the finest Chairmen that BR never had, as effectively setting back the change to diesel traction and higher average speeds in the UK for at least another twenty years. That period was of course extended by the 1939-45 war and its aftermath. We shall never know quite how a decision for diesel traction would have worked, and whether it would have checked the decline of passenger and freight for the nationalised railway.

It seems probable that Wedgwood, on learning of the disappointing response, suggested to Gresley that his Pacifics could match the German unit's performance with a larger train with more comfortable accommodation, and the latter strongly agreed. These were early days and the system of remote control necessary in a multiple unit train for unifying the power output of a number of diesel engines had not been developed to a reliable standard. Neither had the system of distributed power throughout the train that has become a feature of today's express multiple units. One could not accuse Gresley of being narrow minded or living in the past, for although he was a steam man, he embraced electric traction wholeheartedly. At the end of his career, he was alone amongst his peers in producing No.6701, a modern electric locomotive that worked well over the Manchester-Sheffield-Wath route when it was electrified. No doubt he considered the culture change necessary in his Company, and its cost, for the successful introduction of diesel traction and decided that firmer evidence over a longer period was needed to make such a change. It was still only 1934.

An additional advantage was that the LNER already possessed both the engines and the coaches for a steam powered service, and could avoid the financial burden of a substantial international contract. During the 1929-1935 period, the trade recession had affected the LNER's freight revenue severely. The company's coal, mineral and steel traffic – and hence revenue – fell substantially, far more than the other three railway groups. Experience a quarter of a century later would suggest that in buying the

diesel unit without providing the accompanying maintenance personnel and infrastructure, the LNER would have opened a Pandora's box of troubles. One also needs to bear in mind that at this time in the political world the Nazi Reich was flexing its muscles, and making the most of the undoubted excellence of German engineering. The free nations of Europe were only too keen to respond and show that whatever Nazism achieved, they could do better.

I think that the quotation from Maybach must have been received in October 1934. As a result of the Board's agreement and the disappointing response from Germany, Wedgwood felt that a trial was necessary to explore the alternative of steam traction. Gresley's confident assertion was to be put to the test. Acting on Wedgwood's orders, the Southern Area organised the remarkable trial runs of November 30th in that same year. Even so, we know that Gresley, through Bulleid, was still in correspondence with the engineers of the Deutsche Reichsbahn in November 1934.

So we come to the famous trial high-speed run of November 30th 1934. It was intended to explore the potential of the existing Pacifics with a very light train with a similar load capacity to the German railcar over a similar distance. It was decided to test the timings for running between London and Leeds which was a close approximation of distance if not topography. There would be an adequate allowance for rest at Leeds, there would be only one set of men, and all the arrangements could be restricted to the Southern Area. The run was made from Kings Cross to Leeds, using the timings suggested by Maybach, with a 180 psi A1, No.4472 FLYING SCOTSMAN, which at 154.85 tons outweighed its three coach train plus dynamometer car, weighing 147 tons. As it happened, the Divisional Locomotive Running Superintendent, I.S.W. Groom, had wisely picked Bill Sparshatt for the task, and fortunately his regular engine was No.4472 FLYING SCOTSMAN, which was an A1. Sparshatt was known to be one not to shirk an opportunity to amend the record book.

The CCE had operated a weight restriction on Bridge No.60 at Wakefield over the River Calder since the advent of GNR No.1470. Leeds-London expresses were the preserve of Ivatt's large Atlantics, superheated by Gresley, at least as far as Doncaster in most cases, where the Pacifics took over for the run to and from London. Exactly what caused the CCE to be concerned about this

structure is hard to establish some 70 years later. Bridge capacity is an inexact science with masonry structures, especially underbridges, although now far more accurate than in 1930. Since the K3s, with 20 tons axle loading, were allowed to work between Doncaster and Leeds the restriction was more likely due to the overall weight of the larger engine than axle loading alone. The bridge was a brick arch viaduct with a central wrought iron (probably) span over the river. The spandrels of the viaduct arches had been repaired and strengthened, suggesting that there may have been some weakness in the foundations, not unusual in crossing a river valley. The CCE's caution in allowing the A1s over the viaduct in very restricted numbers seems to bear out that theory. New steelwork had been designed for the river span but not installed.

After the repairs to the spandrels had been carried out, A1 Pacifics from Doncaster or Grantham were allowed through in 1932-23 on at least one diagram, but it was not until 1936 that they were given general clearance. Although only 30 miles, the nature of the road from Doncaster was such that there was not a great need for Pacifics, and the K3s and Ivatt Atlantics were coping. It seems that the trial run would have been limited therefore to an A1 Pacific rather than an A3. This must have been one of the first occasions when an A1 worked throughout from Kings Cross to Leeds.

Driver Sparshatt and his mate, Fireman Webster, ran to Leeds successfully in 152 mins, and came back with two more coaches, 207 tons, in just over 157 against a tentative timing of 165mins. These times were considerably faster than anything that had been achieved before, or since, and the record stood for many years until the arrival of the Deltics. Steam traction had a greater reserve of power than the contemporary diesel engine, with its fixed installed HP. On the down run after an unprecedented start and a maximum of 95mph down through Sandy, Stoke Bank was topped at an amazing 81mph, a record that stood for many years. On the return again 4472 was running far faster than was the norm at that time, and for the first time 100mph was reached south of Little Bytham, with the undeniable corroboration of the dynamometer car. Admirers of the GWR have since been somewhat sensitive about this achievement in relation to that for which CITY OF TRURO is famous, but although Sparshatt had to push his engine hard to reach 100 mph, the corroboration of the dynamometer car was vital. The GWR claim to 102 mph is based on highly tenuous evidence and in all the argument for and against, what has been lost sight of is the magnificence of the engineering achievement for its time. The magic 100 mph figure has an emotional significance, but in fact whether the speed was 92 or 102 is neither here nor there.

Considerable credit must be given to the crew, especially Fireman Webster, who had shovelled his way to Leeds and back again. Although the A1 had a very light train, she had to be worked hard at high speed, and her coal consumption was heavy at an average of 54lb per mile, something that was not dwelt on overmuch at the time for understandable reasons. Webster was estimated to have fired nine tons of coal on the day, an outstanding feat of strength and determination, and fatigue must have been a factor in the running of the A1. Although the A1 Pacific could go fast, the trial run required an altogether higher level of speed not only to be attained but also maintained, uphill as well as downhill, and the Pacific had to be driven very hard to achieve such remarkable times. The 180 psi A1 seemed to be capable of just over 90 mph when driven normally, but in order to reach 100 mph clearly Sparshatt had to 'drop the lever', i.e. lengthen the cut-off.

Although the front end layout of the A1 was limited for high speed by comparison with later designs, some felt that there were better A1s that could more easily have achieved the running times and speeds of FLYING SCOTSMAN at Kings Cross. Members of the class had produced some fine runs in the past, and Bert Spencer's long lap long travel valve gear, very similar to the GWR Castle,

was excellent for its time. VICTOR WILD and FLYING FOX were two long-term favourites at Top Shed, and it was considered that either would have done better, despite No.4472's fame. That Sparshatt had to lengthen the cut-off to 40% on the climb to Stoke, at well over 80 mph, supports that view. For a 180 psi A1 with a front end layout that was not good, and 8 ins piston valves feeding 20 ins cylinders, the power absorbed in moving the locomotive at high speed would have been considerable, not to mention that required to overcome the greatly increased air resistances.

A further problem with the A1 was that she was right-hand drive, whereas the A3s had left-hand drive, which made signal sighting far easier. It is perhaps appropriate to remind readers that the vast majority of signals in 1934 were oil-lit and much harder to sight, and on the up journey Bill Sparshatt was driving FLYING SCOTSMAN at speed in gathering November late afternoon gloom. Lights were much fewer, and in those days it was normal for signalmen, when necessary, to lower a signal arm prematurely as a danger signal. There were, after all, many reasons then for stopping trains quickly that have since ceased to exist.

This early venture into high-speed running brought a sharp reminder that such experiments always had an implicit risk. The operating authorities had decided to start the train from the old platform 11 at Kings Cross in order to give Sparshatt a good start. O.S. Nock described him as having something of the showman about him, but whether so or not, Sparshatt was determined take advantage of this

rare opportunity for fast running. He had gained a good speed with his featherweight train by the time he encountered the sharply curved layout at the junction of platform 10 and 11 tracks. At the time as far as I can trace there was a tandem, immediately followed by a double slip, and no doubt there was a heavy lateral impact which caused the wheels of the A1 to ride up on to the railhead leaving flange marks. One could hardly get any nearer a derailment without actually having one. I think that perhaps the jaws of some of the permanent way chairs might well have been broken as the wheels mounted the railhead, giving the game away, and this would certainly have attracted the attention of the ganger, walking round daily. He would have called higher authority at once. A tandem, incidentally, is one single lead within another, sometimes called, incorrectly, a three-way point.

The CCE applied heavy permanent speed restrictions (PSRs) to the tortuous terminal station layouts for very good reasons, but I wonder how they were calculated and more importantly, how drivers were supposed to judge them accurately. Expresses arrived at Kings Cross occasionally at such speeds that one waited for the sounds of an impact from the buffer-stop end, and it was a testimony to the drivers' skill that the train was brought to a stand safely, despite greasy rails and the vagaries of the vacuum brake. Cecil J. Allen was the official timekeeper for the 1934 run, and later observed that he was lucky to reach the south portal of Gasworks Tunnel intact and without further incident!

DOMINION OF CANADA leaving Potters Bar Tunnel with an up express. She was only in this condition from December 1947 to October 1948. The tender is A3 corridor No.5328. (Ted's Dad)

SILVER LINK, brand new, at Top Shed. This photograph is believed to have been taken during a rather fortuitously-timed club visit there on September 14th, before the famous trial run on September 27th 1935. The photograph shows the short buffers originally fitted - seee also page 27. (L.J. Burley, Gresley Society Trust)

Nevertheless, Gresley had demonstrated the ability of his locomotives to run at high speed with standard stock.

At some point it was decided to go ahead with a significantly faster express service. The notion of a new train, perhaps with a new type of locomotive hauling it, seemed to have become accepted by the LNER authorities. It is difficult to trace exactly when this happened, but having successfully demonstrated the ability of the A1 to haul a light load and keep the fast schedule to Leeds and back, the decision *seems* to have been reached in late 1934 or early 1935. This required Gresley to consider whether his A3 would be suitable, or whether a new design was called for suitable for daily sustained and economical high speed running.

His first P2 Mikado left Doncaster Works in May 1934. The order for five more A3s in 1932 to strengthen the Scottish motive power allocation had been cancelled, and one P2 authorised instead. In 1933 there was no building programme due to financial restrictions but in 1934 the five A3s were reinstated together with four replacements for the Raven Pacifics, the latter needing reboilering. Five more Mikados were also agreed. Much has been and could be written about the P2s, Gresley's second attempt to make use of the 2-8-2 wheel arrangement so commonly and effectively used on the Continent and in America over difficult roads. The four cylinder compound 2-8-2 express locomotives of the Saxon Railway

with 6ft 3ins coupled wheels, built in 1918, were most successful in their work. In its primary purpose, the haulage of heavy loads over the difficult Edinburgh-Aberdeen main line, the Mikado design was completely successful. It didn't matter just what was hooked on and how difficult the start, No.2001 and her sisters pulled away just the same. The provision of a fourth coupled axle, and the enormous increase in adhesion that it gave over the A3, eliminated all problems associated with starting and hauling heavy loads on the steeper gradients in Scotland. It is important to understand that point, even if one accepts at the same time that there were other serious problems with the Mikados. Extended tests between Doncaster and London in 1934, however, had shown some worrying inconsistencies in steaming with the prototype. Nevertheless, Gresley was keen to make use of the newly opened testing plant at Vitry-sur-Seine, and he had negotiated with the OCEM authorities in France for No.2001 COCK O' THE NORTH to go there for testing in the late autumn of 1934 for three months.

However, things were not going well at the locomotive testing station at Vitry in late 1934. Staff had experienced a flurry of hot boxes and bearings with all of the French locomotives. No.2001 frequently ran hot and her testing programme was ruined as a result. André Chapelon suggested that they tested No.2001 on the road instead, hauling a number of counter-pressure

locomotives. The Mikado successfully completed two round trips between Tours and Orléans before returning to the UK in February 1935. The Test Report must have been embarrassing to Gresley, and not a little irritating as well. The frequent overheating of the axleboxes and crankpins was not the fault of the locomotive, but the lack of any resilience in the solid concrete foundation of the testing station. The big end had performed perfectly well. However, the testing had revealed problems with the poppet valves due to excessive lead and with the steaming. Little had been learnt of the P2's performance, and indeed the French engineers were quite critical of the design of bearing used at Doncaster. Crucially, the optimum setting for the Kylchap exhaust had not been established in the testing.

Gresley had used the Kylala-Chapelon (Kylchap) exhaust design first on a D49 4-4-0 in 1930, and then on his P2 Mikados, with the exception of No.2005 THANE OF FIFE. This design had been used with conspicuous success on the rebuilt P-O No.3566 and successive rebuilds as both Pacifics and 4-8-0s. It had raised the boiler evaporation rate considerably, at the same time burning the fuel more evenly across the grate and thus more economically. The function of an exhaust system is to act as a pump, powered by exhausting steam from the cylinders, creating a partial vacuum in the smokebox by entraining the combustion gases from the firebox so that they are expelled from the chimney mixed with the exhausting steam. That vacuum sustains the draught from the firebox through the boiler tubes and flues, and if it were insufficient, the fire would die back and the boiler pressure fall. In his early years with the Paris-Orleans company, as mentioned earlier André Chapelon had been given the task of improving the performance of the company's larger locomotives, and he had researched the available exhaust systems thoroughly. He had concluded that the Finnish Kyläla exhaust system, which used a specially shaped device (*ajutage*) suspended over the blastpipe orifice to divide the single exhaust flow into four separate jets, so as to increase exhaust gas entrainment, had performed best. The Kyläla system had been used in the UK on three LMSR 4-6-0s and an SECR 0-6-0.

In Chapelon's Kylchap design it had been associated with the use of a concentric petticoat located between the top of the Kyläla *ajutage*, and the downward extension of the chimney bellmouth, and the whole assembly was precisely located and held together with two strong vertical bars. The concentric petticoat had been used by Legein in Belgium on his Pacifics and 2-10-0s. Separation of the exhausting column of steam into four jets, or with a double Kylchap, eight jets, was assisted by the location of four vee bars as Doncaster referred to them, or in French, *barrettes*. These were sharp case hardened knife edges, secured with set screws in the orifice of the blastpipe at right angles. Placed to register with the *ajutage* above, they were similar to the Goodfellow tips used in the USA on some designs. For the more powerful locomotives calculations showed that the height of the theoretical exhaust system exceeded loading gauge limits, and therefore the exhaust was divided into two jets in the standpipe, or breeches pipe as it is sometimes called. This was the theoretical justification for the use of the double Kylchap blastpipe. The standpipe was equipped with a guiding vane or mid-feather in each branch, placed so as to divide the cross-sectional area into two semicircles. This was to ensure that the exhausting steam from the steam chests was properly directed up through the blast nozzles. In this way the exhaust steam flow was halved in the breeches pipe, and the two streams were then each roughly halved and quartered in the Kyläla *ajutages* before discharging into the petticoat pipe and chimney. Thus the exhausting steam was made to present a greater and uniform surface area in order to entrain more thoroughly the smokebox gases and hence create both a greater vacuum

and more even draught across the tube bank and firegrate.

This was the 1K/1C design: the Kylchap was also developed in a simpler form as the 1K/T design for shorter smokeboxes in which the concentric petticoat was replaced by a longer Kyläla exhaust splitter and a longer downward extension of the chimney bellmouth. The latter design was used normally on lower power mixed traffic locomotives, and was usually a single blast assembly. It was used on more than 4,000 locomotives around the world. The Kylchap exhaust had played a crucial role in the rebuilding and subsequent performance of P-O Pacifics, and no doubt Gresley was interested in using this valuable means of both enhancing the evaporation rate and reducing back pressure.

Andre Chapelon's exhaust design had the added refinement of being able to tailor the area of the exhaust orifice (or orifices in the case of a double Kylchap blastpipe), one of the most critical dimensions in a steam locomotive, to the normal power output which was required of the locomotive. This was effected by varying the size of the *barrettes* or vee bars. There were three or four sets of *barrettes*, numbered from No.0 to No.3, and their effect was to reduce the net cross sectional area of the blastpipe orifice by 5, 10, 15 and 25% very approximately, obviously depending on which size was used. It was important to fit the right set: the design of the locomotive and its working in service could have been affected by other considerations such as smokebox volume. In very general terms, too big a reduction in orificial area and the sharpened exhaust would increase coal consumption disproportionately. If the reduction was too little then as soon as the locomotive was eased the smokebox vacuum could drop, risking a drop in boiler pressure as well. A Kylchap exhaust wrongly set or an engine correctly fitted but not properly handled could certainly burn coal. In theory the size of *barrettes* required varied with each duty, and immediately one can see that the constant adjustment of each locomotive would become impractical. In practice the exhaust system was so superior that the finer points of its application could be ignored, and a general setting was used. The Paris-Lyons-Mediterranée Railway used a variable form of the Kylchap exhaust that could be adjusted by the driver. M. Chapelon's view was that it was pointless, and the driver, despite his technical training (in France) was not the person to make that adjustment. In fact the works setting was usually at the minimum and crews left it unaltered. Changing the sizes of the *barrettes* and the blastpipe orifice of

COCK O' THE NORTH however, had not produced the answer to the steaming problem. One can understand Gresley's quoted remark that 'the first COCK O' THE NORTH will also be the last'. One can understand his embarrassment. In that there were five more Mikados, presumably he was referring particularly to the use of poppet valves.

The problem alluded to above was this: unfortunately Gresley's ideas so far for the new Pacific had leant heavily on the success of the P2, and the start of the new service was then only some seven months away. During that time a design had to be decided upon, drawings produced, detailed and four locomotives built. Also, unfortunately, while Gresley was faced with this dilemma, at much the same time, on January 4th 1935, Wedgwood had presented a long paper to the Board on the investigations so far, the high-speed test, and the scope for further accelerations. No doubt it struck a positive and enthusiastic theme, and as a result it was accepted and the Board gave the project the green light to go ahead. It was subsequently decided to amend the 1935 Building Programme to include the construction of four new A3 locomotives and the necessary rolling stock for a new service between London and Newcastle. There seemed to be growing enthusiasm for the planned new service in the senior levels of the LNER, but I wonder whether that enthusiasm was entirely shared by Gresley at that time, knowing what had to be done in a short time ahead, and what hung on its success?

Meanwhile, during 1935 the experimental 4-6-2-2 compound No.10000 had been stored out of service. A very considerable effort made to produce a reliable machine, but severe financial restrictions arising from the Great Slump of the early 1930s had delayed changes that had been discussed with André Chapelon, namely the introduction of re-superheating and the provision of a special 1K/1C Kylchap exhaust. The use of an intermediate superheater was necessary to raise the steam temperature between the HP and LP stages, to avoid condensation in the LP cylinders. The Kylchap double exhaust had been successfully used previously in a Swiss Railway water tube boilered 2-6-2T built by SLM in 1927. In January 1935 No.10000 had been transferred to Neville Hill, although at the time she was in Darlington works. In March 1935 she was fitted with the Kylchap double exhaust, but this required more modifications to ensure a tolerable degree of smoke deflection with the softer exhaust. No.10000 worked test trains to Darlington and Hull from Leeds with a counter-pressure locomotive, B13 4-6-0 No.761. This presumably was the reason for sending the engine to a new depot where it was almost completely unfamiliar to the staff there. On the route between Leeds and Hull, beyond Selby, there lay some 18 miles of straight and level track where the engine could work up to a steady 60mph for testing. Various loads were simulated and the power outputs at different cut-offs were measured. Even with the largest size of *barrettes* there were still problems with smoke deflection, despite the sharpness of the exhaust. With the smaller sizes the smoke deflection was worse, although significantly with higher power outputs the steaming improved. The engine achieved quite good power outputs, maintaining 14-1,500 DBHP on the level, approximating to about 2,000 IHP. The maximum recorded was 1,702 DBHP, similar to the output of a double chimney A3, about 2,300 IHP.

However, the inherent unreliability still dogged the engine, despite the improvements achieved and, on August 21st 1935, the story ended with the project terminated, and the engine sent light to Darlington works. Gresley had conceived the locomotive, built it with expert advice and assistance, and against all odds, it had run, hauling good loads, and not uneconomically. He had persisted with the experiment sufficiently to make an overall assessment of the use of high pressure, water tube boilers and compounding, but it was clear that further expenditure would gain no reward. He had achieved much more than most of his peers had managed. When one considers the totally different environment of a locomotive with frequently changing power and speed requirements, when compared with the steady requirements in marine use, with high frequency vibrations and shocks transmitted through the frames from the railjoint, it is surprising that the boiler performed as well as it did. The late Ken Hoole, an expert on matters North Eastern, calculated that it had spent 58% of its short life in the works, running just over 90,000 miles. It stood there until over a year later, when on October 13th 1936, it was sent to Doncaster for rebuilding. The boiler returned to Darlington where it remained in stationary service until the works was closed in 1965. No.10000 had been a most instructive experiment, even if not successful in terms of reliability.

Gresley was elected President of the Institution of Mechanical Engineers in 1936, and he was warmly thanked by his fellow senior engineers for having the courage to build No.10000 and to investigate the use of high pressure compounding. A great deal had seemed possible at its outset, and the project actually succeeded to a far greater degree than some of the more exotic experiments with very high pressures or duplex systems. In the end a working railway requires not a sophisticated machine that needs constant attention to produce power and economy, but a simpler, reliable day-to-day machine.

Meanwhile, as far as indications on the form that a new Pacific might take, the situation on the LNER in early 1935 could not have seemed very promising. The experiment with No.10000 had almost run its course without complete success. The prototype Mikado, despite its impressive debut, was not proving very economical, but the second, No.2002 EARL MARISCHAL, completed in November 1934, was doing well, was more economical on fuel, and had become popular. Nevertheless there was already talk of high coal consumption and a tendency to run hot. Expenditure was severely constrained as a result of the general economic situation and as already mentioned Gresley had great difficulty in getting agreement to four additional A3s as replacements for the five Raven Pacifics. Four of the latter needed new boilers, so their early withdrawal was intended. In such circumstances the decision both to proceed no further with No.10000 and not to modify the Mikados is understandable.

Yet the Company was now firmly committed to a groundbreaking new service only months away. There was much to be done and comparatively little time in which to achieve it.

The newly rebuilt No.10000 with a down express taking water, by the look of it, at Langley. The signal in the distance would be correct for the junction and Langley had no troughs on the slow line. The period is probably 1938 and the W1 has her original A3 type corridor tender No.5484, now with UNION OF SOUTH AFRICA.

CHAPTER TWO
Development of the A4 Pacific

A preliminary drawing had appeared in May 1934 showing a Pacific featuring the A3 boiler coupled with a 50 sq.ft. firegrate, poppet valves and a reduced coal capacity for the otherwise normal eight-wheel non-corridor tender. These drawings were the normal method of summarising a proposal in outline and for the designer to decide on the critical dimensions. In March 1935 a new design appeared. The poppet valves had been replaced by piston valves, and the firebox tubeplate had been moved forward 12 ins to provide a combustion chamber, shortening the boiler tubes by the same amount. The tender was changed to a bogie design, now with a corridor, 2 ft longer and nearly 3 tons heavier than the 1928 design. The advantages of rotary cam poppet valves in terms of reduced mechanical maintenance were not considered worth the increased coal consumption experienced so far with No.2001, despite the good results obtained with the D49 4-4-0s. The second Mikado, EARL MARISCHAL, was a piston valve engine, and its fuel economy was superior to COCK O' THE NORTH. The softer exhaust of the second P2 had necessitated a second pair of smoke deflectors, and so the front of the new Pacific had been changed to resemble the 'Hush-hush' rather than the Mikado. In

retrospect, the appearance of the design was not a million miles away from the outline of the SR Pacifics designed by Bulleid a decade later.

With the arrangements for the timetable now in hand, it had been decided to go ahead with the locomotives and rolling stock. As referred to earlier, the company's Joint Locomotive and Traffic Committee met on February 21st 1935 and had authorised the construction of four A3s during 1935. This was probably a financial device to release the necessary capital expenditure, as it seems quite unlikely that Gresley ever intended to build Nos.2509-2512 as A3s. His mind was not yet clearly made up on the design, and the estimate for the new engines would have been based on the existing A3. The rolling stock would have been covered by a block authorisation in Gresley's budget for new building as part of the continuing process of renewing the fleet.

Wedgwood had cleared the way for Gresley to produce his locomotives and train. The test run of March 5th 1935 had been authorised by Wedgwood in order to confirm the proposed four hour overall timings for the new service. The test train was hauled by an A3, and ran through to Newcastle on the new schedule, albeit with no stop at Darlington. It is not clear why the LNER opted for the

longer route after the success of the Leeds trials of November 30th 1934, but it could well be that the first trial was designed to test the estimated timings proposed for the German railcar. No doubt its success encouraged the view that the LNER should go for the larger North Eastern business market which promised higher revenue. I feel that the need to push FLYING SCOTSMAN hard on the Leeds trial run convinced everyone that an A3 rather than an A1 should be the motive power, which was an advantage on the Newcastle road. As the CCE still had work to complete before lifting his restriction at Wakefield to allow A3 operation, the A3s were still barred into Leeds from the south. The Newcastle road was longer by 82 miles, but it was much faster than the sharply graded and restricted route from Doncaster to Leeds and Bradford. Arguably it was a bigger business in commercial terms. Also the A3s were more fleet-footed.

The engine was No.2750 PAPYRUS, a favourite at Top Shed and a distinguished performer on the Non-stop. The train consisted of six coaches including the dynamometer car, 217 tons. Two crews were used, the regular team on No.2750, Driver H. Gutteridge and Fireman Wightman on the down run, and on

The front of DOMINION OF CANADA showing the Canadian Pacific Railway whistle and bell carried. Note also the short access cover originally provided just to the rear of the nameplate. (H.N. James)

the return run, again Driver W. Sparshatt and Fireman Webster. It was thought to be too demanding for one fireman, which might be regarded as something of an understatement! Gresley had evidently noted the publicity generated by the achievement of 100 mph, and decided to see what an A3 would do. After passing Doncaster on the up journey, PAPYRUS was carefully prepared for a determined effort down Stoke Bank, and as they approached Grantham she was gradually opened out, passing Stoke Box at 70mph. The A3 was then let fly down Stoke Bank, and with the boiler pressure actually rising, she covered over 12 miles at 100mph, and reached a maximum of 108mph. It was a magnificent effort by one of Top Shed's favourites, and moreover the A3 was not winded, for she went on to set a record for the Peterborough-Kings Cross section, 76.35 miles in 62 minutes 6 seconds. The schedules allowed four hours either way, but the northbound run, despite a delay caused by a derailment, took 237 minutes, and the southbound 232 minutes. For 300 miles out of the 536.7 miles the A3 had averaged 80mph. Later exploits by the A4s left PAPYRUS' achievements rather in the shade, and that is a pity, for it was a wonderful run.

Again, it was significant that the limitations of the layout of the front end seemed to throttle the A3 at high speed. Again, the cut-off had to be increased to reach the top speed, the larger port opening giving reduced throttling through the exhaust ports. It seems that the steam flow required for high speed through the cylinders at short cut-offs was greater than the steam circuit could withstand without significant pressure loss. Immediately after reaching the top speed, the cut-off was reduced and the pressure rose in the steam chests due to reduced steam demand from the cylinders. It seemed that the A3, although a faster locomotive than the A1, would reach 100 mph comfortably, but needed driving hard to advance significantly into three figures.

The trial was a great success, and at the company AGM on March 8th, three days later, William Whitelaw announced the decision to introduce a high-speed service between London and Newcastle, to be called 'The Silver Jubilee'. I suspect that the magnificent run with PAPYRUS also gave Gresley and his team reassurance that if the new locomotives were not completed in time, a 'green engine', an A3, could time the train.

The run by PAPYRUS led Gresley to revise the March 1935 design once again a month or so later, quite drastically. Feeling perhaps that his ideas for the future needed more development, he turned back to his eminently successful A3. The judgement of railway history is that he was absolutely right, brilliantly so. Gresley was a man who was cautious when necessary, but brilliantly far-sighted. He was open-minded, willing to listen to new ideas, provided always the advocate of those ideas had a case to argue and knew what he was talking about! The final design had the basic A3 boiler barrel reinstated, with the A3 firebox extended forward to form a combustion chamber. This effective modification increased the direct radiant heating surface – evaporation from which is roughly six times greater per unit of heating surface than an equivalent convective area in the tubes. The boiler tubes were shortened by a foot, and the number was reduced by four but otherwise the new boiler, Diagram 107, was very similar to the Diagram 94HP/94A of the A3s. The construction of the firegrate was altered to increase the ratio of free gas area to 56%.

Gresley had developed a neat and compact front end based on three cylinders, concentrated drive on the second axle, and conjugated valve gear: even if he wanted to improve on the design, there was very little time. He kept to concentrated drive, and remembering that the CCE had not yet used transition curves or possibly even realised the necessity, needed to anticipate higher stresses from the guiding action of the leading coupled axle together with heavier

DOMINION OF CANADA standing at Haymarket shed in 1937, carrying the presentation whistle and bell. The tender is A3 corridor tender No.5328. (H.N. James)

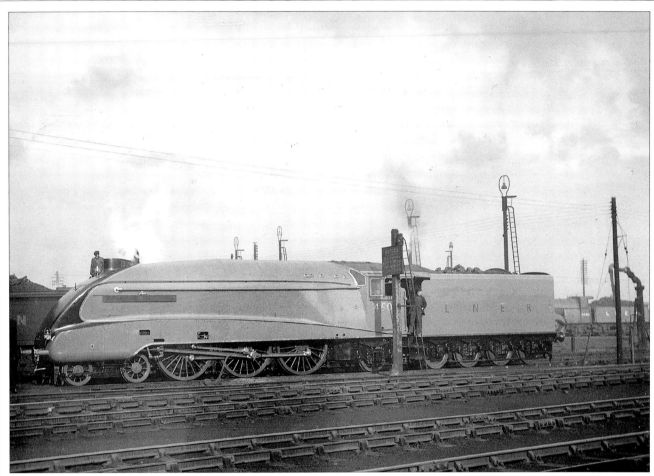

A pristine A4 with the cleaners adding the finishing touches, probably at Doncaster shed. The covered nameplates place the date at early March 1939 when No.4500 was renamed SIR RONALD MATTHEWS. Unhappily so in the view of many for the bird names, even the less inspired ones, suited the A4s better. (The Transport Treasury)

tyre wear. This avoided the use of a leading crank axle, which was structurally weaker than a solid axle. The familiar Gresley three-cylinder layout was used, with conjugated valve gear. The front end layout permitted only 18½ in cylinders with 9 ins piston valves, 27% greater than the 8 ins of the A3, and the boiler pressure was raised to 250 psi to compensate. The reason for the limit on cylinder diameter was that the middle cylinder, being on the locomotive centreline, restricted the available space left between the frames for the piston valve. The new design of valves and cylinders improved the ratio of piston valve to cylinder diameter from 40% in the A1 and 42.11% for the A3 to 48.64%. Gresley took particular care to ensure that tractive effort and adhesive weight were matched and his locomotives were not prone to slipping. Streamlining had evidently been in Gresley's mind, as for the first time we saw the running board pitched on an aerofoil curve rather than in its traditional horizontal position, with valancing over the upper half of the coupled wheels.

The cab was a modernised version of the A3 cab with angled wedge front leading faces as on the Mikados and bucket seats for the crew. This gave a slightly wider vision forward, and avoided internal reflection in the dark. The twin pullout regulator handles, the vertical reverser screw, main brake and ejector, boiler pressure gauge and Gresley's individual touch, the steam chest pressure gauge, were all signs of the A4's ancestry in the A3. One curiosity was the reverser, which worked in the opposite way to the A3 and confused drivers at first. Later, after a predictable series of incidents it was changed to avoid confusion.

A novel but necessary addition was the Flaman speed indicator and recorder, manufactured in France by Atéliers Vaucanson, located under the fireman's seat and driven off the right-hand rear crank pin. This was a mechanical device, and those with experience of it in service speak well of its reliability. It had been used previously by the GNR as early as in 1915, and had been used on locomotive testing since then. It was calibrated up to 120 mph on a segmental scale, and was also fitted with a hand-set needle to indicate the maximum permitted speed, usually 90 mph. The recorder was a stylus below that traced the actual speed on to a vertical drum loaded with a special printed roll of paper. This could then be removed and checked subsequently, and presumably, in the special language of railway discipline, any offender 'would be given suitable advice'. In France this recorder was

a standard fitting on all main line steam locomotives, known universally to crews as 'L'Espion'. The recordings were examined scrupulously, but the drivers' observance of speed limits was extremely good. After October 1937 when all A4s were available to work the streamliners, a late substitution might have meant that unless a paper roll had been loaded, the Flaman speed indicator was not recording, and any resulting high jinks might have gone undetected. Certainly there were occasions recorded by enthusiasts when the driver had let his A4 exceed the speed limits, and one presumes that the recorder was out of action, no doubt for a variety of reasons!

The steam passages were enlarged and straightened, the main steam pipe cross-sectional area increased by 96% and the branch pipes from the header by 24%. The exhaust passages took the form of an intricate but successful 'bridge' type blastpipe base that had been introduced a few years earlier on the A1 and A3 Pacifics. The effect of this was that when working hard with full regulator, the steam chest pressure was almost the same as the boiler pressure in the A4. The footplate is a severe environment, and the gauges have to be robust, so clearly they cannot be as sensitive as those in a testing station, for

An extremely unusual shot of an A4, DOMINION OF NEW ZEALAND no less, hauling what appears to be non-corridor stock, with 'open lights', i.e. an express headcode. At first glance the stock looks like a quad-art suburban set, but it is not articulated and carries roof boards. The location is given as Welwyn but it is the north portal of Potters Bar Tunnel. The date lies between March 1938 when the tender No.5647 was modified with Hoffman roller bearings, and May 1939 when the New Zealand Railways whistle was added. (The Transport Treasury)

example. With full boiler pressure, a white-hot fire and working hard, the difference could be as little as 3-5 psi. Gresley provided steam chest pressure gauges on all of his big engines, and this simple aid was particularly valuable to drivers starting.

The Gresley regulator consisted of a central regulator valve operated by a rod from the backplate. A transverse shaft was mounted on brackets attached to the backplate, linked at the centre to the operating rod, and at the outer ends of the transverse shaft there were two vertical handles. The left one was for the driver and the right for the fireman to assist or when manoeuvring the engine. The regulator handles operated in a quadrant, and operating the regulator handle moved the valve by moving the operating rod forwards or backwards. It could be very stiff depending on whether it was properly serviced and lubricated, or whether the backplate brackets were properly aligned. The driver had to stand up and use his weight judiciously, varying the regulator until the load was moving steadily. Without some indication of the steam pressure in the steam chests a thunderous slip was all too easy, with the concomitant

strain on the motion and wheelburns for the CCE to deal with. SILVER LINK was equipped with a pyrometer when new, but it was later removed: those used in the UK were notoriously unreliable devices in the harsh regime of the footplate and the idea was not pursued on the rest of the class.

Gresley considered using the Kylchap exhaust, but having experienced initial difficulties with COCK O' THE NORTH, instead he decided to use the single blastpipe with a jumper top introduced by Churchward and used on the GWR. Until 1941 the cost of the Kylchap exhaust included not only royalties but manufacture by the Associated Locomotive Equipment Co. (ALE) at Worcester; the total was over 5% of the overall cost of an A4. It was understandable therefore that the LNER was reluctant to pay a substantial sum for what, hitherto, they could do themselves. In the jumper top blastpipe, the pressure of the exhaust beat, having reached a predetermined value, lifted a collar on the top of the blastpipe to expose additional exhaust orifices in the top, increasing the total area and reducing back pressure. Without any running experience with the device, however, Gresley was unaware of the

tendency, in service, for the arrangement to function less certainly when jammed. The jumper top blastpipe required regular cleaning to remove any deposits of carbonised cylinder lubricant and smokebox char that prevented the moveable collar from seating properly on the top face. With higher superheat of the A4s compared with the low superheat GWR locomotives, carbonisation was much more prevalent. This was the reason for the post-war use of plain circular blastpipes not only on the A4s but on the GWR locomotives as well when they were provided with high degree superheat.

The first four engines were attached to new corridor tenders of similar design to the A3 type, but without trim and styled with additional cladding to match the train. The intention was to balance all wheels but those of the tender were unbalanced. It was decided that with the 1936 batch of A4s, the corridor tenders would be removed from the A1s and A3s, and modified to match the A4s. In fact after nine had been used with Nos.4482-4490 (the tenth was still attached to PAPYRUS for the last round trip by an A3 on the 1937 Non-stop) seven new corridor tenders were built for

Nos.4491-4497. By the time the last of the batch was completed, No.4498, the tenth A3 tender was available. The A3s of course received new high-sided tenders or spare GN tenders. The 22nd corridor tender, No.5484, remained with the W1 No.10000 until June 1948, when tenders were exchanged with No.60004 WILLIAM WHITELAW.

All of the corridor tenders had buckeye automatic couplers, which, with a stiff regulator and a less experienced driver, gave the platform-end audience wonderfully entertaining interludes as crew and shunter tried to couple loco and train. Passengers in the leading coaches already settling in their seats were alarmed as some 170 tons of A4 bounced against the buffers of the leading coach, sometimes repeatedly, sometimes with more than usual vigour, until the shunter pronounced that the union was safely completed. The record as far as I remember was six shots at coupling before the deed was done. In contrast one admired the senior men, as they stood off 15 ft or so, while the shunter set the couplers and removed the saddles over the extended buffer shanks. Then a signal from the shunter, the regulator pumped quickly, and a firm brake application and a clink from the buffers as they just touched. No fuss.

As Top Shed and Haymarket used their A4s on the night sleepers, on certain turns one had the risk of a rude awakening at Grantham and Newcastle as well! Gerry Fiennes, in his memoirs, referred to a traumatic moment when the Royal train, no less, having been worked into the terminus, and the train engine, an A4, refused both to couple correctly and to uncouple to permit another try. One of the station's many N2s was summoned to bump the A4 and release the coupling. Peter Townend, who was present at the time, recalled that the incident took a while, leaving no time for the brake testing, but the driver set off and of course everything went as it always did, correctly. The cause was a difference of height between the couplers on the A4 tender and those on the leading vehicle of the Royal train, something which on future occasions was carefully checked. Two out of six inches might seem to the layman nothing to worry about overmuch, but let me assure you that losing the Royal train en route would have been a sure way to end a promising career, probably in the Tower.

The brake controls were much the same as the A3, the braking being solely vacuum on engine and tender, as with the train. The braking system of the A4 was not quite as good as it could have been for a high-speed locomotive. Ironically, in that respect the locomotive was the least well-equipped vehicle in the train. Vacuum rather than Westinghouse compressed air brakes were more restricted in performance,

particularly in the rate of propagation of the brake application through the train, and in the use of variable pressure control systems to match the friction characteristics of the brake blocks on wheel tyres at different speeds. However, vacuum braking remained the standard for locomotive hauled trains until the 1970s.

The vacuum brake needed an experienced hand to finesse the braking and control the level of vacuum: it was unforgiving to the heavy-handed. Whereas Continental practice involved the use of the leading and trailing carrying wheels to provide additional retardation, only the coupled wheels and the tender of the A4 were braked. One had also to recognise in calculating the braking force of the tender that, as the run progressed, the tenders lightened and in the absence of a load control regulator, brake force was limited to about 50% of that for a full loaded tender. As adhesive weight limited the brake force that could be applied on those axles, the braking capacity of the A4 on a lightweight express was limited. On the other hand the addition of brakes to the carrying wheels would have been a major redesign task, and in British practice was unpopular with its need for frequent rigging adjustment. The A4s never seemed underbraked at speed during their working life, although a full, heavy brake application on the streamliners in an emergency would, and did make the

SILVER FOX, now in garter blue livery with nameplates, heads an up express. The date is given as 1938, but the location is not Barnby Moor as quoted, but Markham, some eight miles further south. The structure in the distance is Askham Tunnel, which at 57 yards is the shortest piece of conventional tunnel construction that I can recall on the rail network. (The Transport Treasury)

The first 'Coronation' A4, DOMINION OF CANADA at Kings Cross just after naming. She has the CPR chime whistle, the coat of arms and stainless steel trim, but the famous bell has not yet been fitted. The A3 corridor tender is No.5326. (The Transport Treasury)

blocks extremely hot. And as veteran car enthusiasts will know, the friction generated by brake shoes decreases with heat. The operation of the streamliners was said to be hard on brake block life, as brake applications were more frequent due to the observation of speed restrictions from high speed, compared with heavier trains travelling at lower speeds.

The springing of the A4 was different from the A3 since it was intended for higher speeds. The main coupled wheel springs were similar to those used by Maunsell on his 'Schools' class 4-4-0s, first used by Gresley on the D49 and K3 classes. The springs were the normal laminated type with 16 plates, half an inch thick, but they were lengthened from 42 to 48 ins long. The deflection was thus 0.27 ins per ton, very roughly twice the value for similar sized locomotives. In service the plates occasionally showed hairline fractures which were allowed to run. The bogie was suspended by double swing links with horizontal bearing springing. The Cortazzi axleboxes were used for the trailing radial axle as in the A3. The riding of the A3s had occasionally become jerky, and the fault was found to be the inclination of the sliding top surface. As a result it was changed from 1 in 7 to 10.66, but the sliding faces in plan were tangential to a radius of 12 ft. as with the A3s. In service the riding of the A4s also gave a little cause for concern at the outset,

and the stiffness of the horizontal control springs was increased as a result. To curb rolling at speed, at Stanier's suggestion side checks were fitted to the main and bogie frames. These modifications to the suspension were made pre-war. No further trouble was experienced.

The streamlined cladding was entirely new. It is however difficult to see exactly when the decision to streamline the new Pacific was made, but it was ultimately Gresley's. He had studied the streamlining so far applied, and was attracted to the idea of reducing the power required to move the locomotive at higher speeds. The amount of power consumed by the locomotive due to machine friction, inertia, expansion and thermal losses, plus that required to overcome the effect of gravity varies but can amount to quarter of the whole on average. At higher speeds that proportion increases due to the increased significance of air resistance. Experimental work had already been undertaken at Doncaster on front end design with the objective of deflecting exhaust steam and smoke clear of the crew's lines of vision for signal sighting. The experiments both with CORONACH and HUMORIST, and the high pressure compound No.10000 had contributed to the general understanding of air resistance and air flow round a moving train. Work had also proceeded on the effect of streamlining and trying to quantify

its benefits. From the work so far carried out it appeared to be worthwhile at 70-75mph or more, and this work had paved the way for the design of the A4.

From the time when the German unit was being considered streamlining, by implication, seems to have been part of the project. It was all the rage in all forms of transport, the initial stimulus coming from America, probably first in aviation. The German and French diesel units were stylish and streamlined in which the air-smoothed finish was not so difficult to achieve with the prime mover carried on a coach chassis. In France the Bugatti railcars dominated the fastest regional services by a clear margin, with one exception, the 'Sud-Express' of the P-O between Poitiers and Angoulême timed at 70.4 mph and worked by Chapelon's magnificent Pacifics. At speeds limited to 120-130 kph streamlining had less to offer the French by way of economy, but some experimental rebuilding took place. One of Chapelon's second series of Pacific rebuilds, 231H726, was fully streamlined but no tests took place to establish whether any advantage had been obtained. The German diesel units had limited accommodation however, and the German steam locomotive designers sought a locomotive that could haul a normal express load at similar speeds. In 1935 Borsig of Berlin produced Adolf Wolff's magnificent fully streamlined three - cylinder 4-6-4 with 7ft 6½ins coupled wheels, making full use of the larger Central European loading gauge. From 1935 these locomotives hauled 200 tonne trains from Berlin to Hamburg, 178 miles, at an average of 70 mph. In 1936 an Institution of Locomotive Engineers' visit was treated to a demonstration run, reaching 118 mph. In America, 'streamlining' was applied to anything that moved, and the railways were not slow in applying the principle to the steam and diesel locomotives. When the step change away from diesel back to steam was made, it seems probable that Wedgwood felt that the new train ought to fit in with the genre of new streamlined expresses, and Gresley took it as part of his remit.

The Chicago, Milwaukee St.Paul & Pacific Railroad of America was in competition with the Chicago & North Western and the Chicago, Burlington & Quincy Railroads for the traffic between Chicago and the cities of Minneapolis and St.Paul. It had responded to the introduction of the diesel powered 'Zephyr' high-speed units of the CB&Q by introducing the 'Hiawatha' service. The two, later three special locomotives that were built by Alco, a year before the first A4 in 1934, for the daily 100 mph operation were fully streamlined large 4-4-2s, and they were completely successful. Their schedule was timed at an average of 73.9 mph overall, including 78 miles from Sparta to Portage scheduled at 81 mph start to stop. Interestingly, a year later the Pennsylvania Railroad met the challenge by accelerating its 'Detroit Arrow', using ordinary stock with K4S non-streamlined Pacifics over a fairly level road, to 75.5 mph between Plymouth and Fort Wayne. Later, a larger 4-6-4 version of the CMP's Class A Atlantic was built, the F7 4-6-4. This was also fully streamlined, and in 1943 one averaged 100mph for 25 miles with no less than 800 tons! News of the Class A had doubtless filtered through to Doncaster. It is worth bearing in mind that, brilliant though the A4 was, Britain was a little behind in the race towards higher rail speeds.

It was as easy then as it is now to provide a cosmetic appearance and streamlined ends to what was in effect a rake of carriages with the diesel engine or engines in or under some of them. In America and Germany the new diesel units and some steam locomotives were streamlined, and the transport world seemed gripped by a streamlining frenzy. The infection even spread to the London Passenger Transport Board, which actually produced a streamlined underground train for the Piccadilly Line. As if it had much effect at 30 mph underground, and indeed if anyone could actually measure that effect! It was quite another matter to enclose a Stephensonian steam locomotive in a metal shroud and produce a masterpiece of style. The attempts to streamline the irregularities and excrescences of the conventional steam locomotive at Swindon with MANORBIER CASTLE and KING HENRY VII were unfortunate, and would have made little difference to the air resistance of an express train. If it was to be done, then a streamlined shell or casing had to be designed within which the components could be fitted. While the new Gresley three-cylinder Pacific was the same in outline as the A3, and it was straightforward to replace boiler cladding with streamlined casing and design the rear half of the locomotive cladding, it was another matter entirely for the front half. Gresley had decided that the running board should follow an aerofoil profile, and the Drawing Office was given the task of selecting a suitable shape. Gresley was also concerned that the front of the locomotive should be streamlined, but in a way that gave effective smoke deflection. He was not prepared to build a locomotive that would run fast without affording the driver a clear view ahead.

Gresley himself was convinced of the value of streamlining, but while theory and wind tunnel testing suggested that there was a benefit, that had to be balanced with the cost of the additional work. He left his assistant, O.V.S. Bulleid to push the concept along in detail, checking and modifying at each stage as he saw it necessary, and sometimes teasing Bulleid, to whom this was all meat and drink. No doubt Gresley had other pressing matters to attend to. Wooden models of A3s and putative A4 shapes were commissioned and tested in a wind tunnel in order to determine the extent of any saving in power output and the effectiveness of smoke deflection. The vee fronted cab of the Mikado had been included, and at least one of the A4 models included the inverted horizontal wedge shape used by Bugatti on his high-speed railcars on the Etat Railway in France. On his visits to France Gresley had noticed how effective these were in minimising air disturbance, even lifting the exhaust of passing steam locomotives, and this shape had given the best results in testing. Even so, the model was not completely satisfactory in all wind angle conditions. Eric Bannister, a junior technical assistant in Gresley's office, related the story of the happy accident that solved the remaining problems. The test model was clad in plasticine and needed careful handling, and during wind tunnel testing under the direction of Professor Dalby, Bannister noticed an accidental thumbprint causing a depression just behind the chimney. When tested this minor but critical change proved instrumental in enabling the horizontal wedge shape to cope with all problems of smoke deflection.

The benefit of streamlining was said to be the saving in fuel and power from decreased air resistance. The wind tunnel testing at the National Physical Laboratory not only explored the optimum shape for the A4 casing, but also the likely saving in power. The estimates of power required at 100 and 150 mph showed a saving of 190 and 640 HP for a fully streamlined locomotive and train respectively in favour of streamlining. When one considers the power required to maintain the lesser of these speeds on the level, one can appreciate that the estimated saving is hardly outside the limits of experimental error that existed half a century ago. Experience of model analysis suggests that the relationship between say a 1:40 model and the full size is not necessarily arithmetical, and the results are indicative rather than accurate. The greater the ratio between the model dimensions and the full size design, the greater care must be used in extrapolation. One cannot simply multiply the results by 40. They always required, where possible, a full size test, which then gave some idea of the relationship between the results suggested by model analysis, and those experienced in reality. Suffice it to say that at the normal speeds for heavier expresses, the saving was insignificant.

Another and more fundamental problem was that unless the prevailing wind was head-on, the wind resistance of a train was dependent on the dimensions and nature of the *total* surface exposed to the wind, i.e. the surface of the whole train and not just the locomotive. Of course the benefit of streamlining was not always apparent, if the direction of the wind was unfavourable – indeed sometimes there must have been no benefit at all. The locomotive represented roughly one eighth of the whole surface area for the 'Silver Jubilee', or for the 'Flying Scotsman', nearer one fifteenth. The effect of streamlining the locomotive was far less than was generally supposed, certainly less than 10% and possibly less than 5%. What wind tunnel testing did show was that streamlining the *train* was, if anything, more important than the locomotive. This was the reason why

COMMONWEALTH OF AUSTRALIA at Kings Cross at, or soon after its naming, in June 1937. A4 corridor tender No.5646. (The Transport Treasury)

the train, when viewed by the public on September 27th 1935, looked so very different, with all possible projections, excrescences such as panelling, and gaps between and under the coaches either removed or clad with rubber sheeting.

Having established the shape of the front of the new Pacific, a wooden full size replica was made. It is a pity that some of the numerous wooden replicas made during the steam age did not survive. The smokebox was sealed under the streamlined casing with a door similar to that of No.2751 HUMORIST during the smoke deflection experiments, and the first Mikados. Access to the door was provided by what was universally known as the 'cod's mouth', a lifting angled cover plate in the front casing. The draughtsman responsible for designing the means of opening and closing the casing famously drew lunchtime inspiration from noticing the mechanism used to operate the Doncaster Borough Council's refuse carts. Also famously, the draughtsman dealing with the front mistakenly specified a radius of curvature of 14 ft as 12. This was later corrected when the short buffers were extended.

Gresley was still not happy with his A4, and in retrospect one can imagine that a normally horizontal running board would not sit easily on the emerging A4. He was determined to get the appearance right and

insisted that the running board should have the aerofoil profile as in the April 1935 design. There was something of the artist in him, as there should be in all engineers, not resting until balance and composition had been established. He cared about the appearance of his locomotives. When it came to locating the running board, the Drawing Office suggested the aerofoil of the R101 airship, which Gresley approved. This was transferred to SILVER LINK by marking the shape on planks temporarily secured on the sides, so that the smith could make the supporting brackets. An obvious problem with the partly built A4 was that there were few straight lines and edges to which one could refer. Instead of the drawings preceding manufacture, the necessary supports were manufactured, and the drawings then prepared on an 'as made' basis. There is no doubt that this part of the design was one of the more elegant inspirations, something which was revealed by accident when Gresley's successor, Thompson, dispensed with the side valancing of the A4s as a wartime economy and an aid to access for maintenance. It is of course a matter of taste, but before, the A4 looked very much part of the art deco-1930s world. After, with the span of the driving wheels exposed, they looked superb. Even in preservation, at the turn of the 21st

century, the A4 does not look like a piece of engineering antiquity.

So the streamlined shape emerged, the Bugatti inspired front, the aerofoil running board, the shaped cladding and the Mikado cab. One got used to the shape of an A4 and after a while it seemed perfectly normal. However, the coalescence of the separate aspects of the design of streamlined casing into one harmonious whole is the most remarkable feature of the appearance of the A4. The whole revolutionary look was completed by fitting the locomotives with a chime whistle. These have become very collectable, and their provenance has also become something of a minor science. Captain Howey, owner of the Romney, Hythe and Dymchurch Railway, presented the original to Gresley in April 1934, and he used it on the prototype Mikado COCK O' THE NORTH. It was manufactured by the Crosby Valve Co. of America, and an order for four more for the Mikados was later diverted to the first four A4s. The 4 in. diameter whistle was divided into three chambers of different length, and when sounded produced three notes which merged into a distinctive chord.

The sound of a chime whistle is a very emotive one, especially for anybody who has lived near the East Coast main line for a period. Later, specific engines for the 'Coronation' were fitted with appropriate whistles. One of the experiences of the steam age most sorely missed by people of my generation is the sound of those chime whistles. One did not even have to see the railway, but for example around 17-18.00 the sound of an A4 would drift over the GN main line as the 'Tees-Tyne Pullman', 17.00 Peterborough, the 'Yorkshire Pullman' each made their way north, and the 'Flying Scotsman' came up the last lap. Then as midnight approached, the haunting call was heard across the silent sleeping countryside as the A4 on the up Newcastle-Holloway ECS ambled back from Peterborough, her driver calling for the road.

Half a century ago, a number of recordings of steam trains were marketed by Argo Transacord and the originals were made by Peter Handford. Apart from providing the background sound (approximately) to a generation of videos that were based on ciné films. Peter demonstrated that just the sound of a train could be powerfully emotive.

The new livery comprised three shades of grey, the lightest silver grey being used for the locomotive and tender bodies, a darker shade for the frames and valancing, with the darkest shade used on the wedge front. Gresley and his team were obviously feeling their way with an entirely new design. When the livery of the whole train was under discussion, the Doncaster works shunter, J55 0-6-0ST No.4800 was conscripted as a guinea pig for various shades of grey livery before

the colours were finally decided. Originally, on completion, the name of the locomotive, SILVER LINK, was carried on straight rectangular nameplates with rounded corners on the smokebox sides, a traditional but entirely successful arrangement. Before the locomotive went into service however, these were removed, at the suggestion of Gresley's daughter, Violet, on the grounds that it spoilt the effect of the whole ensemble. Certainly as modified, from the 21st century viewpoint the train has a more '1935' look and the advice was probably good. The name was painted on the streamlined casing in silver with bright blue shading over the driving axle. Later when the livery was changed to garter blue, nameplates were restored, cast in brass and chromium plated. The three shades of grey met at the front buffer level, but later the darkest grey was brought round to each side where it met the body shade in a parabolic curve from behind the plain chimney down to the cylinders. 'Parabolic' was descriptive rather than a precise definition. The plain copper chimney casing enclosed the anti-vacuum valve as well, and was painted black. The effect was completely successful, and this arrangement for the A4 livery prevailed, with various body colours, for the rest of their years in service. It was always amusing to examine the A4s being repainted in Doncaster Works paintshop, carefully observing from head-on, to see whether the two curves either side of

the smokebox were identical. Often they weren't.

The Silver Jubilee was to be a luxury service, revolutionary in terms of speed. Gresley brought it into life brilliantly. The design of the coaching stock attracted much less attention from the public, which was a pity. The interior was sumptuously furnished, but it was the exterior which was novel. Gresley had employed his system of articulation but sparingly, using pairs of coaches carried on three bogies. He was conscious of the operators' coolness towards the system, due to the need to replace not one vehicle but the whole articulated set for just one hot box or whatever. There is no evidence that this was a problem with the operation of the streamliners in fact. The advent of roller bearings was needed to bring home the advantages of articulation, namely significantly reduced construction and maintenance costs together with reduced frictional resistance compared with conventional stock. Wind tunnel testing had produced valuable information that had been used in the design, such as the removal of all external projections and equipment, and rubber sheeting between the coach ends and between the bogies, all to reduce air resistance.

In an age where we are constantly subjected to the clamour of the motor industry, the sight of a new car with its well-nigh perfect paintwork, shape and general appearance is a daily experience. In 1935 before the technology involved in vehicle

WOODCOCK with a down express tops the climb out of Kings Cross at Finsbury Park. Although published in December 1946, the photograph was clearly taken well before September 1942 when the valances were removed and the A4 painted black. It is impossible to tell whether the A4 is apple green or garter blue. The A4 corridor tender was fitted with Skefco roller bearings in 1939.

bodywork skills such as panel beating, filling and shaping had advanced very far, Doncaster had to rely on very basic skills to produce its first A4. That it did so in 74 days from the laying of the frames was quite remarkable. When this is taken into account, the quality of the finished result, especially with the complex shape of the front of the engine, was astounding.

Meanwhile outline plans for the train had been sent to Wedgwood, and the approval of the Board and its CGM had been obtained by the end of March 1935. From then it had all been down to Gresley and his staff. In response to a subsequent enquiry in late 1935 by Wedgwood, after the amazing introduction of the 'Silver Jubilee', as to the sequence of events that preceded it, Gresley's reply was brief and to the point.

March 5th, 1935: Trial run to Newcastle and back. (with an A3)

March 11th, 1935: Outline diagram of the suggested train sent to CGM.

March 28th, 1935: The LNER Board approved the CGM's proposal.

April 17th, 1935: Cylinder drawings were sent for CME's approval.

June 6th, 1935: Outside cylinders cast at Gorton.

June 7th, 1935: Inside cylinders cast at Doncaster.

June 26th, 1935: Frames for the new engine laid at Doncaster.

Sept 7th, 1935: Locomotive finished and put into steam.

It was a masterpiece of understatement.

More than half a century later, I doubt whether anyone would dare, or indeed be allowed to consider starting a prestigious new groundbreaking service with just *one* locomotive at first for nearly three weeks. There simply wasn't enough time to do more, given the dates of the decision to go ahead, and the starting date for the new service. One might feel that the LNER Board was unaware of the risks, but both Whitelaw and Wedgwood must have been, and it is a measure the strength of Gresley's reputation that he was trusted to deliver on time. He was confident in the excellence of his design, its construction and those who operated it, and was justified in his faith. Of course there was the knowledge that the A3s could run the service if required, but the publicity cost would have been high. The second A4 QUICKSILVER was completed on September 21st six days before the trial run. It was available at Kings Cross on September 26th but hardly run-in. Presumably if SILVER LINK gave trouble, it might have been risked, but in the event there was no need.

I am sure that starting the service with only one A4 was not something undertaken by choice. There is no doubt in my mind that the lights must have been on till late in the evenings beforehand at Doncaster

Works! I am sure that, privately, Gresley kept his fingers crossed during those early weeks, even with the second A4 backstage, as it were. Whether he did or not, it was an amazing achievement, a *coup de théâtre* which reached its climax in the astonishing trial running of September 27th 1935. Gerry Fiennes used to argue that the man who wants an idea to succeed is always stronger than those who wish to stop him. September 1935 was an excellent confirmation of his belief.

The situation had been tense, but Gresley had one enormous advantage. He had, at Kings Cross and Doncaster Works, a team of some of the finest and most loyal designers and craftsmen that anyone could wish for, men and women who were proud of the quality of their work. That team had, at its head, an outstanding chief whose engineering judgement and experience were second to none, and it was that which turned the risk of potential failure into a stunning success. It is a tribute to the quality of Doncaster's engineering that the frames of the new Pacific were laid in the last days of June 1935, and the actual construction had occupied 76 days. On September 7th 1935, the first A4, SILVER LINK, was put into steam for the first time at Doncaster.

No.4462 while still named GREAT SNIPE, at Top Shed. It is coupled to A4 non-corridor tender No.5667. The period would be the years 1937-1940.

CHAPTER THREE
The Streamliner Years

On September 7th 1935 the first of four special new Pacifics was completed at Doncaster. To a public and the railway enthusiasts in particular, used to the powerful and yet graceful lines of the A1 and A3 Pacifics and unprepared for such a radical departure from the traditional appearance of a locomotive, it was a shock. For the new Pacific, SILVER LINK, was a completely streamlined locomotive in three shades of grey, a startling enough shape, but in its new livery an astounding sight. Top link Driver Hardiman was sent to Doncaster to bring the new locomotive up light to Kings Cross on September 13th, and many of us would have wished to be there to hear his reaction. No doubt it was the centre of attention as it stood in the Top Shed yard for the first time. The late E.A.J. Neve, an old friend of many of us, and a great expert on matters GN and LNER, rose earlier than usual to see the new

Pacific working its running-in turn on the 7.10 Cambridge on September 14th 1935. A traditionalist by nature, Eric Neve could remember twenty years later the utter astonishment at seeing this strange apparition approaching, sounding like a Gresley Pacific but looking anything but.

In its unique way the A4 was and still is a very handsome and well balanced design, and I am one of many who regard it as the epitome of grace at speed. There were many attempts at streamlining express steam locomotives in Europe and America, but Gresley succeeded better than most, completely and aesthetically in my view. The streamlined casing had to be functional and attractive without obstructing the use and servicing of the locomotive, but as Gresley knew, it had also to deflect the exhaust clear of the forward view of the crew.

The A3 is a handsome traditional locomotive design, but those who

lived by the East Coast main line, we became used to the A4s and regarded them as handsome, stylish locomotives, the élite. Even now, in preservation, the locomotives have a timeless quality, whereas some other designs start to look old. Dirt, filth and neglect never suited them. To others used to the locomotives of other railways, they must have seemed odd. I remember a Crewe fitter telling me that 'they just don't look like a steam engine'. In 1953 British Railways commissioned their excellent film unit, headed by Edgar Anstey, to make a film called 'The Elizabethan'. The film was of course in monochrome, and the less said about its puerile commentary, in rhyming verse, the better. A mobile film unit was accommodated in a brake van on the ex-LMSR line to Stamford and several 'takes' of the train were made. As the 'Elizabethan' appeared, accelerating away past Werrington Junction, the film train

The run which marked the birth of the High Speed Train and, for the photographer, the shot of a lifetime. On September 27th 1935 SILVER LINK raced through Hadley Wood station at 70 mph and this superb photograph was the result, taken from the south portal of Hadley Wood North Tunnel. It has been published many times, but it is still a very fine image of a very historic occasion. The stainless steel trim to windows and doors is well illustrated, and the clean coach roofs and sides are particularly noticeable. Hadley Wood signalbox, by that time taken out of operation, can be seen together with the small yard that existed until the 1950s.

set off ahead. The moving shots of SILVER FOX with Driver Bob Marrable accelerating her train away from Peterborough past Walton are some of the most wonderfully evocative moments of steam traction on film.

It is a tribute to the quality of Doncaster's engineering that although the new Pacific had been constructed very quickly, three months after the frames were laid SILVER LINK had shattered most of the records for sustained high speed on rail with steam traction. It was, in the words of Cecil J. Allen, writing on the history of Gresley's Pacifics, 'a première without equal'. It was a feat of great and almost faultless engineering that many of us in the industry, half a century later, envied.

SILVER LINK had been completed, run in and sent to Kings Cross, where after a few perfunctory trips on the 7.45 and 16.15 'Parleys' to Peterborough, she was returned to Doncaster on September 19th for trial running with the new train. The new Pacific began to demonstrate the increased power and turn of speed that was intended. In the up direction, down Stoke Bank, 100 mph was reached and held for six miles, but more significantly, the Peterborough-Grantham section was run start to stop in 26 minutes with a minimum of 72 mph at Stoke. On September 22nd, five days before the trial run, high-speed braking trials were carried out to confirm the new

A4's ability to stop her train safely within the existing signalling braking distances. Again the new locomotive had shown her potential for speed, having reached 101 mph near Tallington during these tests. The ability to stop safely on normal block signalling was not shown to be the case where wheel/rail adhesion was poor, and on the five occasions when the braking was tested, SILVER LINK overshot the home signal at least twice by a substantial distance. The worst was at Tallington up home by 695 yards from high speed. It would have been extremely optimistic to have expected anything better with a light train travelling at high speed. The train simply had insufficient brake force, as we now describe it.

I would be surprised if the operators had not already anticipated this eventuality. While the 'Silver Jubilee' was a new concept in operating, fast moving light trains and light engines homeward bound were not, and it was known that the latter especially had greater difficulty in stopping. For that reason light engines were limited in speed. Therefore the 'Silver Jubilee' was operated on a double block basis, that is with at least two block sections clear ahead of the train instead of the normal one, to ensure safe running. This complication would have caused a slight operating inconvenience, but it was far too late to do anything else. In practice it was not a great encumbrance, for the 'Silver Jubilee'

moved quickly through the block sections, and it would have been an unwise signalman who let anything get in her way!

The locomotive and train were planned to take part in a trial run on September 27th 1935, the Friday before the train commenced running on Monday, September 30th. Inter-departmental communication, indeed inter-Divisional communication, was not one of the LNER's stronger points. Not only had it been shown late in the day that high speed indeed meant double block working, but there was worse to come. It had been suddenly realised in the North Eastern Area, also at a very late stage, that the train might not be able to stop with certainty from more than 70mph, in *all* foreseeable circumstances, over the brand new colour light section between York and Darlington. A special train, hauled by an A3 piloted by a Raven Atlantic, had run from York to Darlington at speeds up to 100 mph, and had established beyond all reasonable doubt that more than 70 mph was inadvisable. The C7s were fleet-footed but this was above and beyond the call of duty! The Raven engine's predicament, being hauled at high speed by a Doncaster Pacific, was the subject of merriment at Doncaster. This section had been resignalled with three aspects, with the odd signal displaying a fourth aspect where the braking distance was insufficient. With a signal spacing of roughly ¾ mile, in clear

The down 'Silver Jubilee' races north of Hadley Wood North towards Ganwick. As it is an eight coach train, the date must be after March 1938. Ganwick signalbox had been removed, in 1932 I believe, along with Mimms Hall, and Hadley Wood had become a ground frame in an early use of intermediate block colour light signals.

weather a driver travelling at 90 mph would have been able to sight a caution aspect and act promptly without undue risk. But signal sighting and positioning has to assume the worst of all combinations of variables affecting braking, and on a foggy night, for example, a late sighting, wet or greasy rail and slow reaction times to select but three variables, would have spelt trouble. The operation of the railway has always assumed that drivers stop *before* and not just somewhere in the vicinity of signals at danger. Ironically the newest and fastest train on the LNER could not run at full speed on its newest signalling. One could not, and cannot operate double block signalling over a route with continuously track circuited automatic colour light signalling.

As a result, the operators realised that there was little chance of the train keeping to the 37 minute start to pass timing from Darlington to York, 44.1 miles, and had to increase the allowance to 41 minutes on the up journey, and 41½ minutes on the down. This increase required a compensating cut south of York, and the 'Silver Jubilee' was actually required to reach Kings Cross in 157 minutes, and on the down journey, pass through York in 156½ minutes from Kings Cross. This required average speeds of 71.9 mph on the up and 72.2 mph on the down. These were start to pass through York at 20 mph timings, or vice versa, and required an even higher standard of high-speed running. Meanwhile the CCE of the NE Area had to alter his signalling to provide a fourth aspect throughout, a task that took another 2½ years.

Cecil J. Allen, referred to earlier, was the leading writer of the time on locomotive performance, and was compulsory reading. He was not an engineer, but worked as a Materials Inspector for the Chief Civil Engineer of the Southern Area of the LNER, a post that involved a great deal of travelling. He was also, because of his great interest in train performance, the LNER's quasi-official timekeeper, and most if not all that we know about the great pre-war deeds of Gresley's Pacifics comes from his pen. We remain greatly in his debt. Naturally he had to be careful in what he wrote, as an employee of the LNER. He wrote a monthly column in *The Railway Magazine* that was required reading for everyone interested in locomotive design and performance. His style of writing was formal and archaic by modern standards and his prose was littered with Latin tags and classical quotations that were joyfully recycled later by both speakers and wags at railway club meetings.

He wrote many books, but in 1950 produced the small but invaluable *The Gresley Pacifics of the LNER* which was, for many, a bible, the introduction to the story. Despite his style of writing and a number of technical inaccuracies, Allen's magnificent record of the story of Gresley's Pacifics stands among the best of steam age literature. The overwhelming proportion of what we know about locomotive performance at this time comes from him, supported by his regular correspondents, O.S. Nock in particular. One suspects that his normally strictly impartial view conveyed in his monthly articles yielded somewhat when on the subject of Gresley's Pacifics. His account of the trial run of September 27th 1935 as one of the passengers is one of the great passages of literature in railway engineering. One can imagine the sensations of the passengers 'as SILVER LINK blazed away at this enormous speed and more'.

Just as the appearance of GREAT NORTHERN had been met with astonishment, the appearance of Gresley's huge 2-8-2 COCK O'THE NORTH was awesome, so the trial run with SILVER LINK brought incredulity. This was the first occasion when the whole train was presented to the public rather than the odd lineside enthusiast. As a sight the train was something totally new, flush sided with the coach ends and the shielded-in spaces between the bogies. Even the carriage numbers were displayed as stainless steel numerals. A new standard of luxury had been employed in the construction of the train. As already mentioned it featured articulation, with a triplet articulated restaurant set flanked by two articulated twins, one first and one third. The colours used for interior décor were blue for first class and green for third. Cooking was by electricity and the chef had the luxury of *a refrigerator...* Tubular lights were used although whether they were fluorescent is unlikely remembering the need for an AC supply. An electric speed indicator was provided in the first class brake at the London end, but this was moved to the restaurant car where it would have been more useful. The coaches were steel with silver liveried rexine cladding, and the fittings were chromium plated to echo the silver theme. It was a complete contrast to the traditional teak panelled East Coast express stock.

Wind tunnel testing had lessons for rolling stock as well as locomotive design, as already mentioned, and Gresley had gone as far as practically possible in removing any protruding feature which would increase aerodynamic resistance. Gone were the teak panels and panel beading, and instead the coaches were flush-sided. Those who viewed the traditional steam locomotive as perfected in the A3s and their peers were uncomfortable with the strange look of the new engine. On the footplate were the top link crew, Driver Arthur Taylor and Fireman J. Luty accompanied by I.S.W. Groom, Divisional Loco Running Superintendent. In just over an hour's time this strange new locomotive would have smashed most of the existing speed records, not by a whisker, but by a huge margin.

Since late in the day the ability of the train to run fast north of York had been restricted and it was judged necessary on the trial run to explore the speed capacity of the new A4 to the full, to establish the margins in hand on the schedule. The results of that decision were spectacular to say the least. It also exposed another failure of communication. The CCE was apparently unaware of developments in his colleague's department and therefore unaware of the implications for his own, and consequently nothing had been done to prepare the track for higher speeds.

The GN main line was always well laid and maintained, and trains ran at good speeds. Nevertheless the alignment had changed little from the time of construction, and consisted of a mixture of straight and circular sections. On straight track there was no difficulty, but on curved track the train was of course subject to centrifugal force, which is proportional to the square of the speed of the train and inversely proportional to the radius of the curve. The track had a slight degree of super-elevation or cant to offset the centrifugal force, but it was not the practice to use the higher values that became normal a few decades later. The equilibrium speed – that at which the train exerts no lateral force on either rail – was probably no more than 50 mph, at the most 60-70 mph. At each change of curvature there was a corresponding change of centrifugal force, and if the curvature changed sharply, there was an impact which was made worse by the fact that the Silver Jubilee train had rather soft horizontal control springing. It is quite possible that the some of the impacts were heavy enough to throw standing passengers to the floor.

The solution was a transition curve, usually a cubic parabola, over which the changes of curvature and cant took place more gradually and comfortably. The setting of track design parameters for passenger comfort was in its infancy, and was something that could not be introduced ad hoc, for a consequence of inserting transitions was a lateral shift in the alignment. Therefore the whole of a curved alignment had to be redesigned. Permanent Way Inspectors and gangers often 'eyed in' a false transition to overcome the problem, but at the higher speeds of the streamliners this would have been inadequate. Therefore it is hardly surprising that the privileged guests on the trial run were subjected to a number of nerve-wracking shocks.

Whether the CCE's department took the view that its maintenance policy was adequate and had had simply gone to sleep or whether nobody thought it necessary to bring the CCE into the discussions one cannot tell. However, even if he had, I doubt whether any action would have been taken on the ground. The redesign of much of the alignment from London to Newcastle was a major task requiring an enormous commitment in labour and cost. First of all a detailed survey of sections of the line would be required – I doubt whether any accurate and systematic records other than the original constructional plans existed. After the calculation the new alignment would have to be marked or pegged, the track slued under a heavy speed restriction, and then fettled up to full speed running. This task would have taken months if not a year or two, and its cost would have been considerable. There were no track machines in 1935!

The start was fast, and there can have been few that had seen Finsbury Park fly past in 4 minutes 42 seconds from Kings Cross with steam traction. Six minutes was good. The first hint that the level of speed had been raised considerably must have come at Hornsey, where the reverse curves can rarely if ever been taken before at 60 mph by a down express as Taylor gathered speed. On the footplate, according to Taylor subsequently, his Superintendent was concerned that the A4 was not going well enough! Then came a left-hand curve through Wood Green at 70 mph, but instead of the speed gently falling north of Wood Green on the 1 in 200 rising, it continued to increase steadily as the train climbed out of London and Taylor pressed his engine harder. At the top of the climb out of Kings Cross at Potters Bar, the sharp right-hand through the old station was taken not at 45-50 mph, but 75 mph, after which SILVER LINK accelerated rapidly downhill to Hatfield. Already, the passengers must have experienced substantial lateral forces on the curves, but worse was to come.

Unfortunately for those in the train, the old Hatfield station was on a sharp left-hand curve, preceded by a gentler right-hand curve north from

Red Hall signalbox, and limited later to 70 mph. At Hatfield the train must have suffered a very heavy blow at no less than 94½ mph, and further north at Woolmer Green where the down slow turn-in connection was located, unhappily, in the middle of a sharp left hand curve, there would have been another mighty impact. Langley troughs, later restricted to 70, were passed at over 90 mph.

As CJA wrote, at milepost 30, just beyond the summit of the Chilterns, where the descent to the Bedfordshire Ouse starts, the speed rose to over 100mph, and SILVER LINK held this speed and more for the next 25 miles, reaching maxima of 112½ mph twice, at Arlesey and Sandy. I might add that within this distance were four closely sited boxes at Hitchin, three level crossings and two bottlenecks, which called for some very brisk signalling indeed! This tremendous burst of speed no doubt astonished and enthralled most of the passengers, but as the special shot through St. Neots at 104½ mph and accelerated downhill the situation was becoming serious. Had they but realised it, the senior members of the LNER staff were staring possible disaster in the face. At the 55½ milepost by the Bedfordshire Ouse the Offord reverse curves were limited to 70 mph, necessarily, due to heavy curvature. Allen quoted the train's speed at the 55th milepost as 109½ mph, almost 40 mph in excess of the approaching PSR (Permanent Speed Restriction). In the original 1935 description the speed is given as the 54th milepost, and I would have thought it difficult for the driver, with a vacuum braked steam locomotive and a light train, to slow from 110 to 85 mph in less than half a mile. It is as well that Gresley himself went on to the footplate to tell Driver Taylor to 'ease his arm'. The day might well have finished sooner and wetter than it did!

Driver Taylor must have braked hard to bring the speed down to 85mph. Speeds were kept lower after this, but Peterborough was passed in 55 minutes 2 seconds, a time that was never equalled or even remotely approached with steam traction. SILVER LINK was no less than 8½ minutes ahead of the 'Silver Jubilee' schedule! As is well known, the special then caught up the 13.40 Leeds and Harrogate at Essendine, which had left 45 minutes ahead! But for that, the special could well have passed Grantham in just under 80 minutes from Kings Cross. The train turned at Barkston, and very little was attempted on the up run beyond a brief spurt to 94 at Tempsford.

This was the supreme demonstration of sustained high speed in the steam era. SILVER LINK held 100 mph for 25 miles on

end, averaged 100 mph for 43 miles continuously, and from Finsbury Park to Fletton Junction, 72.46 miles, the average speed was 90.17 mph. The maximum speed was at the time a record for steam traction for the world. But for the intervention of the curves at Offord, there is every possibility that the A4 could have maintained 100 mph on the easy road right through to Peterborough. Her start-to-pass average from Kings Cross was 83.25 mph. High speed now had a completely new meaning, for this was the grandfather of the High Speed Train. Post-war, we were sometimes lucky enough to experience a run in which an A4 was unleashed, and we realised how fast an engine they were, and their capacity for sustained high speed, especially the double Kylchap ones. But we were aware of their pre-war prowess, and were not surprised. The astonishment in 1935 at their capacity for speed must have been enormous.

The new locomotive went straight into service on the 'Silver Jubilee' and worked it single-handed for a fortnight and well into the third week before the second A4, No.2510 QUICKSILVER was ready. The latter's frames had been laid a fortnight or so after SILVER LINK, on July 15th, and work proceeded, informed by progress and development with the prototype. The second A4 emerged for running in at Kings Cross on September 26th, but she was not used on the high-speed service until October 17th. One wonders why. There must have been some reason why the engine was held back, for nobody would start the new service with only one engine for nearly three weeks if a second were available. If the engine was completed, then two possibilities exist. Either QUICKSILVER ran warm during running-in, or she was held back to have the Flaman speed recorder fitted. No record exists of her having returned to the Works in 1935, which suggests that the second reason was the more likely. I would imagine that SILVER LINK was examined with more than usual care and not a little anxiety by senior running staff until the second A4 was ready, when they no doubt breathed more easily! There were some anxious moments while the Kings Cross top link got used to the greater speed of the A4 and the higher speeds necessary to keep time. They did remarkably well, considering only Taylor had handled the A4 at high speed previously. The CCE was now painfully aware of the need to adapt his track for higher speeds, although he would have needed time before the transition curves could be designed and slued into the alignment, but the PSRs were re-emphasised. Likewise the CME promptly modified the coach springing.

Other anxieties were minor, principally because the firebox brick arch of No.2509 appeared not to withstand the shocks and vibrations at the high speeds which were being attained and maintained. The arch supports were incorrectly shaped and were altered at the first weekend. No doubt the 'growing pains' of the crews' acclimatisation and the shortcomings of the alignment contributed to those vibrations and shocks. The arch was repaired at night at Gateshead, but there seemed to be no other problems. Gresley, on learning of the repairs carried out on an engine in steam, was concerned: had he known of it, he would have ordered an A3 to deputise. The second A4, QUICKSILVER then joined her sister, and later Nos.2511 and 2512, SILVER KING and SILVER FOX completed the batch, and A4s gradually began to appear on other services, the 'Silver Jubilee' being a weekday only service. The A4 returned south from Newcastle on Saturdays on the 'Flying Scotsman'. SILVER FOX was adopted by Samuel Fox & Co., steelmakers, and was equipped with polished stainless steel boiler bands and two plaques of fox in full flight fitted halfway along the boiler cladding. SILVER FOX was a familiar sight at Kings Cross. She was one of the long term Kings Cross locomotives and only left when the depot was closed in 1963.

The 'Silver Jubilee' ran from Newcastle at 10.00, calling at Darlington, arriving at Kings Cross at 14.00. Departure from London was

at 17.30, calling at Darlington and terminating at Newcastle. Locomotive positioning diagrams were worked on weekends. It was worked by the Kings Cross top link, the 'Newcastle' link, which was increased from six to eight crews to encompass the extra diagram. After some experience of the service it was decided to transfer No.2511 SILVER KING to Gateshead as a reserve in exchange for A3 No.2504 SANDWICH. She stood pilot for the 'Silver Jubilee' and then usually worked to Edinburgh and back on the Leeds-Glasgow service later named 'The North Briton'.

The 'Silver Jubilee' was a success both in financial and operational terms. It was decided to see what coal and water the A4 used, presumably to assess the increased requirement for a second service to Edinburgh or Aberdeen. On November 4th 1935 Gateshead's A3 No.2503 FIRDAUSSI, one of the last series with enlarged steam pipes, was used on the up train with Driver Burfoot, and on the up and down trains on November 19th with Drivers Samwells and Haygreen, to compare her coal consumption with the A4. In fact it was slightly lower. After the CCE's experience with the 112½ mph press run, transition curves came quickly into more general use to ease the sudden changes in centrifugal force as the curvature changed. The operation was profitable at a time of continued economic recession when the 'Big Four' depended on Government grants for new works and the companies were making little profit. The train had only one failure

in its first year and no lost time was booked against the engine. On March 7th 1938, when the colour light signalling had been amended to four aspects to provide for the greater speed, the train was strengthened by the addition of an eighth carriage and the timing from London to York was slightly eased. As drivers became more confident with the brakes of the A4s, speeds rose well above 70mph north of York, especially if the train was late.

In January 1936 17 more A4s were ordered, Nos.4482-4498. The silver theme was set aside in favour of the names of wildfowl for the early engines of the batch. Meanwhile management had started to discuss how the 'streamliner' principle might be extended farther north, to Edinburgh or possibly Aberdeen, and timings based on a six hour transit to Edinburgh were published. The commercial managers had agreed outline plans for another streamliner to Aberdeen, which at that time commanded good holiday traffic, and with no competing air service of any significance, the LNER regarded its services as a priority. It was unlikely that the schedule envisaged would have allowed enough time for engine changing at Newcastle, and the A4 would have to work through to Edinburgh.

More recently, records of braking trials in the Scottish Area have come to light as early as November 1935, not with an A4 but with A3 No.2566 LADAS hauling 250 tons. The trials were carried out between Cowlairs and Grantshouse, to establish the ability of a high-speed express to stop

SILVER LINK, brand new at Top Shed on the day of that visit (see similar picture, page 10). Quite clearly, the Flaman drive is absent - it was almost certainly fitted a month later. (L.J. Burley, Gresley Society Trust)

on existing signalling. From the description of the events, it looks very much as though the trials had been requested by those within the operating department responsible for signalling and safety. They were later known as the Rules Section, and there would have been concern that if in future lightweight expresses were to be timed to run at 80 mph or so, their ability to stop within the existing signalling needed to be verified. At the time none of the express rolling stock were fitted with devices such as the quick service application valve made by Westinghouse, the QSA, which accelerated braking and was later used on the streamliners.

It seems also to have been part of a proposal by the Scottish Area to secure investment to increase the braking distances from distant to home signals in Scotland. If so it was unsuccessful, for eleven months later approval was given to the Southern Area and not the NE or Scottish Areas. The trials were organised between the Divisional Operating and Locomotive Running Superintendents, in consultation with the Divisional CCE. The CME was not involved. It is interesting in that as far as the Division was concerned, not only was Aberdeen being mooted, but Glasgow as well.

As plans crystallised for the second streamliner, it was decided to link London and Edinburgh. It was therefore necessary to establish the likely fuel consumption of an A4 on a 'Silver Jubilee' type of service between London and Edinburgh, but with an increased load. On August 27th 1936 the regular 'Silver Jubilee' train from Newcastle was increased by the weight of the dynamometer car. This was a service train carrying fare-paying passengers, but notwithstanding, it was also decided to see whether the maximum of 112½mph could be increased down Stoke bank.

The engine was SILVER FOX, driven by Driver George Haygreen on the up service, having worked down the night before, while the down train was rostered for Driver Sparshatt with SILVER LINK. As events proved, this was highly fortuitous. On the up journey, Driver Haygreen, well known to enthusiasts as a reliable driver, however, did not handle the A4 at all well, and was content just to do enough to keep time, running with a partly closed regulator with between 130 and 180 psi in the steam chest. Many have speculated as to the reason, for Haygreen was an experienced top link driver who had been on the 'Silver Jubilee' from the start. It was not typical of the way in which the A4s were normally driven, but Gresley no longer controlled locomotive running as he had done on the GNR. Haygreen can hardly have failed to notice the dynamometer car behind the locomotive, and at Newcastle the guard would have given him the details of the load as usual. As it was greater, with the dynamometer car, no doubt there would have some speculation as to the purpose of the test. No doubt having ascertained that it was to establish fuel consumption, I am certain that he was trying to keep the consumption of coal to a minimum by throttling the engine. This would have been understandable but unhelpful in that it would have given a false impression of the normal coal consumption.

It was not until after Grantham that Edward Thompson went through to the footplate, and as the engine accelerated downhill after Stoke Box, he was said to have directed the driver to 'top a hundred'. The regulator was opened fully, but the boiler pressure had dropped to 215-225 psi. This unsatisfactory situation was entirely due to the fact that the driver had not been made aware previously of what was required of him. The speed was 68.5 mph at the summit, which was good if a shade low, but with the pressure down and the fire having to be made up, the engine was not so well prepared as she should have been. As the A4 descended the bank a progressively longer cut-off was used as Haygreen strove to beat the record, culminating in 35% as the locomotive finally reached 113 mph, not north of Essendine as usual but at Tallington, five miles further south, where the track is almost level. There is difference of opinion over whether it was actually Edward Thompson, as stated by O.S. Nock, or J.F. Harrison, but it was a senior member of Gresley's staff.

The consequence of the hard driving and lengthy cut-offs at high speed became apparent half an hour later, as those in the dynamometer car suddenly heard the noise of fragments being dropped from the engine. After the express had passed Hatfield the middle big end bearing

Another familiar shot, taken on the approach to Marshmoor, now Welham Green station. QUICKSILVER is picking up speed quickly, and all the passengers in Class C1 4-4-2 No.4449's train are about to hear is the thump of droplight windows and the noise of the slipstream as the streamliner flies by. The date is 1937, and the A4's tender is the prototype A4 corridor No.5589.

The up 'Silver Jubilee' in autumn 1938 with GANNET pulling hard. Her fireman has been hard at work with a heavy round of firing by the look of the black exhaust! The location is not given but I would guess that it is approaching Great Ponton. Her tender was A4 non-corridor No.5675. (Cawston Bequest, Canon Brian C. Bailey Collection)

metal disintegrated, and the cylinder end covers were fractured. The disabled A4 managed to complete her journey and dragged herself and her train into Kings Cross seven minutes late. It was a frightening experience for those in the know, especially for the crew, coaxing a badly damaged locomotive along at 40-50 mph over the last few miles. It was fortunate that the Doncaster middle big end was a wholly enclosed marine type with a rear strap holding the connecting rod in place. A fork and cotter or 'open fork' type might well not have remained intact and either punctured the boiler or derailed the train at speed with disastrous results for the passengers and staff. C.J. Allen was a passenger in the dynamometer car, and in his book revealed something of his feelings as the badly damaged engine limped home. Once again, lack of communication, it seems, had frustrated the LNER's intentions.

It had been a very near thing. The LNER authorities, Gresley among them, had been lucky, and a trainload of fare-paying passengers had been hauled at a record speed of 113 mph, a feat that has not been bettered with steam traction – officially at least! O.S. Nock knew George Haygreen and his family well, and when the latter reminisced later, he lamented the fact that he had not been told what was expected. One would have thought that the dynamometer car

team would have been in communication with the driver, and advised him of what was required. From the way in which he handled SILVER FOX it seemed that was not the case. Men with bowler hats, it seems, did not speak to men with cloth caps very often or easily in the 1930s. As happened with Bill Sparshatt, disaster, briefly, seemed the more likely outcome, and once again the LNER was reminded that high-speed running needed careful and thorough preparation, consideration of the likely risks and attention to detail.

As a result of this and other instances of the middle big end overheating, a heat detector was fitted to the crank pin. It took the form of a small phial of amyl acetate that broke when overheated, giving off a strong scent of pear drops. Unfortunately the smell stayed with the locomotive even after repair and caused some confusion, and so aniseed was used in its place. The RCTS *LNER Survey* refers to an amusing incident with the heat detectors used on the middle big end – 'stink bombs' in the vernacular. The driver of Doncaster's No.4494 OSPREY reported a hot middle big end, which on careful examination at Neville Hill was only warm. Moreover it was discovered at Doncaster that the engine had not even been fitted with a detector. The probable cause was a nearby cellulose paint factory

at Ripon! It was an unusual example of A4s on the Leeds Northern route which, post-war, was almost unheard of.

The northbound run was made, in much more chastened circumstances, understandably, by SILVER LINK with her regular driver, Bill Sparshatt, who was soon to retire. It was the occasion for a virtuoso performance by one of the great characters of the East Coast main line, a man who knew Gresley Pacifics and how to get the best out of them. The climb to Stoke was carried at an average of 82.6 mph, with no less than 90 mph on the approach to Stoke Bank and a minimum of 74 mph at the summit, using full regulator and 18% cut-off. Strangely, Sparshatt set his cut-off at 18% for much of the run, and drove on the regulator to contain the speed when necessary. While his coal consumption was slightly heavier than Haygreen coming south, his water consumption was nearly 10% less, showing the effect of short cut-off and much more full regulator working compared with the less expansive working of his colleague.

Experience with the 'Silver Jubilee' showed that the benefit of streamlining the A4 that had been confidently expected was in fact quite small. Comparison with the A3 FIRDAUSSI had shown that the A3 had the slightest of edges on coal consumption at least, 36.15lb per mile as compared with 36.7. With figures so close based on one return trip, the comparison was questionable, and it would have been necessary for a considerable number of additional runs to make a valid comparison. Also, one has to allow for human element in hand firing. However, the value of streamlining the locomotive only accounts for about 5% of the train resistance, and as explained earlier the greater benefit was gained by smoothing the train surfaces, reducing the train's air resistance. The average EDBHP required to work the train was as low as 620. An A4, worked with fully opened regulator and 17-18% cut-off, would clear Stoke at 72-75 mph, developing about 1,800-1,900 IHP in the process. The coal and water consumption showed that on this load, the A4s were very economical locomotives. This run neatly summarised the difference between ordinary express running and the streamliners. Expresses of considerable weight could and did run fast downhill, but on the uphill sections, the streamliners were some 20 mph faster.

Gresley, in his Presidential address of 1936 to the Institution of Mechanical Engineers, gave some information about the operation of the 'Silver Jubilee'. In its first year it had run 133,464 miles, of which 115,536 had been at a booked average speed of 70.4 mph. From examination of the Flaman records, over 30,000 miles had been run at 80 mph. Of 498 arrivals, 278 had been before time (BT). In all this there had been only one failure on the road. It was a powerful performance. The financial performance must have cheered management. The operating ratio, the direct cost of operation per £100 income, was 18, a figure from the realms of fantasy as far as anyone on British Railways 50 years later was concerned. 40-50 was very good, and values over 100 (loss-making) were depressingly overwhelming. The high speed supplement alone grossed £12,000, 35% of the £34,000 capital cost of the whole train! High-speed travel was successful and profitable. The cost of the second batch of 17 A4s was £127,500, £7,500 each, a sobering thought! The last to be built, No.4903, cost £8,247.

A month later in 1936, on September 26th, No.2511 SILVER KING worked the 'Silver Jubilee' set plus the dynamometer car, 254 tons, from Newcastle to Edinburgh and back in the charge of Driver Tom Dron, one of the senior and most able men at Gateshead. At this time normally the Newcastle-Edinburgh main line was not the speedway that it has become, and 60-70 mph on the easy descent past Belford was as fast as one could expect. However, the

13.20 Kings Cross-Edinburgh, which had shed some of its load by Newcastle, was booked to cover the 124.45 miles with 330 tons in 130 minutes, and was known to have cut that to 125 minutes. The northbound 'Queen of Scots' Pullman, which at the time was worked from Leeds to Edinburgh by Heaton, had left Newcastle 25 minutes late behind A1 No.2582 SIR HUGO, but had arrived triumphantly in Waverley right time, 119 minutes. Clearly the doctrine of Bill Sparshatt was shared in the Northeast!

The actual times of SILVER KING were 118 minutes northbound and 114 minutes southbound, faster than the normal express schedules at that time. This was an uneventful but successful trial run. The southbound run was remarkable for the powerful climb on Cockburnspath bank, of which the last four miles to the summit were graded at 1 in 96. No.2511 was worked at 35% cut-off and full regulator, the steam chest pressure falling to 210 psi in the process. This was the first occasion when an A4 had been fully extended on test, and when the additional power was calculated for the resistance of the locomotive, the calculated IHP was of the order of 2,500. With the two sets of figures, the requirements for coal and water could now be established with confidence.

The speed at the top is normally quoted as 68 mph, but 61 would be nearer. Gresley was on the footplate and after a sustained 64-65 on the bank, for some reason he closed the regulator himself just before the tunnel. Tunnels were always damp if not wet due to condensation, also with leaks or the normal oil and water dropped by engines, and Penmanshiel was pretty wet. With an engine working hard on a rising gradient, drivers either partially closed the regulator or shortened the cut-off as they entered the tunnel to prevent wheelslip at speed. Perhaps Gresley was apprehensive that an A4 worked as hard as this might fly into a violent wheelslip in the tunnel. Eric Trask, a senior locomotive running engineer, was on the engine in the fireman's seat, and expressed his annoyance as the regulator was closed, and reopened it: imagine his embarrassment at turning to see who the culprit was, and seeing the CME!

The LNER Board decided to introduce two more streamlined expresses, firstly running between Kings Cross and not Aberdeen but Edinburgh Waverley, in six hours, from July 4th 1937. The second service was to be between Kings Cross and Leeds, to be introduced on September 27th 1937, of which more anon. The first was called 'The Coronation' to commemorate the Coronation of King

Edward VIII, and with its unique streamlined observation car used in the summer months, the load was nine coaches, 312 tons tare and 325 tons fully laden. Departure from Kings Cross was at 16.00 and from Waverley at 16.30. A special livery was developed for the A4s working the train, and the train itself.

Although a train is a means to an end and not generally regarded as a work of art, the 'Coronation' was truly beautiful. Skilled designers and craftsmen had worked together to produce engineering art. Gresley had, of course, been Carriage & Wagon Engineer under Ivatt before succeeding the latter. Four pairs of articulated coaches plus the observation coach were in each rake, painted in Coronation, or Marlborough blue below window level and Garter blue above, with the name of the train on the coach sides in stainless steel characters. The locomotives allocated to the 'Coronation', Nos.4488-4492, were given a new livery to match the train. The locomotive body was garter blue, with the now familiar black front drawn round the smokebox sides to finish in a parabolic curve. Red and white lining was used between the black and garter blue, while the wheels were dark crimson. The ninth coach was the streamlined observation coach, one of the few that has run in this country. Of course there were two sets of coaches, and both observation coaches – the 'beaver tails' – were very striking, superbly constructed vehicles, marvellous examples again of the craftsmanship of the LNER's Carriage and Wagon staff. Again, it is difficult to trace who decided upon all this and when. In the 1930s one could be creative and innovative without either trespassing on someone else's responsibilities or calling in serried ranks of experts. It was a brilliant stroke, an inspiration and superbly implemented. Both survive to this day, after a fashion, and it is to be hoped that they will be restored. The coaches were modified in the 1950s to give better rearwards vision, the one shortcoming of the original design, and were used on the Scenic Scottish routes to Mallaig and Kyle. As originally built, while the external shape was quite breathtaking, inside the rear view had to a certain extent been restricted by the rearward and downward slope of the roof. One needed to be seated and not standing to enjoy the experience. We need to remember that glass technology has advanced beyond all recognition since the 1930s. The observation coaches were detached in the winter months.

After the 220 tons tare of the 'Silver Jubilee' Gresley surprised many inside and outside the LNER

The down 'Coronation' speeds through Ganwick with Gateshead's Driver Coates eyeing the photographer. The date is August 11th 1937, and the two months old COMMONWEALTH OF AUSTRALIA has her A4 corridor tender No.5646 which remained with her throughout her existence. (Cawston Bequest, Canon Brian C. Bailey Collection)

by setting his A4s a much more severe test, 325 tons gross for the summer loading and 290 in the winter. The coaches and their interior accommodation were heavier than the 'Silver Jubilee' by an average of some 3½ tons per coach, the eight car winter set being almost a coach heavier. The train boasted two kitchen cars with electric cooking equipment, and the necessary axle-driven dynamos increased the train resistance significantly. These were the days when one expected to dine on a long journey, and the workload in the kitchen cars would have been far higher than today. Nevertheless, although one might wonder whether the second kitchen car was a viable option, we shall never know.

The 'Coronation' was always spoken of as a hard pull. A demanding time northbound was set for the Kings Cross-York section, 157 minutes for 188.15 miles, half a minute slower than the 'Silver Jubilee' initially but with almost 100 tons more and to a stop. This required a start to stop average speed of 71.9 mph, made necessary once again by the signalling PSR north of York that had not yet been lifted. The York-Edinburgh timing for the 204.5 miles was 200 minutes, rather easier, but an additional stop at Newcastle was soon introduced with 77 minutes for the 80.2 miles from York and after a three minute stop, 120 minutes on to Edinburgh. One has to remember that the route north of Darlington contained some stiff gradients, more

curvature, a number of PSRs and a lower line speed. Moreover as far as Morpeth, it carried a large number of heavy freights. North of Newcastle the route was not generally fast, although the section from Lucker troughs to Tweedmouth was favourable in the down direction, and north of Berwick much work had to be done to raise the quality and speed of the track. In the southbound direction the train called only at Newcastle, with 120 minutes allowed for the 124.4 miles, 62.2 mph, and 237 minutes for the 268.3 miles to Kings Cross, 68.0 mph. The train, like the 'Silver Jubilee' before it, ran only on weekdays and not on public holidays.

The 'Coronation' was worked by A4s from Kings Cross and Haymarket, but the opportunity was taken to bring Gateshead's top link into the operation with Kings Cross and Haymarket for this prestigious service. There had been a long tradition of skill on Tyneside, and Gateshead top link had some fine enginemen. In fact the operation was quite complicated. The down train was worked by Gateshead men throughout on Mondays, Wednesdays and Fridays, changing over at York, the second set of men having travelled as passengers from Newcastle. On Tuesdays and Thursdays, it was worked by Kings Cross and Haymarket, again changing over, from London to Edinburgh men, at York.

The up train working was a mirror image, except that crew changeover

was at Newcastle. So on Mondays, Wednesdays and Fridays Haymarket men worked to Newcastle, and were relieved by Kings Cross men, whereupon they travelled to lodge at York. On Tuesdays and Thursdays, Gateshead men worked throughout, changing crews at Newcastle. Two different crew changing locations were a nuisance, involving every crew in some travelling 'on the cushions' in footplatespeak.

As a result the Kings Cross 'Newcastle lodge' link was expanded further from 8 to 10 sets of men, and the Gateshead top link from 6 to 7 sets, although the latter was reduced to 6 sets from March 7th 1938. When the conversion to four-aspect colour light signals had been completed, the down Newcastle stop was added, and the working simplified. Kings Cross worked the down train Tuesday and Thursday Only and the up Monday, Wednesday, Friday Only; Gateshead worked the down train Monday, Wednesday, Friday Only to Newcastle and the up Tuesday and Thursday Only from Newcastle. Haymarket worked both down and up trains between Edinburgh and Newcastle.

As with the 'Silver Jubilee' positioning diagrams were worked at weekends. The hard northbound timing between London and York, however, remained unchanged. A curiosity was that the existing 16.00 departure from Kings Cross, a heavy train, was left in place to make its way out to Finsbury Park on the down slow, by which time the 'Coronation' was two or three blocks ahead. Photographers waited on many occasions for the memorable sight of the two trains bursting out of Gasworks Tunnel abreast. It became quite a game of chance since the drivers were rarely given the 'Right Away' at the same time, and the A4 on the lighter train was usually pulling ahead already. I can imagine that if the heavier train got ahead albeit briefly, the 'Coronation's' driver would have had a hard job in the messroom living the episode down!

The streamlined cladding of the top of the tender restricted the amount of coal carried, and while this was not important on the 'Silver Jubilee', on the longer run it was critical. The A4 ran out of coal on the up run on one occasion, and subsequently greater care was exercised in coaling the tenders. The weather was adverse and the strong cross winds increased the train resistance. There is the possibility that inexperience might also have contributed to the problem. The tender cladding was cut back to allow easier and fuller coaling, and Doncaster carried out the work during the first general overhaul. For the longer run the mechanical lubricators, driven off the rear right-hand crank as was the Flaman recorder, were fitted with two gallon oil reservoirs in place of one gallon. Eventually the whole class moved over to the larger size.

From the second series of A4s, as already stated, Nos.4488-4492 were assigned to the 'Coronation'. The livery and application of embellishments of all sorts to the A4 class is something of a minor science that is summarised in each individual locomotive history. The first engine of the second series, No.4482 GOLDEN EAGLE had been turned out in the normal LNER express locomotive livery of apple green, fully lined out, with black front and sides corresponding roughly but not exactly to the outline of the dark grey of the first four A4s. Since it was thought that the heat of the smokebox might have affected the apple green paint adversely, Nos.4483-4487 had black painted smokebox fronts and sides back to the first boiler band at first, but this was not an attractive solution, and the livery reverted back to the parabolic curve. No.4488 was held at Doncaster while No.4489 was turned out in lined works grey for a few weeks. The new Coronation livery was complemented by the external fittings such as nameplates and window frames being chromium plated, and the numbers and 'LNER' initials were in stainless steel relief. Names on an 'Empire' theme were chosen, and the cab side carried a superbly hand painted panel with the coat of arms of the country concerned,

the works plate being moved to the inside of the cab roof. Both Nos.4488 and 4489 were recalled and repainted in the new livery. There was some doubt about No.4489's name: originally intended to be BUZZARD, it was changed to WOODCOCK before it emerged from the Works, and then to DOMINION OF CANADA once the naming theme had been decided. The others were No.4488 UNION OF SOUTH AFRICA, No.4490 EMPIRE OF INDIA, No.4491 COMMONWEALTH OF AUSTRALIA and No.4492 DOMINION OF NEW ZEALAND.

Various whistles were presented and carried in place of the normal chime whistle, No.4488 with one from South African Railways & Harbours, No.4489 with one from the Canadian Pacific Railway, No.4491 (as late as 1960) with one from the West Australian Railway, and No.4492 with one from New Zealand Government Railways. The low note of No.4492 DOMINION OF NEW ZEALAND was a common sound in my youth, and it is preserved forever on one of Peter Handford's recordings. One could identify that A4 several miles away from the East Coast main line. No.4489 DOMINION OF CANADA carried a presentation bell ahead of the chimney. The bell could be operated from the cab at first, but after the inevitable malfunction it was silenced. During the war it was removed but restored after. When the double Kylchap was fitted in 1957 it was finally removed.

After the five 'Coronation' A4s came Nos.4493-4495, also in apple green similarly to No.4482, before it was decided in October 1937 to bring order to replace chaos, and paint all A4s in the 'Coronation' blue livery. This move also allowed any A4 to be used on the streamliners, not just in emergency. The A4s had been renamed over the years, and the early names were changed, largely as a result of the introduction of streamlined services. BUZZARD was never reused. Before and after the war some of the names were removed and replaced by company directors' names, never a happy change except for those worthies so celebrated. The A4 names were later reused in most cases on Arthur Peppercorn's A1s.

The inauguration was preceded by a press trip on June 30th 1937 from Kings Cross to Grantham and back, turning on the Barkston triangle. Driver G. Burfoot with No.4489 DOMINION OF CANADA had the full summer loading of nine coaches, 325 tons gross. The special ran on the day after the LMSR had introduced the 'Coronation Scot', a rather less ambitious duty, and their new 'Princess Coronation' Pacific No.6220 CORONATION. The LMSR, like the

LNER a year before, had nearly wiped out most of its senior staff with its recklessness in making the 114 mph sprint so close to Crewe, but that is another story. A response from the LNER was confidently expected the following day, although I gather that given the LNER's record of high speed trial runs, that the confidence was not without apprehension!

William Stanier's new Pacific had run magnificently on her 263 ton train. While recorders had timed her at 113 mph on the descent of Madeley Bank – or rather the approach to Basford Hall sidings might be more accurate – the Hasler speed recorder in the cab indicated 114 mph briefly, and that was the basis for the speed claimed by the LMSR. In my experience electric speed indicators were 3-5% high, which given their environment was an extremely good performance, but it was when one read low that one needed to worry! The earlier mechanical counterparts such as Flaman and Hasler were set on mean wheel diameter, were accurate, and the LMSR claim was well founded. It was the return run to Euston that was superb, 119 minutes for 158.1 miles with 100 mph at Castlethorpe, no less than 79.7 mph start-to-stop, a foretaste of the electric timetable to come three decades later.

Gresley was all for putting his good friend William Stanier in his place, and there was no doubt that the LNER would attempt something spectacular. No.4489 ran to Barkston splendidly, and set out for London. The layover at Barkston may have been a welcome break, perhaps with refreshments, but it was felt at the time that it might have been unwise. The rate of combustion in the firebed had been reduced as the engine completed the climb to Stoke, and the fire probably required building up prior to the maximum effort to follow. In retrospect, 9.6 miles or so of uphill running was not a good preparation for a dash down Stoke, now with 320 tons, and the speed at Stoke needed to be at least 70mph and nearer 75mph. It would have been better to extend the run to Doncaster, even if it meant turning the observation car. No.4489 topped Stoke at 69 mph, and the maximum at Essendine of 109.5 mph was good work, although it was regarded as a disappointment by the LNER. It remains the highest speed achieved in the UK with steam hauling more than 300 tons, just, at least as far as authenticated records are concerned. One can understand the disappointment since 22 years later, a double Kylchap A4 achieved 108 mph with no less than 435 tons. Again, the continuation to Kings Cross was an excellent piece of running, but the disappointment was understandable. Significantly,

No.4489 was losing steam pressure at the time she was eased, and perhaps it was moments like this that convinced Gresley that he should think again about using the costly Kylchap double exhaust on an A4. Subsequent experience with No.4489 with a single chimney was that she was often shy of steam, inexplicably so despite passing through many general overhauls and changes of boiler.

The inaugural 'Coronation' was hauled by No.4491 COMMONWEALTH OF AUSTRALIA in the charge of Driver Tom Dron, and Fireman C.R. Charlton, a name not unknown in the North East. Considering that apart from driving Gateshead's only A4, No.2511 SILVER KING, from Newcastle to Edinburgh and back on the test run the previous September, and on normal services, it was his first run on this searching timing, it was a superb run, and one that was probably never bettered. C.J. Allen had the delicate task of recording the run in the knowledge that his chief, Charles Brown, the CCE of the Southern Area, was also on the train, frequently enquiring as to the extent that Dron was exceeding his newly defined speed limits. In fact his excesses were less than Taylor's, although 86½ mph at Hatfield was a bit strong! Tom Dron reached York 1½ minutes early on this demanding schedule notwithstanding a TSR to 25 mph north of Grantham, making his net time about 152 minutes, a benchmark that stood unbeaten as far as we know.

It was a demanding operating task, and when one examines the official records of the train operating for the short spell of two years or so when it ran, an enviable record of punctuality and reliability emerges. No.4491 COMMONWEALTH OF AUSTRALIA worked the 'Coronation' for 48 out of the first 51 turns, for example. Of course it was being achieved at a cost in thorough checking and supervision, but in later days the railways would have paid a very high price to emulate this feat. Night after night the train ran to time, summer and winter, and the number of delays was small considering the level and duration of high speed necessary for punctual running. On one occasion, as mentioned previously, in adverse weather the locomotive ran out of coal, principally because the tender capacity was limited by streamlined plating. When the tenders were modified the problem disappeared. Special attention was paid to the coaling of the tenders, as was the case after the war with the 'Capitals Limited' and the 'Elizabethan'. Careful packing could ensure that another ton or two could be loaded.

The coal consumption was heavier than the 'Silver Jubilee', naturally, but was normally still about 40lb per mile.

There was considerable variation between the weights of the A4 tenders, none of which conformed to the normally stated weight. The A4 corridor tender had bowed rear ends and no cantrail beading, to match the streamlined stock. The top sheeting to the tenders not only limited coal capacity as mentioned above but caused the death of a locomotive inspector riding on the footplate. The plating was cut back to allow easier coaling, but greater priority was given to coaling more carefully to ensure a fully packed tender. The unfortunate man was struck as the two expresses passed on Wiske Moor troughs and the resulting deluge of surplus water smashed the right-hand forward cab window. This was the second fatality with the A4s, the first being caused by inadequate space at the front of the A4's streamlined casing with short buffers, fatally injuring a fireman.

At her first general overhaul, SILVER LINK had exchanged tenders with QUICKSILVER, and in 1938 it was decided to experiment with the use of roller bearing axleboxes on the tenders of A4s Nos.2509, 4492 and 4493. Tender No.5590 (2509) received Timken roller bearings, 5647 (4492) Hoffman and 5648 (4493) Skefco. The experiment was completely successful and one wonders why it was not extended. Cost perhaps, or the onset of the 1939-45 war. The history of engineering is however littered with good ideas that withered on the vine once the prime mover behind it moved away.

Meanwhile there was some concern that, in service, the A4s rode well but tended to roll, and the wear on the leading coupled wheels showed that the bogie was not guiding the locomotive into curves as effectively as it ought. Roland Bond, a senior LMSR engineer who had travelled on the A4 footplate, reported this to Gresley. Stanier had encountered similar problems with leading bogies on the LMSR following his chairmanship of the Indian Pacific Locomotive Committee investigating derailments caused by inadequate lateral control forces. There were a number of experiments conducted with the bogie and the angle of the Cortazzi sliding surfaces, just before the outbreak of war. In late 1938 the bogie was altered to conform to the D49 design, with roughly double the initial lateral force in the control springing. To combat any rolling tendency, at the suggestion of Stanier's senior assistant Roland Bond, check plates were fitted to the main frames above the bogie and on

the frame itself. The Cortazzi truck alterations were abandoned during the war and never taken up again. The bogie originally carried dust shields similar to the A1s and A3s, but in 1941 they were replaced with a single plate across the bogie. The advent of ATC/AWS receivers, fitted to the bogie, altered the dust shield, and a protecting plate was fitted between the receiver and the front coupling. The A4s had always ridden exceptionally well, and when one considers their normal speed range of 70-90 mph against the inadequacy of the track alignment, the tendency to roll is not to be wondered at! In the post-war years, their riding was superb, even when their mileage was high, and there was little of the rail-end battering that one got used to with the first generation diesel traction.

The LNER management had every reason to be encouraged in what were otherwise dark days economically and politically. The 'Silver Jubilee' had a good average load factor, but the 'Coronation' was less fortunate and more seasonal north of Newcastle. Maybe Glasgow would have been a good idea, for although the distance from London was nearly 39 miles longer than by the LMSR route, there was no fast service from Euston in the late afternoon – the 'Coronation Scot' left at 13.30. The plans for a service to the industrial cities and towns of the Leeds and Bradford area had been around for a few years, and once the CCE's load restriction on the Calder viaduct at Wakefield was eased, they were implemented. The river span was the subject of further design work in 1937, but the date of reconstruction is not known. On September 27th 1937 the third streamliner was introduced, 'The West Riding Limited', serving Leeds and Bradford. The time allowed for the 185.7 miles from Kings Cross to Leeds Central was 164 minutes. It left Bradford at 11.10 and Leeds at 11.33, running 15 minutes behind the 'Silver Jubilee' from Doncaster and arriving at 14.15. In the down direction it left at 19.10, reaching Leeds at 21.53 and Bradford at 22.15. The train was similar to the winter 'Coronation', an eight coach train of four twin articulated coaches with two kitchen cars and electric cooking weighing 279 tons. The new train did not merit a beavertail observation saloon due to its late departure from Kings Cross.

The restriction on axle loading having been eased, and although there were now two A1s at Copley Hill and A3s at Doncaster, for the first time, an A4 was working into Leeds. The Doncaster-Leeds road was quite sharply graded and littered with PSRs of various types for curvature and underground colliery workings, and as the service had no equivalent of the fast running to be had north of York, it was a hard job. It had a clear run southbound, on the tail of the up 'Silver Jubilee' but northbound, with the evening freights starting to roll, it received a less kindly treatment from the operators. Insofar as timekeeping was concerned, the down train was the hardest among the three streamlined services after March 1938. The 'Coronation' schedule had been eased north of York with the introduction of four aspect signalling. The train was worked between Leeds and Bradford by a pair of 0-6-2Ts, in delightful contrast to the 'state of the art' A4 that took it out and brought it in from London. The 'West Riding Limited' was worked by Kings Cross men, but not from the No.1 Newcastle lodge link. The old 1A Pullman link that existed earlier was revived as No.1A link, and four senior men from No.2 link and two men from the No.3 Express Goods link were promoted into it.

The two dedicated locomotives were Nos.4495 and 4496, GOLDEN FLEECE and GOLDEN SHUTTLE, the former having been hastily retrieved as GREAT SNIPE having been just run-in, was renamed and repainted. The press trip from Leeds to Barkston on September 23rd was hauled by No.4495, now GOLDEN FLEECE, but there was little opportunity to demonstrate the speed capacity of the train and certainly no attempt was made. The inauguration was not so blessed organisationally as the earlier two. No.4495 was sent on the Sunday evening 18.10 to Leeds positioning turn, but she ran hot at Doncaster, and Haymarket's indefatigable No.4492 DOMINION OF NEW ZEALAND was sent light to Leeds to be used instead. This locomotive had come almost straight from working the 1937 Non-stop, the first year in which the A4s took over from the A3s, and had dominated one leg of the duty, working 62 turns of which 52 were consecutive. After three legs of the duty, she took over the 'Coronation' and was replaced by yet another Haymarket A4, COMMONWEALTH OF AUSTRALIA. One wonders whether the Haymarket Shedmaster quite appreciated the extent to which his A4s were underpinning the streamlined services!

The opportunity was taken with the introduction of the 'West Riding Limited' to vary the route of the 'Yorkshire Pullman'. Instead of travelling directly from Harrogate and Bradford to Leeds and then to Doncaster, the new operation was from Bradford to Doncaster via Wakefield, from Harrogate to Doncaster via Knaresborough and York, and from Hull to Doncaster where the three portions were joined.

The train used this route until the Pullman services were withdrawn at the outset of war; post-war, it reverted to its original route. The introduction of the third streamliner brought five sets of coaches into use: one each for the 'Silver Jubilee' and the 'West Riding Limited', and two for the 'Coronation', the latter three being specifically lettered. The spare set was brought into use occasionally, but otherwise it was used for special events, carrying special matching blue roof boards.

The hundredth Gresley Pacific was No.4498, and as a tribute to the Chief Mechanical Engineer who had served them so well, it was given his name at the suggestion of an enthusiast, K. Risdon Prentice. Always a good performer, No.4498 is of course still with us, preserved by the Sir Nigel Gresley Trust. The order for 17 A4s was increased to 31, and the further 14 were numbered 4462-4469, 4499, 4500 and 4900-4903. The third batch was paid for by a Government grant for the renewal of obsolete equipment. They were coupled to new non-corridor tenders similar to those of the Mikados built the year before. They were based on the later A3 design fitted to the 1930 batch but with no cantrail beading, some of which found their way on to A3s. The Mikados had given trouble with smoke deflection, and Gresley decided to fit the A4 cladding to Nos.2003-2006 in 1936. This was applied from the front tubeplate forward, and was successful despite the fact that the P2s normally ran at much lower speeds.

In January 1938 there was a proposal to fit a W1 Diagram 111 boiler to the A4s, with the larger 50 sq.ft. grate, which would have required an extension of 12 ins or so to the A4 frames. Various design proposals were discussed within the CME's department from time to time, but I would imagine that Gresley felt that this expense was unjustified. It was soon succeeded by another proposal, to increase the A4 Diagram 107 boiler to 275 psi, but that required thicker plate to withstand the higher pressure, with some increase in locomotive weight that would have been prohibitive on certain routes. Development was then concentrated on the proposed 4-8-2 but war caused that to be aborted, along with the 275 psi A4, both of which were intended for building in 1940-41.

The 4-6-2-2 compound had been an instructive experiment albeit unsuccessful but Gresley had decided to rebuild it as a conventional simple expansion engine rather than spend more money on it. The W1 had been built as part of Gresley's research budget as mentioned earlier, and not as a part of the locomotive building

programme. The rebuild which emerged from Doncaster in November 1937 was a heavier locomotive than the A4 that attracted a number of restrictions, but No.10000 was a fast, free-steaming and very powerful locomotive with the larger P2 firegrate and a tractive effort 17% greater than the A4. Critically, it was fitted with a new and larger Kylchap double Kylchap blastpipe, replacing the special 1935 design, a new one designed specifically for the simple expansion rebuild. In most respects the cost of conversion had been contained by using components that were already extant, cutting out the need for expensive patterns. It was presented to the public as an improved A4, and there were certainly some aspects of the W1 that might well have been carried forward such as the exhaust and the larger grate. A number of names were considered for the engine, but none was ever used.

Gresley was not alone in believing that in future heavy trains would have to run faster and greater power development and possibly fuel of lower quality would necessitate a larger grate and firebox volume, so that fuel in larger quantities could be used. In fact it was not necessary to enlarge the grate further, although a lengthened combustion chamber would have usefully increased the firebox volume. With hindsight we can see this now, but at the time there seemed to be little concern about the practicality of firing the larger grate. The Mikados acquired some unpopularity in Scotland for this reason, although almost all French compound Pacifics and the Est 4-8-2s had grate areas of 46-48 sq.ft. with hand firing, and an 8ft length was not considered a problem. Express locomotives generally received better quality coal, and while the railways continued to plan for 600 ton trains, they only materialised in exceptional circumstances. Certainly grate size was not a limiting factor in the development of a more powerful A4. In France, Chapelon's compound Pacifics and 4-8-0s developed higher power outputs using fuel more efficiently. It is a pity that Gresley did not reduce the frame length to the A4 design. As a result, generations of firemen were saddled with the demands of a larger grate and the need for an extra pace from the coal door to the firehole.

Following the successful use on No.10000, it was decided to fit an A3, No.2751 HUMORIST, and a new A4, No.4468 MALLARD similarly with a Kylchap double Kylchap blastpipe and chimney. This was to increase the maximum sustained evaporative capacity of the boiler and to reduce back pressure loss, which reached up to 15-20% in large American locomotives with conventional draughting. The detailed design for each class was slightly different, the orifice diameters being 5 ins for the A4 instead of 5¼ ins for the A3 with the longer 94HP boiler tubes. The modified locomotives had a very different sound from the familiar bark of a single blast A4 worked on full regulator and typically short cut-off. It was a thin rasping exhaust that was reminiscent of the wheezing exhaust of some of the more ancient GNR locomotives still around, although sharper, and one that became all too familiar in later years. It was something that perplexed crews, since many were very dependent on the sound and feel of the locomotive in judging how to work it. To those who travelled abroad and had encountered 'Les Chapelons' on the 'Flèche d'Or' it must have been a familiar sound.

So we come to the crowning point in Sir Nigel Gresley's career insofar as posterity has judged him. The immortal MALLARD was released from the Works on March 3rd 1938 and went to Carr Loco, where it was run-in and put to work on the 'Yorkshire Pullman'. It was Doncaster Loco's first A4, and by comparison with their A1s and A3s, MALLARD must have been a revelation. With her regular driver Joe Duddington, fairly new to the top link, she quickly gained a reputation as a strong, fast and free steaming locomotive. Doncaster, at that time, powered

most of the expresses from Yorkshire, Copley Hill having only acquired A1s Nos.2553 and 2555 in 1936, as mentioned earlier. They were nominally for the 'Queen of Scots' Pullman, but also served as reserves should the A4 be unfit for service on the 'West Riding Limited'. Joe Duddington was made of stern stuff, and could run hard when needed, as witness his marvellous run with SOLARIO on the inaugural 'Scarborough Flyer' of 1936. The 180 psi A1 achieved a net time of 162 minutes for the Kings Cross-York run, only five minutes more than the 'Coronation' but with 395 tons!

Gresley had fitted the 'Coronation' set with the latest Westinghouse QSA valves to accelerate the application of the (vacuum) brakes, with a view to reducing the train's braking distance. They would have made no significant difference to the braking force, but an important consideration in braking is the speed at which a brake application is transmitted or propagated from the driver's brake valve down to the back coach. The train is travelling at full speed during that period of transmission, before the brake blocks come into contact with the wheels progressively down the train, and the distance covered at speed is a significant contribution to the full braking distance. It was the speed of transmission that Gresley hoped to accelerate with the new valves. Previously it was given as 10 seconds from application to

effective braking on the rear coach, and the new valves actually cut that delay to 3 seconds. That represents, at 90 mph, a reduction of over 300 yards in the braking distance.

No doubt the use of double-block working on the streamliners was an operating impediment, and a better standard of braking would have been a great advantage in dispensing with this handicap. The LNER's freight managers did not always share the general enthusiasm for the streamliners, since the double-block working delayed their services, and there were customers who were quick to point out the shortcomings of the LNER's freight services. However it would have taken a remarkable reduction in braking distances to allow high speeds on existing signalling using normal absolute block. History has failed to relate whether and by how much the valves made a difference in service, for obvious reasons, but they were fitted subsequently to all sets. It was better to have the best that technology could offer at the time. So the new valves were fitted to a Coronation set and three twins from the set were tested between Kings Cross and Peterborough on a special test runs on a number of occasions in 1937/38. The test run on July 3rd was different in that instead of Top Shed providing the locomotive, it was Doncaster's engine and men. It was decided to use their new A4, MALLARD, with six out of the eight streamlined coaches,

The up 'Silver Jubilee' south of Grantham hauled by SILVER LINK in autumn 1936. Pre-war photographs of the train often show the A4 in an apparently darker livery than the train. Often this is because the engine has been repainted in blue but here we know that SILVER LINK was in silver grey livery before she had nameplates refixed. The reason for the darker shade may have been due to the emulsion used in the film, or simply that the train was more carefully cleaned than the locomotive. (Cawston Bequest, Canon Brian C. Bailey Collection)

together with the dynamometer car. Nearer the time Gresley decided to extend the special to Barkston triangle, and see what the new locomotive could do down the bank.

Opinion regarding the new A4 was that it was so much freer running that it could well reach 130 mph. The Kylchap exhaust would have stimulated a much higher evaporation rate as well as lowering internal resistance in exhaust back pressure. The improvement over the A1 and A3 steam passage design was beginning to be appreciated. The intention to turn the train at Barkston and stage a high-speed descent of Stoke Bank was kept secret. This was unfortunate, for the CCE had planned to repair the up track at Grantham station on July 3rd and imposed a 20 mph TSR. Had it not been for this, there is no doubt the record would have been a shade higher. In fact Gresley learnt of this beforehand, but let the arrangements go ahead since it was probably too late to change. The down run was successfully accomplished, the train was turned on Barkston triangle, and the engine was given a last minute check to ensure that all was ready. As the RCTS LNER Survey Part 2A records, 'at Barkston the Westinghouse team (present for brake testing) were informed of the impending high-speed attempt and they were offered the opportunity to go by taxi to Peterborough to rejoin the train after the attempt – this offer was declined'. Most of the illustrations of that famous day came from the camera of Max Hoather, one of the Westinghouse team. Part 2A also records that the footplate team 'drowned' the middle big end in superheater oil, nothing better being to hand. Quite how, without a pit and with streamlined casing, is an interesting thought! The load was fairly small, the six coaches and the dynamometer car making 240 tons. Joe Duddington had his regular fireman, Tom Bray, and they were accompanied by Locomotive Inspector Sam Jenkins on the footplate. In view of the unknown speeds they hoped to achieve and the possible consequences of that speed, they were brave men. The LNER's high-speed adventures so far had not been a totally unblemished record of success without risk!

To accelerate from 24 mph through Grantham platforms to 74 mph at Stoke summit required a cut-off of 40-45% with full regulator. This required an unprecedented acceleration in the evaporation rate from the boiler, and an enormous power output. As the train swept south the acceleration was phenomenal, and as has been related many times, MALLARD reached a peak of 125 mph just before the 90th milepost, a place which is now marked for posterity by a commemorative sign, placed by The Gresley Society Trust. However, a peak of 126 mph was subsequently claimed, and it is that which is quoted on the commemorative plaques carried by the locomotive. The exact figure has been discussed many times, but the report of the Mechanical Engineer (Design, Testing & Performance) at Darlington in 1964 confirmed a fleeting figure of 126 mph from the speed curve of the dynamometer car roll. The brake test was carried out before the train reached the switches and crossings and slight curve at Essendine itself. The results of the brake test and any influence on the running of the streamliners it may have had was lost in the euphoria of the achievement of a world record speed, understandably.

Congratulations came from all quarters, especially from William Stanier. The train stopped at Peterborough where the A4 was removed with an overheated big end. The overheating was probably caused by the regulator being closed for the flat curve at Essendine, while working at full power at 125 mph, with the sudden removal of load through the piston and connecting rod. Adolf Wolff of Borsig had three similar middle big end failures in similar circumstances with his O5 class 4-6-4s, and instructions were given that the regulator should not be closed completely at speeds over 160 kph (100 mph), and the driver should use increased braking instead. After careful examination, remetalling and running-in, MALLARD was back at work after nine days. When the CCE was told of the record run, he drew Gresley's attention to the fact that there were 40 ft rails laid in 1910 in the up main near Tallington – hardly suitable for two miles a minute. As they had been there during the trial running of FLYING SCOTSMAN, PAPYRUS, SILVER LINK and SILVER FOX and more than few high-speed sprints with the streamliners presumably they were thought fit to remain. With the plans and preparations for the streamlined services being discussed in 1934/35, I would have thought it wiser for them to be removed for use elsewhere. For jointed track with 40 ft rails on softwood sleepers, 28 years in the main line is a very long, indeed exceptionally long life. In fact the speed had been reduced to 70mph well before Tallington with the knowledge that the engine had run warm, as the A4 made for New England depot at Peterborough. But at least they had learnt their lessons of 1936 and had used a special train on a Sunday for the attempt.

There is no doubt that a conventional single blast A4 could not have achieved a speed of this order. The maximum power output for a single chimney A4 was 2,600-2,700 IHP. Whereas the A3 needed pressing to exceed 100 mph down Stoke Bank, the single blast A4 could reach 110 mph without undue effort, if not restrained.   MALLARD's performance, despite the lengthy cut-offs used, suggested that the double Kylchap had lifted that expectation significantly higher. While this capacity was unusable normally on express work, the double Kylchap A4s were able to time services with a much greater ease than their sisters. The enhanced rate of evaporation and the lowered back pressure allowed the locomotive to develop some 400-500 IHP beyond the maximum for a single blast A4. A reduction of 5 psi seemed small, but as a percentage of a mean effective pressure of say 60 psi with an A4 developing 2000 HP at 75 mph, it represents 8% of the power output. Of course much depended upon the skill of the crew in preparing for a special effort. This was the first of very few occasions on which a Kylchap A4 had developed over 3,000 indicated HP, and the exact figure is open to argument since an A4 could not be indicated due to the presence of streamlined cladding. The estimate of power developed, a large proportion of which is required to move the engine at such a speed, depends on the formula and constants used, and the quality of the recordings on which it is based.

Gresley was sufficiently encouraged to authorise the expense of fitting the remaining A4s with a double Kylchap, Nos.4901-4903. He told Col. Kenneth Cantlie, then managing director of ALE, the British Kylchap licensees in 1940, that all future large locomotives including the proposed 4-8-2 should be fitted with Kylchap exhausts, and all existing Pacifics and Green Arrows would be fitted retrospectively. It was said that Gresley intended to make another attempt on the world speed record in 1939, but the outbreak of war prevented a repetition. Use of the Kylchap exhaust was protected by André Chapelon's patents and it included manufacturing costs by ALE. It attracted licence fees of some £400 for its use, a considerable sum in 1938. Fitting Kylchap blastpipes to the remaining single blast A4s would have cost the LNER the equivalent of two more locomotives, and that at a time when the construction of the second batch was financed by a Government grant to the LNER. Gresley knew that the patent rights would expire in 1941, and planned to convert all Pacifics after that time, with Class V2 as well. Although France fell to Germany in May 1940, André Chapelon was a friend and fellow engineer, and

Top. SILVER LINK in the first few weeks of her existence, in platform 4 at Kings Cross waiting for the road to Top Shed. If (repeat, 'if') the notes on the photograph are correct, it was the A4's first day in service at Top Shed. The tender is A4 corridor No.5589 and the date is given as September 14th 1935.

Below. The ECS loco, N2 0-6-2T No.4610 (later BR No.69494) backs on to the 'Silver Jubilee' – the date is given as September 14th 1935 but this seems unlikely. The train was recorded in use for the braking tests on the weekend before the record run, but it was not presented to the public until 27th September. (Both H.N.James).

Gresley was not prepared to take early advantage of the situation. Sadly, by 1941, Gresley had died and the war had imposed other priorities. His retro-fitting programme had to wait another 16 years, although 81 of the 90 post-Gresley Pacifics were equipped with double Kylchap exhausts.

Another 16 years were to elapse after Gresley's death before the rest of the class together with the A3s gained this improvement. Meanwhile over 120,000 tons of coal had been burnt and a generation of firemen laboured unnecessarily. Gresley led the way very much in this country in using a much more efficient and sophisticated exhaust system, but it proved curiously difficult subsequently to convince a largely conservative group of locomotive engineers to follow suit. His successor, Edward Thompson, for all the changes that he made, understood the value of the Kylchap exhaust, did not interfere with Gresley's edict and used it on all of his Pacifics. But elsewhere there were concerns about access to tube banks for sweeping, and in the smokebox generally, which was nonsense since the need for tube cleaning was actually reduced by the strong and even draught. There were still drivers who lengthened their cut-offs in a vain attempt to hear the noise of the exhaust they were used to, burning more coal rather than less. Engineers, who, in other respects were able and competent managers, obstinately refused the evidence before their own eyes due to their hostility to costly bought-in equipment. There was clearly a failure of communication between some of those in charge of design and those in charge of locomotive running. Late in the day there was even an offer by the BTC to convert the double Kylchap engines to single, something which must rank as one of the most stupid ideas in steam locomotive history! Patent royalties were always a problem and the reluctance of Stores Superintendents (who normally made any external purchases for the company) to buy in any equipment which could equally well be made in-house (as they saw it) was well known. A short-term advantage was obtained but in the long term the railways suffered.

So the LNER proceeded royally, with its three streamliners, the Nonstop et al, making outline plans for a super A4 with 275 psi and a 4-8-2 for the heavy expresses. The streamlined trains, with their aerodynamic cladding, were much quieter than normal. Those who can remember them speak of their speed and relative quiet as they passed. They carried twin tail lamps as an insurance against being stopped by a vigilant signalman, and the sight of the twin lamps speeding into the dark is a fond memory of those days. The sets were cleaned and serviced each night at London, Leeds, Newcastle and Edinburgh. The coaches were steel with a rexine cladding, and in days before carriage washing machines and Exmover detergent, there was no option but to wash manually with soap solution, brush and water. With signalling improvements in 1938, for the winter months all three streamliners were of similar formation. The Garter blue livery became standard for the class, and for the W1 4-6-2-2. The zenith of steam operation had been reached in Britain, and although post-war recovery enabled the Gresley engines to do great things, steam would never again enjoy the prominence of the pre-war streamliners. We would have to await the arrival of the diesel engine in the shape of the 'Deltics' to advance significantly on the standards set in 1939. An emergency timetable was introduced from September 1st 1939, and so the streamlined trains finished on Thursday August 31st, never to run again as complete units. Things were never going to be the same again.

When John Robertson visited Kings Cross, one would expect a super photograph. It is May 13th 1961, and I suspect DWIGHT D EISENHOWER is starting the 14.00 to Edinburgh. Tender: non-corridor No.5671. (J. Robertson, The Transport Treasury)

CHAPTER FOUR
War and Post War

War came on September 3rd 1939, and all of the golden age of high speed travel with steam traction finished. With the declaration of war, the world changed irreversibly, slowly at first but inexorably. The streamliners had been withdrawn, and their motive power, the A4s, had been stored either in the misplaced belief that this would be a short, sharp diplomatic spat and that things would return to normal, or the LNER authorities simply did not know quite how to react. As time wore on it was realised that all locomotives were needed in the general effort. In peacetime, information as to what the railways were doing was freely available, but now under wartime security regulations, it slowed to a trickle.

An emergency timetable had been devised leaving much of the railways' resources for the war traffic. Made for understandable reasons, there is no doubt that the emergency timetable cut back the number of passenger services too heavily, with the inevitable result that individual loads rocketed. Very soon, the weight of travelling passengers and the volume of goods carried on the East Coast main line in particular had escalated to unprecedented and unsustainable levels. By Easter 1940, six months later, express loads had grown to 7-800 tons and often more, as troop movements, evacuation and dispersal of government functions added to the weight that the railways had to carry. The question 'Is your journey really necessary?' became as much part of the nation's vocabulary as the admonition that 'There's a war on, you know'. Without doubt, at such a worrying time, family reunions were indeed necessary, and the wartime loadings were exacerbated by Easter. The limit on train weight was not the capacity of the locomotives, for Gresley had provided the LNER with a fleet of big locomotives, but the ability to handle such huge formations at the stations. A famous example occurred on March 31st 1940. The 10.45 from Newcastle had accumulated more portions at the principal stations, and was finally increased at Peterborough to no less than 26 coaches, 764 tons tare and probably at least 850 tons gross. No doubt the crew of Gateshead's famous A1 No.2569 GLADIATEUR were thankful to pass the task of haulage to Kings Cross to the crew of brand new V2 No.4800!

Another famous event occurred six days later when the prototype A4, SILVER LINK herself, driven by Driver W. Carman of Grantham, was set the task of hauling the 13.00 from Kings Cross to Edinburgh as far as Newcastle. The story has been told many times, but it is worth considering for a moment how it was actually done. The train was made up in two platforms. The Buckeye coupling has saved many lives but in steam days it required skill and a straight track to make a secure and safe coupling first time. Those readers familiar with Newcastle Central for example, with its curved platforms, will understand the problem. The leading portion was drawn into Gasworks Tunnel and

Reading Shed, and the unusual visitor is the World speed record holder for steam traction, MALLARD. I suspect it is April 27th 1948, when an overheated middle big end resulted in her being replaced by SEAGULL for the Western Region tests. The engine is in garter blue livery with LNER cut-out letters and numbers, but with the tender declaring the identity of the new owner. She had just been transferred to Kings Cross from Grantham. The fitter is no doubt reflecting how easy servicing outside Walschaerts valve gear must be, by comparison with the local products. The A4 had just been coupled to A3 corridor tender No.5323 no doubt to aid footplate access in the Exchanges. (Maurice Earley)

The three views of MERLIN, temporarily renamed after the children of FitzHerbert Wright, when he became a Director of the LNER.

coupled to the second portion. History does not record how it was done, whether it was backed on to the rear portion or whether that portion was propelled forward to make the connection. Reversing a loaded train was not normally allowed but the power signalling provided the necessary locking to allow the move. The train then totalled 25 coaches, now some 850 tons gross. By the time the coupling had been successfully made, the brakes had been tested, the doors had been checked (no easy task on 25 coaches), 'Right Away' had been

successfully conveyed to the driver inside the tunnel, and the overloaded Pacific had staggered past Finsbury Park, at least some 16 minutes had passed. From thereon matters were less onerous, the 103 miles to Grantham taking 123 minutes, and only 4 minutes were lost on the 207 minutes running time allowed from there to Newcastle. Presumably as up trains increased in size as they travelled south, so northbound trains discarded portions down country in the same way.

The operation of such huge trains must have caused enormous problems. Special instructions were no doubt issued to deal with such difficulties at the principal stations. With train lengths approaching double, there was the inevitable requirement to draw up at least once intermediately. Then there was the concomitant nuisance of having staff trudging down the track to convey the 'Right Away' to a driver at least ¼ mile and sometimes nearer ½ mile away, while restraining late arrivals from opening all the doors again! And

at the journey's end, there was the process of marshalling and disposing of such enormous trains, which must have posed daunting problems. Half a century ago, it was common practice for the station pilot to add or remove coaches at the main stations, both passenger and non-passenger. Inevitably the problems were greatest in London.

Just consider the practicalities of unloading thousands of passengers from a train that stretched from the buffer stops at Kings Cross out to some way through Gasworks Tunnel, and then getting the empty stock away. Difficult enough in peacetime but in wartime conditions with blackout and air raids it called for the greatest care and experience. There were a number of special instructions, which probably originated in those hard times, that provided for the operation of trains far longer than the platform could accommodate. Where the length of the train exceeded that of the platform track circuit and thus occupied the adjacent one through the connections as well ('blocking back') the Signals & Telecomms (S&T) lineman was authorised to lift the locking so that, provided the train was clear and stopped, the connections could be reset. This allowed either the train engine to couple on or draw up, or an engine to come on the rear.

The Belle Isle signalman, if the preceding express was too long to clear the Kings Cross up main home signal, was authorised to allow another engine into the section, under caution and having warned its driver of the position ahead and having advised the Yard Inspector that a

shunter was required to meet the engine at the rear of the train. If the Yard Inspector required the ECS engine, having coupled on to the back of the train, to draw off part of it, then the Belle Isle signalman had to instruct the driver when authorising him to enter the occupied section. Where the down trains were too long for one platform, departures used two platforms at Kings Cross, as in the case of SILVER LINK earlier. The ECS locos were permitted to assist as far as the middle footbridge (at the north end of the roof) provided a clear understanding had been established with the driver of the loco at the head of the train. In the same way the incoming engine would assist the ECS loco to get away

Half a century ago the railway was far more dependent on pieces of paper signed by the Appropriate Authority to legitimise an operation that was contrary to normal operation. The administration of wrong line orders, securing of unlocked trailing connections, shunting part of trains in and out were all possible, but only given time, written authority and competent staff that were now in short supply. Even in wartime railways had to work to rules which were and are laid down for safe working and not industrial cussedness.

Then of course there would be the problem of starting with the locomotive cranks awkwardly positioned, and the need to set back with the hazard of unlocked trailing points behind. The LNER, and indeed the country, had cause to remember Gresley's policy of building big engines with gratitude, big engines which could move these enormous

loads unaided, the A4s among them. By 1941 more services were restored to ease the loading situation, but main line trains still loaded in excess of 700 tons for much of the time. And there were still enormous numbers of freight trains to be accommodated as well.

And yet, with all of this confusion as the country grew used to wartime conditions, news came through later of a startling performance. The locomotive was Gateshead's Kylchap A4, No.4901 CAPERCAILLIE, which was the regular engine of Driver G. Hannah. Taking over a huge 21 coach train, 665 tons tare and some 730 tons gross, at Newcastle, No.4901 was let rip south of Darlington. This remarkable locomotive averaged 75.9 mph for 25 miles, with a maximum of 78.5 mph. A facilitating factor was that the Gateshead crew was relieved at York. There was little understanding of mathematical modelling of all the resistances that No.4901 overcame, and the Johansen formula, which was derived from LMSR wind tunnel testing of 1:40 models, tended to give high values for still air conditions. At the time it was thought that No.4901 had developed 2,200 DBHP continuously, necessitating an IHP of the order of 3,000, but the DBHP value was probably nearer 1,700, depending on the strength of wind resistance on this notoriously exposed stretch of line. Nevertheless it was a magnificent piece of work requiring some 2,500 IHP, possibly more, sustained for roughly 30 minutes. It was a telling demonstration of what the Kylchap A4s could do if put to it.

The last three years of Gresley's life were occupied by the design of his

The first 'Capitals Limited' on May 23rd 1949 is launched at Kings Cross by Anne Crawford, an actress born in Edinburgh. As one can see, the A4 is in garter blue livery, and is spotless. It was a unique experience at that time, and one can understand why the Non-stop was such compulsive viewing for enthusiasts. As a result of the war, the younger enthusiasts seldom saw a clean locomotive. Notice particularly the Doncasters painter's ornate cross for 'Kings +'.

V4 2-6-2 and the first main line electric locomotive, No.6701. There was some brainstorming already mentioned, that produced outline designs for a 4-8-2 heavy passenger locomotive, and an improved A4 with higher boiler pressure. The nation was heading towards a war with Germany, although hopes for peace remained high. The Pacifics were beginning to work long diagrams that improved utilisation and increased the rate of mileage accumulation. There were signs that Gresley was concerned about the standard of servicing and maintenance of his locomotives, and he explored options for improving the valve motion. An outline design for the use of the earlier form of conjugated gear in an oil bath was prepared, but Gresley's death occurred before any experiments could be carried out.

When in 1941 Sir Nigel Gresley died, it was clear that an era had ended. In the last few years of his life, his health had deteriorated. Latterly he had not been well, although he was keen to continue until he was 70. Gresley had been a very good chief. He had taken the LNER to great

heights of achievement, while working within severely constricting financial limits. He had a remarkably wide overall view of locomotive, carriage and wagon developments in Europe and the USA assisted by his membership of the International Railway Congress Technical Committee. He had been cautious at times, had made his mistakes, but when he was convinced of the correctness of a course of action, he took it. He had managed to hold six disparate railway engineering establishments together and despite some hostility, made it work positively. The LNER workforce liked a winner, and he had shown an instinctive will to win, to move forward. He was also a kind and courteous chief, very loyally and fondly regarded by his staff.

The LNER had to find a replacement for a man who was regarded as well-nigh irreplaceable, and quickly. Bulleid had gone to the Southern in 1937 and Gresley's principal assistant, Edward Thompson, was only five years younger than Gresley himself. But in days when promotion rarely went

beyond the immediate successors in the 'Big Four', there was only one possible choice in the circumstances. Thompson knew the LNER CME's organisation well, the locomotives and rolling stock, and the system for maintaining it. So it was Thompson who was promoted to CME, ironically when his hopes of high office must have all but evaporated. Edward Thompson was an unfortunate man. He seems, from the views of those who worked for him, to have been the antithesis of his confident and relaxed predecessor, a troubled man normally difficult to work for and aloof to the point of arrogance. Yet he could be as charming, helpful and courteous as he could be difficult. In his short tenure of office, he introduced a 4-6-0, 2-8-0 and laid the foundations for a post-war 2-6-0 and 4-6-2, good and straightforward designs which served the LNER and its successor well. He possessed considerable academic ability and a logical mind. Although he had risen to become Mechanical Engineer (Doncaster) with the authority that the post conveyed, he had perforce to spend nearly all his working career in the shadow of Raven, Gresley and also Bulleid, men with whom he would not have been wholly in sympathy. It happened, and no doubt still does. Now, very late in his working life, when the chief's post had all but gone from his grasp, it was his.

Thompson was concerned with many issues, for the LNER was in a difficult state. The war had brought severe limitations in the availability of materials and skills, with as much as possible being diverted to the war effort. As a result the supply of spare components was severely limited, and as much use as possible was wrung out of existing components. Gresley had managed carefully with the limited investment given him and in the main, had built wisely. The LNER could not afford the rate of reinvestment required to keep all of its infrastructure and rolling stock in first class condition. When Gresley reached high office he inherited a considerable number of designs that were obsolescent but far from life expired. These had continued in traffic but whereas they were once quite capable of good service, they were now at or approaching the end of their usable life. The Pacifics and V2s were fine, although in wartime conditions they ran hot far too often, and the worn wartime replacement bearings of the conjugated gear made them sound far worse than they already were. Some of the smaller engines were a considerable burden and Thompson's B1 4-6-0 was an excellent replacement that was long overdue. The B1 was essentially a two cylinder version of the B17 4-6-0 with 6ft 2ins coupled wheels, driven by two improved K2 cylinders as used on GN Atlantic No.3279 and with a B17 boiler of thicker plate to withstand 225 psi.

Edward Thompson had an academic aversion to the conjugated gear, preferring three cylinders with divided drive, separate sets of valve gear, and connecting rods of equal length as in the GWR four cylinder engines. One of his first initiatives was to propose the rebuilding of the A4s to remove the conjugated gear, although the fitting of an inside set of Walschaerts gear would have necessitated driving on the leading coupled axle and extending the frames accordingly. He was dissuaded early on: the cost, the commitment in terms of design, material and labour would have been considerable, and the Railway Executive Committee would have certainly put a stop to any such ideas in wartime. In retrospect it would hardly have simplified maintenance. One might have been tempted at the time to think that in view of the A4s' wartime and post-war troubles, it might have been a good thing. But

Thompson's divided drive would not have achieved that alone, and the real culprits, the middle big end and jumper top blastpipes, would have remained. In fact he allowed orders for the building of Gresley designs to continue, fortunately. The country was in dire straits and it was no time to dispense with haulage capacity for whatever reason.

So apart from removing the side valances of the A4s and, temporarily, most of the chime whistles, he left them to work the main line. Their chime whistles were removed in most cases since they were easily confused with the air raid warnings, and like all locomotives, the A4s were painted black. The Flaman recorders, no longer required, were stored at Doncaster and then most were scrapped. The 'LNER' initials were reduced to 'NE' as an economy measure, and one can imagine Thompson's father-in-law, Sir Vincent Raven, would have enjoyed that. Their condition, like that of all other engines, deteriorated. Stripped of the skilled manpower to clean, maintain, overhaul, fire and drive, with spare parts and replacements in short supply, frames, axleboxes and then motion wore badly. The railways were given 'directed' labour from occupations not deemed necessary for the war effort, which required the depleted staff not only to use unskilled recruits but to train them too.

By its nature, the conjugated motion required that all clearances and tolerances should be within laid down limits: if they were not, then the aggregated slack was amplified in the operation of the middle piston valve. The situation was made far worse by the shortage of critical replacement parts, especially bearings. The functioning of the conjugated gear depended critically on the main bearing of the heavy 2:1 lever, which normally was a needle bearing and gave little trouble. In wartime supplies were impossible and plain bearings had to be used instead, which wore rapidly in service and were not renewed as frequently as they should have been. Engineers working at the time recalled elliptical and kidney-shaped worn bushes, which had resulted in the valve events bearing only the slightest resemblance to what was, in theory, supposed to happen.

Thompson, in these conditions, had some justification for his views. He had inherited a locomotive fleet that contained a large proportion of designs that were by now obsolescent if not obsolete, as mentioned above. He was also confronted by a large number of three-cylinder locomotives that featured Gresley's conjugated motion and which were not performing at all well in wartime

conditions. Although an excellent design, which eliminated the need for an inaccessible inside set of valve gear had three sets been used, some were more complicated than an equivalent two cylinder locomotive for peacetime work. At some depots there was neither the experience nor the manpower to support them and in war conditions things simply went from bad to worse.

Thompson sought independent advice from William Stanier to support his contention that the conjugated gear was the cause of many of his problems. The Gresleys and the Staniers, however, had been good friends, and the latter, when asked, was placed in a delicate position. He had to choose between loyalty to his old and late friend and supporting a colleague. Of course we have no record of any verbal briefing that always occurred on such occasions. Very reluctantly he deputed his Personal Assistant E.S. Cox of the LMSR to report on the question, a man with no love for Gresley's locomotives and their achievements. Cox regarded the 2:1 gear with distaste, but reported that the principal cause of the problems was in fact the design and performance of the middle big end, and not the valve gear. For an engineer often regarded as partisan, it was a perceptive observation, and history has since proved Stewart Cox right.

The valve gear had little in his view to commend it, vulnerable as it was to wartime maintenance conditions and imparting unequal cylinder outputs when it needed repair. The LMSR CME simply accepted and signed the report, which was not the endorsement that Thompson was seeking. It did not, however, deter Thompson from inviting Cox to move to a senior position on the LNER with the unusual title Mechanical Engineer (Commercial) a move which the latter, on Stanier's advice, turned down. As he observed later to George Carpenter, he was aware that 'Not all was sweetness and light in the LNER CME's department under Edward Thompson'! Having received the Report, Thompson did little with it. War imposed severe restraints on what could be done, focussing on support for the war effort, although on the Southern Railway, Bulleid was building, whatever his protestations to the contrary, a main line express Pacific and a lighter version for secondary lines. I suspect O.V.S. Bulleid was a far more persuasive and charming man than Thompson, someone who could make his case far more successfully than most, and who could get away with bending wartime restrictions.

Then disaster struck. In a German air raid, the depot at York was bombed, and Gateshead's No.4469 GADWALL, which by then had been renamed SIR RALPH WEDGWOOD, was destroyed beyond repair, on April 29th 1942. Ironically, it was only at the shed returning north after general overhaul. While the A4 might have been rebuilt in peacetime, there was no question during the hostilities. Both metal and the skilled craftsmen to work with it were in short supply. The war continued and express work settled into a steady grind. Expresses of 600-700 tons were very much the rule. *Yeadon's Register* shows that, although conditions during the war were extremely hard, the A4s continued to be shopped regularly. Quite what that meant in terms of quality, with a shortage of material, many men away in the forces, directed labour, and part of the railways' works given over to armament production, one can only guess. Those men in reserved occupations worked long hours, added to which were hours spent on Air Raid Protection and Fire patrols in their rest time. People were tired. Photography was forbidden in the war years, but those few illustrations of A4s that have been published show them in lamentable external condition. If an engine was usable, it was used until it failed; then it joined the queue waiting minimal repairs to get back into service again.

Gateshead's favourite, No.4901 CAPERCAILLIE, was fitted with an experimental open fork big end but it shattered in service and damaged the middle cylinder after only 13,000 miles. This engine was a magnificent performer, and was used on the up 'Flying Scotsman' for long spells during the war. The war years brought their own fears, but the railway scene was depressing. Certainly some locomotives got into strange places, although the A4s rarely left the main routes. Grantham's GOLDEN FLEECE and even Haymarket's No.4488 UNION OF SOUTH AFRICA were among strangers to appear on the GC Section at Nottingham and Gorton Depot, Manchester, no doubt causing temporary cardiac arrest amongst the Lancastrian enthusiasts who saw them. But with the adult population involved in the war effort and censorship forbidding photography or any untoward interest, news of what was going on was limited. Even after the war, locomotives generally were filthy, noisy, and it became more common to see the halt and the lame among their number hauling slow freight, or laying dead on some lineside country depot. Most of the main line depots had a casualty or two. The rebuilt W1 came into its own, her enormous tractive power,

17% greater than the nominal figure for the A4, being a great advantage in hauling 700 ton loads.

A few weeks after D-Day, on August 10th 1944 while the Allies were fighting their way through Normandy, No.4486 MERLIN was temporarily renamed and renumbered at Doncaster Works on one side during the day in order to be photographed. The reason was that a new Director had been appointed to the LNER Board, Fitzherbert Wright, and in act of extraordinary indulgence by Peppercorn, the A4 was successively given the identity of 1928 BRIGID, 1931 DAVINA and 1934 BRYAN. The details first became generally known in the RCTS 'Green Guide' Part 2A in 1973. Eleven of the class were renamed after members and officers of the LNER, and a further two were considered for renaming at the time of partition of the Indian sub-continent. EMPIRE OF INDIA was to become a Dominion, and GUILLEMOT was to become DOMINION OF PAKISTAN. The nameplates were actually cast for the latter but never used. In preservation, UNION OF SOUTH AFRICA became OSPREY for a while as the first name had unsavoury political associations, but reverted when the country became politically acceptable again. The details are in the Appendices.

End of an A4. The scene at York after the bombing raid on April 29th 1942. SIR RALPH WEDGWOOD lays wrecked among the debris. In peacetime the engine might have been repaired, but in wartime conditions the option was not available. The A4 tender No.5672 was not so badly damaged, and became No.703 as part of a Thompsonian renumbering, and reused with the first A2/1 No.3696

The proportions of the boilers had changed slightly due to wartime shortages and maintenance problems. In 1943 the number of tubes was reduced from 121 to 111, and then to 105. The reason was that the smokebox tubeplates were suffering a number of fractures, and the problem was cured post-war by using a thicker tubeplate and a fuller flange radius. Another wartime measure was the shortening of superheater elements by 1ft to prevent return end burning, which reduced the boiler dimensions, particularly that of superheat, as below:-

Year	1935	1943	1943
Firebox area	231	231	231
Tubes	1281	1175	1112
Flues	1064	1064	1064
Sub-total	2576	2470	2407
S'heater	748.9	706	706
Total	3324.9	3176	3113

There had also been proposals to renew fireboxes where necessary in steel due to the difficulty in importing copper, but this was dropped. It was difficult to achieve effective water treatment during the war, and this was essential to avoid corrosion wastage in the steel firebox plates. Those familiar with the problems of maintaining locomotives in service and later in preservation will appreciate the measures that had to be taken to ensure that fireboxes were safely stayed and locos kept in traffic. Towards the end of the war, 18 A1s and A3s needed new frames. Thompson had mooted the standardisation on the A4 boiler for these engines, during rebuilding, which would have been a sensible move, especially if the locomotives could have been modified and strengthened to work at 250 psi. The outcome eventually was the rebuilding of No.4470 as a new A1. Ten years later a number of A3s were fitted with Diagram 107 boilers. Thompson disliked the Gresley banjo dome extension, and drawings for a round dome appeared. A batch of ten new boilers was built in 1944, and nine were Diagram 94HP rather than 94A. Nothing further happened. He also had a design prepared for a new regulator valve as the original had suffered from leakage, but again the war prevented action on a broad scale. A second design was produced in 1946 and this was introduced. It is interesting to recall that The Superheater Co. had pressed Gresley to try their multiple valve smokebox regulators in 1938.

A multiple valve regulator comprises a casting containing, rather than a single or double-beat valve, a small *number* of valves of increasing size, opened and closed by the operation of a camshaft. The latter is normally worked by external rodding with a compensator at the midpoint to ensure that the camshaft operation remains true to the regulator setting. It is placed on the superheated side of the header. Its advantages are threefold.

Firstly it is lighter and easier to work, not passing through a steam-tight gland, and allows greater precision in controlling the steam chest pressure, especially at starting. Secondly, the amount of steam left to drive the engine when the regulator was closed is reduced as far as is practicable. Thirdly, it allows the superheater elements to remain charged with steam and thus prevents burning at the smokebox ends.

The effect on the exterior of the locomotive can be seen on BLUE PETER. Clearly it would not have been possible to fit one to an A4 without ruining the streamlined appearance. It was possible to fit one into a cylindrical smokebox, as on some of the BR standard locomotives, provided there was adequate space, but it is doubtful whether the external linkage could be successfully fitted between the boiler barrel and the cladding, the space normally filled with insulation.

The accident whenby the regulator was jammed open on BLUE PETER, with expensive consequences, was not caused by any shortcoming or malfunction in the design.

The regulators were fitted to V2s Nos.4804-4808 instead. The A4s had been limited to a maximum cut-off of 65%, but this had caused some difficulties in starting the greater loads in wartime. It was agreed in 1943 that No.4499 should be altered to 75%, although this slightly altered the steam lap at normal cut-offs. Following a favourable report, the remainder of the class were altered similarly. There seemed to be no urgency in carrying out the modification and it was no less than 14 years later that the conversion was completed.

Then at long last came peace with victory in 1945. Once the celebrations were over, the extent and the cost of six years' war was brought home to us. The war had permanently changed the face of Britain, and it had certainly changed the face of the railway industry. A General Election brought the Labour Party to power, a party that had espoused nationalisation, and was now determined to carry it out. Men who had seen action in the war, suffered its fear and trauma, and experienced its horrors, were less likely to settle for the hard railway life of slog, Dickensian conditions and low pay, and what we now call unsocial hours. In addition to the shortages of well nigh everything to run a railway, there was also a sense of anticlimax as a weary nation contemplated the price of war. The post-war railway was a sad shadow of its former self.

There were two trials in 1945, the first to compare the rebuilt Mikado, the A2/2 and the new class A2/1 (the latter created by the modification of the last four 'Green Arrows') with an A4, SILVER FOX. The second was to compare the new A1 GREAT NORTHERN with an A4, this time SIR RALPH WEDGWOOD. The first trial had to be repeated as the results were bad, and the weather was extreme. The A4 was the most economical on express work, but the smaller-wheeled Pacifics had the edge on fast freight work. The newer Pacifics were of course built with double Kylchap exhausts. The trials with GREAT NORTHERN were almost a dead heat, both engines running economically. As both had the same boiler, grate, pressure, and stroke, apart from ½ in greater cylinder diameter in No.4470, the outcome was no great surprise. The A1's Kylchap exhaust appeared to make little difference in comparison with the single blast A4, insofar as records of the tests show, but in its daily work it was clearly superior despite a more tortuous steam circuit. At the performance levels current in 1945 its role was not specifically recorded or commented on. It was more a comparison between the locomotive with conjugated gear and concentrated drive versus divided drive and independent valve gear for the middle cylinder.

Edward Thompson was an orderly man, and he had introduced a new numbering scheme in January 1946 that brought order and sense in place of the previous random allocation of numbers for new building. The new numbering was varied slightly at first, which meant that a few locomotives carried an intermediate number before getting the final version. Gradually the A4s were overhauled and repainted in LNER garter blue bearing the new numbers allocated under Thompson's system. Some were renumbered before overhaul. The stainless steel cut-out numbers and letters reappeared as the A4s passed through Doncaster Works at general overhaul. In 1946 after the end of the war, Edward Thompson retired and was succeeded by Arthur Peppercorn. The latter had even less time in office than his predecessor. State ownership was imposed by the new Government from 1st January 1948. He did, however, restore much of the Gresley 'team', such as Bert Spencer, who had been 'seconded' as Materials Inspector and Outdoor Machinery Engineer. He substituted a more compact and successful divided drive layout for the elongated and awkward design produced by Thompson. He was a kindly, courteous and popular chief very much in the Gresley tradition. In his short term of office, however, he produced a powerful 6ft 2ins Pacific followed by the magnificent A1 Pacific express design, both with divided drive.

On May 21st and 22nd 1946 a test train was run to Edinburgh and back to establish whether the running of the 1930s could be restarted. It was significant that it was an A4, No.17 SILVER FOX, that was used, and not the new A1, GREAT NORTHERN, but possibly the corridor tender of the A4 was a factor in the choice. The load was 6 coaches, 207 tons, and the drivers were Messrs. G. Kitchener of Kings Cross and J. Leonard of Haymarket. The London man had worked on the streamliners before the war. The timings from London to Grantham, York, Newcastle and Edinburgh were 98, 77, 77, and 124 minutes, 376 minutes in total. The southbound timings were similar and both allowed for PSRs and TSRs that did not apply to the pre-war streamliners. The A4 was fresh from general overhaul but still in unlined black livery and the train was loaded with sandbags to simulate passengers. To test the quality of the track alignment the CCE took a Hallade recording. However, he was not happy with the condition of the track, and it was no less than ten years before anything like pre-war speeds were restored other than on certain services like the 'Tees-Tyne Pullman' and then only with certain drivers. I think in retrospect the CCEs of those days were worried about a rash of derailments for one reason or another, and the mood was not one of optimism. The loss of manpower to the services had a severe effect on track maintenance, and the recruitment of staff post-war was a big problem in city and urban areas. CCEs were also looking for a higher track standard for high speed running than hitherto. The quality of track geometry had still some ground to make up from the increase in train speeds of the 1930s.

The railway industry had been changed permanently by the war and its aftermath. There was also a new problem beginning to make itself known – formation failure. The foundation of the main lines, in places, was beginning to break down due to the accumulated arrears of drainage and reballasting. The mechanical plant of the day was woefully inadequate to deal with the problem within the confines of the weekend possession, and so, in the meantime, manual means of repair had to serve. But now men were not content to slave away in poor conditions for a poor reward, and left the industry in numbers after wartime labour controls were withdrawn in 1949. I am also quite sure that the restrictions imposed by the LNER's financial condition pre-war had resulted in an infrastructure that was run down in places, but it was all blamed on the war.

From 1945, for those growing up fascinated by railways and engineering, life was dull. There was a shortage of steel and coal, and the railways, which had served the country faithfully during the war years, were now subservient to political expediency, something that was to last half a century. But there were now new minds determining the way forward however, and Gresley, Doncaster, the LNER and the streamliners were no part of it. Arrears of track repairs and signalling limitations prevented a return to high speed. To be honest, moreover, the Silver Jubilee of 1935 and the Coronation of 1937 as events had long since been forgotten by many as history moved on. It would have been inappropriate if the streamlined services had recommenced using the same names. There was a post-war 'West Riding' service but the schedule, for an admittedly far heavier train, was 28% longer.

The Pullman trains were restored after the coal shortage, together with a third new train, the 'Tees-Tyne Pullman', which was a very second-rate 'Silver Jubilee' in speed terms, but no doubt the best that could be done at the time. Small boys, yearning for the return of the streamliners, didn't understand. The 'Yorkshire Pullman' restarted using its original route via Wakefield on November 4th 1946, and the 'Queen of Scots' followed on July 5th 1948. The 'Tees-Tyne Pullman' started on September 27th 1948 and, surprisingly, was worked by Heaton Depot. The engine was remanned at Grantham until May 1949 when Kings Cross took the duty over. It was always regarded as one of the principal services. The Non-stop was reintroduced in 1948 as the 'Flying Scotsman' but in 1949 it was the first portion that ran non-stop, named 'The Capitals Limited' and departing at 9.30 from Kings Cross and 9.45 from Waverley.

The ten years of war and austerity, followed by a slow recovery, were not fruitful years for the A4s. There were signs of some improvement, but the class had suffered from a lack of skilled maintenance and from the few but critical points of weakness, namely the big end design and the right-hand driving axlebox. Performance had been inhibited by the 60 mph overall wartime speed limit, and reliability had fallen generally from the pre-war standard, and at times drastically. On the occasions when youngsters travelled north behind one of the Gresley Pacifics, mindful of their great deeds, the result was invariably disappointing. Sometimes one had a good engine and crew, but with an unchallenging schedule, unless there were arrears to be recovered, results were unexciting. All too often, the crew settled for a quiet day's work with an engine not in the best of form. Added to this were the constant checks from signals on a congested railway, or from 'the Engineer' relaying track, repairing bridges, or whatever. Much of the romance and excitement of one's first long journeys was lost in dismal running. Nor was it peculiar to the old LNER: everybody seemed to have caught the disease. Occasionally there were heartening signs of recovery. The new Divisional Motive Power Superintendent at Kings Cross in 1949 was Kenneth Cameron, an inspirational engineer trained at St. Rollox who had commanded a major railway workshop in the Middle East during the war. He put on his boiler suit and demonstrated to his fitters how jobs should be done, which encouraged them greatly.

Another small but important change was brought in at this time. The blastpipe orifices for the Kylchap engines were, as described earlier, fitted in each case with four *barrettes* or 'vee bars' at right angles. The *barrettes* were of case hardened steel. They were secured with set screws and brazed to prevent the screws loosening and the *barrettes* from dropping into the valve chests, where they would cause serious damage. It was decided to cast future Kylchap blastpipe tops with four wedge shaped inserts integrally, and dispense with the radially adjustable *barrettes* altogether. It was an understandable economy, but the quality of the castings deteriorated and something of the original design was lost. However, the superiority in performance of the double Kylchap engines over the single blast engines was such that the refinements of the original design were not obvious. The same design was used on 81 out of the 90 post-Gresley Pacifics, and then on the redraughting of the remaining single chimney Gresley Pacifics in 1957-59.

There had been concern in some people's minds about the inequality of power output in the Gresley Pacific. Indicator diagrams taken from A3 No.2751 HUMORIST had shown that there was an inequality between the cylinders that changed with speed and output. There seems to have been a lack of understanding that despite theory, cylinder outputs differed in practice as wear occurred in the valve gear linkage, often quite significantly, even in what one might call symmetrical designs of two or four cylinders. The differences in power output arising from quite minute variations in valve timing could be quite large. In an attempt to equalise the power output of the three cylinders of the A4 in 1947 it was decided to line the middle cylinder down to 17ins on five engines, originally six. They were Nos.3, 12, 14, 20 and 31. The experiment was quite inconclusive, although drivers had to use longer cut-offs to compensate, and the modified A4s were regarded as weak. The reduction in the thrust of the middle piston was considerable at 15.5%.

Up to about 50 mph it was in fact No2751's right-hand cylinder that produced the most power, which might have been the cause of excessive wear and overheating in the right-hand driving axleboxes. As the right-hand valve was driven directly by the outside Walschaerts valve gear, this was difficult to understand. There was a great deal of running at or below 50 mph in the immediate post-war period. At the speed at which maximum power was developed, the three 18½ ins cylinders were fairly well in balance. At higher speeds however, the middle cylinder gradually developed more power, and if the indicated results of testing on HUMORIST were anything to go by, the discrepancy would have been significant. The weak link was of course, not the cylinders nor the conjugated gear, but

the middle big end bearing itself. No.14 reverted to normal after only two years, followed by No.60003 in 1954 and No.60031 in 1959. The dates of reversion of Nos.12 and 20 are either unknown, or they remained unaltered until they were withdrawn. As the post-war schedules, if not the loads, were well within the speed capacity of an Ivatt Atlantic, a B1 or a K3, it was unlikely to make a dramatic difference. Looking back at the HUMORIST figures, there was a facetious and totally impractical argument for leaving the middle cylinder alone and enlarging the left-hand cylinder to 20 ins!

In 1948 the new Railway Executive of the British Transport Commission behemoth was created. In retrospect one can see the fingerprints of the Civil Service all over the concept of this huge bureaucracy. It also provided a heaven-sent opportunity to find a home for the many high-ranking service officers who had been demobilised. There were, within their numbers, Royal Engineer officers from the Transportation Division who had been railwaymen in peacetime. The operating and civil engineering functions at the Railway Executive were claimed by the LNER in the private scrummaging that occurs at such times. Michael Barrington-Ward and the happily named Landale Train were the fortunate beneficiaries. The larger LMSR took the Mechanical

and Electrical engineering, which was unfortunate for the LNER, since it brought the entire LMSR cadre into power, with the one exception of J.F. Harrison of the LNER, Peppercorn's assistant and the LNER's CME-elect. The other senior M&EE figures retired or found work in private industry. It might have served BR far, far better if Regions had been allowed autonomy in day-to-day operations and the provision of motive power and rolling stock, especially for design in mechanical engineering. Most had modern designs that were competent and economical, and the depots held the necessary stocks of spare parts.

However, as with all things designed by people who do not have the responsibility of making the system work, the nationalised railway had the familiar triangular structure. If there were six Regional heads of department, clearly there must be an overall chief at the central organisation, although what that person was to do was far from clear. G.F. Fiennes, on appointment to the Centre as Chief Operating Officer, enquired 'Operate what?' The new system of operation was that the central organisation, the Railway Executive, would manage the whole network and the Regions merely answered their master's voice. Even the Regional CMEs were stripped of the 'Chief', becoming simply Mechanical Engineers. Despite

The 'Atlantic Coast Express' hauled by MALLARD winds through Vauxhall on June 8th 1948. This was the first of two test runs on the Southern Region, MALLARD having replaced SEAGULL which latter had run hot. MALLARD herself ran hot the next day on the up run. The dynamometer car is, I think, the Darlington Car now in the NRM. (The Transport Treasury)

protestations by Robert Riddles and his team that the designs of the 'Big Four' would not be swept aside in favour of their largely LMSR common user designs, and that there would be a series of Exchanges to establish best practice, that is precisely what happened. It seemed that Doncaster and Darlington's days of influence were at an end.

The A4s had emerged from the unlined black of the war to regain their pre-war garter blue livery, black front and parabolic curves and maroon wheels. The provision of cut-out numbers and letters pre-war was affected by wartime conditions, but Doncaster had continued for some while with garter blue before changing to unlined black. A number of A4s continued with cut-out numbers and letters and with the end of the war the 1939 livery began to reapplied, albeit with the new numbers as mentioned earlier. The silver foxes carried by No.2512 and the different chime whistles started something of a fashion for ornamenting individual A4s. On May 26th 1946 Haymarket's MERLIN had plaques depicting the badge of HMS Merlin fitted to the cab sides, later transferred to the centre of the boiler sides. It became a simple matter to identify the Scottish visitor on the Non-stop on seeing the single chimney and plaque of the approaching A4. Commemorative plaques recording MALLARD's achievement were also fitted in a similar position on the engine in March 1948. Here there was some interference by the newly created Railway Executive, which wanted the credit for the achievement, but officers of the old LNER insisted that the name of the engine's builders and original owners should be recorded. So it was, rightly. Next it was the turn of No.60009 UNION OF SOUTH AFRICA, happily still with us. C.J. Fourie, a Bloemfontain newspaper owner, donated a single plaque of a winged Springbok in 1953, which was mounted on the driver's side of the boiler casing at overhaul in April 1954. Finally, No. 60024 KINGFISHER was fitted with the badge of HMS Kingfisher in the same position, on October 21st 1954. In preservation, SIR NIGEL GRESLEY, then restored as No.60007, was fitted with similar plaques to those of MALLARD, commemorating the post-war official speed record of 112 mph on May 23rd 1959.

Most of the chime whistles had been removed in the war years and no doubt melted down. Since import restrictions prevented the LNER from recourse to the Crosby Valve Co., the replacements had to be manufactured under licence in the UK. Inevitably the British version was different; it was not exactly of the same metal or the same wall thickness, and produced a note higher in pitch.

With nationalisation, the new administration was concerned to emphasise its ownership, and both 'BRITISH RAILWAYS' and the appropriate numbering were quickly applied widely but not comprehensively. A change in livery was heralded by some experimental use of a purple livery and a red, cream and grey lining, and Nos.60024, 60027, 60028 and 60029 were turned out in these colours. After some A4s had carried painted numbers at the front, the familiar numberplate appeared just below the top lamp iron, complete with Doncaster's own version of the Gill Sans 6 and 9. By the spring in 1949, the new express locomotive livery of dark Caledonian Railway blue with black and white lining had been decided on, together with the first BR totem – the 'Ferret and Dartboard'.

LNER No.4496, renamed DWIGHT D EISENHOWER but not yet renumbered under the Thompson scheme. It was based at Grantham and is heading a down express south of Hatfield. The period is June 1946 and the A4 has her original A4 corridor tender No.5651. The local ganger is doing some spot re-sleepering on the down main, by the look of the sleepers in the ten-foot (K. Pullen, The Transport Treasury)

The Railway Executive of the BTC decided to have a series of exchange trials, as had been announced, to assess the requirements for the new standard locomotives to be built by British Railways. These exchanges were inadequately prepared and too short and superficial for any firm conclusions as to the merits of the competing designs. On the footplate the situation was inevitably different from running a normal service, with pilotmen and inspectors. No doubt the testing crews and footplate staffs played their part, but there is no doubt that a much more searching test programme and stronger footplate discipline to achieve greater uniformity in running would have been of far greater benefit. The effects of the style and standard of driving was difficult to quantify in scientific terms, but it had a significant impact on the running. Driver Harry Byford of Camden Depot, for example, used a lighter hand on his Stanier Pacific during the test running, apprehensive lest its powerful exhaust when worked hard should impact on the coal consumption. At the other extreme the Southern drivers drove their 'Merchant Navy' and 'West Country' Pacifics with a gay abandon and ran well, but at considerable cost to their fuel consumption. In any case despite the A4 recording indisputably the best figures for coal and water consumption, official minds were made up according to the gospel preached at Derby and the requirements of the industrialised LMSR. Accordingly the outcome of the tests was never likely to have any significant effect on future designs.

Why we needed a fleet of standard locomotives was something of a mystery, which is not within the scope of this book. No doubt Robert Riddles and his team, too, may have wanted their moment of glory. The Exchanges were certainly a waste of money in commercial and financial terms. However, for the engineer and enthusiast, it was quite the opposite. It was not hard-headed commercial judgement so much as a few weeks of sights that were unprecedented and undreamed of at the major London termini and on the main lines. In those days the locomotives of the Big Four rarely strayed from their native heath, and so it was a wonderful treat after so many long years of misery and austerity. There were the unforgettable moments of the 1948 Exchanges such as when the 'West Country' left Blair Athol and charged up to Druimachdar, leaving her banker, winded, well and truly in her wake. Or CITY OF BRADFORD in the preliminary running, for once opened out spectacularly on the Southern, reaching 88 mph with the up 'Atlantic

Coast Express' near Woking. The photographers had a magnificent opportunity to photograph unprecedented events, and many a grandmother's funeral must have been pleaded in those few weeks.

The LNER locomotives selected were A4s, Nos.21 WILD SWAN, 25 FALCON and 26 MILES BEEVOR. They were all single chimney engines of which only No.25 was later a regular top link locomotive. At a late stage Bert Spencer, formerly Gresley's Chief Technical Assistant (Locomotives) intervened and at his suggestion the three Kings Cross double Kylchap A4s were substituted. Nos.22 MALLARD, 33 SEAGULL and 34 LORD FARINGDON, now E22, 60033 and 60034 to be strictly accurate, had been given a general overhaul within five months of the trials, coupled to a corridor tender and were given a brief check up before the running. Then Higher Authority intervened and proclaimed that the world speed record holder, now with her commemorative plaques, would open the batting for the Eastern and North Eastern Regions. On the Western Region Driver Joe Burgess and MALLARD started the trials with the preliminary running but ran hot and SEAGULL took over. On the Southern Region's South West Division, Driver Bob Marrable had SEAGULL at the start but she too ran hot and was replaced by MALLARD, which in turn also ran hot. Repaired in the meantime, SEAGULL then took over. Driver Ted Moore drove LORD FARINGDON on the Eastern and London Midland Region test trains without any trouble. Although the conjugated gear was widely held to be the cause, it was actually the relative susceptibility of the Doncaster middle big end, not for the first time. It simply illustrated the lack of understanding in the technical press of the time. Perhaps the wish was father to the thought? It was said that the big end retaining nuts should have been slackened half a turn after tightening, but that the foreman fitter would not allow this. This was before K.R.M. Cameron (of earlier note) became DMPS at Kings Cross in 1949.

It was a pity that for many, these three incidents should have obscured the ability and economy of the A4, for they emerged as the most efficient of the express classes, despite a formidable opposition. Their coal and water consumption, specific to the load hauled and distance covered, was the best of the group. This was not at the expense of performance, for unlike some crews in the tests, experienced men like Joe Burgess and Bob Marrable of Kings Cross were not afraid to open the regulator fully and run with generally short cut-offs when necessary. Ted Moore,

with LORD FARINGDON, was less inclined to run hard. SEAGULL did particularly well on the Western Region, with a superb climb to Hemerdon from Plymouth, and fast running up from Taunton. On her home ground, LORD FARINGDON returned the best figures of the tests, her coal consumption being as low as 2.92lb/DBHP.hr. The coal and water consumption measured in lb per DBHP-hr for the competing designs were as follows:-

Class	Coal	Water
LNE A4	3.06	24.32
LM Duchess	3.12	27.08
LM Scot	3.38	25.81
GW King	3.57	28.58
SR M Navy	3.60	30.43

The result was understandable since the A4 had the most efficient draughting system and the smallest clearance volume at 7.7%, except for the GWR 'King' at 5.5%. In fact the latter value resulted in excessive compression, especially after high degree superheat had been added. The Stanier Pacific had a clearance volume of 12.5%. However, all of this was in vain, and ideas from farther west than Doncaster prevailed.

Those enthusiasts who met the A4 SEAGULL at Paddington with her last run on the WR were overjoyed to hear the WR loco inspector descend from the footplate and remark 'We have nothing to touch this engine'. Peter Townend has told the account of the Western's Chief Traction Inspector and his memory of the Trials: 'Your A4 climbing Hemerdon Bank with a full glass of water, both injectors on, and still making steam. You could not do that with one of ours. You dare not put the second injector on and when you got to the top you were looking for the water in the bottom nut.' This frank admission was greatly enjoyed by a man who later had nineteen of the class in his care. Certainly the work of Joe Burgess with SEAGULL was one of the lasting memories of the Exchanges. The mechanical engineering leadership of the Railway Executive were of course primarily concerned with the problems of serving industrial areas where maintenance staff were in short supply, and took the view that three cylinders amounted to one too many. They concentrated on simple two outside cylinder locomotives with Walschaerts valve gear, using the Doncaster type of slidebar, and needed little persuasion to ignore the Gresley Pacifics. In their position at the time, one can understand their view. However, one might have hoped that, given the excellence of the performances of the A4s and the familiarity of the problem to E.S. Cox in particular, the problem of the middle big end might have merited more urgent attention.

In 1948, as mentioned earlier, the three Regions constituting the old LNER agreed to restart the Non-stop, albeit to a far easier timetable. It was of course, the 'Flying Scotsman' as in pre-war days. This was the first lodging turn by Kings Cross and Haymarket since before the war. The first trains were headed by Nos.60034 LORD FARINGDON in the down direction and 60009 UNION OF SOUTH AFRICA on the up, the latter being delayed twice, not for the last time. It was good to see what a clean A4 looked like, for some of us had never seen one before. The Non-stop A4 was always well turned out and a treat for sore eyes. The burnished buffers fitted to the A4s were a novelty post-war, only seen briefly when the locomotives emerged from Doncaster Works. The double Kylchap A4s at Kings Cross were often used on this duty, and worked it with an ease not often found with the single chimney sisters. Two of the A4s used, Nos.60028 and 60029, wore the experimental purple blue livery.

The year 1948, however, had another surprise in store. On August 12th, after six days of rain, there was a cloudburst in the hills north of Berwick and the resulting inundations brought down seven arch bridges spanning watercourses of different sorts, mainly the unfortunately named Eye Water. The state of the railway system on the Borders as a result of this and other flooding beggared belief. Trains were stopped, sent back and re-routed. As an illustration, Edinburgh Control was called by the driver of the 10.05 Kings Cross-Glasgow, which had been halted and diverted over the Waverley route. He was at Tynehead and could go no further. The Haymarket top link driver, Bill Nairn, was, at the time, waist deep in water! In retrospect, it is a wonder that the lineside phone still worked.

The non-stop 'Flying Scotsman' was halted at Alnmouth, and after returning to Newcastle, set off for Carlisle and the Waverley route. The Waverley route now being blocked at Tynehead with the 10.5 ahead, the Non-stop had to return for the second time, now to Carlisle, before it finally arrived at Edinburgh Waverley, from the wrong direction via Beattock and ten hours late! Subsequently the train was diverted via Selby, Leeds and Carlisle, which provided some amazing sights – a Midland Compound piloting No.60025 FALCON and thirteen polished teak coaches, for instance.

From Sunday August 23rd, the Waverley route having been cleared, all Scottish expresses were diverted from Tweedmouth via Kelso and St.Boswells to Edinburgh with an extra allowance in the schedule for water stops and banking south up Falahill Bank, 9 miles at 1 in 70. On the 24th, Driver Bill Stevenson was rostered to work the southbound train, and reasoning that the total mileage had been increased by only some 15 miles, 408.65 in all, and the junctions all lay in his favour, decided to try to run non-stop. His engine was No.60029 WOODCOCK, not always a free-steaming engine, but by running hard at Falahill bank, and then easily, necessarily, over the Tweed Valley route, he was able to reach Lucker troughs, 92 miles, without stopping. It was a masterly feat of enginemanship, for the climb to Falahill was one of the hardest on a main line. Immediately after leaving the main line at Portobello at heavily reduced speed, there was 15 miles to Falahill Box of which 1 mile was level, 3½ miles averaging 1 in 200, and 10½ miles largely at 1 in 70! There was no opportunity of charging the bank at speed and it was a sheer unremitting slog to the top. The 'Flying Scotsman' of 1948 was not a light train: it comprised 13 new all-steel pressure ventilated coaches weighing 475 tons, one of the heaviest loads to be lifted up the bank, let alone run for another 390 miles afterwards. Fortunately St.Boswells and Tweedmouth Junction lay correctly for a through run and were clear. With careful use of water he was able to hand over to Driver John Brown of Kings Cross at Pilmoor also without stopping. No.60029 drew into Kings Cross having run the 408.65 miles non-stop, a world record for steam power, and a magnificent testimony to the skill of both crews, especially Bill Stevenson. This remarkable performance was replicated by Bill the following day on No.60028 WALTER K. WHIGHAM with the northbound train, physically somewhat easier but harder on the nerves with only two sets of troughs in over 200 miles, at the end rather than the beginning of the run.

Now this simply would not do at Haymarket, and Bill Stevenson's colleagues accepted the challenge. By now the tale had got around, and his peers at Haymarket, notably Jimmy Swan, were keen to show that they too, could run non-stop. On no less than 17 occasions was this remarkable feat performed, seven times by Jimmy Swan and six by Bill Stevenson, prompting the boast that the A4 could have gone farther still had it been necessary. Haymarket top link drivers knew their engines, and with fully expansive working they often ran between Edinburgh and Newcastle without taking water at Lucker. There were some very fine drivers at Haymarket in those days, and they were justifiably proud of 'their' A4s. The late Charles Meacher told me that if there were rails laid from Haymarket Shed, they would have taken their A4s home with them!

The drivers at Haymarket and Gateshead, and possibly others as well, had to live with the fact that there were only two sets of troughs north of Shaftholme Junction. A timely filling of the tender, together with good enginemanship, especially in the careful use of water, made the North Country crews expert at running good distances without taking water. In 1948, when attempts were being made to discourage overtime at stations due to engines taking water, Driver Bill Hogarth of Gateshead, showed how economical a well-driven A4 could be. He ran from Grantham to Newcastle with SILVER KING on the 470 tons 'Flying Scotsman' without taking water at all, 162.9 miles, just over 30 gallons per mile. The injectors stalled at King Edward Bridge as the A4 rolled the train into Central Station. The average DBHP was about 600 with an IHP of 1,100 and the average evaporation rate was about 15,000 lb/hr, making running under power possible for the 200 minute schedule, at an average speed of 52-53mph. Bill Hogarth was one of the most outstanding drivers on the East Coast route.

So the decade of the 1940s drew to an end. It was a different LNER from that of the 1930s, not even in the same form but part of British Railways. The company had gone with the 1947 nationalisation, some of its directors retired to the City or commerce. Its precarious financial existence had gone, but in many ways the body that was the LNER had been pitched out of the frying pan into the fire. There were now no worries about insolvency, for nationally owned concerns cannot be bankrupted, but now as plaything of Government they were entirely dependent on its charity for their existence. The decisions and policy were imposed from without, and the CMEE and the Motive Power department now had to bend the knee no longer to Doncaster, but to BR Headquarters at Marylebone Road.

CHAPTER FIVE
The Last Decade

The 1950s brought a recovery of the former LNER principal main line to something like its pre-war self, although it began imperceptibly. Speed restrictions were slowly eased although, due to curvature, until the end of steam the East Coast main line was always limited by heavy Permanent Speed Restrictions (PSRs) through most of the major stations. Post-war, the up main line from Hatfield to Kings Cross was limited to 60 mph, or less in places such as Hornsey curves. In the down direction it was not a problem until well beyond Potters Bar, since drivers were reluctant to press their engines until the fire was well built up and burning well. An up express with steam on, however, would have soon exceeded the limit. It was generally assumed that this restriction was due to the condition of the track and certainly the CCE had difficulty in recruiting staff for the maintenance of the track, as was the case for all CCEs in the Home Counties. However, the track looked pretty fair north of Wood Green, and rode well. From a signalling point of view, though, the braking distances looked inadequate for a heavy train travelling fast in a number of places. For example, from

Barnet North's distant to the home was barely half a mile.

As this section was usually timed with additional 'recovery' time, late running services could benefit from some excessive speed running downhill into Kings Cross. Some of the drivers at Top Shed and depots farther north, who knew the road into London very well and were acute judges of the vacuum brake, were notorious for their precipitate arrivals at the terminus. Gateshead men, starting to learn the road south of Peterborough in 1956, were genuinely apprehensive of landing amongst the produce on Walton's Fruit Stall behind old platforms 4 and 5. Contrariwise and somewhat ironically, I remember a very respected member of the Kings Cross top link on SIR RALPH WEDGWOOD drawing carefully to a halt with the 14 coach 9.50 from Leeds in old platform 8. The A4 was about to stop a length short, and the driver gave her a breath of steam to move closer, but the wheels picked up on oily rails and with all but 500 tons pushing behind, she slithered into the buffer stops. Buffer stops were for emergencies, and drivers were supposed to stop short. In those days

the stops beneath the asphalt concourse were quite insubstantial, and were not the same again. Nor was the concourse behind!

By the end of the decade in some respects things were even better than before the war, but the growth of competition was steadily moving the railway further into decline. In 1950 things were much as 1949, but in 1951 the Festival of Britain took place. This was celebrated on BR by the naming of a number of services. The existing named services, many of which were worked by A4s, were also provided with new decorated headboards as well. On the East Coast this was principally the 'Heart of Midlothian', the afternoon service between the British and Scottish capital cities. It was introduced with two immaculate sets of the new BR coaching stock, nowadays referred to as the BR Mk1 stock, an eminently successful design which has recently passed its half-century of service. It was based on the Bulleid steel coaches for the Southern Railway, which in turn were developed from the Gresley and Thompson 'Newton' stock, but carried on simple bogies and not the Gresley pattern, which were no doubt more costly. As a

MALLARD at Kings Cross on June 25th 1950. The world record holder is in BR dark blue livery, and has the road via Main Two through Gasworks Tunnel to Top Shed. I would guess that she has brought in an up express, remained at the stops while another Pacific coupled on at the country end of the train, and has now been released after the northbound departure. Turning the stock round in the station was a frequent practice at Kings Cross, a relatively small terminus for the traffic handled. To the best of my recollection, it was only done with the West Riding services. The A4 is in splendid external condition, and has the prototype A3 corridor tender No.5323. (Cawston Bequest, Canon Brian C. Bailey Collection)

The up 'Capitals Limited' on August 22nd 1950, with GOLDEN PLOVER working hard on the climb to Stoke, south of Grantham. The tender is A4 corridor No.5650. (Cawston Bequest, Canon Brian C. Bailey Collection)

consequence its riding, especially over 30,000 miles when the tyres were worn, was not the equal of Gresley's stock. Later versions with Commonwealth or B5 bogies were better riding vehicles. The original lighter bogies had a disconcerting tendency to 'hunt' at 60 mph or so when worn, especially on Continuous Welded Track (CWR) whereas the heavier bogie did not at any speed.

The gradual increase in the number of turns between London and Tyneside peaked in 1951, but this concentrated work and therefore locomotives at a small number of depots. As a result they were usually overwhelmed and the workload of keeping Pacifics maintained for lengthy duties without running hot was proving too great. Hot boxes and other failures proliferated. There was simply a shortage of experienced staff available, and often materials as well, to keep the A4s going as of yore. There were certainly signs that things were getting better, and it was not unusual to see a clean, good-sounding A4 at the head of an express. Unfortunately it was also not unusual to see dirty, off-beat and ill cared-for engines as well. Hitchin loco yard usually had a temporary resident, relieved on an up express with a hot box or short of steam. Occasionally the lineside youth would be rewarded for their vigils by the sight of a Hitchin B1, L1, or something very much older and smaller in charge of a late-running up express. We had become used to the sight of a 'Retford Pacific' – a B1 – on such as the up 'Tees-Tyne Pullman' or 'Queen of Scots', but a 'Hitchin Pacific' was something much smaller – and much older!

In the early days of AWS, then called ATC (Automatic Train Control), a test section was installed between

New Barnet and Huntingdon, and a number of Pacifics were fitted with the equipment, together with classes at Kings Cross. The equipment was tested but the project lost impetus, until the tragedy of the Harrow collision in 1952 brought greater urgency. Within a very short space of time full-scale trials were organised with MALLARD and LORD FARINGDON. As 500 ton trains were to be worked and tested at high speed, the choice of Kylchap A4s was significant. The equipment was approved by the Chief Inspecting Officer of Railways, but difficulty was experienced in making the equipment reliable, and trials were still going on in 1956. LORD FARINGDON was turned out once again to haul a train of 422 tons including the dynamometer car, the tests taking place at 90 mph with full regulator left open, to assess the braking distances. Eventually, as we know, the system was approved.

The installation of ATC/AWS required an enormous investment in signalling in order to bring it up to date, and that is no doubt why the gestation period was unnecessarily long. It is a consequence that has always dogged safety systems. As one example, before the AWS system for a route could be signed off, all braking distances provided between distants and home signals, or between successive colour light signals, had to be regularised. That required them to conform to the currently laid down distances that trains using the route in question needed to stop from the currently permitted speeds. One might think, well, of course, but that was not the case, as the problems with the introduction of the streamliners showed. The signalling system was not reconfigured every

time a new locomotive, rolling stock, or faster train service was introduced.

Nevertheless, if the Kings Cross grapevine was correct, there were occasional moments of excitement during the testing as some well-known drivers with a taste for speed used the occasion to indulge themselves. They had the locomotive, the opportunity, and a clear Sunday afternoon with little to get in the way. Then there were the amusing highlights. A Kings Cross A4, GANNET, was hauling the up 'Mark Lane Flier', which was the 7.35 from Nottingham via Grantham, arriving in London at about 10.50. The train was always known by this old GNR name, derived from the fact that South Midlands businessmen used this service to reach the City of London by late morning. It was usually a train of at least 10 coaches, sometimes as many as 14 coaches, and I suspect it included some ECS returning to London. The last stop was Huntingdon North, but on this winter's morning, with snow on the ground, GANNET ground to a halt between there and Hitchin, and would not move. The ATC equipment had malfunctioned and applied the brake. Driver Joe Howard tried to disable it, but to no avail. The only relief engine was one of Hitchin's old ladies, shunting one of the station yards nearby, a GNR J1 0-6-0 as I recall. I gather that the sight of the two top link enginemen, of shall we say fuller figures, in the almost non-existent GNR cab with a minimal seating, with the GNR pull-out regulator and lever reverse, struggling along with a good load behind, was a collector's item!

At that time in the south there was a pick-up goods that ran from New England to Ferme Park, '1111up', which called at every possible siding. There were no doubt other equivalents on the main line. It was often worked by a WD 2-8-0, but it was also used as a means of returning a failed engine to Top Shed. Youngsters watched as, one by one, their favourites limped past, filthy black and run down. Some Pacifics were confined to slow freight duties until reaching their shopping mileage. Fuel was not always as good as pre-war, and shed staffs were very often short on establishment and experience.

In September 1951 the Eastern Region's Motive Power Superintendent, L.P. Parker, had decided to concentrate all of the ER A4s at Kings Cross, moving the A1s and A3s to Grantham, Leeds and Doncaster. As a result the A4 class was confined to Kings Cross, Gateshead and Haymarket. In association with this, engine changing at Grantham and also to a lesser extent at Peterborough and

DOMINION OF NEW ZEALAND heads the 15.30 Kings Cross-Newcastle through Greenwood on June 5th 1950. The A4 is in BR dark blue livery with her usual corridor tender with Hoffman bearings, No.5647. Greenwood's down main home was a GN somersault signal and it was a feature of many photographs, good or not so good, for many years. For lads at the lineside, the clank as the signal cleared brought a sense of anticipation as to what was coming! (Cawston Bequest, Canon Brian C. Bailey Collection)

Doncaster was introduced. At Kings Cross and Grantham the top link crews were allocated regular engines in a similar fashion to the system at Haymarket, one Pacific to be shared between two crews. In this way the locomotives would run for two-three hours and then be relieved, so that bearings that might be prone to overheating or failure on a long run would stay only warm. Lubrication could be checked and fires cleaned and refreshed. So, after a few brief years of through working we had to get used to a different railway, with less variety but better reliability. At Gateshead the Peppercorn double Kylchap A1s, which were preferred by the DMPS, held sway, together with the double Kylchap No.60005 SIR CHARLES NEWTON (née CAPERCAILLIE) and sometimes their first A4, No.60016 SILVER KING.

There was a very good argument for moving most if not all of the Gateshead A4 fleet to Haymarket in exchange for its A1s and three A2s. It was difficult to avoid the impression that several of the A4s at Gateshead were poor things, and would have benefited from the move to a depot where they were liked. Problems would have been addressed

and they would have been well maintained. Certainly they would have been useful with the Non-stop, although Haymarket always seemed to manage comfortably. None of the Gateshead A4s were coupled to a corridor tender, so there would need to have been some transferring between engines. SIR CHARLES NEWTON, with a corridor tender, and Haymarket's favourite MERLIN would probably have dominated the Non-stop duty! The timetables demanded little, and performances were uninspiring as a rule. Meanwhile youth fretted in its impatience at the lineside.

Haymarket had 12 top link crews sharing 6 A4s regularly, the seventh, usually No.60012, working in the second link with Peppercorn A1s unless one engine was away for overhaul. The top link at Kings Cross had steadily enlarged, and the 10 sets of men were increased to 18, by now regularly allocated to 9 A4s. The remainder were spare 'pool' engines, engines stopped for examination or repair, or away for overhaul at Doncaster. The crews worked through 18 weeks on different duties, and then worked round again.

Gradually reliability and performance improved, and the crews

of the A4s began to be familiar to many enthusiasts. Several became well known for their determination to keep time, and indeed some would run hard to recover time lost. The world record holder, MALLARD, was in the hands of Drivers Joe Burgess and Alf Smith, with Joe Howard replacing Burgess on the latter's retirement in 1952. Joe Howard had been in charge of B1 No.61251 OLIVER BURY in the 1948 Exchanges and had got very good work out of her. Indeed at Kings Cross, it was said that he was the only one who ever did! Both crews were proud of 'their' A4 and ran her reliably and well. She was supposed to have a jinx when on the Non-stop due to various trivial accidents that had befallen her, but in the hands of her regular drivers she ran well. During the middle 1950s they were justly proud that together they had run over 100,000 miles with no failure in traffic, a powerful endorsement for regular and skilled manning.

Two Kings Cross drivers earned an enthusiastic following, Ted Hailstone with the original A4, SILVER LINK, and Bill Hoole with SIR NIGEL GRESLEY. Both had their own simple version of what later was called 'The Passengers' Charter'. Both took a late arrival as something of a personal criticism. They were at the peak of their profession, and willing to run fast in places, perhaps faster than they were supposed to, in order to regain time. I knew both well and there is no doubt that they enjoyed the experience of driving express locomotives at speed. If they were delayed or took over late at Grantham or Peterborough, it was welcomed as an opportunity for even faster running. Their fame – perhaps notoriety might be more accurate as far as management was concerned – diverted attention from the fact that many of the other top crews, for example Harry Willers and Bert Green, were just as capable of fast running but were usually less inclined to do so, and respected their hardworking firemen and locomotives. The two other London double Kylchap engines, SEAGULL and LORD FARINGDON were at this time the regular engines of Jim Edwards and Bert Green, and George Graham and George Tee. Every now and then, one of the drivers would be presented with the instrument and the opportunity for regaining time, and spectacular running resulted. Looking back, how curious it was that men in their grandfather years should be unable to contain the still-burning fires of youth! There was a very healthy rivalry among the crews in the 1950s, and many a heated debate about the relative merits of their steeds.

The same could be said of Haymarket's top crews where the standard of driving skill was very high, and keen competition ensured that it stayed high. The locomotive maintenance was also of a high standard under the DMPS, Kenneth Cameron, formerly at Kings Cross, and later to become the Scottish Region's MPS. Bill Stevenson and Jimmy Swan, mentioned earlier, were two of a number of skilled drivers, well known amongst professionals and enthusiasts alike. No doubt a similar level of excellence was present at Newcastle, although apart from such as Bill Hogarth and Archie Waugh, little was known of the other Gateshead and Heaton crews down south until the advent of the 'Talisman'. The only men to work lodging turns were volunteers, forming the sadly named Gateshead 'Blackleg Link' of three crews which worked the 'Night Scotsman', usually with the roller-bearing A1s.

The 1950s wore on and, as conditions improved, performances began to suggest that the A4s were as good as ever. The operating authorities however continued to time even the principal expresses at an undemanding level. Loads were 12-15 coaches, but the number of passengers rarely seemed to justify such capacity. 'Recovery time' was loaded into the schedules to offset the many causes of delay. Just to take one example, the southbound 'Flying Scotsman' was allowed over two hours in the winter from Grantham to Kings Cross, when with a clear run and the right incentive, a keen crew could gain twenty minutes. Harry Willers with WILD SWAN, on a heavy 13 coach train of 518 tons, ran from Grantham to Kings Cross in 101 minutes, recovering 14 minutes late running and arriving 8 minutes before time, 22 minutes less than the schedule. The main line between Doncaster and Grantham offered plenty of scope for delay once a driver had lost his path, and the London crew usually had some time to regain.

There were no motorways at the time, and journeys by road were lengthy. For a reliable and comfortable car one had to buy a more expensive and usually foreign model, and the run-of-the-mill became unreliable with age, suffering particularly from overheating on a long run. One needed to be lucky to average more than 30mph. Therefore the railways found no significant commercial gain in accelerating schedules at that time, but a decade later with diesel traction, it was a different story. There was a reluctance to cut schedules with steam traction despite it being quite clear that the locomotives were capable and the crews would respond to a challenging proposition. The

railway of the 1950s, by comparison with the industry in more recent times, was managed by older men. While those in charge lacked little in experience, there was a reluctance to innovate and to accelerate trains, in short to take what were perceived as risks. There was the probability of increased maintenance costs, and a sceptical attitude to the commercial benefits that faster and more frequent services might bring. It was an attitude that cost the railway dear in the long term. Those who wanted speed, reliability and good service could not find it on the railway, and went elsewhere.

In 1951 the maximum line speed was restored from 80 to 90 mph over a number of sections, and consideration was given to cutting schedules. The feasible section times with each increment of load were calculated, and then the times were tested practically using an A3, CENTENARY, between Kings Cross and Doncaster with a variety of loadings. The A3 had run 70,000 miles and was not far short of the mileage for general overhaul. It was selected by L.P. Parker himself rather than allow a less run-down or newer locomotive to be used. The timings would then leave a margin in favour of newer and less run-down locomotives. The crew was Driver Ted Hailstone and Fireman Lincoln, and the timings required that the engine be driven hard. The latter was not impressed at the implications of harder timings for his colleagues! The timings became the basis for the new timetables, but substantial allowances in the form of 'recovery time' were added to allow for engineering speed restrictions.

The Kings Cross top link of 18 with each pair of drivers allotted a regular A4 was thus in about 1954, for example:

60003	Shirley Frost & Harry Willers
60007	Charlie Simmons & Bill Hoole
60013	Sid Tappin & Alf Guymer
60014	Ted Hailstone & Arthur Ferrington
60022	Alf Smith & Joe Howard
60025	Percy Heaven & Fred Deeley
60028	Bert Cull & Fred Dines
60033	Jim Edwards & Bert Green
60034	George Graham & George Tee

(Obviously at times drivers retired and new men moved up to replace them.)

The Depot had 19 A4s and some pairs regularly used a second engine once the first had become run down. Drivers Simmons and Hoole, for example, switched to No.60015 QUICKSILVER when she came out of shops, and No.60007 SIR NIGEL GRESLEY became a pool engine. Others used what was given them, although not without protest, especially if the allocated engine was

not highly regarded. The drivers' grapevine was very effective and there was an understandable concern that one's steed should not be wanting. Bill Hoole, if he could not use SIR NIGEL GRESLEY, regarded an alternative as an opportunity if not a challenge. I remember Eric Neve asking Harry Willers how he was getting on. His regular A4 was away at Doncaster and he had been given DWIGHT D. EISENHOWER, not one of the favourites and known to be a tricky steamer, for six weeks. He had run her without any trouble, and his reward later was to be given none other than DOMINION OF CANADA, the well-known black sheep. Again, he had managed to run her regularly for a few weeks. He dismissed the question: 'It's not difficult. There's more to it than tearing downhill!' He could run as hard as the better known drivers, when required. Ted Hailstone normally preferred SILVER LINK and ran her up to good mileages. It was always his ambition to take his beloved A4 with him on the Non-stop, but alas he never managed it. She had a very long spell on the Non-stop in its last summer, and Ted would have greatly enjoyed that. A pair of burnished buffers was fitted to SILVER LINK for a Royal duty. Before long, most of the Kings Cross A4s had all gained burnished buffers as they passed through the Works, which added that finishing touch to their appearance.

At Haymarket the men became better known in the south with the operation of the Non-stop. Of course they used the A4 prepared for the duty and not their own. The following is not a complete list but comprises some of the better known drivers and their regular locomotives in the mid-1950s.

60004	Jim Swan
60009	Jim Paterson
60011	Bill Nairn and J. Craik
60024	Tony and William McLeod
60027	Bill Stevenson
60031	Tom Smith and Willie Bain

In addition there were Drivers Bell, W. Gemmell, D. Smith and later, Redpath whose regular engines were not known to me. Willie Bain became well-known due to his insistence on a very high standard of cleanliness in the No.2 link with the A1 ST. JOHNSTOUN. To describe the A1 as immaculate was an understatement!

Gateshead was then the only other depot to have A4s but, as mentioned, preferred to use their Peppercorn double Kylchap A1s. The Gateshead single blast A4s tended to remain in the background for the early 1950s. Here locomotives were operated on set duties as far as possible. The depot had three diagrams for its A4s, but on the day it was as likely to be an A1 as an A4, or even an A3. The first was the 10.05 Kings Cross-Glasgow from Peterborough forward to Newcastle, and the other two were the up 'Flying Scotsman' and 'Heart of Midlothian' from Newcastle to Grantham, each with its balancing turn.

At Haymarket the normal practice was to couple a return trip to Newcastle with another to either Dundee or Glasgow, or even Aberdeen. The Kings Cross A4s had lodging turns to Newcastle and Leeds, plus a number of heavy express out and back turns to Grantham and Peterborough, and a few lighter jobs. The normal form was for a locomotive to run to Grantham twice in 24hrs, 422 miles. The lodging turns were interspersed with 'filling-in' turns of the same sort. The remaining 'pool' locomotives would run to Leeds, Doncaster and Grantham with lesser expresses, and would be handled more widely. Kings Cross had a second link comprising the senior men who would not lodge, for one reason or another, but there was a great deal of experience and good enginemanship in the link.

In 1951, in a series of moves intended, it seems, to break down the insularity of the former 'Big Four', the new CM&EE appointed at Doncaster was K.J. Cook. Kenneth Cook was a Great Western man, with extensive experience in workshop management at Swindon. It would have been difficult for someone so steeped in one culture to change easily to another at 55, but Cook was an open-minded

man, and was not alone in facing this problem. An Eastern man, R.A. Smeddle, was sent to the Western Region as CM&EE, via Brighton, to face the same problem in reverse. As it happened, both men achieved considerable improvements in their new environments. Cook was said to be prepared for faster services, and was ready to provide the power for it, but the operators of the three Regions of the East Coast main line were not of the same mind.

Cook, as an outstanding workshop engineer, was used to the relative robustness of the Swindon 4-6-0 frame construction, and there an optical system of greater precision was used in repairing and re-erecting locomotives. He decided that a similar optical system was needed at Doncaster, and eventually a suitable one was located and installed, manufactured by Taylor, Taylor & Hobson. It used the same method as the original Zeiss optical system, so that the principal components could be precisely aligned relative to the frames. Eyepieces were attached to the main frame members, and allowed the operator to sight through and measure the position of horns, axleboxes, cylinder blocks, etc, with greater accuracy. Cook was keen to use practices, techniques and tolerances from the automotive industry where appropriate and possible. At the same time bearings were machined to tighter tolerances. There is no doubt that in time this enabled a reduction in the clearances

as a result, so that the repaired locomotives ran better and more quietly. In the short term however, the number of cases of overheating actually increased, and the reduced tolerances had to be eased.

In particular, the design of the big end bearing, which Gresley intended to improve but was prevented by the war, was at last tackled. Experience of the Swindon and LMSR designs led to the use of continuously white metalled bearings instead of the previous use of white metal crowns, and the brass gluts or distance pieces were replaced by steel gluts to prevent wear. The pin trimming that regulated the oil feed down to the bearing was replaced by a hard felt pad. Gresley's semi-circular retaining strap was retained so that the bearing was held firmly together, also because in cases of failure it had continued to hold the bearing together. It had been strengthened with an additional rib on the back of the strap. With the 'open fork' type referred to earlier, the whole assembly could dismantle, probably needing more extensive attention before the failed locomotive could be moved. The Swindon 'open fork' bearing was fitted to about six A4s, but the performances of the modified Gresley design had been sufficiently good to obviate any further use of the GWR type. Experience showed that at the regular dismantling of the big end at 12,000 miles intervals, as laid down in the BR maintenance instructions, it was necessary to

The down 'Tees-Tyne Pullman' at Hadley Wood station on July 6th 1954 behind SIR NIGEL GRESLEY. The driver, unmistakably, is my old friend Bill Hoole, and therefore the train will have been going rather faster than usual. The old Hadley Wood signalbox survived for two decades after being reduced to ground frame status, even after closure and removal of the sidings. The A4's tender is A3 corridor No.5324. (Cawston Bequest, Canon Brian C. Bailey Collection)

The 17.00 from Kings Cross, with its complement of commuters, heads for the north behind ANDREW K McCOSH from Wood Green Tunnel. She had lost her corridor tender by then, having gained non-corridor No.5670. (P.J. Coster)

replace the lubricating felt pads in order to pre-empt failure. Remetalling was usually only necessary at 24,000 miles. It was also laid down that only the main works would machine the big end brasses since they had the equipment, but as standards improved at some depots that was neither always necessary nor possible. It was the close attention to running in service that complemented the care with which Doncaster had overhauled the A4, and produced such an improvement in reliability.

However, the Gresley Pacifics differed from the Swindon 4-6-0s in their frame construction. Gresley, no doubt because of the need to restrict the weight of the finished Pacific, and also because of his insistence on concentrated drive, had used a frame structure that flexed much more. The throw of the centre crank prevented frame bracing being placed adjacent to the driving axle. His Pacifics were long engines, and the main frames

The A4 and the train. SIR CHARLES NEWTON was a regular sight on the up 'Flying Scotsman' between Newcastle and Grantham both during the war and after, and was also a familiar sight in the 1950s. Here she is leaving York, passing over a newly relaid switch and crossing layout with the up train. The date must be between late 1952 and the mid-1950s as the long guard irons have been removed and the train is still in red and cream livery. The non-corridor tender is No.5641. (Transport Treasury)

SIR CHARLES NEWTON and crew wait for the Right Away at Peterborough North with the 10.10 Kings Cross-Glasgow in July 1957. The A4 travelled south with the 21.35 Glasgow-Colchester. Tender: A4 non-corridor No.5641.

and vibration from jointed track, and as mentioned earlier, they were subject to unusually heavy lateral thrusts in running over heavily curved layouts in depots and at stations. I know that depot track was given little if any priority for attention by the CCE or his District Engineer, and it was usually in poor shape. The curvature could be very severe, down to 5 chains (100m) or even less, much sharper than the design allowed for. The problem was dealt with in the same way as the middle big end – timely inspection and renewal. Why the right-hand side should be more susceptible is not clear, but remembering the comparison of cylinder power outputs with HUMORIST, and how the right-hand cylinder, despite its valves being directly driven by the outside valve gear, produced more power at speeds up to 50 mph, perhaps the conjugated valve gear was the cause. It was an asymmetrical design, and the right-hand valve tail rod operated the longer arm of the robust but heavy 2:1 'lever', which was virtually a tapered beam. In the early years, the 2:1 lever of the K3s tended to shear the fulcrum bolts until the whole assembly had been redesigned and strengthened. The power required to drive the conjugated gear seems to have been significant and unequally divided between the two tail rods. The moment of inertia of the 2:1 lever would be considerable, especially at 6-7 cycles per second. Very small differences in valve events and cylinder dimensions caused quite large differences in cylinder power outputs, and this seems the most likely cause.

Whilst matters in the locomotive world were improving slowly, the A4s were no longer used on high-speed services as was the original intention. The prestige services were far from high-speed by pre-war standards. Any suggestion that the streamliners might be reintroduced would not have been well received at all by the BTC. The reintroduction of speed recorders was vetoed by a difficult trade union, and management were not prepared to wage an industrial war on what was seen as a minor issue. The sound of an A4 working hard with a load nearly twice the size of the streamliners became the normal sight and sound. They managed well, for such was the versatility of the well-designed steam locomotive. Drivers adapted their style of driving over the years, so that on the long climb out of London, engines were not pressed as they might have been with lighter trains and tighter schedules. Once the heavier load was moving, then the A4's turn of speed could be put to good use. But gone was the protection of double block, and on a crowded main line with trains of

extended beyond the cylinder blocks. As did all locomotives, they spent a small but significant part of their life moving around depots and across layouts characterised by sharp curvature, but the length of the Pacific frames meant that they had to endure a measure of flexing and lateral thrust. It was the practice in the Works to correct any misalignment discovered in the frames at overhaul by 'peening', and this continued some while after the introduction of the optical system. 'Peening', by way of explanation, was the process in which the metal surface was hammered with a shaped head. It was usually a rounded 'dolly' held in a pneumatically powered hammer. At Doncaster, the tool was called the 'pom'. Its purpose was to broaden the surface area being worked by spreading the metal. With slightly distorted frames one face of the frame plates had become microscopically longer than the other. By 'peening' the shorter face would straighten. It is a treatment that, like so many of those used in steam construction and repair 50-70 years

ago, has been either superseded by better ones such as heat treatment or welding, or has simply disappeared as unnecessary.

Instead of standard axleboxes being fitted as was the practice hitherto, with the new system the thickness of the horn slide varied slightly. Each overhauled Pacific had an individual set of axleboxes, and repairs or replacement involved sending the part to Doncaster. To remedy this problem each engine was returned to its depot with a pair of spare driving axleboxes. The store at Kings Cross was filled with numbered axleboxes. And, as these things always happen, when a particular A4 was repaired at Top Shed, the axleboxes were wrongly transposed. The engine entered service, and ran happily despite the error.

One of the curiosities of the A4s already mentioned was that the right-hand driving axlebox tended to fail before the left. It was a strange problem that was dealt with but not solved. The axleboxes had to withstand quite considerable wear

Top. **MALLARD stands at the buffer stops of platform 4 at Kings Cross one foggy evening in December. Time exposure in such poorly lit conditions required care and experience but a successful result such as this conveyed something of the sight, sound and feel when the romance of the railway was less obvious than usual.** *Above.* **MALLARD joined by LORD FARINGDON at Kings Cross in the fog. The two Top Shed double Kylchap A4s make an impressive picture – locomotives built for speed, with their streamlined outlines showing well in the poor light. (both George Heiron, courtesy Mrs Shirley Heiron, The Transport Treasury)**

driven by Joe Howard, and the second was LORD FARINGDON driven by George Graham. It goes without saying that the A4s and their trains were absolutely immaculate. The trains were composed of BR standard first class open and catering stock from the Eastern or London Midland Regions, but those who turned out to see them were lucky enough to see the 'Coronation' beavertails. The 'Plant Centenarian' and these specials were the only occasions that I remember on which they appeared on the East Coast main line after the war. The A4s returned on Sunday, and I believe LORD FARINGDON in particular was checked and diverted so many times that there was little left in the tender after Potters Bar!

An A4, like all steam locomotives is an assembly of parts, and each should have been identical with the others. The drivers' experience was that some engines could be relied on for a trouble-free trip while others could not. Inevitably some were regarded as black sheep. It depended of course on what had been recently overhauled, and which A4s were within sight of general overhaul. The four double Kylchap engines were in a class of their own. I never heard mention of them ever being short of steam, and when opened out they could outrun the single chimney engines.

The single chimney locomotives ran well when newly shopped, but as the mileage mounted the steaming could become less reliable. Some definitely steamed and ran less readily than others. The reputation of a particular locomotive, strangely, would survive its visit to Doncaster Plant, where the boiler and a number of components had been changed and the engine had been carefully re-erected and aligned. The reason that it did so was that although the boiler was changed, and the whole barrel was lifted as one piece and moved to the Boiler Shop, the items within and attached to the smokebox were marked or labelled and usually remained with the locomotive. Therefore if there was any slight defect in the smokebox arrangements that for some reason had not been corrected in reassembly, it would remain in the overhauled engine.

The significant parameter was the locomotive's steaming ability, and there is little doubt that the exhaust design of the single chimney A4 was susceptible to quite small variations in any of the salient dimensions, the quality of the coal or the skill of the fireman. A locomotive is a machine, and if it is deficient in some respect there is a simple engineering reason for it. Obviously crews preferred engines on which they had enjoyed a good run, and vice-versa. Several of the Top Shed single chimney engines

different types and speeds, signal delays were far more common. The Greenwood-Potters Bar bottleneck remained the biggest problem, since the normal secondary traffic was inflated by the number of inner suburban trains. The working of a cramped station layout such as Kings Cross was very dependent on the availability of empty stock locomotives and their ability to get ECS up the bank out of the terminus. Delays at Holloway and Belle Isle, the latter surely one of the most outrageous misnomers on the railway system, were almost mandatory, and reference to 'Star Brush Halt' and Belle Isle featured in many a record of an up run. A number of expresses loaded up to 15 coaches after the war,

but by the 1950s the 17.15 from Leeds and the 22.35 Edinburgh sleeper were normally the heaviest trains of the day, 15 coaches, some 550 tons loaded, and both were usually headed by an A4, being Top Shed turns. The sound of the A4 blasting up the hill from Grantham to Stoke, or pounding up Holloway Bank, was something to remember for a long while.

On May 22nd 1954 we had a very brief glimpse of what might have been. The International Railway Union visited the UK and two special trains were run for the delegates. Starting at 7.55 and 8.05 from Kings Cross the two 11 coach specials, Nos.366 and 367, ran non-stop to Edinburgh on a 405 minute timing. The first was hauled by MALLARD

could be tricky, as previously mentioned, probably the worst being DOMINION OF CANADA. I have seen her in Kings Cross with 180 psi on the boiler pressure gauge, the highest it had read since going off Copley Hill Depot in Leeds. Yet if the fireman could make her steam, she would run. I suspect that there were several at Gateshead with much the same sort of reputation. GOLDEN EAGLE was one such, but eventually the trouble was traced to a leaking smokebox. This would have prevented the engine from developing sufficient smokebox vacuum to draught the fire effectively, which would then have impacted on the steaming, as probably most Gateshead crews at the time would have testified!

The jumper top blastpipe seems to have been one cause of trouble. No doubt it was fine when an A4 so fitted left the works. Carbonised lubricating oil and char tended to obstruct the operation of the moveable collar and if jammed, the additional orificial area was blocked when the engine was working hard. Later the collar was bolted down. In addition the blastpipe could suffer from a build-up of carbon which reduced the net diameter, and restricted exhaust flow further. The blastpipe in such cases should have been removed and the carbon burnt out, the casting cleaned and reinstated. It was essential for the operation of the exhaust as a pump that the column of exhausting steam should just fill the chimney liner. If the carbonisation was severe the shape of the exhaust stream could be altered, affecting its sealing effect in the chimney liner. If the size of the orifice was too small or was deflected by the jammed jumper top, it would fail to fill the chimney, and the smokebox vacuum on which draughting depended critically would not have been created. Some judged the jumper top more nuisance than it was worth, and removed it, substituting a home-made top. One had to be careful to replace it before the A4 went for attention at Doncaster. When one was mistakenly left on an A4 when it went for general overhaul, the Regional CMEE gave instructions to ensure that it should not happen again. One would have thought that people on the ground should have been given credit for knowing what they were doing, and that if the engine was not steaming properly then this required attention, not indignation. Clearly, one needed to be within the culture to understand the attitudes prevalent at the time.

The rebuilt W1, now BR No.60700, had been allocated to the Southern Area and moved between Doncaster and Kings Cross, apart from a fortnight during the war at Haymarket. There, I would imagine the arrival of a seventh 50 sq.ft.grate in Scotland was not viewed with enthusiasm, war or no war, and she was returned to Top Shed where she worked for more than 11 years. In 1953 she went to Doncaster where she was highly regarded as a free steaming and conspicuously powerful locomotive. Visits to the Works were always prolonged since the locomotive had an unique boiler, frames, rear truck, and after the conversion of SIR VISTO, unique cylinders. If any of these items required repair the engine would have been detained until they were ready. At a non-classified repair in December 1956 she was fitted with 19 ins cylinders, presumably similar to the A3 cylinders. In theory the 8 ins piston valves would have limited the flow through the cylinders and hence the speed, but in the immediate post-war years the running speeds would not have taxed the engine. The valve size never seemed to inhibit the W1 at speed. At Kings Cross the large grate and distance from coal gate to the firehole door made her far less popular than the Kylchap A4s. Bill Hoole told me that he would like to have run her for a spell. At Doncaster with only the single chimney A3s and V2s for competition, the W1 was well liked, and the 9.00 from York and 15.50 return from Kings Cross were her usual task. Now and again the W1 was urged up to speed, and 90 mph with 500 tons on the descent from Stevenage to Offord seemed to call for no unusual effort. It was on the 15.50 when on leaving Peterborough, at Westwood Junction, the bogie frame fractured and derailed the engine, as I recall, uncomfortably close to the signalbox at Westwood Junction.

In 1953 the Testing Team at Swindon under S.O. Ell had studied a 'Green Arrow', as there had been numerous complaints that the provision of self-cleaning screens in the V2 smokebox had affected the steaming. New England's No.60845 was considered to be the worst of the modified engines, and was sent for investigation. The single blastpipe had been modified by Swindon and the steaming rate improved considerably by altering the proportions and positions of the chimney liner, cowl and blastpipe. There is no doubt that the V2, despite being recently overhauled, was in poor shape, its valves having been set without the expansion allowance normally used at Doncaster. Indeed some of the indicator diagrams made one wonder that the locomotive could pull anything! H. Holcroft criticised Swindon for not having corrected the valve setting before testing. There was no point in testing an engine that was obviously in a defective condition. At the time, for all the undoubted experience in the Team, Swindon had achieved improved steaming with small diameter blastpipes that restricted the exhaust and increased back pressure. That view is not one with the benefit of hindsight, either, since the Region applied the same principle to its King 4-6-0s and, despite improving steaming, the high back pressure resulted in an epidemic of hot driving axleboxes. Fortunately under R.A. Smeddle double chimneys were fitted to them.

The Railway Executive and its successor guarded its responsibility for locomotive design obsessively and, while it was happy to allow modifications to be carried out in Wiltshire, it would not hear of anything to do with double Kylchaps from France! Swindon had cured the poor steaming of the Ivatt 2MT 2-6-0s by fitting a Dean 0-6-0 blastpipe in place of its own poor design. There seemed to be a distinct prejudice against ex-LNER locomotives and everything about them. K.J. Cook, a thoroughly Western man, sought to apply S.O. Ell's new blastpipe proportions to the A4s. The two fitted with the new arrangement, SIR RALPH WEDGWOOD and QUICKSILVER, steamed satisfactorily but no better, but the coal consumption rose. The original blastpipe orifice was 5.1875 ins, which was increased to 5.375 in 1954. This was reduced to 5.125 later in the year, but the engines so fitted were noisy and less free-running due to the increased back pressure. I remember seeing Bill Hoole with No.60015 QUICKSILVER, just overhauled, on the 14 coach 'Northumbrian' passing milepost 7, making an unbearable noise, but not travelling particularly fast. I had first heard the A4 south of Wood Green Tunnel, two miles and a tunnel away! No.60008 DWIGHT D EISENHOWER, another pool engine with a reputation for erratic steaming, was also modified to little effect.

The BTC continued to experiment at considerable cost and with little success for three years. It is a measure of the lack of understanding by the BTC, that, as mentioned earlier, at one point they even asked whether the ER management wanted the double Kylchap locomotives converted to single blast! The NE and Scottish Region management were no help and preferred to keep their heads down, not having had any problems with their locomotives or (more likely) not having realised that there were any.

L.P. Parker had enjoyed a cool relationship with the CMEE at Doncaster, and his technical section had asked for the conversion of the single chimney engines to double

No.60700 passes Finsbury Park with the 15.52 express to Leeds and the West Riding. This was a Doncaster turn, and the W1 was a popular choice for this duty. It is summer 1955, and she has her usual non-corridor tender, No.5639. (P.J. Coster)

Kylchap. Cook, whose experience leaned towards workshop management, would not hear of it and dismissed it as being too expensive – as he thought. When asked to comment on the A4s fitted with WR exhaust design arrangements, Parker replied that all that was required was to fit Kylchap exhausts to the single blast engines. In response Doncaster then modified the WR proportions, which made the engines noisier than ever, the increased back pressure curbing the engines' capacity for speed. Matters had reached an impasse, with nobody of seniority willing to commit themselves. Peter Townend, on appointment as Shedmaster at Top Shed, was familiar with the problem, and took the initiative. In deciding to make an investment case, he had to provide the necessary information, and conduct a series of tests at Kings Cross to prove the economy in coal consumption. The first task was to establish what was entailed in conversion. Contrary to Works opinion, it was simply a matter of fitting the new breeches pipe and Kylchap assembly, after first enlarging the chimney aperture to take the double Kylchap casting. The cost per engine was estimated at just over £200.

The second task was to compare the coal consumption of a single and double Kylchap A4. Denied, for obvious reasons, the use of the dynamometer car, it had to be a 'weighed on and off' trial. The principal difficulty was in getting the engines to work identically on the same load so that the amount of work done was approximately equal. Moreover, firing is not a precise science, and a good fireman will use less coal, run for run, than a less skilled man. The Kylchap A4 continually gained time with the same cut-off while the single chimney A4 had to work harder to keep time. Eventually a satisfactory comparison was achieved and the economy in favour of the Kylchap engine was about 7lb/mile. This provided the justification for the investment of the relatively paltry sum to convert 31 A4s. The Eastern Region was fortunate in that its Assistant General Manager was T.C.B. Miller, a fine locomotive engineer who had good experience in the Motive Power organisation and was only too aware of the problem. The staff at Kings Cross were not hopeful but, in May 1957, No.60017 SILVER FOX returned from overhaul at Doncaster with a double Kylchap. Peter had moved quickly and within a few weeks the A4 had shown what she could do by taking the 'Morning Talisman', 8 coaches, over Stoke summit at 78mph, a post-war record at the time. But once the single chimney engines were redraughted with a double Kylchap and chimney, the number on the cab side ceased to matter any more, for they all ran superbly. As mentioned earlier,

sixteen hard years had elapsed since Gresley's unfortunate death, simply because, though he had ordered that all future Pacifics should have double Kylchap exhaust, he had not made that order retrospective before his death.

Back in 1953 the non-stop 'Capitals Limited' was renamed 'The Elizabethan', a very happy choice of name. The train ran for exactly ten years, the tenth being diesel-hauled. It was progressively reduced to a timing of 390 minutes for 392.7 miles, with a load of 11 coaches, 425 tons fully laden, later reduced to 10 coaches, 390 tons. The 'Elizabethan' was a testing proposition, and in reality it could be regarded as the fourth streamliner of the East Coast Route. The schedule was well within the capacity of a single blast A4 in good condition, but what made it far harder was the level of delay and speed restriction meted out to what should have been a premium service. It was unusual to suffer delays less than 15 minutes, and 20-25 minutes were unfortunately common. For the 46 runs in the Appendix E the average delay was just under 21 minutes. For that reason it stands, deservedly, alongside the pre-war streamliners as an example of the A4s at their best. It was the showpiece of the East Coast main line, worked by Kings Cross and Haymarket A4s. It was 100 tons heavier, and although not timed so fast as the 'Coronation', net of the many delays suffered on its run, in fact it fell little short of the pre-war train. The timing gradually reduced to 60mph, but with the increase in relaying due to the adoption of CWR, its was eased to 395 minutes. The train was mainly composed of late LNER 'Newton' or 'Thompson' coaches in superb condition, and the A4 at the front was always magnificently turned out, resplendent with burnished buffers.

I remember as a lad, waiting at New Southgate after a scrambled dash from school, peering anxiously northwards. It was touch and go to get there in time – had she gone already? From the platform there was a dead straight two miles to the north, through Barnet Tunnel and then Oakleigh Park, to the right-hand curve into New Barnet. Normally on a sunny afternoon up expresses were only visible in silhouette as they entered the tunnel, but the Non-stop, with its gleaming A4, was visible immediately as she rounded the curve south of Barnet, the sun catching the streamlined nose. As the A4 drew nearer, excitement mounted and, as the train emerged from the tunnel, the sound could be heard. Were we due for a surprise? Then this incredible vision of a beautifully groomed A4 and train swept past, SEAGULL, MERLIN, or some such engine in charge. For those of us who

grew up in the post-war years, it was a treat that money could not buy.

The A4s were reliable and individual locomotives achieved some remarkable periods of continuous operation of the duty. The stars at the London end were usually the double Kylchap engines, but the single chimney A4s also ran well. In late spring the engines going to works for general overhaul were noted with interest, since they were likely to be used on the Non-stop. The A4s used at Kings Cross were usually some of the regularly manned engines, but in 1954 two 'pool' engines, GOLDEN FLEECE and GANNET were used and ran well. Apart from the Kylchap trio, SILVER FOX and WALTER K WHIGHAM were commonly used and ran well. The two drivers running WALTER K. WHIGHAM, Bert Cull and Fred Dines, looked after their A4 well and she was always one of the most consistent A4s at Top Shed. I remember Fred Dines' reaction when I pulled his leg over No.60028 running hot, unusually, when just back from general overhaul. "Tell the other crew when you see them that we find that it always helps to do a bit of oiling round before a run."

The Non-stop A4 came down to Kings Cross station, and was followed by a standby, which waited at the Station Loco Yard and took a later

train, the 10.18 Leeds or, more usually, the 12.18 'Northumbrian'. At Haymarket there was less of a choice, and while the Non-stop A4 was usually a low mileage engine, the standby A4s might well have a considerable mileage accrued. Haymarket's No.60027, known down south as 'Magnificent MERLIN' was the undoubted star performer, with John Cameron's preserved UNION OF SOUTH AFRICA as the next most frequent visitor. I recall in 1956 travelling on COMMONWEALTH OF AUSTRALIA, which had run 55,000 miles since the last overhaul according to the Haymarket men, but one would never have guessed from her performance. The reserve A4 at Edinburgh usually took the 8.35 from Glasgow forward from Waverley to Newcastle where she was available should the down service run into trouble.

With an A4 in such splendid condition, the temptation to let her go was great. On occasions drivers, understandably, gave in to that temptation, usually on Stoke Bank where their worries about having enough water had been left behind. Bill Hoole was quite frank: the A4 could gain time easily over most sections despite the length of the run. His practice was to let the engine go on selected sections, and then run

A magnificent view of the up 'Elizabethan' pulling out of Waverley on Saturday July 25th 1953. I consulted my notes to find that, later that afternoon, WILLIAM WHITELAW passed New Southgate on time. The crimson and cream livery on the leading 'Newton' full brake seems to be incorrect, to judge from the adjacent FK. The A1 on the far side of the station is on the 10.00 'Flying Scotsman', and it was usually a Gateshead duty. Tender W1 corridor No.5484, and the A4 still has the Flaman drive. (J. Robertson, The Transport Treasury)

The 15.52 to Leeds emerges from Wood Green Tunnel behind the W1. She worked this duty involving a fairly heavy train in each direction, and I never could recall any signs of it being driven hard. Of course the double chimney would have disguised any great effort, and her starting tractive effort was greater than a Gresley Pacific. The period is 1956-57, and the tender is the usual No.5639. (P.J. Coster)

more easily in between. He also fired to Stoke himself from Werrington in the south or Newark in the north, when the engine was working hard, so his fireman had little cause for complaint! The ease with which the A4 swept up to 90-100mph and held it with 425 tons of train always made me wonder why on earth the CCE couldn't lift the permanent PSRs a little, even for that one service. The value in publicity would have been enormous.

The great problem was of course that while the streamliners had the protection of double block working, the 'Lizzie' did not. Clearly, it should have done, along with the other prestige trains. 'The Non-stop' was not non-stop all too often, almost always because of signals. Even in a less litigious society, there was a danger that the advertised ideal and reality were often quite different. Double block working would have forced a path through congested areas, as well as providing braking protection. There were delays due to permanent way and bridge works, and when the wartime arrears had eased off, there came the rush into continuously welded rail (CWR). The BTC had been convinced – rightly – that this was a good investment, and the LM, E&NER and WR all adopted heavy programmes. Possessions and

hence TSRs grew longer, which delayed trains further.

In 1956, at last, the timetable had the dust beaten out of it. Loads were reduced to a scale sufficient to cope with passenger loadings and timings were reduced. A new afternoon service was introduced between London, Newcastle and Edinburgh named 'The Talisman', departing at 16.00 and calling only at Newcastle, but taking 40 minutes longer than the 'Coronation'. The news spread swiftly down the grapevine, and soon, sure enough, we saw Gateshead crews with their distinctive NE Region orange cap badges riding with the Kings Cross men, learning the road. An immaculate No.60025 FALCON headed the first train northwards, and Gateshead's No.60019 BITTERN brought the southbound train into Kings Cross. It was a welcome return to the south for the Gateshead A4s, which had been infrequent visitors since 1951. The up train was awaited with interest to see Gateshead's A4s once again and often the engine had even been cleaned, although the paintwork left much to be desired. It did not take the Gateshead men long to learn the tricks of the trade. With a light train, the A4s offered a more comfortable ride compared with the A1s and the greater power of the latter was not required. The up train

was last in a row of some four or five expresses, together with the first, if not the second fish train from New Clee as well. One evening at New Southgate the signalman remarked that 167up (The Talisman) was telegraphed forward as passing Hitchin at 22.16, running 20 late. Shortly after, Hatfield telegraphed 167 at 22.25, a remarkably fast time. Listening in to Control, from subsequent times reported it was clear that 167up was going fast. Then Cemetery offered four bells, with the telephoned comment that she was flying. It was a cold night with a sharp frost, and I crossed to the down platform, to get a better view. On the long straight from Cemetery, one could hear the wheel beats on jointed track, and I was able to time the approaching A4 with her train approximately, at 90 mph. SIR RONALD MATTHEWS flashed past in a flurry of flying ash, and was gone. Control later confirmed that arrival had been right time! I fancy 24 minutes (allowing for signalbox times) from Hitchin would have taken some beating!

In 1957 the equivalent morning service was introduced as the 'Morning Talisman'. The Talisman trains were to some extent the streamlined trains in a later form, with similar loading but somewhat slower, recognising that they had to cope with a certain amount of delay on a busy railway. There were certainly some exciting moments with the service, and many drivers were able to enjoy fast running again, legally, and without half-killing their mates! It was very clear that a double Kylchap A4 driven by a good crew could gain a considerable amount of time on the 'Talisman' schedule without undue effort. Sadly, the level of delay was such that they often had to.

The weaknesses which had emerged in the A4 design in post-war conditions were the design of big end, the single exhaust and the persistent problem of hot driving axleboxes, usually on the right-hand side. The big end was redesigned as already mentioned and provided it was correctly lubricated and regularly serviced at the correct mileage, overheating became a thing of the past. The coupled axleboxes, especially the right-hand driving axlebox, also needed to be examined and serviced at the appropriate mileage. The lubrication was now by felt pads in the middle big ends, but they gradually compressed with service, and needed to be changed regularly. By attention to detail in examination and maintenance, overheating was pre-empted, the A4s gradually shed their post-war problems, and mileages began to rise

higher and higher. With the whole class converted to double Kylchap quickly, as mentioned earlier, it became a matter of indifference as to which locomotive the crew was allocated, for they all ran well. At the same time the first generation of diesel locomotives had been introduced but in their early years performance was not very reliable. In theory, diesel locomotives should operate far more reliably than steam since there are roller bearing axles and there is no fire needing cleaning, no lubrication to refresh, no water refilling and a totally different order of cleanliness. However the designs were far from ideal, underpowered, and operating initially from the Victorian environment of steam locomotive depots, which were far from conducive to good diesel engine maintenance.

The A4s, and the other East Coast Pacifics, were pressed into service with extended diagrams and shorter allowances for servicing beyond anything ever dreamed of in 1935. Locomotives were running Newcastle or Leeds and back in the same day, and the daily mileage of an A4 in good condition rose from 350-400 to 500-600. Top Shed now had many locomotives, A3s and Peppercorn A1s as well as the A4s, and the workload in keeping the Pacifics running was considerable. An important change was the transfer of cyclic

examinations of A3 and A4 Pacifics at 36,000 miles, together with the renewal of driving axleboxes, to Doncaster Works where the expertise and the capacity lay, and the additional work was welcome. The A4s were now running much higher mileages, and on occasions the Shedmaster at Kings Cross was asked why various engines, which were overdue for general overhaul, had not been sent in. At the time SEAGULL, which was still working the principal express turns, had run more than 130,000 miles, and five others had exceeded 100,000 miles. If the cost of a general overhaul can be amortised over 120-140,000 miles instead of 80-90,000, there is a considerable reduction in the annual traction cost.

The greatest achievement of the class post-war in terms of speed was the special run in 1959 to celebrate the Golden Jubilee of the Stephenson Locomotive Society. The operation of the train was in the best traditions of the streamliners and in several respects surpassed it. The A4s continued with reliability and economy to cover for the ailing diesels, but slowly and remorselessly the newcomers' performance improved. When the wedding of the Duke of Kent to Miss Katharine Worsley took place on June 8th 1961, four immaculate A4s were prepared for the duties. The Royal train was

GOLDEN PLOVER had been to Doncaster Works, and was returning north via Kings Cross. The visitor is backing down on to the 14.00 to Edinburgh on August 13th 1958. The tender was A4 corridor No.5650. (J.F. Aylard)

headed by WALTER K. WHIGHAM, the standby was SILVER LINK, and the two additional special trains were headed by ANDREW K McCOSH and QUICKSILVER. Enthusiasts and railwaymen had a very special treat as the cavalcade went north. Needless to say, the whole day's running was perfectly executed.

Too much money had been invested, and across the Atlantic and in Europe there were many examples of diesel locomotives running reliably and accumulating very high mileages. The arrival of the Deltics was the turning point. Large and powerful machines, built at an enormous cost which was heavily censored by the management, the 3,300 HP Deltics were the first diesels to emulate and improve on the work of the A4s. With that one class of diesel locomotives, express speed moved way beyond the reach of steam traction in much the same way that the A4s had moved it on in 1935. With a management that had sold its soul to modernisation, with good reason in most respects, everything of the old railway was cast aside. The established order had remained in place for a quarter of a century, but change was coming, and abruptly so. The first inroads had been made into the A3s three years earlier, but it was a tremendous shock when five of the Kings Cross A4s were withdrawn at the end of 1962. What was worse was that they were some of the finest and most famous – the first, SILVER LINK, along with SEAGULL, WALTER K WHIGHAM, ANDREW K McCOSH and GOLDEN FLEECE. There was an indisputable case for the retention of SILVER LINK as one of the most famous of all British express locomotives, a loss still regretted. But with a British Railways Board intent on a de minimus programme of preservation – if one at all – it cut no ice. By now, some in senior management were contemptuous of past railway achievements, feeling that *they* had created a modern railway.

Shortly after, sister QUICKSILVER and MALLARD herself were condemned, followed by an embargo on steam south of Peterborough applied with near-religious fervour. The remaining A4s went to New England at first, then, after a few more had been withdrawn and No.60008 had been despatched to America, to Scotland where they joined the remaining Gateshead and Haymarket A4s. At the suggestion of the Scottish General Manager, James Ness, the A4s were put to work on the Glasgow-Aberdeen services. The trains were light and timed quite sharply, and the antics of some of the smaller prototype diesels were causing more disruption rather than less.

Ferryhill men knew Gresley Pacifics and took to their A4s. The same could not be said of the Perth men, and still less of the Balornock men who seemed to think that the A4 had two cylinders too many! I recall the Ferryhill Shedmaster referring slightingly to the Perth and Glasgow men as 'the hydraulic gang'. Their disavowal of the use of cylinder cocks resulted in the cylinder covers gradually being forced off and the A4 condemned in each case, the latest being the famous No.60005 SIR CHARLES NEWTON formerly of Gateshead.

So enthusiasts and photographers who flocked to the north were rewarded by the sight of A4s in the evening of their career. They were driven hard, sometimes they were cleaned, and as a result they looked splendid. The long, fairly flat road through Strathmore was good for speed, and they crossed the Tay at the speeds of their youth. On one occasion I was waiting at Aberdeen for the 13.30 to Glasgow and seeing the English Electric Type 4 first approach the station and then, after an anxious lineside phone call, retire hurt to be replaced by WILLIAM WHITELAW. The grin on the driver's face said it all. He drove his A4 with great vigour, and we ran into Perth having recovered most if not all of our 21 minutes of late departure.

One by one they went, until they were all gone. DOMINION OF CANADA, now a double Kylchap flier, was sent to Canada. DWIGHT D EISENHOWER had already gone to America. SIR NIGEL GRESLEY, UNION OF SOUTH AFRICA and BITTERN were saved by enthusiasts for posterity. MALLARD herself now rests at York in the National Railway Museum, in pride of place, joined by her old shedmate, FLYING SCOTSMAN. I cannot hide a smile when I think of DWIGHT D. EISENHOWER and DOMINION OF CANADA, the two recalcitrant A4s which Harry Willers was given in quick succession so long ago. Who would have thought that, out of the treasury of famous locomotives at Kings Cross, those two would survive?

In the UK we have the most famous one in the NRM nearly in working condition, two under general overhaul, and one hauling special trains for our delight. Long may they continue to do so, and thank you, ladies and gentlemen of the supporting teams and societies, for your hard work and generosity!

No.60700, as she became, probably hauling the 15.52 down express, at Greenwood in 1954. The tender has been changed to a non-corridor type, No.5639. (Cawston Bequest, Canon Brian C. Bailey Collection)

CHAPTER SIX
Looking Back to the 1930s

Looking back at the exciting events of the 1930s with the luxury of 70 years of hindsight, one gains the impression, uncharitably, that the LNER was naïve, and had quite underestimated the risks and implications of high speed. It was lucky, very lucky to have achieved its goal without a disaster. That may sound a trifle harsh given the euphoria of the pre-war achievements, but any sober assessment of the incidents where danger suddenly threatened would reach the same conclusion. One cannot use a mass transport system for high speed experiments without very careful attention to safety. The lessons learnt from those experiences have since been enshrined in the rules that govern the safe working of the railway, and it is safer as a result – or should be. A Rule Book is always a chronicle of past mistakes and failures.

In considering the events leading to the introduction of the A4 Pacifics, a number of things run through the mind. It is particularly fascinating for anyone acquainted with the operation and management of the railway to look back and try to piece together the decisions and actions which led to the events of September 27th 1935 and July 3rd 1938. Much of what we know of those years in fact comes to us not so much from the engineers

themselves as from dedicated and knowledgeable enthusiasts. The industry has changed and what took place in the 1930s seems hardly credible in today's culture. I am sure that the well-known story of the introduction of the A4 is the tip of the iceberg, and many railwaymen must have played unsung but vital parts in the story. That in no way diminishes the magnitude of the achievement; indeed it enhances it.

Overall, one is looking at a time when a major initiative was led by a small, expert team of senior staff. Half a century later a similar project would be led by a large group of people representing the many different levels in the railway organisation. To me it is axiomatic that the smallest team practicable, provided it is comprised of expert and experienced staff, will always be better than a committee. This was a vivid demonstration of such a truth in 1934-35.

The period from the LNER's first adventures into faster running in late 1931 to the introduction of the 'Silver Jubilee' was not particularly lengthy, but when one considers the astonishing change in the appearance and performance of the British express train that was witnessed on the afternoon of September 27th 1935, a number of questions arise in the mind. When one looks back at the

events of the 1934-35 period, we are looking at what would comprise a major project today, with a director or manager, engineers, planners, and a financial backup, together with a network of computers, software and so on, all specific to that one project. There would be vacuous explanations or honeyed words to explain the inevitable delays and the malign presence of those inseparable twins, under-estimating and overspending. In the 1930s things were so much simpler.

One needs first of all to understand the way in which the LNER Company operated. The railways' organisations were based very much on the military, and the names used reflected that link. Seventy years ago the chief officers, all experienced railwaymen, took it in their stride and, when one considers what was achieved in such a short space of time, the quality of that achievement is obvious. Indeed the language and the very names changed over the years, and a senior manager was a Superintendent or Agent in the days of yore. With the 1939-45 war, many superintendents became 'officers', but now we are all managers.

The LNER Board of the 1930s comprised busy, inevitably wealthy and influential people, but it was not their practice to involve themselves in the operation of the company

A cabside detail of DOMINION OF CANADA showing the Canadian coat of arms carried, and the fox on the boilerside. (H.N. James)

The up 'Coronation' about to leave Edinburgh Waverley behind EMPIRE OF INDIA. The date is not given but must be summer 1937-39. The detail of the A4 cladding is particularly good.

with staff and company matters. The CGM had no corresponding all-line chiefs of operating and civil engineering, a disadvantage that was corrected in the war years. The operating department was normally the senior department in a railway, both before and after the 1939-45 war. Therefore Gresley had no counterpart at HQ responsible for train planning and motive power, or civil engineering, which introduced the risk of poor communications. Perhaps Wedgwood felt that it would be wiser in any case to leave the operational responsibility delegated to the Divisions – which were in effect the pre-Grouping companies – rather than impose new centralised authority. In the Southern Area, in fact, the situation became worse as the pressure on operations became excessive. The operation of the former GER section, including the busy Liverpool Street suburban service (the 'Jazz') was hived off in 1930 from that of the East Coast main line and the quieter pastures of the old GCR, creating the Eastern and Western sections of the Southern Area.

So while Gresley presided over the mechanical and electrical engineering of the LNER as a whole, his department being centred on Drawing Offices and Works, the operation and maintenance of his locomotives and rolling stock was divided among the three Locomotive Running Superintendents. On the GNR, Gresley had controlled locomotive running, but on the LNER, organisationally, it was removed from him. On the GWR the CME controlled locomotive running until nationalisation. The LNER Locomotive Running Superintendents were responsible to their Divisional General Managers for the provision of motive power to meet operational needs, and surprisingly, not even subordinate to the Divisional Superintendent who was in charge of operation. In technical matters, of course, they remained subject to the CME.

This was a legacy from the Grouping Act. Sir Vincent Raven, who was the highly respected and successful CME of the North Eastern Railway, was too old to be considered for the post of CME of the LNER and in the event Gresley was appointed. Raven's wisdom and experience were felt to be valuable to the new company and he was retained for a period as Technical Adviser. His advice was that locomotive running and maintenance should be separated from the CME, as had been successfully done on the NER, and the LNER had taken that advice. So Gresley had little control over the use of his locomotives, and feedback on their operation was variable. He and the Superintendents met regularly

overmuch. For all its impressive directorate and chief officers, however, the LNER was not a company to invest in, and its financial position was usually poor. Indeed by contrast with practice today, most of the LNER Directors were 'hands off' rather than 'hands on'. Most of the decisions fell to the strong Chairman, William Whitelaw, or to the very able Chief General Manager, Sir Ralph Wedgwood. Locomotive matters were dealt with by the Locomotive Committee, chaired by B.A. Firth until his death in 1928, when he was succeeded by Andrew K. McCosh. The Locomotive Committee usually met jointly with the Traffic Committee rather than independently. The Company was divided into three Areas, Southern, North Eastern and

Scottish, each led by a Divisional General Manager, with Divisional officers for operating, locomotive running, passenger, freight and civil engineering. Signalling and Telecommunications were not the complex science that they are today, and the responsibility for signalling in the 1930s still lay with the Divisional CCE, assisted by a specialist Signal Engineer to discharge that responsibility. Wedgwood's rule was simple: the Divisional staff ran the *railway*, while he and the Board ran the company and its policy.

Nigel Gresley was employed at company or all-line level rather than Division, under the CGM, along with the Chief Accountant, Chief Stores Superintendent and those dealing

DOMINION OF CANADA with the up 'Flying Scotsman' at what looks like Peterborough North. The bell is being rung as the A4 approaches the platforms. The period is 1937-39, and the tender is A3 corridor No.5328, possibly No.5326 if before December 1937.

and there were good professional contacts through the engineering institutions. However, we are talking of a time when it required timing, care and diplomacy to address some senior engineers, and I can recall in a sister discipline that it was all too easy to blight a promising career with an injudicious word or emphasis.

It was a pity. Railway history is littered with examples of how the CME and the Motive Power Department consistently failed to communicate, especially on the LMSR where the motive power department was subordinate to the operating department. Their failure, of course, meant that the railway as a whole suffered as a result. Gresley himself often talked to the drivers and engineers in the Running Department. For example, firemen laboured with temperamental locomotives for generations, yet there were exhaust systems designed not only in France, but by the Master Mechanics in America which removed much uncertainty where they were applied. The vast amount of written and anecdotal evidence of steam traction in America never referred to a design being shy of steam. It would not have been tolerated.

If the CME were wholly responsible for the Motive Power Department, the responsibility for handling budgets, addressing that department's problems and their performance targets would be his too. In France the CME was wholly responsible for the motive power until 1971. M. Camille Martin, the Director of Motive Power from 1956 to 1971, felt that it was essential to ensure the free exchange of knowledge unhindered by inter-departmental 'Chinese walls'. Arguably it would have made the CME's department both large and powerful, and maybe in railway politics some felt that was not a good idea. Gresley was already in charge of what then would have been equivalent to a major engineering group. But it would have simply meant that the Divisional staff would have reported to Gresley rather than their General Managers, although they would still have had to work with the Operating Superintendents for day-to-day operations. That would have forced the creation of a clear line of communication, authority and responsibility. There were certainly occasional signs that Gresley's successors were not as au fait with locomotive running as they needed to be.

While we have reflected on the rapid development of the A4 and the streamliners, unless they could be woven into the fabric of railway operation, they would have remained only a good idea. The timetables were changed at approximately the beginning of May and October in the 1930s as has once again become the case today. If the surmised timescale of late 1934/early 1935 for the decision to go ahead is right, then the May 1935 timetable, when one would have thought it was preferable to introduce a new high-speed service, especially one celebrating the Sovereign's Jubilee, was already quite out of the question. It was already a very late revision for the September 1935 book. One could not simply shoehorn the new service in, for there was already a 17.30 Kings Cross-Newcastle express and it was a popular service for returning Northern business travellers, and as such a good revenue earner. This had to be retimed (to 17.45) along with the many services pathed through the well-known LNER 'bottlenecks' which were affected. The same applied to the up service as well. This decision would certainly have needed the personal authority of the CGM.

To anyone with experience of the railway industry, one's thoughts now turn to the process of timetable production in the 1930s. It is clear

UNION OF SOUTH AFRICA at Edinburgh Waverley in garter blue, pre-war (it had gone new to Haymarket principally for the 'Coronation'). The weathering is characteristic, especially of the garter blue – highlighting the 'joins'. (K.J. Macdonald, The Transport Treasury)

that the decision-making processes of the LNER were far quicker than they were half a century later, but the routine process of running a railway in the 1930s did not have the advantages of modern business machines and systems. Normally, half a century later, BR took a year from the initial skirmishing to the introduction of a timetable, and I would guess that the timescale was not dissimilar in the 1930s, but for very different reasons. For example, staff consultation had become much more adversarial and very protracted, not least due the politicisation of the trade unions. In the 1930s timetables were not altered nearly so often, but there was the slow compilation and consultation with specialist sub-sections, hand written drafts, typed, consulted and agreed, and then the printer's copies, and finally the printed timetable. Interleaved between all of these stages were the repetitive mind-numbing checks and proof readings, for these were the days when standards were impeccable. All this took weeks not days. They were also days when the timetable was on sale well before it took effect, not always something that BR managed!

Therefore there was some point, probably early 1935, at which it was decided to plan and then firm up on a new streamlined service. As a service with dedicated locomotives and rolling stock, operated by footplate staff, guards and on-train staff independently of other services, it could be injected into the timetable later in the process than usual, once the Chairman had decided to go ahead. It is also clear from the speed of events that by comparison with its nationalised successor, the LNER Divisions were not saddled with a bureaucracy, and they could decide and implement far more rapidly. Orders were for obedience rather than an invitation to discussion. Provided late alterations were properly worked out, they could be authorised and enacted. Nevertheless, the timescale for the inclusion of the 'Silver Jubilee' service that was set, by instruction or by implication, was alarmingly short, and within a few decades would have been regarded as wildly impossible.

Examining the operation of the streamliners, again one has to remember that this was a very different railway. With almost the entire railway controlled by absolute block mechanical signalling, adequate for speeds of 40-70 mph, the LNER had to devise quickly a means of operating the faster services safely. It was no use issuing a sheaf of local instructions. The system used had to

pass the scrutiny of His (then) Majesty's Railway Inspectorate. The method adopted was 'double block' for operating the 'Silver Jubilee', an approved device that was normally used only for the Royal Train.

In fact no provision for 'double block' per se existed as far as one can trace. The 1934 LNER Signalling Regulations for absolute block were the Law and the Prophets for signalmen, and there is no reference there. Normally one used Regulation 3, which regulated the use of absolute block for normal running. However, Regulation 4(e) did provide that, in fog and falling snow, a train should not be accepted from the signalbox in the rear unless the block indicator for the signalbox in advance was 'line blocked' (i.e. section clear). This would have given the additional protection of two block sections rather than the normal one. When the section ahead cleared, without waiting for 'train on line', the streamliner would have been offered to the signalbox in advance where the signalman, in his turn, would not have accepted until *his* advance block instrument was at 'line blocked'. The instruction issued for the streamlined trains would have laid down the special bell code for them (4 pause 4). In order that this should work without locking up the line ahead too

GOLDEN FLEECE in an earlier incarnation as GREAT SNIPE in LNER apple green livery. This can be tied down accurately to August 27th 1937, just before the A4 was repainted in garter blue livery. I doubt whether the posed cleaning gang had to work very hard! Here the operating handle for the cod's mouth can be seen. The tender was new A4 corridor No.5650.

DOMINION OF NEW ZEALAND brings the 1937 down non-stop 'Flying Scotsman' across the magnificent Royal Border Bridge. The train was equipped with new stock in 1938 which continued the panelled teak exterior, but with greatly improved interior. The A4's tender No.5647 had not yet been fitted with Hoffman roller bearings.

SIR NIGEL GRESLEY on a down express. A Kings Cross engine, she was coupled to A3 corridor tender No.5329. The location is a mystery. There some places where an up slow or goods loop existed without a down slow or goods, but most were at or in the vicinity of a station. The number of places which fit the description and had a siding or running line some way away on the up side would be far fewer. It could be Connington or Barkston, but if not, I pass! (The Transport Treasury)

KINGFISHER, waiting to take out an express to Glasgow or the north at the west end of Waverley. She was nearly new in 1937, in LNER apple green with a black smokebox. The tender was A3 corridor No.5332. (Dr R.A. Read, Gavin Whitelaw Collection)

far, regulating boxes had to be nominated. In practice signalmen were well aware of those trains which were a priority, and took good trouble to make sure the road ahead was clear in good time. Failure to do so invited the certainty of a 'Please explain' from District Office followed by a painful interview!

Regarding the problem of the NE Area colour light signalling, the development of the A4 and the 'Silver Jubilee' was so rapid by comparison with the normal progress of such major initiatives that something like this was bound to happen. Colour light signalling had many advantages over absolute block, but it lacked the flexibility of absolute block, the inability to work with two clear block sections ahead being one disadvantage. The resignalling would have been carried out on the basis that each of the several junctions then extant would have been protected by a colour light home signal, with the next colour light in the rear being at braking distance from the home. With the proximity of some connections, if the braking distance of roughly 1,300 yards could not be achieved, the second signal in the rear would have had a fourth aspect to give an approaching express preliminary warning.

No doubt the road was cleared ahead, and, knowing that the trains had priority, a driver could have run

at full speed, but a moment's inattention and an unexpectedly adverse signal could cause problems at higher speeds. Despite the care that went into organising such a service, with a railway still populated by hordes of timber wagons from the days of George Stephenson with grease-lubricated axleboxes, hot axleboxes daily were a fact of life, as were broken couplings and consequent runaways. When a signalman received a 'Stop & Examine' or 'Attention Danger' bell code, *all* approaching trains had to be stopped. The cause might be a door on the catch of a passenger train, or the problems mentioned above with freight, even a derailed wagon. It might have been unassociated with the streamliner, yet a potential source of danger on an adjacent track would have required it to stop at once. In fact once the service settled down, some drivers ran in excess of the speed limit, knowing that if they were called on stop, they could still do so safely – just. The normal signalling intervals were 1,300 yards, and the distance required to stop the 'Silver Jubilee' from 90 mph was 1,250 yards – in normal conditions.

The railway of 1935 differed from today's in another quite critical sense. It was one in which the *operation* of the railway was almost entirely in the hands of the artisan and semi-skilled staff. Those staff were not lacking in

experience, indeed it would put many contemporary staff to shame by comparison. The engineers specified equipment, set the standards, and then stood back to let the inspectors, foremen, gangers, instructors, etc, run the railway. By the 1960s, the technical staff had gradually come into day-to-day operations, a process that continued to the present day, by which time the inspectors of yore have disappeared. One may debate the whys and wherefores, but it is not within the scope of this book to do so. However, it remains a major influence on the events that are being considered here.

So we turn to the astonishing trial trip of September 27th 1935. If there was a defining moment in which Doncaster finally exorcised the ghost of the 1925 Exchanges, it was this. In fact the A3 had achieved it already, quietly, but now there was no question. The 'Silver Jubilee' train was, for the East Coast main line, a very light train but the performance still has an air of unreality about it, so far were the speeds in advance of what had been experienced up to that time. Some aspects of the performance demand further discussion. But first of all it is essential to realise that but for one factor, the run would have been rather less spectacular. All of the circumstantial evidence points to the fact that SILVER LINK was not

SPARROW HAWK at Waverley station in 1938-39. The A4 is adding three coaches to its train, which must be heavy since she has a pilot engine, D49 4-4-0 No.264 STIRLINGSHIRE. The train was probably the second part of the 'Flying Scotsman' since the Non-stop is visible on the left-hand side of the picture. The NE Area practice was to couple the pilot inside, so the senior driver retained the brake and the responsibility for correct observation of signals, and the junior driver on the pilot simply provided the assistance. Or so it should have been, but in my experience the crew of the second engine usually didn't make much of an effort until something serious was called for. (H.N. Shepherd, The Transport Treasury)

equipped with a working speed recorder on Friday, September 27th 1935.

It is when one looks at the speeds that were achieved and where they were achieved, that we come to the first clue. The GNR main line was well maintained and drivers could run fast downhill, even occasionally exceeding the speed limits slightly, in relative safety and comfort. But in this particular case we are considering speeds 20 mph or more in excess, and the CCE's reported restiveness is hardly surprising. He was within a year of retirement at 65. Described as 'a nervous man' by C.J. Allen, he would have been all too aware from Allen's timings of the extent to which his speed limits were being put to the sword. These were the days of jointed bullhead track, without the heavy ballasting and concrete sleepers of welded track, and the track was far more susceptible to misalignment from excessive speeds. In an age when communications were at a more gentlemanly level, he would have made his views known to his colleague of 25 years, courteously but firmly. Allen never revealed overmuch of the conversation in his compartment, but having known a number of CCEs, I am quite sure that Brown had told Gresley to tell the driver to ease up. After braking heavily for Offord curves, Taylor was very much more restrained.

It is the matter of discipline that is also intriguing. In 1935 the PSRs were known, but the lack of any strong enforcement seems strange by comparison with the railway two decades later. The measuring of train speed was not easy or quick and drivers were left to use their judgement. Partly due to the lack of transitioning and partly due to the drivers' approximate judgement of speed, passengers would have had to endure a lower standard of comfort at speed. It was very different later, when enthusiasts were cautioned by drivers to lessen their recorded speeds for fear of disciplinary action following publication. In 1935, Taylor had been instructed to press the engine harder in order to establish what reserve of power she had. The schedules had been tightened by 2½ minutes south of York to compensate for the signalling speed restriction beyond. A request from the CME was an order, and no matter as to the chain of command, one did as one was told. It is clear, however, that Driver Taylor, an experienced top link driver who drove all through the streamliner years, had been misled by the riding of the A4. One can imagine the surprise for him on seeing the CME on the footplate, and the surprise – alarm might be more accurate considering where he was – on hearing that he had not been running at 90 mph but 20 mph or so faster. Although the trial run must

have been the sort of coup that Publicity Officers dream about, in fact it was not much use in its requirement to establish what the reserve of power was. Clearly SILVER LINK had the power to gain time considerably on the schedule, but it had involved speeds that would not have been permitted in ordinary service.

The official description of the A4 and the 'Silver Jubilee' train issued at the time states that there was a speed recorder fitted to the engine. I am quite certain that there was no working speed recorder fitted to SILVER LINK on September 27th 1935. It is a detail but quite important. The photographs of SILVER LINK new, at Doncaster and Top Shed, show that the drive to the recorder was not fitted at that time. The photographs of SILVER LINK at Top Shed are believed to have been taken during a club visit on September 14th by Leslie Burley.

The apparatus was a speed indicator *and* recorder, and it was driven mechanically, off the right-hand rear crankpin. The small primary gearbox was suspended by a special bracket over the wheel centre, and the drive was taken back to another secondary gearbox directly under the cab, from where a vertical shaft drove the device. It was a bulky machine and the convenient location was beneath the fireman's seat where the driver could glance across at it, at least in daylight. One can see the arrangement on MALLARD in the National Railway Museum. Driver Taylor, in a subsequent broadcast, referred to a speedometer on the train. There was an electrical speedometer on the train for the benefit of the first class diners, and maybe it was that which Taylor was referring to. Otherwise would all three men on the footplate have ignored a speed recorder – unless it was not working? And if the latter was the case surely that fact would have been communicated back to the train? Surely the novelty of a speed recorder would have attracted attention rather than go unnoticed? A driver of Taylor's experience and seniority would not have knowingly treated the speed limits in quite such a cavalier fashion. Nor would his Divisional Running Superintendent, Groom, in the cab with him, have allowed him to do so. One might speculate as to why it was missing, or present but not working, but it is unlikely to be known now. I have little doubt that it was left off in the general haste to deal with the main drawings and to complete the engine.

As a result, the trial run was a very startling demonstration of the capacity of the A4 for high speed. In fact, because there was no available measure of the speeds being attained (though Gresley was checking the speeds with his stopwatch) it was the record being produced by Cecil J. Allen as the official recorder that must have alarmed Brown. The LNER had published copies of the Flaman recordings made on all of the other auspicious occasions, but significantly, there is nothing for September 27th 1935. As a result of the record run, I think that Flaman recorders were fitted to QUICKSILVER before she entered service on the 'Silver Jubilee', and to SILVER LINK as soon as possible, probably a month later in early November when she visited Doncaster Works.

It was a fairly simple matter to fit a Flaman recorder to an A4, although the instrument had to be purchased from France. Only the bracket from below the aerofoil running board carrying the primary gearbox would need modification from that used on tests with the A1 and A3 Pacifics. The mechanism was well understood at Doncaster, and two drawings were produced endorsed 'October 1935'. It was the practice in mechanical engineering for drawings to be produced quickly for fairly minor tasks as well as the major ones, and while the fitting would have been a straightforward matter, it would normally have to wait for the appropriate drawing before proceeding. The two drawings produced in October 1935 were

superseded in 1937 by a set of identical drawings prepared in the Drawing Office. W.B. Yeadon, probably with the old files with him, wrote in the authoritative RCTS LNER *Locomotive Survey* that although Gresley had agreed to the A4s being fitted in March 1936, it was not until October 1937 that the decision was ratified and it took effect. I think that correspondence referred to the decision to fit the whole class and not just the dedicated locomotives. When the locomotives were built for the 'Coronation' and 'West Riding Limited', they too, were similarly equipped. Indeed I suspect that the whole of the order EO 340, Nos 4482-4498, were fitted. It is difficult to be specific since the majority of photographs of the time tend to have been taken at the lineside or on shed from the driver's side. The earliest photograph that I have found in researching this book, clearly showing the Flaman drive is that of No.4489 in her early works grey as WOODCOCK in April 1937. No.4487 SEA EAGLE was photographed by Gordon Hepburn at Grantham with the up 'Flying Scotsman' in May 1937, a month old, and the Flaman drive is clearly illustrated. The three streamlined trains were worked almost exclusively by the locomotives that were built for them until December 13th 1937, when brand new A4s GOLDEN PLOVER took the down 'Coronation' and SIR NIGEL GRESLEY brought the up 'Silver Jubilee' into Kings Cross. Of course except in emergency their individual liveries would have confined them to the duties they were built for, until October 1937 when garter blue became standard.

The LNER introduced three streamlined services. Of these the 'Silver Jubilee' was the first and most successful both in financial and operating terms. There was a good growing commercial business linking London and the North East, and South West Yorkshire as well as the country recovered from the recession after 1935. The 'Silver Jubilee' and 'West Riding Limited' both put travel to the capital and back in one day well within the reach of businessmen, affording a reasonable period of time for meetings, etc. The introduction of the 'Coronation' was slightly different, since the Anglo-Scottish traffic included a larger proportion of holiday and residential travel and was more seasonal. However it also offered an earlier return to York and Newcastle, and a late evening service from Newcastle to London. Whereas Gresley and the Divisional Running Superintendents set the A4s a reasonable task in the first and the third service, that of the 'Coronation' was significantly harder, especially in

summer when the observation car was added to the train.

The general view of the 'Coronation' has been that it was the zenith of British steam traction as referred to earlier, and more specifically, that it was the most demanding proposition in the United Kingdom set for a steam locomotive by the operators. There can be no doubt as to the truth of that claim. The quality of the work was outstanding, but the only doubts some may feel concern the increased number of substitutions en route. There were 46 occasions as far as I can trace on which the A4 was replaced or assisted for one reason or another in the train's 26 months of operation, and on the face of it, it is higher than one would like. One may disaggregate the failures and dismiss those caused by operating problems or faulty servicing, but a substitution is an operational failure whatever the reason. The mileage per failure in service based on that number of replacements/assistances was less than one third of the 'Silver Jubilee' figure at 9,300. I and many of my former colleagues would have been apprehensive at having to defend that rate of failure to a General Manager, especially in the knowledge that the 'Silver Jubilee' figure was three times better.

However, in order to make a comparison, with what does one compare it? There was nothing comparable in the UK, and the nearest competitor was the same company's 'Silver Jubilee' which was both lighter and operated over 70% of the distance. When one considers the likely contenders from other companies for comparison, one naturally starts with the 'Cheltenham Flyer' of the GWR. Despite the undoubted quality of its running, it was generally a lighter train hauled by a smaller locomotive running less than half the distance on Britain's flattest and finest main line. The 'Princess Coronation' Pacifics of William Stanier were larger and more powerful than a single chimney A4, and the 'Big Lizzies' would certainly have timed the 'Coronation' comfortably. In terms of sustained running they had a higher specific steam consumption (14.5lb/IHP/hr minimum) than the single chimney A4 (13lb), which would have led to a higher fuel and water consumption. It was a pity that they were never really taxed for long by what the LMSR operators asked of them.

When the records are examined in detail, it is clear that the greater demands on the locomotives reflected on the crews and maintenance staff, and the performance in general improved once experience had been gained. The original A4 design had a

defect in that the streamlined cladding prevented the tender from being fully loaded, and that was quickly corrected. There were two other areas of risk, namely the design of middle big end, and the exhaust design for the single blast engines. Neither normally gave trouble. When one considers that the service brought two depots newly into the operation with no previous experience of the streamlined services, perhaps it is not surprising. Fourteen of the failures and replacements occurred in the first winter. The number of failures per quarter continued to fall from 8-9 in the first winter so that by summer 1938 and 1939 was 2-3. The six monthly figures showed an uneven but steady reduction, and had war not intervened there was every reason to expect that the mileage per failure would have increased to the 'Silver Jubilee' overall standard. For similar reasons, the latter may well have moved towards 35,000 miles per failure. Almost certainly, had war not intervened and Gresley continued in office, the Kylchap A4s would have been more numerous and would have taken a greater part in the running of the streamliners.

When one looks at punctuality, the record of timekeeping of the three streamliners was immaculate in practical railway terms, and I am sure that the Flaman speed recorder was a valuable aid to that end. Several decades later, BR would have paid dearly to achieve the standard of running of the 'Silver Jubilee', even with diesel and electric traction and speedometers! For those who learnt

I could not resist this Dickensian gathering of lads, standing in front of SEA EAGLE at Kings Cross. There is even a Faginesque character with his bowler, as well as an Artful Dodger or two. Clearly there was more to running a depot than repairing hot axleboxes and bearings! I wonder whether we are looking at lads who eventually became the aristocrats of the Top Link?

One for the Health & Safety Executive! Our Fagin, precariously placed, clears the smokebox of SEA EAGLE in front of that gaping 'cod's mouth'. Just think what he would need to wear and use today!

or assumed to be full – mistakes such as these risked trouble or even failure on the road. Excellent staff training and discipline minimised potential troubles. The record of performance on this demanding duty was outstanding, although it involved a greater number of failures by comparison with the two other services. It was clear that the engines could cope easily with the load and the schedule, and did so economically.

However, one can argue further that on 12 occasions the effect of the replacement did not cause a late arrival as defined as within 5 minutes of right time. On others, with experience drivers took the standby locomotive at Newcastle or elsewhere rather than persist with poor steaming. Changing engines where a replacement was ready was a wiser course of action than persisting and then having a complete failure out in remote country. On one occasion A4 No.4496 GOLDEN SHUTTLE on the up 'Coronation' was replaced at Doncaster by A3 No.2743 FELSTEAD since a derailment had necessitated diversion via Lincoln, and the water crane there was too low for the streamlined tender. Full marks to someone with local knowledge – something that is, alas, too rarely found now. On two occasions and probably a third, reported as 'SOS' (shortage of steam), the engine ran out of coal, because the streamlined cladding of the tender referred to above prevented its being fully laden. More worryingly, on six occasions, five in the first winter, the A4 came off the up train at Newcastle 'SOS' with less than a third of the run completed. As the engines involved were from both Kings Cross and Haymarket, it would seem to indicate that the firemen were having trouble, possibly because Haymarket were not yet aware of the need to check the jumper top's functioning.

Casting an eye over the record of replacements and breakdowns, the occasional operational hiatus stands out. Normally another Pacific standing pilot, usually at Newcastle, replaced the A4. Sometimes things were less straightforward, especially if the A4 failed out in the country where no replacement was available, bearing out the old railwayman's adage that however bad things have become, they can always get worse and probably will. Driver Auger must have realised the truth of that on May 17th 1938 when SILVER FOX ran hot at Grantham. The pilot was an A1, SOLARIO, but as luck would have it, she was one of the two Pacifics fitted with a special steam operated scoop, and most firemen were unfamiliar with it. Inexplicably, SOLARIO was turned out by Haymarket for the up service on May 18th and worked through to Kings Cross. One would

about railways in the 1950s when running varied from day to day, the record is uncommonly good. Perhaps we forget forty years on how much unwanted baggage there was to affect steam operation – brick arches that occasionally collapsed, fires that needed cleaning, injectors that stalled, shortages of steam and bearings of all sorts that might overheat, while coal and water availability and quality were ever-present worries. And all that together with the timekeeping at the mercy not of the Hailstones, Hooles and Swans, but of the poorly paid and unmotivated run-of-the-mill crews. The lack of reassurance now given by AWS in running at speed after nightfall is noticeable. There was no doubt that the A4s could and did run these challenging schedules, day in and day out. When one looks at the amount of delay encountered, despite the protection of double block working, the amount of delay time recovered is remarkable. The 'Silver Jubilee' operated in two Areas, and the route of the 'Coronation' passed through three Areas. In the latter case one would expect at least three

TSRs for track renewals in the summer and one or two more at times in the winter. Using the SR approach, 2½% of the six hour schedule meant that every driver had to face the certainty of delays of nine minutes, and regularly a run would have to achieve a net time of 350 minutes or less to arrive on time. In fact the normal allowance of 3 minutes per TSR seems, from experience, a shade parsimonious. Relaying took place over shorter sections in those days, but even a short 15-20 mph TSR would cost nearer 4 minutes, rising to 4½ minutes for a ½ mile TSR. Even with a light train the acceleration was unlikely to reduce those times substantially.

The record of the 'Coronation' in particular illustrates how much more the A4 design was tested by this hard duty, especially the single blast engines. Every so often one can see where attention to detail seems to have lapsed, with inevitable results. The 'wrong sort of cylinder oil' might have predated BR by half a century, but the wrong size trimming, a worn felt pad, a jumper top blastpipe sticking, an oil reservoir wrongly said have thought that Haymarket could find a replacement A4, or even Gateshead, which had three by then, or Heaton which had one. Although sixteen minutes late, taking water at Newcastle took extra time, and four TSRs accounted for more than the lateness. A month later Driver Taylor fared worse still, when WILD SWAN ran hot at Hitchin with only K3 No.2428 available as a replacement. By Grantham he was no doubt glad to take an A3 for the rest of the run. 1939 started badly. GOLDEN EAGLE ran hot at Grantham on January 4th, and Driver Ferguson took over the W1 4-6-2-2, No.10000. At Durham the replacement ran hot, and the train was hauled to Newcastle by G5 0-4-4T No.1837 where A1 GALOPIN took over for the remainder of the run. Then on January 12th WILD SWAN ran hot at Claypole, where only J6 0-6-0 No.3580 was available to continue to Grantham. A1 DONOVAN continued to Kings Cross arriving 71 minutes late.

But the two most remarkable substitutions came two months later. On March 22nd 1939 COMMONWEALTH OF AUSTRALIA had run hot with the up train at Newcastle, so Driver Nash took the pilot, TRIGO. Starting 8 minutes late, despite two TSRs, he reached Kings Cross in 230 minutes, 7 less than the schedule, 225 net. The TSRs cost 5 minutes, an underestimate in my view. Two days later, WOODCOCK was removed at Tweedmouth with piston trouble. Occasionally one of Tweedmouth's Atlantics was pressed into action, and C7 No.2205 took the train to Newcastle, on this occasion arriving

26 minutes late. Driver Nash – again – took SINGAPORE as replacement, but there was a further delay due to the fireman and shunter coupling the steam heating pipe but not the screw coupling, with disastrous consequences. The two TSRs were still in force, and there were two signal checks, but Nash made a record run in 228½ minutes, 222½ net. Again the net time was probably less. The work of Driver Nash and his fireman was remarkable, but we need to reflect on its context. Both runs were made in darkness, the signals in the vast majority of cases were oil-lit, there was none of the assurance of AWS and no speedometer – only the protection of double block. No doubt the speeds downhill were high, but the two runs represented enginemanship of the very highest quality.

These unusual and fascinating incidents formed a minority when compared with the overwhelming number of punctual and reliable runs, as can be seen in Appendix H. Adherence to schedule was therefore important especially when TSRs were in operation. The run to York obviously could not benefit from the high-speed section farther north where the schedule was easier and useful time could be recovered. After the climb out of London came the high-speed section down to Offord and on down to Stilton Fen where the schedule was tight anyway. With the timetable demanding high speeds, it was hard to gain much more than seconds, and the bridges over new roads in the suburbs injected delays from TSRs that took a long while to regain. A little more time could be

gained if a driver was prepared to risk censure for excessive speeds, but it was even better if there was no record of the speeds! But beyond Peterborough it was all hard work, with the climb to Stoke with the harder pull, and the more congested two-track section from Stoke northwards. Although the road was no more than undulating, if a driver was late at Grantham it was that much harder to arrive on time at York, due to the number of permanent speed restrictions for flat crossings, water troughs and major stations. The protection of double block was invaluable, and signalmen usually, but not always, kept a clear road.

If the service had been reinstated in a suitable guise after the war, I have no doubt that senior motive power officers would have insisted on changing engines at Newcastle. The use of one A4 throughout was felt to be unwise by more than a few at the time, and the mileage per failure bears this out. Engine changing would need six minutes, comfortably, although on a good day one might cut that down to five or a touch less. The extra minutes could be recovered, particularly with a fresh engine, between Newcastle and Edinburgh. Although the maximum speed permitted over the northern part of the East Coast main line was lower, especially beyond Berwick on the old NBR main line, and the incidence of PSRs greater, the timings were easier. In the railway industry medals are not won for overcoming difficulties so much as avoiding them.

A detail of the stainless steel fox and clothing bands carried by SILVER FOX.

CHAPTER SEVEN
Recovery and Triumph

Interest in the railway scene during and after the war naturally took second place to concern for surviving hostilities and their consequences. What interest there was lay in seeing novel sights, such as the American and new War Department 2-8-0 freight engines, occasionally strange visitors when a hard-pressed District appropriated someone else's power for work farther afield and unfamiliar heavy freight activity. The express locomotives were a depressing sight, and just when one thought that things could get no worse, they did.

Gresley had sought a means of widely applying three cylinder drive rather than two larger outside cylinders, which in some cases would have restricted availability. The three cylinders achieved a more even turning moment, and his simple method of conjugating the outside valve gears had enabled the third inside valve gear to be dispensed with. The alternatives as used at Swindon and Darlington involved the use of inside valve gears, in the latter case with three sets of Stephenson gear driven off six eccentrics. It enabled the building locomotives of

greater power for their size, and it was present in a number of classes with a more general use such as the B17 4-6-0, the D49 4-4-0, the K3, the O2 heavy freight locomotive and the V1 and V3 2-6-2 tanks. Gresley had indeed built small classes of relatively sophisticated design for special tasks, such as his P2 Mikados and K4 2-6-0s. It was effective in normal peacetime circumstances but now, deprived abruptly from 1939 of some of the skilled staff to maintain it, and replacement parts, it now created difficulties for the Running Dept. Some of the staff were returned under the 'Control of Engagements' legislation, but the hours were long, and the blackout, austerity and constant air raids were wearying. The time when the conjugated gear could be used generally and without difficulty at all depots was passing.

His great friend William Stanier had been given the investment to restock the LMSR, and had produced a number of excellent modern, simple but economical designs. The LNER could not afford to do the same, and Gresley operated in three areas, improving the old but not life-expired, building powerful new engines, and

for special work producing small groups of engines. It was difficult for everyone, but one can understand how the LNER was plunged into wartime conditions for which it was less prepared than the other big companies.

The division between the CME and the Locomotive Running or later, Motive Power Department, became obvious. Gresley had built good, powerful and advanced designs but they depended critically on the depots to service, maintain and operate them. Moreover standards varied from depot to depot, and at some they left a great deal to be desired. Not all depots could cope well even before the war, but now the fat was in the fire. One could also sympathise with Edward Thompson, now CME, who disliked the arrangement, and must have wished dearly that he were rid of it. Whether one accepted the conjugation of the drives for the outside valve gears to provide the operation of the middle cylinder valve or not is a matter of engineering opinion. Gresley did, Thompson did not. That accepted, however, the time to do something about it is not in the middle of a desperate war, in which

SEAGULL at the head of the 'Atlantic Coast Express' at Waterloo on June 1st 1948, the first familiarisation run for the A4 crew. Driver Bob Marrable is waiting for the 'Right Away' while an Authority of trilby hats looks on. The tender is adapted A3 corridor No.5325.

at the beginning survival itself seemed doubtful. Not every depot was so fortunate as the Haymarkets of this world, and it has to be admitted that there were depots where even two cylinders taxed the staff almost beyond endurance, and some Gresley engines were not well served or regarded. Nevertheless, Gresley's locomotives were strong and resilient, and although they were often in deplorable condition, they kept going. The A4s were largely left alone.

Once peace had been achieved, the situation surveyed, and remedial action planned, things started to get better. The war had reduced the number of passenger trains but increased the loading. With peace the LNER timetable slowly began to resemble the services if not the speed that it had once carried. Time had moved on, and some of the more delightfully ersatz portion working was not resumed. So it was a very pale shadow of the pre-war LNER that was taken into national ownership at the end of 1947. The A4s had started to return from Doncaster in garter blue with their new numbers, but the original reason for their introduction – the streamliners – had gone forever. Loads were more often double, but the steam locomotive is adaptable, and they coped.

Schedules that in 1946 were slow enough not to have taxed the speed capacity of a B1 4-6-0 were gradually shortened until by 1953 the Eastern, North Eastern and part-Scottish Regions of British Railways could start to boast a reasonable mileage of expresses timed at 60 mph or over start-to-stop. The 44.15 miles from York to Darlington had always been a good stretch of straight, easily graded main line and it was here, especially in the up direction, that drivers could let the engine go without extending the fireman unnecessarily. Schedules had now become quite sharp, and some good performances could be enjoyed. In the south there was always Stoke Bank, where however dismal the uphill work may have been, there was always the prospect of a good gallop and a few minutes regained, provided Peterborough North was ready to receive.

The old LNER had an excellent reputation for the operation of fast freight, and some were no slower than the expresses, it seemed. Some, with a returning top link crew with home and bed/refreshment in mind, and with a Pacific or V2, were decidedly faster! The network was carrying a great number of freight services, some fast but many at low speeds in virtually unbraked trains, running trips from the railhead to concentration points, or long distance heavy hauls. The punctuality of freight services was of a different order to passenger. The slower ones – if they were not cancelled or retimed – might start late and just lose more time.

It is easy in retrospect to apply the lessons learnt after the event. When Arthur Peppercorn became CME, and the design of the A2s and A1s was discussed, clearly the subject of roller bearings was one of the design improvements considered, and as we know, applied. So was the provision of Kylchap exhausts, hopper ashpans and rocking grates, to ease the burden of servicing. The LMSR had learnt and applied the lesson of manganese steel liners to wearing parts such as the axleboxes. Why, I wonder, did British CMEs usually prefer to build new rather than apply the benefits to locomotives with a decade or two of useful running ahead as in Europe? It is a thousand pities that the A4s were not so modified with these, together with the exhaust conversion intended by Gresley in his last year or so. Of course the disruption of nationalisation was in full swing, and Peppercorn was about to retire. It would not have been a cheap task or a quick one, but it would have been time and money well invested, and would have eliminated the majority of the locomotives' failures at a stroke. Even if Peppercorn had little time to act, his successors did, and it was a pity that they concentrated on relatively mediocre standard designs – with two notable exceptions – rather than improve the fleet.

Added to all this were the consequences of deferring wartime relaying, which resulted in numbers of temporary speed restrictions (TSRs) due to the state of the track or relaying. The mixture of widely varying train speeds, together with the effect of TSRs on the slowest and the bottlenecks on the East Coast main line, combined to make smooth traffic regulation and punctual running something much to be desired but seldom enjoyed. The bottlenecks were places where the four track layout was reduced to three or, more usually, two, and I have listened as signalmen carefully calculated their margins to avoid delaying an express before letting a slow freight go. One could not trust the judgement of the driver, who was anxious to get moving (and get home) despite the fire having died back and the falling boiler pressure. With mechanical signalling it was more difficult to handle trains quickly and once a train had passed the protection of the advance starter, it was beyond signal control until it reached the next section's home signal. All that having been said, the majority of disruption was managed successfully by the signalmen, and but for their skill things could have been much worse. Nevertheless, on the footplate or on the train one peered anxiously ahead at certain points on the main line, praying that the signalman had got it right. Usually he had, but one only noticed when he hadn't! As a result, such trains as the Non-stop were often not truly non-stop. It took three tries before I enjoyed a non-stop run from Edinburgh to Kings Cross.

Quite why the LNER had not tackled some of the worse bottlenecks before the war is difficult to understand. With 70 years' hindsight, a layman can see clearly what should have been done in the past, but the officers of the LNER had to judge the best use of funds at the time, bearing in mind the economic conditions of the time. The new designs of the 1930s may have been excellent, but they had a cost, and that capital might have been better employed in relieving, say, the two track sections between Barnet and Potters Bar, and between Digswell and Woolmer Green. These were, and still are in the second case, costly operating obstacles. It is odd that a good investment case was not made for a Government grant once the recovery was under way after 1935; despite having 100 Pacifics, the LNER preferred to build another 14 A4s. But had it taken this logical approach, there have been no Kylchap A4s, no MALLARD, and no world speed record. Perhaps it is as well that the LNER did not always take what seems now to have been the most logical course of action!

It will be understood from the foregoing that delays on the East Coast main line were rife, and the time lost on planned delays had to be added into the running time. The expresses naturally lacked the protection of double block working that the streamliners enjoyed, and drivers of the principal services could no longer count on a clear run. The old LNER used sectional timings related to loading, and to these were added 'recovery margins' to allow for an assessed level of delay. In the 1952 trials with CENTENARY passing times were established with different loads. The timetable planners' practice was to insert blocks of recovery time on specific sections, so that a down express would have 2 or 4 minutes extra between Huntingdon and Peterborough, and again anything from 2 to 6 minutes between Retford and Doncaster. On the up road things were even less distinct. The up 'Flying Scotsman', with 500 tons, was expected to run from Peterborough to Hitchin, 44.4 miles largely against the grade, in 43 minutes. The remaining 31.95 miles, mainly downhill, was expected to take 45 minutes, including 5 minutes recovery time!

The problem for the train planners was to match delay with recovery time. Of course it was impossible. It would have required a weekly amendment to every service as soon as the pattern of TSRs changed, that is, with the CCE changing them at short notice as well! On the Southern Region the practice was to inflate section timings by 2½%, which seemed to work very well. A TSR near the start or termination of a journey was always going to throw the system out anyway but I think, overall, it would have been better. The result was that drivers regulated their train's progress, knowing where the TSRs were, to avoid working their engine – and fireman – unnecessarily hard. The disadvantage was that the carefully calculated times for critical junctions such as Retford or York, or the London approaches, were not observed accurately. Trains were checked by signals or even stopped. Running south of Hatfield was always a matter of luck as the inner

suburban service was then encountered, together with the infamous bottleneck between Barnet and Potters Bar and then south of Finsbury Park the empty coaching stock (ECS) joined in the fun too.

In the 1950s and 1960s the speeds of trains were watched carefully. As the hobby of train timing grew, certain drivers caught the eye, noticed for their relaxed view of speed limits. One can understand the Motive Power authorities' view: either a rule is a rule, or not. The railway organisation was divided into departments that worked together on a clearly understood basis, but relationships inter-departmentally were rigid and formal. What communication existed was formal, and rarely critical. One did not trespass on another department's responsibility, and while this was understandable, it prevented joint action in solving or simplifying something to the benefit of all. It is a great pity that there was not a more

open understanding between the Motive Power and CCE departments regarding speed, since it could have worked to the railways' benefit. As far as the civil engineer was concerned in steam days, straight track itself requires no speed restriction. Whether the riding of the locomotive at speed would necessitate a speed limit due to nosing, hunting, undesirably high rotational speeds or uncontrolled lateral movement in the case of a steam locomotive, was a matter for the CME and the Motive Power Officers to judge. There is also the possibility, albeit rare, of a signalling speed restriction such as the one of 70 mph between York and Darlington from September 1935 to March 1938.

On curved track there is a design speed at which the cant is matched with the centrifugal force. Trains are allowed to exceed that speed by a controlled amount determined by comfort criteria. The rates at which actual and theoretical cant were

GOLDEN EAGLE leaving York during the war with a northbound train of 610 tons. The third man on the footplate is O.S. Nock, whose footplate dress was unmistakable. She has a bad blow on the left-hand cylinder, but in wartime that was the least of the crew's worries. The date is summer 1945 and the A4 has exchanged her A3 corridor tender for an A4 non-corridor No.5667, which she kept for the rest of her time. (W. Hubert Foster)

changed is also governed by comfort criteria: it was not considered a good idea to introduce 'wall of death' sensations to heighten the impression of speed! In practice therefore, the maximum permitted speeds were and are determined by comfort rather than purely safety. For the permanent way engineer, high speed was perfectly acceptable where the track was suitable, such as on Stoke Bank or the York Plain. I remember the CCE of the BR Eastern Region, in diesel days, dismissing the Motive Power Department as being unable to go fast enough to worry him. On a fast stretch, safe running largely depends on the condition of the rails. There are criteria for preventing rails becoming so worn that on curved track, centrifugal force might cause the wheel flanges to mount the rail head *au Sparshatt*, and cause a disaster.

Which reminds me of an amusing story. There was an occasion when, as a colleague related to me, the ganger at Hornsey complained that he was weary of sluing the reverse curves between Harringay and Hornsey back to their correct alignment. They were limited to 50 mph at this time, and constant excessive speeding had moved the track laterally. The CCE had a prehistoric ancestor to today's commonly-used radar gun, called the Everett-Edgcumbe speed recorder. This was a large (heavy) box housing an electrically driven recorder, powered by car-sized batteries, and two clamps attached to the track in question at a set distance apart. It was placed at the lineside at a site to be checked for a week or so.

Three things then happened. Firstly most drivers on seeing or hearing about it became models of good behaviour, and this only took a

few hours to become common knowledge. The operational GN grapevine was far quicker and more effective than the Internet today. Secondly it was used for target practice by passing firemen with a handy lump of coal, and therefore was often disabled. Thirdly, when the record was examined, interpretation was far from easy, requiring special scales and conversion before a speed could be established.

The recordings showed that indeed the general level of speed was excessive, but the wrath of the District Engineer was aroused when one train was recorded at 85 mph! The record of course did not identify trains, and an anxious search of the signalman's train registers was started to identify the train and hence the miscreant. At about 1615-1630, the Non-stop was completing the last few miles of her run, and no doubt with a gleaming A4 in full flight in mind, the wheels of discipline ground round inexorably. When the member of the top link aristocracy was identified and accused, he stoutly denied any such thing, citing the guard's log as evidence. Sure enough, he was vindicated, and the hunt was renewed. In such cases the spirit flags, and the operational railway was very good at obfuscation. Eventually, very eventually, a Cambridge man on a B17 with the following Buffet Express was found to be the culprit!

Countless cases exist of speed limits being exceeded – mainly by A4s – in safety and comfort. It was a great pity that the technical chief officers, the CCEs, the CS&TEs and the CMEs and the Railway Inspectorate did not agree that, over certain sections, the speed limits could be raised for certain trains and locomotives. It would have given drivers a 10%

dispensation in order to make up time. The additional cost of maintenance of the fast sections would have been imperceptible, lost among the more costly congested sections. It would have dispensed with the involvement of engineers of all sorts who had much more important things to do. In practice, it was a margin added by permanent way engineers before drawing attention to the Motive Power authorities that a quiet word was needed.

In looking back both pre-war and post-war, various questions have been asked as they appear over half a century later. One might well wonder what might have been. Whatever the answers, although they may be intriguing, they are unimportant now. The railway industry was slowly changing even then, and has changed since with increasing rapidity. What has not changed is the excellence of a great railway engineer, his great team, and his greatest design – and the great depth and variety of memories they have left us with.

WILLIAM WHITELAW in garter blue livery in early 1948. The location is not given. The date must lie between February and May since that is the only time she carried the temporary number E4, and was coupled to a non-corridor tender, No.5639. (J. Robertson, The Transport Treasury)

CHAPTER EIGHT
Of Men and Machines

Although this is a book about the A4 Pacifics, it would be incomplete without recognising the people that drove, fired and maintained them. The whole of the LNER's advance into high-speed travel in the exciting pre-war period depended entirely on drivers and signalmen, those who supported them, and the skills of their crafts. For example the signalmen were trained, especially on the signalbox telegraph, for the simple reason that otherwise they would have been unable to carry out their work. Doncaster had produced a beautiful locomotive, they invested in it the skills of designer and builder, but it needed the skill and experience of the crew to make it come alive and run to time.

The driver of an express locomotive was presumed to have not only a detailed knowledge of the road but an accurate judgement of speed as well. Of course, their work required them to have some understanding of speed. The successful implementation of the timetable depended on it. However, Driver Payne was expected to step on to the footplate of SILVER LINK on September 30th 1935 at Gateshead, leave Newcastle at 10.00 and drive a new locomotive on a lightweight train over a road which he knew in minute detail. Moreover, he was expected to do so at considerably higher speeds and with considerably less total braking power than had been his experience previously. And he was expected to arrive at Kings Cross at 14.00, on time, an hour earlier than

he was used to, too. In the evening Driver Taylor was expected to do the same, much of the journey in darkness with mainly oil-lit signal lamps to look out for, and without the comfort of AWS. He had the advantage in that on the previous Friday, he had an electrifying introduction to the qualities of the A4 Pacific. The two drivers, however, did all that was required of them, as did their colleagues in the succeeding weeks. Without doubt there were locomotive inspectors riding with the crews at frequent intervals if not regularly, and these may have been checking the speeds until the Flaman instruments were fitted. Gresley's achievement in his A4 was unsurpassed, but it was the senior drivers and firemen who brought them to life and achieved such a wonderful record of reliability and punctuality with it. Later on, the 'West Riding Limited' in particular required men from the No.2 and 3 links to form a new 1A link, and with no previous experience of the streamlined services, to step straight on to an A4 and keep time. So much rested on the ability of largely self-trained craftsmen, with little to assist them in their work and no formal training, a prospect that would never be countenanced today.

Enquiries among those who worked with enginemen confirmed that they were given little or no formal instruction in how to proceed with their craft from entry in their teenage years. Indeed as Norman McKillop has related elsewhere, it was only through their own interest and enthusiasm that enginemen, in their own time, started their own formal instruction that later became known as the Mutual Improvement Classes. They were of course examined in their knowledge of rules relevant to operation, and their accumulated knowledge was tested as they progressed. Their knowledge was gained from their elders and managers, although not all were willing to teach a youngster and not all were very good at it! Experience was slowly gained over a long period; the feel of an engine, its movement, the association of the sounds at different speeds with successful timekeeping, and the lineside – all this came over the years. Speedometers were very rarely in use, watches were a rarity, but at least a clock was visible on most stations. And, of course, the Rule Book was drawn up on the basis that drivers knew exactly where they were at all times, night and day, in all

Bill Hoole poses on the front of SIR NIGEL GRESLEY in old platform 6 at Kings Cross before the SLS Jubilee run on May 23rd 1959. (P.J. Coster)

Tommy Smith of Haymarket poses beside an immaculate DOMINION OF NEW ZEALAND at Haymarket before taking the southbound 'Elizabethan', July 24th 1955. The unique whistle is well illustrated here. (J. Robertson, The Transport Treasury)

weathers. The judgement of speed therefore depended on the sound of the locomotive – principally of the exhaust – and the speed at which the landscape passed, mainly telegraph poles and sleepers.

In fact the period from 1953 to the end of steam was a golden autumn on the East Coast route, especially for us in the south, the years of Ted Hailstone, Bill Hoole, Bill Stevenson, Jim Swan and their colleagues. It was my good fortune to know many of them in the 1950s, and to travel with them in that holy of holies to the enthusiast, the footplate. As I have said in the preface there was no other place to compare with it. A busy signalbox, especially an old manual semaphore box, on a busy day was a enthralling experience, and there was a satisfaction in handling the workload to the best of one's ability, but even that yielded to the footplate. Although one understands the

problems of administration, for someone learning how a railway operated, both the footplate and the signalbox were nonpareils.

The first occasion on which I rode on an A4 was a normal run on a summer Saturday, and I was to meet the engine returning from Leeds with '937up', the 10.00 departure express at Grantham. The journey down was on a 'Parley' with its Grantham top link A1, BONGRACE, toying with a load that would be well within the scope of a 4-4-0. On the up platform at Grantham, with mounting excitement I watched a number of trains arrive from the north, change engines and get away before I heard the familiar high-pitched sigh of a Kylchap exhaust, and over the crowd of passengers, saw SEAGULL sail majestically in from Leeds. I must admit I could hardly believe my good fortune, and it was with a growing sense of unreality that I made my

way through the front brake and climbed over the fire irons through the tender corridor. The A4 was picking up speed on the 1 in 200 with her 13 coaches, some 450 tons.

Then, there was the footplate, just as one imagined it, the fire pulsating strongly, the gauges and fixtures juddering with the effort as we accelerated towards Great Ponton, the regulator about half open and that strange sound of the exhaust heard through the boiler and not from outside. Jim Edwards was the driver and Bill Watts his fireman, with their regular engine. The latter was firing easily and sparingly. The Grantham A1 which had relieved a York 'Green Arrow' on the 8.30 from Sunderland was only just in front, and the regulator was shut as we missed Highdyke's distant. Jim instructed me simply and clearly: 'Sit in the fireman's seat unless he wants it, don't move about, keep out of the way and when you're standing, mind the fall plate. It took off a fireman's heel the other month. Watch what you touch: it's likely to be hot or sharp! Don't lean on the doors, and don't make yourself obvious.' A footplate was a potentially dangerous place.

When the regulator was reopened one could see the power of the draught: the fire was white and the heat from the small firing trapdoor was strong even six feet away. The gauges were easy to read, the position of the regulator in the quadrant easy to see, but one had to stand behind the driver to see the cut-off indicator clearly. SEAGULL's safety valves lifted at 240 psi, and the boiler pressure gauge seemed stuck on that figure. All around were the vivid impressions of great heat, power, and the pervasive smell – perfume indeed to the enthusiast – of hot steam and oil, the smell of burning coal. As Bill examined his fire by using the shovel as a shield, one could see the steam, and perhaps smoke, coming from his overalls. When the injectors were turned on, there was that other unique sound that reminded me of the steam locomotive's ancestor, the domestic kettle, singing as it boiled. Bill was firing to the back corners, the normal method, I learnt, for the Gresley Pacifics, and his skill in flicking the shovel blade through the small trap door was fascinating to watch. No doubt it was hard manual work, but he made it look easy. Then, after a round of firing, to keep the footplate tidy every so often the 'pet pipe' or slacker pipe was used to jet scalding water to clean the floor, and the feet of the unwary.

As the A1 in front cleared Stoke and started to run fast, we ambled through the tunnel and round the curve and began to accelerate as Jim opened the regulator more to ¾, and shortened the cut-off from 30 to about

George Spilsbury of Haymarket beside COMMONWEALTH OF AUSTRALIA at Eastfield depot, June 25ᵗʰ 1955. (J. Robertson, The Transport Treasury)

to the East Coast Pacifics. It all seemed easy.

We caught the Grantham man in front as he slowed for Peterborough, but the running was good from there to Tempsford. There is always a noticeable community feel about the footplate, as crews wave to one another, with a touch on the whistle for good friends. There is also that feeling of being involved in the running of the railway, seeing it at close hand. It was noticeable that when SEAGULL's regulator was opened, the fire turned quickly from a reddish bed of burning coal with a few flames into a furnace full of white flame. Full regulator had been used, giving 235 psi in the steam chests, with 15% cut-off and the A4 had gone like the wind, reaching over 80 mph before we saw that Tempsford's distant was on. From then on we had some distants and not others. Our pace was being dictated by the A1, which in turn was being paced by the second part of the 9.20 from Cleethorpes with the Boston men on their B1 in front of him. Nearer London signal checks became more of a nuisance. It was a good but not remarkable run, 136½ minutes gross for 105.45 miles. The overriding impression, however, was one of ease, of two craftsmen completely on top of their work with a machine that required skill and little effort to make it run fast. Jim was known to the irreverent firemen as 'Economy Edwards', a driver in the best GN traditions. Certainly SEAGULL had not been a drain on the Regional coal figures on this run!

There were two lessons for me. One was that the permanent way might look good, but it felt rough. Clearly a different scale of assessment was needed! Secondly, I found that producing a record of any great accuracy of the run and the handling of the locomotive demanded a concentration and singleness of mind that excluded anything else. And yet there was so much to see and absorb. Especially trying one's hand at firing à la Dick Hardy, to the considerable amusement of the crew. Even on an A4 the firehole door could be hard to hit at first!

Later, I had three runs on the Non-stop, only the last being truly non-stop. The first was with Bill Hoole on GANNET, referred to earlier. We took over from Tom Smith of Haymarket at 75 mph approaching Northallerton, the Kings Cross fireman having taken water at Wiske Moor. The sound of a single chimney A4 was quite different, the noise of the blast being much greater both through the engine and from outside. This caused the level of vibration and noise to increase significantly by comparison with SEAGULL. The single chimney engine was working

22%. By Corby the A1 was away, we had the distant, and the cut-off was shortened to 15%. The regulator was still at ¾, 180 psi in the steam chest and 240 psi boiler pressure. By now the juddering had quietened into a steady rattle, and the movement of the locomotive was a smooth and steady stride with no need to hold on (other than near the doors!). My first reaction was curiosity that an express locomotive, that seemed from the lineside to sail sweetly along, certainly did not confirm that impression in the flesh or, rather, metal. Now, riding on one, it felt at low speeds as though the loco was running on the ballast. But as we accelerated it changed, and the feel of the engine became smoother. Although the fittings rattled, the footplate was very steady, only the occasional poor railjoint causing the engine to shake. One gradually acclimatised and developed 'footplate legs'.

In the fireman's seat with the view ahead, one felt the full thrill of a machine built for speed, accelerating steadily, the motion bearings just visible, circling, the mechanical lubricators clicking away and a faint haze from the chimney lying back over the boiler. I realised immediately the value of the cabside glass that Gresley provided in deflecting the strong slipstream. By now the cut-off was back at 10% and the regulator about 25% giving 150 psi, and the boiler, as ever it seemed, at 240 psi. The speed had now crept up to 86 mph, the fireman was in the driving seat, and the driver was enjoying a cup of tea in front of the firehole door warming his back, although I noticed that he checked every semaphore signal as it passed above the tender. The engine was riding quite steadily, and the exhaust was quiet enough to hear the railjoints, especially the characteristic rat-tat-tat-tat of the eight wheel corridor tender, unique

Bill Nairn of Haymarket stands by HUMORIST at Haymarket on October 12ᵗʰ 1957. The late Charles Meacher told me that Bill was a Sergeant-major in the First World War, and a well polished pair of shoes seems to bear that out! (J. Robertson, The Transport Treasury)

hard, as A4s always seemed to be doing with Bill.

He asked me what I thought of it, and I replied that I thought the track was rough. He disagreed. 'This is good. I'll show you rough track!' In a few minutes we tore through Thirsk at 80, and even now I can recall the sensation as it felt as though the engine had hit a speed hump, bounced in the air and landed back on track. Bill grinned: 'That's rough track!' My hair stood on end. Earlier, in the compartment, he had asked whether I had ever travelled at 100 mph, which I hadn't. Our approach to Grantham was checked to 40 mph at Barrowby Road. GANNET sounded ragged and I had noticed that she had made heavy weather of Cockburnspath Bank with Tommy Smith earlier. I must admit that my hopes of something rather special as we raced down the hill from Stoke had been given up by then. Despite full regulator she had laboured on the climb to Stoke, hardly gaining any speed, passed at 45 mph. But now the controls were left unaltered, full regulator and 30% cut-off, and the sound of the A4 changed from labouring as the gradient changed, and the speed rapidly picked up. What followed then was unforgettable, as we made a headlong flight down the hill, Bill shortening the cut-off slowly, urging the engine faster and faster. Stoke Bank was still laid with jointed track, and the noise of the railjoints going faster than I had ever heard before added to the vivid impression of speed. GANNET accelerated to 75 at Corby,

96 at Little Bytham, and then, the magic 100, held for some miles through Essendine. Although by New England we were now hard on the heels of the Leeds express in front, we overtook it on the Excursion Road at Peterborough. Unfortunately, the Grantham fireman on his A1 had taken water at Werrington and the troughs had not yet refilled, and we had to stop at Huntingdon to take some water. We restarted with Bill determined to arrive on time, and the A4 was being worked flat out through Sandy. I remember my astonishment at noting the time at Biggleswade, and realising that it was one second under two minutes for the three miles from Sandy. I can still hear the sound of the A4's blast reverberating from under the two overbridges just north of Biggleswade!

There were many trips on the Non-stop, normally much less eventful. With Ted Hailstone, first in 1955 on DOMINION OF NEW ZEALAND, then a year later with COMMONWEALTH OF AUSTRALIA, we had two

characteristically fast starts. My principal impressions of the run with No.60013 were the riding of the tender, and the delight in timing two successive quarter-miles at 100 mph. The A4 tender was a heavy vehicle mounted on four closely spaced axles, and at over 80 mph over junctions, climbing through the corridor with its fire irons and the like, possibly rather hot, was not a good idea. It was a bruising experience. It was not made any more comfortable by the number of angle iron stiffeners waiting to be struck with the head. Ted eased the engine a little as we hit the rise to Langford Bridge, but we were through Peterborough in just under 70 minutes, some going. Later he asked me to tone down the top speeds as some of the hierarchy would not approve. His return run was a model of restraint, and we ran in eight BT (eight minutes Before Time).

In some ways the later run in 1955 with Bill Hoole and Jimmy Swan on SEAGULL was more remarkable, for while the time to Peterborough was over 2 minutes more than Ted, the climb to Stoke was probably a record with this load. The average speed from Tallington to Stoke was 73.0, and the minimum at Stoke was 69½ mph. This called for full regulator and 35% up the 1 in 178, 2,200-2,300 IHP, increasing to 2,700 over the last three

Ted Hailstone of Kings Cross stands beside his beloved SILVER LINK at Kings Cross before taking the 'Yorkshire Pullman' north. Date, summer 1955. (P.J. Coster)

Willie McLeod and Fireman G. O'Lara with their regular A4, KINGFISHER, at Haymarket. (J. Robertson, The Transport Treasury)

it must have felt on that Sunday in July, 1938. The sensation of power and speed were vivid in the extreme, and one wished for it to continue. The cut-off was shortened, although the regulator was left wide open, but as we reached 90 well before Little Bytham, the cut-off and regulator were eased to halt the acceleration. Then we braked for a 60mph TSR at Essendine. It was a brief glimpse of what the Kylchap A4s could do when given their head, and it was difficult to realise that we had 425 tons behind, not 225!

There were many other occasions, always exciting but not always so spectacular. By sheer good luck, I was rewarded with an experience that I treasure. I had arranged to travel with Ted Hailstone to York on the summer Saturday 9.40 Newcastle, which then was the lodging turn to Newcastle. Imagine my disappointment on seeing the 'Norseman' racing north through Hornsey behind SILVER LINK – Ted's engine! I made my way to Kings Cross thinking that I had made a mistake, but as the A4 backed down on to the 9.40, a familiar shape leaned out of the cab, and I felt a great deal better. Then I noticed the A4 – the world record holder herself, MALLARD. Ted was disappointed, for an A4's injectors had failed on shed, and the morning's allocated engines moved up one place. SILVER LINK had gone in her place, and we had the A4 for the 10.18 Leeds. So we had Joe Howard and Alf Smith's regular A4, and meanwhile steam was being raised on a fresh A4 for a later duty. 'We've got to manage with this old thing this morning.' Ted said gloomily. Some 'old thing'!

With 14 coaches, 490 tons, we pulled away, and as we passed Holloway, the distant was on. We stopped in Finsbury Park, the cause being a door on the catch. Ted turned to me and slowly grinned. 'Now we'll have a chance to see what she's like' he said. 'Joe Howard's always blowing his trumpet about her, but now we'll see!' We pulled away, and built up speed. Les 'Enoch' Booth was MALLARD's regular fireman, and he was big, strong and very experienced. He had previously selected a pile of large lumps of coal, about the size of the bucket, and opening the main firehole door, used his shovel to place them carefully in the back corners. Then a few more were posted in just under the door, and the main door was closed. A number of men brought up on single chimney engines were unfamiliar with the Kylchap exhaust, which could tear the fire if the engine was worked hard, and Enoch was taking no chances. He continued to fire through the smaller trap door. The A4 seemed to need the 'little but not very often' firing approach. The

miles or so. This was part of a nominally non-stop run of nearly 400 miles. Farther north at Ranskill a tractor driver on a farm crossing had left a trailer load of hay too long in the path of Bert Green with SIR RALPH WEDGWOOD on the up 'Tees-Tyne', and both that and the Non-stop were detained while the shattered remains of the trailer were cleared away. Restarting 11¼ minutes late, Bill Hoole and then Jimmy Swan steadily reduced the arrears to 2¾ minutes at Newcastle, and arrived 1¼ minutes early. The net time was 365 minutes, no less than 25 minutes less than schedule.

The following day was the last run by Jimmy Swan on the Non-stop, and it was a great privilege to ride with him for a while. He was a small man, prematurely white after a serious accident, and he looked sad at the end of a brilliant career. He had the gift of a master driver, namely that of anticipating everything and making it look easy. Good drivers were rarely taken by surprise. I sensed his

sadness, and remembered how keen and expert were the Haymarket men. It must have been sad to retire and leave it all behind.

Bill had declared that he was going to try to top Stoke at 70 mph in the up direction as well, much to the fireman's distress. Bill had replaced Jim Edwards, and had the latter's regular fireman rather than his own. The fireman was not used to this vigorous style of driving and said so, but it seemed to make no difference. The twenty minutes or so that followed were unforgettable. Bill was working SEAGULL hard up from crossing the Trent up through Grantham, but his speed fell short, and we passed Stoke at 66. The tremendous effort up the hill from Newark had been magnificent, but what followed was breathtaking. The controls were left at full regulator and 35% cut-off, and we accelerated down the bank. The vibration of the engine and searing roar of the exhaust went faster and faster, and for a few minutes I realised that this was how

Bill Hoole of Kings Cross whilst driving at speed on SEAGULL. His hand is on the regulator, which is wide open. The main brake valve handle is behind. (P.J. Coster)

Bill Hoole of Kings Cross, in the cab of SEAGULL before coupling on to the 'Elizabethan', September 1st 1955. (P.J. Coster)

needle hardly wavered from 250 psi on the boiler pressure gauge when the engine was pulling.

MALLARD was opened out steadily; by Hatfield she was going well and by Woolmer Green she had certainly got into her stride, with UNION OF SOUTH AFRICA on the 'Elizabethan' now well ahead of us. We were 7 minutes late at Hitchin, but by now MALLARD was going fast. The regulator was about ¾ open, 210 psi in the steam chests and 15% increased to 18% cut-off. As we neared Sandy, the regulator was fully opened as was Ted's habit. From Hitchin to Offord the speed ranged continuously in the 90s, up to 96 at Arlesey, until the Offord curves, taken at 70 mph. The hump through St. Neots seemed to make little difference to the speed. The average speed for the Hitchin-Huntingdon section was exactly 90 mph, the fastest that I had noted. That we were travelling fast was obvious, but the engine didn't seem at all taxed. Having been checked by a 20 mph TSR north of Abbotts Ripton, again MALLARD was worked up to speed again on the falling grades, reaching a maximum of 92 north of Holme. Peterborough had put something ahead, checking us, but after Werrington MALLARD was opened out again, to make a superb climb to Stoke with a maximum of 77 at Essendine and a minimum of 61 at Stoke – with almost 500 tons! Much of it was with 200-215 psi in the steam chests, with the cut-off at 20%, lengthened to 22% with full regulator for the last three miles. My impression at the time was that it was effortless, and it was difficult to believe the speeds I was recording. The sound of the engine simply did not give any suggestion that she was pulling hard, yet she was. It was not until I examined the times and speeds more closely that I realised the quality of the run. Yet all through it 'Enoch' had kept the pressure up to the mark, with little effort. MALLARD impressed me as being a particularly strong and powerful A4.

By Grantham we were now 2½ minutes early, and there was no need to push the engine hard. Retford was, as often the case, not ready, and we were checked, but we stopped at York 2 minutes BT. 'Well, what did you make of her?' I asked. 'Oh she's a good engine, very good, as good as mine' was Ted's reply. Then the admonitory finger, 'Don't you go telling Joe Howard I said that – I'd ever hear the end of it!' MALLARD was just like her sister SEAGULL which I had ridden many times, strong, powerful, free-steaming, and had made the haulage of a fourteen coach express look easy. On another occasion I rode with Jim Edwards on the Non-stop with SEAGULL, and with a clear

Jim Edwards of Kings Cross with his regular A4, SEAGULL, before taking the 'Elizabethan' north. To my regret I cannot trace the name of his fireman. (P.J. Coster)

road with only a few TSRs, the A4 sailed along serenely, running into Kings Cross early with enough coal left in the tender to go to Grantham and back!

My return journey from York was with Fred Dines, one of WALTER K. WHIGHAM's regular drivers, another charming and expert driver who lived on the WR at Hayes. It was a very competent run with DOMINION OF NEW ZEALAND hauling 475 tons. We were waiting for the Non-stop but, surprisingly, York let us go ahead of it. 'I mustn't hang about otherwise I shall delay Mr Heavens on the Non-stop' were Fred's words as we pulled away. We made a good run, running in seven minutes BT, the crew relieved before GOLDEN FLEECE and her regular crew stepped off. Fred dined out on his run among his WR neighbours for some while after.

The up 'Flying Scotsman' in the days when engines were changed at Grantham was often an experience to be savoured, a point made earlier. It was usually worked by a top link crew with their regular engine, but sometimes a pool engine or the roller bearing Gateshead A1 was used. In extremis an A3 or even a Green Arrow could sometimes be seen. Fortunately the timing overall was fairly easy, due to a generous allowance of recovery time south of Hitchin, but the timing from Grantham to Hitchin was fairly tight. All of my experiences, apart from the run with SEAGULL described above, were with single blast engines, and it was clear that a different approach applied. A big fire was built up as the A4 got under way, necessary for the 9-12 minute slog up to Stoke with this heavy load. In less promising weather the cut-off was eased at Stoke Tunnel if the driver

judged that wheelslip was a risk, but once over the summit at Stoke box controls were usually left unchanged until the A4 had picked up speed. That invariably meant a maximum in the eighties or even nineties, sustained for some miles before the PSR at Werrington and then Peterborough, by which time the fireman had picked up his shovel again and was building the fire up once more. The A4 was opened out on leaving Peterborough, and the driver would have been using the short drop from Yaxley to gain as much speed as possible for the 4-5 miles at 1 in 200. Offord was taken with the A4 accelerating through the PSR, and then followed some mighty efforts, again to reach and hold as high a speed as possible over the undulating but largely level road to Biggleswade. Bill Hoole maintained that if the A4 seemed to be heading straight for the church door at Offord D'Arcy the speed was about right. The rate of firing over this section was heavy, and as most of the line from Peterborough to south of Hitchin was across flat country and therefore exposed, a good south-wester could make the load significantly heavier at the drawbar. I remember QUICKSILVER in just those circumstances, going very hard with the water in the gauge glasses looking like dirty milk, and Albert Leech firing non-stop all the way to Stevenage.

There was at one time a signalman at Everton, north of Sandy, who insisted on every jot and tittle of the Signalling Regulations being observed. Everton had particularly long gates on its level crossing which all added up to the onward transmission of absolute block taking much more time than it should. It was very easy, on his shift, to catch the distant or, worse, the home signal. Bill Hoole, working a heavy overnight sleeper back from Grantham, trying to make up the inevitable lateness that was inseparable from the operation of overnight services in steam days, caught the distant each night, and was not amused. However, there is a god of engine drivers, and on the Friday Bill was handed a note to say 'URE 99'. Translated from telegraphspeak it meant 'See that no avoidable delay occurs to 99up' (the 20.00 from Edinburgh). It meant that a VIP was travelling on the train, and it was also Bill's means of retribution. So he determined to have his revenge. In the early hours the A4 came down full blast from the gentle hump at St. Neots and, sure enough, there was the distant on. He made a full brake application, hard enough to bring the train to a rapid stand before the home signal cleared, no doubt disturbing the passengers in the process. The

Jimmy Swan of Haymarket at Waverley with SEAGULL, about to take the southbound 'Elizabethan'. I believe his fireman was Davy Booth, but it was long ago. It was his last up run on a train on which he had achieved many fine runs. The date was September 2nd 1955 (P.J. Coster)

Top left. **A poignant photograph of Jimmy Swan at the regulator of SEAGULL, taking the train up Cockburnspath Bank for the last time. (P.J. Coster)**

Middle left. **With the regulator closed for the restriction through Berwick and over the Royal Border Bridge, Jimmy Swan casts an eye round the cab to see that all is well. (P.J. Coster)**

Bottom left. **The team. Tommy Smith and Bill Hoole together at Waverley with GANNET in the background, July 23rd 1954. (Canon Brian C. Bailey)**

problem disappeared shortly afterwards.

Both Ted Hailstone and Bill Hoole competed hard on this duty, and I remember one of Ted's last runs, when he pushed his beloved SILVER LINK as hard as he could, more than he would normally have done. In a number of runs with SILVER LINK, the doyen of the class never seemed to want for speed, and rode smoothly. The sight of the familiar box at Stoke, followed by a gradually accelerating sound, the exhaust, the railjoints, the vibration in the cab, and the general sound of speed, as each pressed the engine hard down the hill. South of Peterborough the going was harder, and as the gradient became stiffer, the cut-off was lengthened, but there were limits to which they would go in chasing the speed. Then the troughs at Langley, the work eased, and the engine picked up speed downhill into London. But as described earlier, the 'Scotsman' had to run the gauntlet into Kings Cross, and the hard work farther north was thrown away as often as not by poor regulation and the want of an appreciation of priorities. The flagship train of the East Coast main line would be delayed by some less important service, and I felt that this was no way to run a railway in the second half of the 20th Century. Hard work was so poorly rewarded and work of the calibre that I had watched was rapidly becoming unfashionable. The cleanliness and convenience of diesel and electric traction were beckoning, and soon they would be the staple form of traction all over the world's railways. The A4 was a very economical locomotive, but any steam locomotive worked very hard will burn a lot of coal, and without mechanical stokers, it was sheer hard work.

There were many other similar occasions, but I have tried, within the limits of the written word, to bring to life some times and scenes in that special place for the railway engineer and enthusiast, the footplate of an express steam locomotive. It was dirty and uncomfortable; what was hot was too hot, and what was cold was freezing. It was a place for prudence – I remember having to spend a wet evening in Haymarket Depot with a hole in my shoe exactly the same size as the red-hot washout plug that earlier offered itself as a convenient footrest in the cab! It was a dangerous place, because if anything untoward happened, one was involved immediately. A lookout waving his yellow flag, standing by a welder repairing a crossing, for example. As if we could stop 600 tons at 60 mph in a hundred yards! But the Rulebook was clear, a flag waved quickly at a driver was a danger signal, and we braked hard, twice in one run. It led of course to a spirited and frank exchange of views at Kings Cross between the driver and the head steward, the latter speaking with considerable feeling about the difficulties of serving the last lunch as the A4 stood on her nose! I remember too pulling the coal forward in the tender and on one occasion turning to see an arch bridge approaching rapidly! It was also dangerous for other reasons, as I reflected when I looked down into the Tweed from the Royal Border Bridge with no cabside doors to save me if need be. Or as I leaned out of the cab window at Potters Bar to find myself looking straight at Locomotive Inspector Jack Goodhand! But for all that, it was magic and there was nowhere else to compare. I hope that it will bring back very happy memories of days gone by.

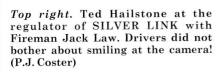

Top right. Ted Hailstone at the regulator of SILVER LINK with Fireman Jack Law. Drivers did not bother about smiling at the camera! (P.J. Coster)

Middle right. Davy Booth firing SEAGULL. He is not firing through the firehole door, but through the smaller trap door, as was invariably the case, to restrict the rush of cold air on to the firebox tubeplate. (P.J. Coster)

Bottom right. The tutorial. Jimmy Allen is driving QUICKSILVER, but Bill Hoole checks the signals for himself as well. The fireman was urged to drive the engine hard, keep time in hand and not to spare the driver, despite his age. It was certain that, when the roles were reversed, the driver would not spare the fireman! (P.J. Coster)

Above left. Bill was unusual in that he would take the shovel, despite his years. He was a fit man, and made light of the work, and still had time to check his fireman and the signals. Here he is firing to QUICKSILVER on the 10.40 semifast to Grantham. (P.J. Coster)

Above right. In the mid-1950s someone had the idea that drivers' names should be displayed on the cabside. Certainly it helped to identify names when the driver was incommunicative or embarrassed, but it soon died out, because the trade union was dedicated to frustrate management and discouraged interest. There were also some who felt that they might become known too well by the public as poor or unfortunate runners. It doesn't seem to be worrying Percy Heavens as he poses on the cab of the 'Elizabethan' at the launching of the scheme. He was an expert driver who shared FALCON with Fred Deeley, reliable and quite capable of running fast when necessary. Again, unfortunately, I have no record of the fireman's name.

Bill Hoole, Albert Leech and the President of the Gresley Society, Allan Garraway, MBE, in an earlier incarnation as Technical Assistant in charge of ATC. DOMINION OF NEW ZEALAND on 31 August 1954 forms their background. (Canon Brian C. Bailey)

Approaching Berwick from the north, with SEAGULL on the 'Elizabethan' on September 2nd 1955. (P.J. Coster)

Alan Pegler, a name inseparable from the story of the Gresley Pacifics, organised a number of special railtours under his company's name, the 'Northern Rubber Specials'. SILVER LINK was one of his favourites and in May 1956 the first A4 was brought to Edinburgh where John Robertson took this superb photograph. I regret that I cannot identify the driver and locomotive inspector but they seem surprised at, presumably, the gallery of photographers attracted by the stranger. Tender: Timken bearing A4 corridor No.5590. (J. Robertson)

The down 'Flying Scotsman' hauled by MALLARD strides effortlessly northwards from New Barnet in early summer 1961. The tender is A3 type corridor, No.5330. (P.J. Coster)

CHAPTER NINE
Work and Performance

We have examined the history of the A4s and the questions that continue to intrigue. I have related memories of footplating on A4s and tried to convey something of the magic in that special place. We now look at the work of the A4s in general, where they worked and on what, and their unique record of high speed exploits. But above all, a railway company requires of its locomotives that, apart not being excessively costly, they should be economical and reliable, and competent to deal with those tasks for which they were built.

The work of the A4s was confined to the East Coast main line to a much greater extent than their ancestors, the A1s and A3s. They did not work regularly on the GC Section, and only worked over the Waverley route and Newcastle-Carlisle occasionally. As Heaton and Neville Hill shared the Leeds Northern route through Ripon, an A4 was an infrequent sight both pre-war and post-war. From Haymarket they worked to Glasgow, Perth and Aberdeen along with the A3s. With the introduction of diesel traction, and the 'Deltics' in particular, those that were not withdrawn were sent to Scotland. Here, their work consisted mainly of the Glasgow-Aberdeen expresses, together with less important passenger and the occasion parcels or fast freight on their former stamping grounds. It was from these routes that the class was eventually withdrawn.

Although they were designed in haste in some respects, one would never have suspected without knowing their history. They were intended at first purely for the 'Silver Jubilee'. Judged by the parameters of the tractive effort formula, they were an improved A3, but they were considerably more powerful. A single chimney A3 could be expected to develop 1,700-1,800 IHP, whereas a single blast A4 could develop 2,600-2,700 IHP. The addition of a double Kylchap improved both outputs by a further 400 HP or so. Many parts of the design were probably started whilst the more contentious parts were being debated. In retrospect it should have been no surprise that a steam locomotive built for one purpose should be suitable for another. Their greater power and economy led to them supplanting the A3 as the LNER's principal express locomotive. It is worth making the point that whenever their economy in fuel and water was measured, it was

never less than good, and often unsurpassed.

They were built for the streamliners, and a dozen or so would have comfortably covered the four diagrams. Gresley was careful to ensure that the class were kept in good condition, and their shopping mileage was 80,000. When it was realised that they were superior to the existing Pacifics on heavier duties, more were built for general duties, and with the company in financially murky water, it was not surprising that there was pressure to work longer diagrams and get more work out of the fleet. After the war the class was generally occupied on the heaviest express duties, assisted by the newer post-war Pacifics. The wheel had turned full circle, since there were no lightweight flyers for the A4s, but plenty of mundane 450-550 ton East Coast expresses in their place. Once the Peppercorn A1s became more numerous, they tended to displace the A4s on some of the expresses, although drivers favoured the 'Blue 'uns' as better riding locomotives. As has been mentioned already, Gateshead preferred the new A1s, and the impression was given that A4 maintenance was not so attentive. Gateshead relegated its A4s normally to lesser duties until the advent of the 'Talisman', and it seemed to have more than its fair share of A4s that could be unreliable at times. The introduction in 1956 of A4 haulage on the 'Talisman' was followed with more than usual interest to see how they would cope. The Gateshead A4s rose to the challenge and worked the train well. It was significant that the Gresley Pacifics were used on the lighter and faster duties, no doubt because the riding was easier and the grate was smaller.

The conversion to double Kylchap made an enormous difference, and some of the best running of the class was witnessed then. Within a few years the work of the A4s on the East Coast main line was finished, and the surviving members of the class moved to Scotland, working the Aberdeen-Glasgow services as well as those routes north of Edinburgh. With the introduction of diesel traction the survivors were used on a variety of excursions and specials. Occasionally they had worked well outside their sphere, such as over the GC section, but now they visited such unusual places as Exeter, Weymouth, and even Blackpool.

There were in fact few depots that housed A4s. Kings Cross, Gateshead and Haymarket had most of the fleet for most of the time but Grantham, Doncaster and, strangely, Heaton also had a number pre-war and during the war. Afterwards, Doncaster and Heaton lost theirs, and then Grantham, too. Four went from Kings Cross to Grantham for the summer of 1957, but returned in the same year. When the diesels came in numbers and the great throwaway started, those not withdrawn went to St. Margarets, at the opposite end of Edinburgh, no doubt to the accompaniment of the sounds of former drivers at Haymarket turning in their graves! From there some went on to St. Rollox and Ferryhill. A number went to New England, but only as a halfway house to withdrawal. It was a very sad sight to see the elite of the LNER and its successor stored out of the way at New England, Gateshead and St. Margarets. Indeed the Scottish depots seemed to have little room for them and Pacifics were outbased at such strange places as Galashiels, Dalry Road, Bathgate and Bo'ness Sidings. I remember seeing the sad sight of 'Magnificent Merlin', dirty, cold and unwanted at the back of St. Margarets, and wondering what Bill Stevenson would have said about it.

Over the length of their history it must be admitted that reliability, for the middle period of their existence, was the least of the attributes of the A4s overall. Until the outbreak of hostilities, given good maintenance, they were fine. Once their weaknesses had been addressed in the 1950s they became, if anything more reliable than in their prime. What could not be removed by modification could be intercepted without failure on the road. But in the middle decades of the 1940s and early 1950s, it was not the same.

Moving to the performance of the A4s on specific services, the 'Silver Jubilee' ran for just under four years, 2½ years with seven coaches, 225 tons tare, and 1½ years with eight, 254 tons. The seven coach train had the fastest timing to York, but the first and only intermediate stop was at Darlington and the load was well within the A4's capability. In just under four years there were only 16 failures recorded, a wonderful record of reliability especially when one considers that it involved well over 200 miles of high speed, with no roller bearings, just plain bearings, oil lubricated. The locomotives were lubricated with special oil with lower viscosity at running temperature, known as 'Jubilee oil'. The A4 ran 536 miles in 24 hours with comparatively rare exceptions, much of it averaging 70mph, and the record of punctuality was superb.

The train ran without failure for just under a year as mentioned before QUICKSILVER had to be relieved at York by a poppet valve NER Atlantic. This was unsuitable and was exchanged at Doncaster for the pilot, hopefully a Pacific. In fact, the only substitute readily available was an Ivatt Atlantic No.4452. Driver Samwells made a tremendous run with the magnificent veteran with a net time of 139 minutes for the 155.95 miles, an average speed of 67.3 mph. Would that someone had recorded it!

Of the 16 failures, 12 resulted in the pilot Pacific or Atlantic being substituted at one of the principal stations. Four times Nemesis struck out in the country requiring a nearby pilot locomotive to come to the rescue. The remaining seven were more colourful to those of us looking back. On April 14th 1937 Durham had nothing more than a G5 0-4-4T No.1752 to take over the streamliner from SILVER FOX for the remaining miles to Newcastle, a sight heartily enjoyed by the Tyneside railway fraternity and not calculated to improve the LNER's image there. In 1938, first of all Driver Samwells had to exchange the comfort of SILVER LINK's cab for Ivatt Atlantic No.4403, piloting sister No.4400 from Peterborough to Kings Cross. As if that were not a sight for sore eyes, six weeks later Driver Burfoot had a trip down memory lane in taking GNR D2 4-4-0 No.4379 as pilot to another Ivatt Atlantic, No.3293, QUICKSILVER having failed. The Ivatt Atlantics took over on six occasions and with a light load, in the right hands, could be relied on as very effective substitutes.

Aside from the moments of light relief, the original quartet dominated the train. The statistics for the 'Silver Jubilee' quoted in the RCTS Survey gave the total number of runs as 1,952. Of these the three London A4s worked 1,429 and the Gateshead A4 was called upon 80 times. 22.6% of the turns were worked by other A4s. The record of the first A4, SILVER LINK, was outstanding. Of a total of 4,004 runs made by the three streamlined trains, she worked 608, 15.2%. The mileage per failure in traffic was 30,800, good for the UK. Half a century later, on the Waterloo-Exeter service this was twice, even sometimes thrice the mileage that contemporary main line diesels had descended to.

Analysis of the records of performance shows that at high speeds and/or high power outputs,

the accuracy of the recording is vital. Distance, time and speed must correlate exactly as a basis for more complex calculations of such as acceleration, and if they do not, the inaccuracies stand out. At higher speeds and power outputs, seconds matter, as does the exact point at which time is recorded. I was one of many who logged locomotive performance in steam days, but it required a very rigorous approach that eluded many, certainly myself, for various reasons. For example, it was difficult to measure the speed *at* a station, since mileposts were often obscured by sidings, if not missing altogether. Railjoints were not exactly 60ft apart due to the presence of S&C layouts. Speeds measured before or after a station were somewhat misleading, causing an inexplicably high estimate of power developed well beyond the known ability of the locomotive.

Looking at the amazing debut of SILVER LINK, it is clear from the analysis that, no doubt at the urging of Groom, Taylor pressed the A4 significantly harder from Wood Green onwards. As mentioned earlier, a time of 4 minutes 42 seconds at Finsbury Park, however, hardly implied any hanging around on his part! The A4 then appeared to be worked at a steady 2,000 IHP, (depending on the assumptions used in modelling the performance), increasing to 2,200 IHP as the speed rose, until Gresley intervened. That would equate to 20-22% cut-off with a fully opened regulator. Out of curiosity, in the Appendix for comparison I have extended the run additionally to Grantham as if it were unchecked by the 13.40, using a similar power output on the climb to Stoke.

Apart from the trial run of September 27th 1935, the drivers achieved a remarkably high and uniform standard of running, as examination of Appendices E and F show. There were occasional variations in high speed but the consequences on the overall journey time were small. Occasionally a driver would set about arrears of running with vigour and the results were spectacular – for example when the construction of a new underbridge at New Barnet imposed a heavy but short TSR, even on the 'Silver Jubilee'. Circumstantial evidence points to June 17th 1936 as the date when Driver Peachey took Gateshead's SILVER KING north, QUICKSILVER having been detained at Gateshead for attention. Passing Potters Bar some 15 mph slower and three minutes behind, Peachey set about recouping time on the long descent to Offord and on to Peterborough. And he did it in style! Before Stevenage the A4 was up to 90, 96 at Hitchin, and no less than

five times did she exceed 100 mph before passing Peterborough 2½ minutes early! The maximum at Arlesey was 103, followed by surges up to 102 at Sandy, 103 at Tempsford, 100 after St. Neots, and remarkably, at the dip through Holme. The speed across the Stilton Fen was unchecked and the speed was maintained at 90 up to Fletton. The Hitchin-Huntingdon time was 17 minutes 44 seconds against a scheduled time of 19 minutes, an average of 91.2 mph. SILVER KING sailed on at rather a steadier rate, arriving at Darlington just under 7 minutes early, 10 minutes under schedule net. It was one of the fastest, if not the fastest run on the down 'Jubilee' on record. I have often wondered whether Gateshead were very diligent about replenishing their A4's Flaman recorder before use! The Flaman would continue to indicate speed, but unless a special paper roll was loaded, there would be no record to be scrutinised.

The fastest net time belongs to none other than SILVER LINK, which on another occasion suffered more delay than her sister, but the net time was no less than 10¾ minutes under schedule. The net time to York allowing for the 'Coronation's' stop was 148 minutes, 9 minutes less than that schedule. The speeds were not so spectacular, but the climb to Stoke, as defined by the time for the 15.25 miles from Tallington to Stoke box, was the fastest on record. Since the run was timed by Allen himself, I am surprised that he did not realise the exceptional nature of the climb. The troughs were taken at a rising speed of 74 mph, followed by no less than 92 at Tallington and 90 at Essendine, falling to 80½ before Corby and recovering to 82, and 76½ at Stoke, and average of 84.7 mph!

A third run bears mention, although the passing times were recorded only to the nearest half minute and the details of running were comparatively few. On December 28th 1938 QUICKSILVER was replaced on the up journey at Peterborough by Ivatt Atlantic No.4446, so in the evening Driver Ovenden had the good fortune to find that the replacement was no less than Gateshead's Kylchap A4 CAPERCAILLIE. The train was delayed at Kings Cross and then badly delayed further at Hatfield and Hitchin by 15 mph TSRs. Ovenden seems to have used the engine's power in making an immediate and rapid recovery. The train was on time at Newark and Retford, but ran into further signal delays at Doncaster and Selby, making the train 3 late passing York. By this time of course the load was eight coaches, 270 tons, and the permanent speed restriction had been lifted to 90 mph north of

York. The speed over the Plain of York rose to 90 mph and more, and that speed was held up to the Darlington stop, where the arrival was punctual. The continuation to Newcastle was 1 minute early despite more signal delays and a TSR at Lamesley.

The recorder claimed a maximum of 94 at Arlesey and 104 mph at Connington, but unfortunately no details were given of accurate passing times to verify the speeds claimed, particularly the latter. The time quoted from Huntingdon to Peterborough certainly does not suggest so high a speed, at least without some elucidation. Also few details of the climb to Stoke were given. The overall Peterborough-Grantham section time was 22½ minutes, and the minimum at Stoke was given as 75 mph. The Peterborough-Grantham time was therefore very similar to the run by Bill Sparshatt with SILVER LINK in 1936. A net time is not quoted, and 65 years later it is not easy to estimate with so little information. The TSRs could have not cost less than three minutes, and the signal delays seem to have caused at least 4 minutes loss of time, so I have quoted 188 minutes in the appendix, but the true value may have been even less. Clearly this was an exceptional performance that deserved to be recorded more accurately.

When one turns to the 'Coronation', the increase in the work expected of the A4 is obvious. The train was 100 tons heavier in the summer months at first than the 'Silver Jubilee', and the A4 had to run nearly 800 miles in two days to complete the diagrammed duty. The coaching stock was not only heavier but more resistant than the 'Silver Jubilee' as mentioned earlier. There were two catering vehicles, each with axle-driven electrical equipment, for example. The 'Coronation' was remarkable not only for its speed and reliability, but the performances of individual engines. The most outstanding was that of No.4491 COMMONWEALTH OF AUSTRALIA, which worked 48 out of the first 51 trains. There are few detailed records of running by the 'Coronation'. In 1937 a trip to between the capitals was expensive and people could not take leave so easily mid-week. One was the inaugural run was handled by one of the senior Gateshead drivers, Tom Dron, on COMMONWEALTH OF AUSTRALIA, and he set the fastest net time on record to York. It was his first run on a streamliner apart from the test run with SILVER KING, and with a very fast start he passed Finsbury Park in just over 5 minutes with the heavier train, and then was 5 seconds inside the very tight timing

of 18½ minutes to Hatfield. He was only 1½ minutes early on the 157 minutes schedule, but had a TSR at Grantham and had eased the engine north of Doncaster. The net time was 154 minutes, but I feel that Allen was over-harsh and 152½ would have been fairer.

O.S. Nock had a return trip to Edinburgh which again circumstantial evidence indicates as taking place on August Bank Holiday 1937. The down run was with EMPIRE OF INDIA, credited by Nock to Driver Auger. Despite a clear run and good speeds, due to a slow start the A4 was a minute late at Peterborough, but by virtue of a mighty effort up to Stoke and a fast run down to Newark he gained 2 minutes on schedule. Selby wasn't quite ready, but again with good speeds he arrived exactly on time.

The up run was with Driver R. Walker, another of Gateshead's senior drivers making his first run with a streamliner, on COMMONWEALTH OF AUSTRALIA. Walker was the driver involved eleven months previously in the astonishing run by Ivatt Atlantic No.4404, which replaced the failed A3 TRIGO at Grantham on the heavy 585 tons 13.20 Kings Cross-Edinburgh. Notwithstanding the fact that he was a NE man, and as such had a limited experience of the GN locomotive, and that he was so grossly overloaded, he cut two minutes from the 90 minute schedule to York, and would have happily gone on to Newcastle unaided if it were left to him. Fortunately C.J. Allen was on the train and, famously, he had to check three times to see whether the Atlantic had been replaced or piloted, or the load reduced, such was his incredulity. He was honest enough to say that if the log had been sent in to him, he would not have believed it. Of such stuff were our forebears made.

The up run was fairly straightforward but by Doncaster, Walker was 2 minutes down. The speeds at Ranskill and Carlton were high, but nothing compared with the mighty dash down Stoke. Breasting the summit at 64½, with 15% cut-off and almost full regulator, he let the A4 go, touching 106 twice and maintaining over 100 mph until close to Werrington troughs. It was one of the great sprints down the famous bank. I hope that the authorities treated it as a first offence! It is worth pointing out that this feat of speed took place at about 21.00 in the gathering gloom, albeit with double block working but with oil-lit signals and without the protection of AWS!

Train timing as a hobby had far fewer devotees in the 1930s, but one described by Allen as the most careful and reliable that he knew was R.E.L. Charlewood, an officer of the LMSR.

Charlewood no doubt used his travel privileges regularly, and he recorded 20 runs down to York on the 'Coronation' that give us a better picture of A4 performance. The slowest run was 161 minutes 41 seconds, but the net time was much less, and the slowest net time was 159 minutes. The fastest net time was 154 minutes. Although he recorded two maxima of over 100 mph, the schedule could be kept without exceeding 90 mph. The climb to Stoke in five cases out of 20 was completed at 70 mph or more, the remainder achieving the high 60s. In the up direction he recorded 17 runs from Newcastle to Kings Cross. Of these one suffered a loco failure, but the latest arrival otherwise was only 4½ minutes late. The fastest net time was 231½ minutes, 5½ minutes BT. Charlewood's timings give us a picture of a service that was fast, reliable, and one in which the running was unusually consistent by comparison with normal and later services.

There were of course some exciting moments when the speed rose to three figures. The long descent from Langley to the banks of the Ouse at Offord was a tempting means of regaining some time. Cecil J. Allen several times quoted a number of high speeds, and we rely on his experience in accepting their authenticity without fuller supporting evidence. No.4491 COMMONWEALTH OF AUSTRALIA made a leisurely start, losing 2½ minutes, but then the driver let rip with two 100 and a 101 mph maxima, and passed Peterborough ½ min early despite having observed the Offord PSR scrupulously. No.4497 GOLDEN PLOVER averaged 102.5 mph from Hitchin to Biggleswade, twice touching 105 mph in the process. Nearer Peterborough there was the descent from Abbotts Ripton to Stilton Fen, six miles or so before the PSR over the Fen itself. The same A4 reached 107 mph on this bank on another occasion. In the southbound direction the descent of Stoke bank was always fast, but tightly timed so that high speed had to be sustained to gain time. Driver Walker's run referred to earlier was a classic example. Another involved Haymarket's No.4497 GOLDEN PLOVER yet again, with a top speed of 104 mph, but more importantly, an average of 100.6 mph from mileposts 95 to 80.

The 'Coronation' ran 1,084 times in its short life, and its punctuality record was 57.5% early or right time and 81.5% if one includes up to 5 minutes lateness. For steam traction and a 400 mile run, the latter figure is very good. When we move on to the third service, however, 'The West

Riding Limited', we find that comparatively little attention has been given to its operation. Perhaps familiarity with the first two was the reason. The press trip ran from Leeds Central to Barkston, which gave little opportunity for displaying the A4's ability to accelerate and run fast. Two A4s were allocated to Top Shed for the duty, Nos.4495 GOLDEN FLEECE and 4496 GOLDEN SHUTTLE. It was remarkable that these two A4s accounted for 27 and 29% respectively of the 968 times the train ran, a total of 56% altogether.

The service ran for a month less than two years and in considering the record of its running, the shorter distance and the freedom, in particular, from overheating, are clearly interlinked. The up train travelled in the slipstream of the 'Silver Jubilee', 15 minutes behind, and had a good run. The down train departed Kings Cross at 19.10 and had a more perilous run, jousting with a couple of outer suburban semi-fasts in the first 20 miles, and the evening freights north of Stoke. As far as is known, there was only one failure on the train during that time, when K3 No.1166 was summoned to replace No.4489 DOMINION OF CANADA at Carcroft. The A4 borrowed on the following day for the up service was Doncaster's four week old No.4468 MALLARD, which was the only time she worked one of the streamliners: sister No.4903 PEREGRINE did not work any at all. Copley Hill depot had a pair of A1s for the 'Queen of Scots' Pullman service, which were also used as pilots for the 'West Riding Limited', and on four occasions an A1 worked the train. Three of Doncaster's A1s and A3 No.2750 PAPYRUS were also used either from Leeds or as replacements, probably the former. One of the A1s was No.4473 SOLARIO, which had the distinction of working two of the three streamliners. The 'green engines' as Gresley called them, ran well, but were always replaced by an A4 for the down service. On her last appearance A1 No.2555 CENTENARY actually ran in one minute early.

There were two unusual incidents when the engine on the down train failed at Kings Cross just beforehand, and had to be replaced. In the first, the most suitable replacement at very short notice was Top Shed's brand new V2 No.4789, which only lost four minutes. In the second the replacement was none other than FLYING SCOTSMAN. Most of what we know about the service came from C.J. Allen's monthly articles in *The Railway Magazine* for November 1940. The train was handled by Kings Cross men, but a new 1A link was formed there, similar to the old Pullman link that existed between

1926 and 1935. The six sets of men came from the No.2 and No.3 express goods link, and considering they had no experience of high-speed running required on the streamliners, their work was remarkable. Ten recorded runs were published. Two of the four down runs were late and two early: all suffered signal checks at Doncaster and TSRs, and one had got the earlier and slower 17.50 train in front as far as Wakefield. The incidence of TSRs seems variable, for one run had no less than five and another had none.

As mentioned earlier, due to failure of GOLDEN FLEECE on the Sunday 18.10 down at Doncaster, the first up service was hauled by No.4492 DOMINION OF NEW ZEALAND, which was actually a Haymarket locomotive at the time. In fact the service was worked by Haymarket and not Kings Cross throughout the first week! It was Driver Long's first run on a streamliner, and he can hardly have had much experience on a fast service with an A4 before. Perhaps his previous years on fast freight with lively K3 2-6-0s had prepared him for the sensations of high speed running. He passed Doncaster 3½ minutes late due an understandable caution with the restricted road from Leeds. From here it is clear that whatever lack of familiarity he had, Driver Long had worked out how to make an A4 run fast. He made a magnificent run, with 100 mph at Crow Park, down the bank from Markham to the Trent valley, topped Stoke at 71-72, and reached 101 down the hill. The very best of a superb run was the climb to Stevenage, started with 93½ at Biggleswade and finished at 81½ mph, an average speed from Sandy to Stevenage of 89.43 mph. As Allen remarked, it was a time that would take some beating. A remarkable maiden trip and his time over the adverse road to Stevenage was never beaten by steam.

Interestingly, the only up run on the 'West Riding Limited' by Gateshead's No.4901 CAPERCAILLIE, on July 25th 1938, was logged. It suffered three TSRs and signal checks inevitably at Doncaster, and was 5¼ minutes late at Grantham. No time was regained by Driver Waite down the bank and only a little to Huntingdon, but then No.4901 was opened out, reaching 95½ on the level at Tempsford, and averaging 90.25 from Huntingdon to Hitchin, uphill! Driver Waite was also in charge of No.4493 WOODCOCK when, despite four TSRs and a signal check, he arrived 1½ minutes early. A feature of the running of all three streamliners was the high speed reached, not only on the down at Arlesey or the up at Essendine, but on the level and gently rising grades

approaching Stoke and Stevenage banks, the brief favourable sections down to Connington, Claypole, Carlton and on the level and clear roads between Doncaster and Darlington.

Although I have concentrated on the streamliners, the A4s almost immediately began to work with the A3s on the slower and heavier East Coast expresses, firstly as positioning turns, and then as normal duties when there were enough locomotives to cover and stand by for the streamliners. Naturally these duties attracted less attention than the high-speed services, but the standard of the A4s' work was good. O.S. Nock and C.J. Allen recorded some splendid running with heavy trains, and it seemed that the A4's capacity for speed was unaffected by the load on the tender coupling. The new 'Flying Scotsman' train introduced in 1938 weighed 503 tons tare. A special ceremony was devised whereby the preserved Stirling Single, No.1, hauled a vintage train from Kings Cross to Stevenage, the passengers then transferring to the new train for the journey on to Grantham behind No.4498 SIR NIGEL GRESLEY. The A4, blessed with an easy start for once, quickly worked her 14 coach train up to 90 mph twice, and the minimum at Stoke was 53 mph. I daresay the top speed would have been higher but for the weight of bowler hats in the train!

Nock travelled on the footplate of No.4902 SEAGULL, which he described as one of the most puissant locomotives he had ridden on in Britain. Having ridden on her many times I can endorse his view. The load was 480 tons and the start a fast one; speed was still nearly 60 mph before signals intervened at Potters Bar. With the regulator less than half open and 16% cut-off, SEAGULL reached 95 at Arlesey, and a powerful climb to Stoke was spoilt by signals down to 10 mph before Little Bytham station, the minimum being 48½ mph at the summit.

Perhaps the most remarkable pre-war performance was recorded by Allen but never published by him, and it is thanks to O.S. Nock that we saw it later. It was on the 'Flying Scotsman', with Driver Dalrymple of Gateshead on No.4490 EMPIRE OF INDIA. In steam days train formations could be varied, and were. At this busy time the 14 coach train was strengthened to 17, 593 tons tare and 635 tons gross. A minute or so was lost in getting the train going, and there was no point in extending the A4 and pulling at the fire when a perfectly good high-speed section beckoned beyond the Chilterns. The maxima at Arlesey and Connington were 91 and 85 mph, and Stoke was cleared at 48 mph. The running beyond was steady and fast, and the train arrived at Newcastle, after two scheduled stops, 4 minutes late. A signal check and heavy station work at York cost 6-7 minutes.

With the war came the end for the streamliners, and the normal loadings increased rapidly. After over six years in declining mechanical condition, hauling huge loads, things began to ease. In 1946 came the test run with SILVER FOX, with a very light load, to assess the suitability of the track for the restoration of pre-war speed limits. With the lighter loading the speeds were at times even higher, especially north of York where the A4 maintained over 90 mph on a gently rising road. Indeed the Coronation schedule from York to Newcastle with cut by no less than seven minutes. On the up run, the time was two minutes faster still with some 25 miles at 90 mph over the Plain of York. Driver Kitchener was allowed to reach 102 mph on the descent of Stoke Bank, a welcome but solitary glimpse of the past. There were three stops intermediately, Grantham, York and Newcastle, and the schedule laid down for the sections was 98, 77, 77, and 124 minutes, 376 minutes total running time northbound. The southbound timings were similar. The A4 gained ten minutes going north and no less than 20 coming south. A signalling colleague saw the train, and remembers the running time from Huntingdon to Sandy, 9 minutes for just over 14 miles, 95 mph. Block times are only approximate, but clearly the A4 was going fast. C.J. Allen was on the train, and noted an average of 82.5 for the 52.3 miles from Holme to Welwyn Garden City, and 87.7 from Tempsford to Three Counties.

From then on, it was a long while before we were able to experience the sight and sound of Gresley's A4s at speed. The Plain of York, Stoke Bank, and the descent from Stevenage to Offord were the principal sections where one could enjoy the experience of express steam locomotives at speed, as they were designed for. Often it was thanks to the drivers who believed in running hard to recoup time lost through delays. That is not to say that they were necessarily better at their craft, for there were men of great skill in the senior links. Perhaps the appreciation of railway enthusiasts stimulated them, for it is good if someone takes a keen interest in one's work and enjoys the exercise of great skill. But the protection of double block had gone, and the level of delay was greater as the CCE attacked the backlog of relaying and ancillary track works, and expresses were checked by conflicting movements and slow-moving freight trains. The

situation was greatly worsened by the presence of the various bottlenecks and other shortcomings of the main line. It has to be said, too, that the timetablers were no help. It seems that with nationalisation the industry settled for an easy, mediocre and unchallenging life, and this was certainly apparent in the timetables set. The East Coast operators seemed to be determined not to set mile-a-minute schedules if they could possibly help it. The old joke about the Midland Railway's Society for the Prevention of Cruelty to Locomotives was no longer funny.

When the permanent speed limit was restored to 90 mph, drivers could let their locomotives run fast once more, at least for some sections. Although the timetable contained relatively heavy loads, it required little more than 70-75 mph on an average day to keep time comfortably. Now and again there would be a demonstration of what could be done when the men, the engine and the opportunity came together. Performances of pre-war quality began to appear in the monthly performance articles.

One who came to people's notice was Edward Charles ('Ted') Hailstone, a previously mentioned North Countryman who had transferred to Kings Cross from the West Riding, and because of his seniority, soon reached the Top Link. When regular manning was instituted, he was given the first A4, SILVER LINK, to share with Driver Arthur Ferrington, also mentioned earlier. The first A4 was always highly regarded at Kings Cross where pre-war memories of a locomotive built and maintained in superlative condition lingered on. Ted was very proud of 'his' A4 and there was a deal of banter among the crews as to the attributes of their charges. He could be intolerant and gruff – or worse – if 'his' A4 was not available, or the work he had requested had not been completed. Somehow one felt that a request sounded very much more like an instruction at times! Yet he could be kindness itself to anyone interested and eager to learn – strict, yes, but kind.

George Carpenter explained to me how Ted had been put on his mettle by another colleague, Alf Smith, who had taken the very heavy Sunday evening 1800 from Kings Cross to Leeds and Bradford up Stoke Bank from Peterborough to Grantham in an exceptional time. Ted was determined to put Alf in his place, and I can imagine there was a gleam in his eye that evening. With SILVER LINK hauling 560 tons, he swept into Peterborough in 79 minutes, 11 minutes early despite 2 minutes delay from a TSR. After waiting time for more than a quarter of an hour,

the train got under way and, notwithstanding this big load, the A4 thundered over Stoke summit at 53 mph with the regulator wide open and 25% cut-off. The time to Grantham was 4¾ minutes inside the 37 minutes schedule. The continuation to Doncaster was slightly easier, 52¼ minutes, 8¾ minutes early, making a total of 24½ minutes gained, or 28 net. He always seemed to have very good firemen, and on this run it was Jim Wilson, one of the best. No doubt the news went down the grapevine rapidly at Top Shed. One might deplore the waste in making such an effort, but to an engineer it was magnificent, and no doubt the driver had a satisfied smile!

In September 1953 Alan Pegler, with Messrs. Bailey and Smith, organised two special trains using the preserved Atlantics, GNR Nos.251 and 990. The two drivers were none other than Ted Hailstone and Bill Hoole, the latter recently having joined the Top Link, with their regular firemen Jim Wilson and Albert Leech. The Atlantics ran from Kings Cross to Doncaster, and the following week worked up from Leeds to Kings Cross while Ted, with SILVER LINK, worked the return duties in each case. The whole programme, even by today's standards, was amazing and worked to perfection giving many happy memories. Many could hardly believe their eyes as the two Atlantics were run-in on the 1700 to Peterborough and Cambridge days beforehand. The fact that two of Top Shed's most popular drivers (with the enthusiasts) were in tandem gave the whole exercise extra spice.

It was clear that after a wonderfully nostalgic down trip, on the first up run Ted was going to give us something to remember. Our load was 425 tons, and the anticipation grew in the train as SILVER LINK roared up to Stoke. Then came a prolonged dash down the hill, with all but 90 mph from Corby Glen to Werrington, 17.6 miles and a maximum of 97.5 mph, a fine effort. It would have been higher but for the intervention of Higher Authority, to the driver's disgust, not for the last time! The time from Doncaster to London was 147 minutes 7 seconds. On the second weekend, there was better to come. The down run, now with 410 tons, was made in driving rain on a dull Sunday afternoon, and I can recall an immaculate SILVER LINK streaking north at a speed not normally seen in the North London suburbs.

It was a pattern of Ted's driving that he used the falling gradient from Langley troughs to Offord to run fast in order to get some time in hand. In so doing, he used about ¾ regulator with a shortish cut-off until reaching the level near Sandy, whereupon he would open the regulator fully to use the full boiler pressure, 20-30 psi extra, to maintain speed. At more than 90 mph, to the uninitiated, this seemed alarming to put it mildly. It must have seemed alarming too to the Inspector who had been despatched to the footplate at 97 mph to tell Ted to desist! Remember that at this time the A4 had no speedometer, although I am sure the driver had a good idea of his speed. This was only a preliminary, however, to a tremendous climb to Stoke fully in the tradition of the streamliners, but with a much heavier load. The speed remained in the high 70s for three-quarters of the distance, and the summit was passed at 70 mph. The power developed by SILVER LINK from Peterborough northwards increased to 2,400-2,500 IHP for over ten minutes, possibly more up the final three miles at 1 in 178, a maximum effort for a single chimney A4. These two runs, together with performances on the 'Tees-Tyne Pullman' and the Non-stop marked the resumption of running – occasionally – to a pre-war standard, sometimes even beyond it.

At about this time the top link gained another name that became even more famous, the Engineman Extraordinary, Bill Hoole. He was an open, friendly man who was a fine driver. He had become well-known locally, but it was when he formed his partnership with Charlie Simmons with SIR NIGEL GRESLEY that people began to take notice. He was working the up 'Elizabethan' with KINGFISHER, a last-minute replacement for the regular A4, and as she had not picked up enough water at Wiske Moor, stopped north of York to take water. From thereon the running was of the highest quality, with fast running where possible, and a 100 mph sprint down Stoke. Unfortunately a late running train ahead from Everton onwards, combined with some hopelessly optimistic timetabling plus the Potters Bar Widening, delayed the Non-stop, but the crew managed to run in on time nonetheless. The net time was 164 minutes, which with 425 tons, compares well with the 'Coronation' schedule.

The partnership between Bill and Albert Leech, his fireman, worked well. Bill was excellent at training, and shared the driving once he was confident of his mate's ability. In his more senior years he was still able to fire an A4 going full throttle. Firemen, watching him fire and mindful of his years, would ease the engine until Bill, indignant, would put his cap over the boiler pressure gauge and yank the regulator wide open again! In 1954 C.J. Allen

published a marvellous run on the down 'Tees-Tyne Pullman'. With 340 tons gross, Bill ran from York to Darlington, 44.15 miles, in 36 minutes 33 seconds start to stop, with 26 miles at just below 90 mph, and maxima of 91 and 92 mph. There were then two slight checks and a careful approach to the stop at Darlington. Allen described the time as one he had never seen equalled or even approached. When I mentioned this amazing run to Albert, his reply was 'Yes, but two nights later I was driving and beat him by a minute!'

Another man who was sought out by those who appreciated good running was Jimmy Swan at Haymarket. Each summer partnerships on the Non-stop between the Haymarket and Kings Cross drivers were studied so as to ensure that the cost of a Scottish trip would be worthwhile, especially when Jimmy or one of his colleagues was paired with Ted, Bill or one of their colleagues at Top Shed. The running was usually of a very good quality. One such occasion proved baffling when Driver Ferrington with an immaculate LORD FARINGDON passed York 17 minutes late for no obvious reason and the A4, despite its usual impeccable mechanical condition, had dropped time in addition to the delays caused. Arthur Ferrington was another friendly man, but he was usually firmly against running hard or fast to pick up time lost by others. He made a few exceptions – one of his last runs was with DWIGHT D. EISENHOWER, on the occasion of the opening of the Manchester-Sheffield-Wath Electrification, from Sheffield to Kings Cross. The representatives of the Press were delighted if not ecstatic, but Authority was mortified as the steam age A4 was let go down Stoke Bank with a rousing 100 mph! The late running LORD FARINGDON was taken over north of York by Jimmy Swan and matters improved a little, but at Newcastle they were now 20 late. But thereon matters changed, and there followed a master class in effortless fast running. By reaching Edinburgh in 113 minutes 2 seconds, 15 minutes were cut from the schedule. Jimmy Swan had the perfect instrument for the task, and speeds were significantly higher than usual for this section, and ran into the 90s twice. The road north of Darlington was restricted, and the limit to Edinburgh at no point was higher than 80 mph. But for a signal check at Joppa, the time would have been 111½ minutes, a record time between Newcastle and Edinburgh despite the 425 tons load. The 'Coronation' schedule had been cut by 8½ minutes with 100 tons more.

By 1954 the running of the 'Elizabethan' was certainly comparable with the pre-war streamliners. The difference lay in the treatment operationally and, whereas the 'Coronation's' transit on average met with 8-10 minutes delay, the 'Elizabethan' got distinctly rougher treatment despite attempts to keep a clear road. The summary of published runs shows that the average expectation of delay was at least 15-20 minutes, often more, and even 30 minutes was not unknown. Once the down train passed York the road would be clearer, but Darlington was often the place for signal delays. The Doncaster-Newark section seemed particularly prone in either direction, with a number of slow freights ambling along the route at the same time. If it was out of path at Hitchin in the up direction then all manner of services were likely to get in the way nearer London, especially the 1315 from Peterborough 'Parley'. This was a service that dawdled up the main line getting in the way of faster services, and the receipts probably never paid for the fuel to run the service let alone anything else. Why on earth it was not retimed out of harm's way I cannot imagine. The preponderance of recorded runs show a net time of 375 minutes or less, some of which are only a few minutes more than the 'Coronation' – with 425 tons, not 325.

In 1954 Bill Hoole, with the up train hauled by GANNET, was checked at Grantham as related earlier. There followed a mighty dash down Stoke reaching 100 mph, but we had to stop for water at Huntingdon. After a tremendous effort to Hatfield, we ran into a string of signal checks, the Potters Bar widening having been started, and ran in 8¾ minutes late. Later Tony McLeod and Jim Edwards did rather better, but Lucker troughs were also low and we had to stop at Newcastle for water, making arrival 5½ late. Then later in the summer Messrs. Swan and Hailstone made a perfect run, arriving 2½ minutes early.

In the 1955 summer Ted Hailstone made one of his fast runs with DOMINION OF NEW ZEALAND, and passed York most unusually 5¾ minutes early. His time from Hitchin to Huntingdon was half a minute inside the 'Silver Jubilee' schedule, with almost *twice* the load. The return trip arrived 8 minutes early, 370 minutes net. In some ways the later runs described earlier with Bill Hoole and Jimmy Swan on SEAGULL were more remarkable with their climbs to Stoke. The net time for the down run was 365 minutes, no less than 25 minutes less than schedule. The up run was delayed and took 396½ minutes, 370 minutes net. Jimmy Swan and Ted

Hailstone made a fine run with SEAGULL as well that year, and the climb to Stoke was completed at 66mph, exactly the same as with Bill Hoole earlier. The A4 ran in 7 BT, 383 minutes, 365 minutes net. Two more runs with SEAGULL were notable, a comparatively uninterrupted down run with two TSRs and a slight signal check, and an up run with no less than five TSRs plus two signal delays. The first, with Joe Howard and Tom Smith, took 378 minutes, 370 minutes net, while the second with Willie Gemmell and Bert Green had no less than 33 minutes delay (including a stop at Drem for 7 bells) on a 390 minutes run, 357 minutes net.

Although the records of runs build up a picture of the work of the class, it is only a sample, and maybe not a representative one. Now and again a run, like that of Driver Samwells with Ivatt Atlantic No.4452, begs to have been recorded. Quite a few exceptional efforts have gone unrecorded, although anecdotal evidence is invariably prey to exaggeration, and the discipline of a supporting and reliable recording is essential. In the guard's or Control's records, again the nearest minute is not accurate enough, but it is tempting to speculate. In 1953 for example, Ted Hailstone was said to have reached a very high speed on Stoke Bank with SILVER LINK on the 'Tees-Tyne Pullman'. As it happened, on August 11th of that year I saw him at Finsbury Park, and he was 12 minutes early, unusual if not unique. Clearly he had done well, but it is a long way from proving the tale. Again, on July 5th 1955, as I went to see Bill arrive on the 'Flying Scotsman', he was already in (old) platform 4 on SIR NIGEL GRESLEY, waiting for the relief crew. He arrived 5 BT, but had been 18 late at Doncaster, a remarkable running time of 135½ minutes even allowing for the relatively rough timings entered by the guard in his log. The train had been delayed slightly at Potters Bar as well. A month later, now with FALCON, he made a similarly fast run passing Grantham 22 late recovering speed and arriving 2 minutes late, 88½ minutes. At the time the train was 12 coaches, 434 tare and 460 tons gross. In all these cases the speed down Stoke must have been high.

Later in 1955 there was talk of Bill Hoole having attained a very high speed, and at the first opportunity I asked him about it. It had been alleged that whilst working the 'Tees-Tyne Pullman' he had reached 117 mph on the descent of Stoke Bank. At a distance of almost 50 years, the facts are hard to remember, but I am quite clear that he had received a hefty rebuke from higher authority.

However, after all had been said and done, he was told that it was a first class performance, it put the Western in their place, but don't do it again! At the time double chimneys were being fitted to the ex-GWR 'Kings' and some equally unlikely speeds were being claimed. As I remember it, the Pullman had extra coaches, and was said to be used by the CCE for one of the periodic Hallade runs. On this run a speedometer was in use as well, as I recall. Bill had behaved himself on the down run, but seeing two young engineers left in charge for the up run, decided to give them something to record. The railway authorities could not discipline a driver without hard evidence, if for no better reason than the disciplinary procedure and the trade union representatives would demand it. It seems that there was none.

On Wednesday November 16th 1955 the train was strengthened to 10 Pullmans, 400 tons gross, and the running times exist, albeit only to the nearest ½ minute. The train had been retimed due to the increased loading. The train was 1½ minutes late at Grantham and 5 early at Peterborough, but the running time of 23 minutes unchecked seems unlikely to support an unusually high speed. The continuation shows that it was an unchecked run of exceptional quality, and the train, although retimed, rolled to a stand at Kings Cross 18 minutes early!

Confusion arises however, from a note at the time that gives November 18th and not the 16th as the likely date of the Hallade run, when the load had returned to its normal 325 tons gross, and a high speed would be more feasible. For a Hallade run all that is required is a compartment or a brake van for a machine roughly the size of a small spin dryer. A comprehensive list of speeds exists, probably for this run, taken off the Hallade record perhaps. It shows that the train was checked by TSR to 28 mph at Little Barford, which was not the case two days earlier. The maximum on Stoke Bank is given as 108 mph, and the speed was 70 mph or rather more all the way from Biggleswade to Harringay apart from the last mile of Stevenage Bank.

Both runs would have involved the same driver, and there can be no doubt about his identity. It seems likely to me, therefore, that a speed of 108 mph was recorded on the Hallade trace, but as speedometers usually read high, a figure of 117 mph might have been noted by the CCE's staff. The speed had to come from somewhere, and this seems the likely source. It would certainly stimulate the CCE to complain to the Motive Power authorities. The CCE's sense of grievance presumably atrophied with time, the Motive Power Dept.

could not act without firm evidence, and as there was no disciplinary action, I would assume that it was dealt with informally. A maximum of 108 mph seems more likely for a single chimney A4 than the anecdotal 117 mph.

There were at the time a number of young enginemen being made redundant through closure of branches in East Anglia, but their seniority was such that they went into the top links. Jim Edwards' fireman, Bill Watts, came from Kings Lynn, for example. When Jim Wilson became a driver, Ted Hailstone's new fireman was Jack Law, who was within a few weeks of becoming a driver. He came from the Mid-Suffolk Light Railway, hardly a bigger contrast with SILVER LINK in full flight! On the occasion of Bill's run with SIR NIGEL GRESLEY on the 'Flying Scotsman', he had an ex-GE fireman, acclimatising to the main line on his first week of lodging. Perhaps his state of mind can be imagined!

If 1955 was a good year for A4 enthusiasts, then 1956 was even better. There was some very fast running on the 'Elizabethan', and in the autumn a new service was introduced, 'The Talisman' between Kings Cross and Edinburgh. I had another fast run north, this time with COMMONWEALTH OF AUSTRALIA, driven by Ted Hailstone and Bill Stevenson. The down run was very similar to that of DOMINION OF NEW ZEALAND with a fast run, touching 101 at Arlesey, only this time signal checks were more numerous, including a dead stand from full speed at Sandy for a light WD 2-8-0 running through the bottleneck.

Of a number of good runs in 1956, it is once again SEAGULL, driven by Ted Hailstone, which takes the eye. In 1955 we thought the southbound climb to Stoke with a minimum of 66 would take some beating, but Ted, in one of his last runs on the Non-stop, thought otherwise. After crossing the Plain of York in the high eighties with a maximum of 91½, matters continued relatively quietly until after Muskham troughs and the Newark level crossing. Then came a tremendous climb to Stoke, topped at 69½ mph, followed by a 100 mph descent with an average of 93.2mph from Corby Glen to Helpston, 15.2 miles. The Huntingdon-Hitchin section took 21 minutes including two signal checks, and arrival was 7¼ early, making a net time again of 365 minutes from Edinburgh to Kings Cross. The run was logged in detail and the net time of 90½ minutes from passing Grantham, at 70 mph, to Kings Cross was probably a record for steam traction with over 400 tons.

With the introduction of the 'Talisman' on September 17th 1956, an eight roller bearing coach load of 272 tons tare and usually 290 tons gross load, something of the 'Coronation' service at last was recreated. The service was slower, but without special measures such as double block, a much tighter schedule might have been difficult to deliver regularly. As it was, a number of services were timed to avoid the 'Talisman' only with the smallest of margins. It presumed near-perfect operating, and the level of delay experienced on the 'Talisman' as a result was hardly surprising. To make matters worse, the 1955 Modernisation Plan included the conversion of the country's main lines to CWR (Continuous Welded Rail) and the concept of premature track renewal was introduced. We need not be concerned here as to the nature of this, but its effect was the lengthening of TSRs to ¾ mile or even more, with a consequent escalation in delay.

The inaugural down train was timed by Cecil J. Allen. The drivers were Percy Heavens and his regular A4 FALCON to Newcastle, and Tommy Smith on his A4 GOLDEN PLOVER on to Edinburgh. FALCON ran very well when the road was clear, and arrived at Newcastle in 271¼ minutes, but the alarming feature was the time lost to delays, 23¼ minutes, giving 248 minutes net. GOLDEN PLOVER was more successful, arriving 2¼ minutes late. This I might add was the inaugural service, which, one might have thought, should have had special treatment! On his return the following day, GOLDEN PLOVER ran well to Newcastle, arriving 3 early despite delays. One of the great pleasures of the 'Talisman' service was the sight of Gateshead's A4s handling fast trains as in their youth. They had for so long been crowded out by the Peppercorn 'A1s', and it was good to see them running fast again. The run to London was continued by SPARROW HAWK with Driver Kipling, and the running was every bit as good as we had become used to with southern crews. The time was just under 261 minutes, 4 minutes BT, but again the level of delay was enormous, 25 minutes, giving a net time of 236 minutes.

There was no doubt that the A4s could still run fast, and all of the crews were not slow to take advantage of the lighter load, where the road allowed. It was an opportunity to show what they could do if really put to it, and it was not long before one did. On Monday November 5th of that year, the ECS for the 16.00 departure was badly delayed into Kings Cross, and the train eventually left 23 minutes late.

The engine was MILES BEEVOR, the driver was Bill Hoole, and opportunities such as this did not find him wanting. Efforts were made to give him a clear run, and the 'Talisman' ran into Newcastle Central 6 minutes early, giving a running time of 1 min under four hours. The A4's net time was 231 minutes.

Quite incredibly, four days later, the train was again subject to heavy delay. This time it was a hoax bomb threat that detained the down train at New Barnet for 26½ minutes. The A4 this time was FALCON, and again the driver was none other than Bill Hoole. Gerry Fiennes, reflecting, never seemed fully convinced that it was entirely accidental, involving as it did the driver who, above all others, would rise to the challenge. Suffice it to say that after getting his A4 into shape after the long stop, Bill took his opportunity and set about recovering 28 minutes late running. The average from Hitchin to Peterborough, 44.5 miles, was 80.1 with 98 sustained for ten miles from Arlesey to Tempsford and 100 at Sandy, and 98 at Connington. A fast climb to Stoke followed with a minimum of 66, and then a dash down to the Trent, and a fast run of the generally level road on to York and beyond, but such was the onslaught of delays that the train was still 22 minutes late at York. This time the train was checked again and again, and despite Bill having put the schedule to the sword, signal checks and TSRs threw it all away again. A fast run north of York and good speeds from Darlington to Newcastle brought the arrears down to 13¾ minutes. Such skilled work and sustained speeds ought to have achieved a better result. The cost of four TSRs and four signal checks, two being signal stops, came to a truly appalling 53¾ minutes, the net time being no more than 228 minutes. So, in a strange parallel, the operational problems of one week in 1956 were answered by a resolute crew in exactly the same way as those in one week seventeen years earlier in 1939. Driver Nash had been succeeded by Driver Hoole.

Another train on which some grand work was done was the up winter 'Flying Scotsman' from Grantham to Kings Cross, which I referred to earlier. It was a superb but heavy train with pressure ventilated 'Newton' stock, 13 coaches, about 475 tons tare and 495-500 tons gross. Most of the two sets of stock were switched to the Non-stop for 12 weeks in the summer, and replaced by similar spare coaches. Both sets were always kept in splendid condition. For some years Grantham worked both turns from Kings Cross to Newcastle changing engines at Grantham, and Haymarket

continued to Edinburgh. Gateshead men worked the up train from Waverley, and another set worked on from Newcastle to Grantham. Later, in the summer months Kings Cross worked both trains between London and Newcastle with the 'Tees-Tyne Pullman' as two lodging turns, and then in 1957 it was extended to cover the whole year. For the winter book in 1956/57 New England worked the down service to Grantham, returning light to Peterborough, and we were treated to the astonishing – indeed unprecedented – sight of New England's A2/3 Pacifics having been cleaned.

Through no fault of the Gateshead crew, it often ran into Grantham late, usually having had delays on the two-track sections, and most of the Kings Cross top link accepted that a special effort had to be made for the East Coast flagship train. I cannot recall anyone beating Ted Hailstone's 96 mph down the hill from a standing start with nearly 500 tons, but after 1957 when loads reduced, it became quite possible to reach three figures. With a keen south-west wind, the pull could be a heavy one. If the train was running to time then one had the cushion of recovery time south of Hitchin to enable an easy run in. If it was late at Hitchin, as it often was, Cambridge Junction's colour light distant was sought anxiously, with the driver's hand not far from the whistle lever. Once through Hatfield, the traffic grew heavier, and the likelihood of a delay grew with it. The Potters Bar Widening project was protected with a TSR, but some delay seemed almost inevitable there. Often a fine effort was ruined by bad regulation in the suburbs. Looking at the last sentence I am tempted to alter 'often' to 'always'! Several of us had some fine runs on the 'Flying Scotsman', fast running with a heavy load which had no parallel pre-war. Ted Hailstone, with SILVER LINK, completed the trip in 92 minutes 35 seconds with a reduced load of 460 tons but before he retired I recorded another run with the full load of 500 tons in 101 minutes 41 seconds. This was a faster run over the harder stretches, with a net time of 93 minutes, with SILVER LINK being worked harder than I had seen before. Bill Hoole was not to be outdone, of course, and Brian Bailey recorded a tremendous run by SIR NIGEL GRESLEY on 495 tons, completing the run in 101 minutes 54 seconds, 97 minutes net. This was on the same day, August 28th 1954, as my run with MALLARD, and it must have been a marvellous sight as DOMINION OF NEW ZEALAND, then GOLDEN FLEECE on the Non-stop, and then SIR NIGEL, in hot pursuit, came up the main line! Later I recorded a fine run by Bill on

QUICKSILVER referred to earlier, which was actually undelayed, in 97 minutes exactly. It was spring 1957 and there was a strong side wind all the way, making the work of the A4 much harder than usual.

So the Indian Summer of the Gresley Pacifics continued, with lighter loads and faster schedules, so that the streamliner principle was now extended, maybe in a lesser form, to many more expresses. High speeds became more frequent with the A4s, especially if there was time to be recovered. Ted Hailstone and Jimmy Swan had retired, but Bill Hoole continued to give his master classes in fast running, not always appreciated by the management. As his retirement drew near in 1959, any remaining inhibitions disappeared and his enthusiasm for fast running continued unabated. Two years to the day after his exploits on the 'Talisman', he was on the 'Morning Talisman' with ANDREW K McCOSH. The A4 was rather run down and had a good mileage, but she had been recently inspected at Doncaster and a double Kylchap had been fitted during her visit. Starting late from Kings Cross he made the most of his opportunity, with a maximum of 107½ mph down past Sandy. The double Kylchap masked most of the signs that might suggest that she was due for overhaul and a broken gauge glass, he was through Peterborough in 61 minutes, Grantham 90, Doncaster in 138, York in 180, and arrived at Darlington in 214¼ minutes. With eight delays, the net time was 187 minutes. The note is endorsed 'Not to be published'! Just before his retirement he was working the second portion of the 'Flying Scotsman' – known before the 1939-45 war as the 'Junior Scotsman', or simply 'The Glasgow' with SIR NIGEL GRESLEY. He was timed at 108 mph descending Stoke Bank, and ran into Peterborough 10 minutes BT. The continuation to London with the 12 coach train, 435 tons gross, was in the net time of 72 minutes.

So we come to the outstanding post-war performance by an A4. The Stephenson Locomotive Society, for its Golden Jubilee in 1959, arranged a special train on May 23rd from Kings Cross to Doncaster, northbound via Grantham and Lincoln, and southbound on the main line. The train of eight coaches, 295 tons gross, was given a tight schedule, 97 minutes to Grantham and 144 minutes returning from Doncaster. It was intended to give Bill Hoole the chance of a final flourish before his retirement on July 8th of that year. In anticipation of this the CCE had agreed for this special train to raise the speed limits north of Hitchin to 100 mph and south from Stoke to 110

mph, as I remember it. In anticipation of what this final flourish might amount to when he was unable to do anything about it, Gerry Fiennes, the Line Traffic Manager, exacted a promise from Bill that he would not go after MALLARD's record, on pain of having three or four more coaches hooked on to slow him down! I doubt whether it was a coincidence, too, that a speed indicator was fitted to SIR NIGEL whilst in the Works beforehand.

Looking back, I know that Bill would have loved to try to beat MALLARD's record. I am also quite sure that over the years he prepared for such an eventuality methodically with fast running over sections of line to establish how they were to be tackled. The preparation of SIR NIGEL GRESLEY, just returned from Doncaster Works, was thorough. A week before she worked the down 'Flying Scotsman' to Newcastle, returning two hours or so later with the 17.00 to Kings Cross. The '10.00' had shrunk to 410 tons no doubt to cater for underpowered diesel traction, but it gave the A4 a chance to run fast. The engine was pronounced a shade stiff, despite having reached 95 mph, but she was opened out on Stoke Bank with remarkable effect. A long 20 mph TSR just north of Tallington was a considerable obstacle, but the engine recovered to 61 at Essendine, 70 south of Little Bytham, 68 before Corby and 74 after, and a mighty 72 minimum at Stoke. That would have been good with the 'Coronation', but this was with nearly 100 tons more. Doncaster Works, when it overhauled its Pacifics, produced some magnificent work, and the valve setting in particular was inspired in its accuracy.

The day dawned perfectly, a fine sunny day. Old platform 6 was packed, and everyone was admiring the immaculate A4 and her driver was the centre of attention. We were off, and with a light train, the regulator wide open and 40% cut-off we raced through the suburbs at a significantly higher speed than usual. The long rise to Potters Bar needed a longer cut-off than I would have thought, 20-23% considering the minimum was 57 mph. The speed was rising, but the acceleration at Hitchin from just under 90 to 101 mph at Arlesey was electric. The regulator was closed and the cut-off lengthened, and after 90 at Tempsford matters were taken more easily. It was taken as read that Bill would make a big effort up to Stoke and so it proved.

We encountered a TSR north of Peterborough, but from there on the high-pitched roar from the double Kylchap stilled conversation as watches were consulted and speed

rose. We accelerated to 73 at Tallington, 80 at Essendine, and 83 was held on the rise to Corby Glen. We recovered slightly to 84, at which point the cut-off was dropped to 40% for the last three miles, and we roared past Stoke in triumph at 82 mph, the fastest ever by steam. What a sight it would have been for a photographer!

After a presentation and a visit to the Works, we rejoined the special. Promptly at 18.00 we left, the whole of the passengers now being in a state of high anticipation at was to happen within the hour. Bill had no reservations about using full regulator normally, and he was using quite a long cut-off for a short while to get very rapid acceleration away from TSRs. The signalling, it must be said, was operated to perfection on this special day. The speeds were very good but not exceptional as far as Newark, where a 30 mph TSR checked us, and at Barkston we were only doing 66 mph. Then came the big effort, with 76 before Grantham and a brief 81 after, 78 before Stoke and 75 minimum. Then he was away, 95 at Corby, 110 before Little Bytham and a maximum of 112 beyond, following which Bill was prevailed upon by Alan Pegler and Chief Inspector Bert Dixon to ease off. One sensed that not only Bill felt a degree of reluctance, but the GN management had co-operated outstandingly in making it a day to remember, and limits had to be respected. The speed tailed off to 103 at Essendine and was still 90 at Helpston. The train rode perfectly throughout, as those who knew East Coast main line knew it would. There were a few routes as good as the East Coast, but never one better.

After Peterborough the buffet car, which had been virtually deserted so far, was now under siege as thirsts were slaked. However, Bill had not done, and we gathered speed and charged up Abbotts Ripton bank accelerating to 76, and reached a brief 86 before the Huntingdon 70 mph PSR. On this occasion he kept to the 70 PSR at Offord. Afterwards there was the unmistakable sound of full regulator and 35% cut-off as we took off uphill, as if it were flat, with 78 at Paxton, an amazing 85 after St. Neots, 92 before Tempsford, and for the third time in the day, 100 mph past Everton. With this impetus we flew up the bank to Stevenage, 80 at Hitchin and the bank was topped at 77mph. Now the hard running was done, and we sailed into Kings Cross 6½ minutes BT on the 144 minute schedule. It had been a memorable day and an outstanding performance. The GN management had done us proud, the A4 superbly prepared, the operation was in the finest traditions of the East Coast and the A4's namesake, and a day to be remembered long after.

Bill was not happy and felt he could have done better. I have devoted space to his running not because it was typical of the A4s' Indian Summer, but because it gave us occasional glimpses of what Gresley's finest design could do. He told us that the A4s were better than ever, and he showed us that, with the improvements to the design, they were. He would have loved a crack at Joe Duddington's record, and I think that he could certainly have gone faster on May 23rd, say to 117-118 mph. But although in May 1959 he was a mite faster over Stoke summit, I doubt whether he could have reached 120 mph. In comparing 1938 with 1959, MALLARD was equipped with a Kylchap exhaust specified by M. Chapelon, through his agents, the Associated Locomotive Equipment Company. It had case hardened, sharp *barrettes* and the breeches pipe was fitted with mid-feathers to stream the exhaust, whereas the 1957 conversions had the combined orifice and *barrette* casting and no mid-feather. One would expect this to affect the evenness of burning across the grate, but whether this gave a marginal advantage in exhausting large volumes of spent steam is impossible to say. We know that Joe Duddington had 55 tons less and used cut-offs of 40-45%, and that made the difference. Sadly but realistically, no railwayman in

authority could have agreed to a second attempt with a trainload of passengers, particularly at very high speeds with lengthy cut-offs.

One more run needs to be mentioned, and it again the immortal MALLARD that was involved. But first, I had travelled behind her with an old friend, Driver Sid Piggins, on a midweek excursion to Doncaster. He was a No.2 link driver of long experience, and it was good to see him handling such a fine locomotive. Again it was the power of this particular A4 that impressed, and after a severe mauling by the operating and CCE departments, she was opened out on the climb to Stoke. With 290 tons she maintained 80 mph up the 1 in 178 to Stoke, only falling to 79 in the last half-mile. This magnificent effort was overshadowed by the subsequent run. It was not long before the A4 was taken out of service for preservation, and she was rostered for the 14.00 departure from Kings Cross. Driver Coe was said to be in charge, but I have a suspicion that Inspector Frank Knight's hand was the one on the regulator. Frank Knight was a remarkable man who made a quiet but very valuable contribution to smooth running at Kings Cross. The train had 14 minutes of delay to Grantham from the usual contributors, but good running had limited the delay to three minutes at Peterborough. As with my run, there was a 20 mph TSR before Tallington, but now

MALLARD had 415 tons. Yet the speeds were higher as she recovered, reaching 82 at Little Bytham, dropping to 80 before recovering to 82 at Corby Glen. Up the last three miles she dropped to 78 at the summit. For 15 minutes MALLARD had been developing over 2,600 IHP and the last 3-4 miles saw the power output increase to more than 3,000 IHP. The estimation of power developed is not a precise science, but on two occasions an A4 has probably exceeded 3,000 IHP, the same engine, once in 1938 going down Stoke, and another the 1960s, going up.

This can only be a selection of performances to give an idea of the best work of the class, and there were no doubt others where determined crews retrieved delays with hard running. The remainder of the class to survive the accountants' axes went to Scotland, where they were gainfully employed from Aberdeen to Glasgow and occasionally Edinburgh. The loads were light, the schedules brisk, and the Caledonian road from Aberdeen to Stirling had easy, fast stretches. Those who had not enjoyed them in their prime joined others who wanted to savour the thrill of an A4 at speed for a last few times. Certainly high speeds became a more common experience, and for a year or two enthusiasts travelled to the new Jerusalem north of the Border before the end came.

MERLIN in her purple livery, off to Glasgow with a down express on April 24th 1949. Note the WD 2-8-0, an unusual sight at Haymarket, with its LNER Class O7 number. The tender was A4 corridor No.5652. (J. Robertson, The Transport Treasury)

CHAPTER TEN
Looking Round

The A4, as a later design and a shorter-lived one, underwent rather fewer alterations than its ancestors, the A1 and A3. Being a streamlined locomotive, changes were less obvious anyway. Starting at the front one could appreciate the shape of the Bugatti wedge shape with its broad brow at chimney level due to the full width of the boiler, waisting down to buffer beam level and curved underneath. The front casing has two doors, the larger opening upwards and the smaller lower door opening downwards, the mechanism driven from either side just ahead of the cylinders by inserting a special handle. The 'cod's mouth' when open reveals the usual Doncaster smokebox door, the top segment omitted as was done with HUMORIST and the Mikados. One can see all too clearly that removal of smokebox char, one of the most unpopular of tasks, was much worse with the A4 than an non-streamlined locomotive. The only embellishment on the front other than the chime whistle was the bell carried by DOMINION OF CANADA while a single blast engine. Pre-war, it was worked with a steam supply, but as mentioned earlier, after an incident it was fixed.

The chime whistle generated much interest since it first appeared, and its sound has a special place in our memories. It combines three different notes into a musical chord, and it has sired a minor science concerned with the provenance and the musical characteristics of each variation. The originals were manufactured by the Crosby Valve Co. of America. Some of the 'Coronation' A4s carried special versions.

The early whistles possessed a brass finial nut, but a plain brass nut made its appearance later, certainly post-war. We know that most of the chime whistles were removed during the war in most cases, and melted down. When it became necessary to replace them, due to import controls post-war, they were made under licence in the UK. The whistle structure is such that a variation in the alloys used in its manufacture, or slight variations in wall thickness between the three chambers have imparted slight differences in pitch. The sound of the chime whistle changed with the new manufacturer post-war, and again with the BR version used on the early standard locomotives.

On the sloping front are the usual four lamp irons and the number and shed plates. Headboards, if used, were usually carried on the lower middle lamp iron, but not invariably. The plain copper stovepipe chimney – shades of Swindon – is painted black. It is the one feature that remained the same through all of the many changes of livery that the class endured. The chimney casing contained a small single chimney liner with the anti-vacuum valve enclosed behind louvres in the rear of the chimney. The double Kylchap engines have a similar but larger chimney of course. Under BR ownership the numberplate replaced the painted numbers, and the familiar elliptical shedplate announced the engine's home depot. The first four had standard buffers and the coupling was recessed, but as the streamlined casing was carried forward of the buffer beam, there was insufficient room with normal length buffers for a shunter to couple up. As the A4s used their front coupling much less it was some while before the problem surfaced, but sadly a man was killed as a result. Longer buffers were provided which solved the problem. The buffer shanks are not painted red, unusually for a locomotive.

WILLIAM WHITELAW, with John Cameron's UNION OF SOUTH AFRICA inside Ferryhill shed. The electrification flashes and the scruffy condition make 1961 or after. The small sand filler door under the nameplate is open. W1 corridor tender No.5484. (The Transport Treasury).

A close-up view of the cab of the A4, SIR RALPH WEDGWOOD in this case. The difference from the A1/A3 cab with the angled forward faces is clear, and the builder's plate, the traditional Doncaster plate, is on the cab side. On the 'Coronation' A4s the latter was fixed inside the roof to make way for the cabside insignia. The vertical handrails were lengthened from 4ft 3ins on the first four to 4ft 6ins. The detail of the Cortazzi axlebox and angled horn faces can be seen here. 'RA9' refers to Route Availability, and was the highest category, as one would expect with one of the heaviest locomotives in service. No date is given but the non-corridor tender (5675) fixes it as post June 1954. (The Transport Treasury)

The front bogie originally had dust shields similar to the A1s and A3s, but this was altered to a horizontal plate. This obstructed the drains for the middle cylinder, and they were diverted, to be clipped to the outside drains, one to each side. Later the horizontal shield was altered to allow fitting of the ATC/AWS receiver, and a guard plate was provided to protect the receiver from the front coupling. The plate was replaced by a larger version when AWS replaced ATC. Doncaster also fitted two pairs of life guard irons, one on the bogie and longer ones just ahead, carrying the drain pipes. The longer ones were removed post-war. At the front only the brake pipe connection is carried.

Moving round to the side, one can see the slight depression in the streamlined profile behind the chimney. The casing runs horizontally for some 4-5 feet, before rising up over the banjo dome and continuing to the wedge-fronted cab. The major alteration was the removal of the

valancing over the coupled wheels by Edward Thompson during the war. It was removed both from ahead and behind the cylinders over the coupled wheels, but in an aesthetically pleasing way. There were second thoughts with No.4462, which had the casing restored ahead of the cylinders, unhappily, but wiser counsels prevailed. The casing ahead of the cylinders had a hinged examination cover to allow inspection and lubrication of the 2:1 gear. It was interesting in 1986 to see MALLARD at work, with the original valancing, with SIR NIGEL GRESLEY. It is of course a matter of taste, but the first engine had a dated appearance, something of the 1930s that the sister A4 No.4498 did not have. The post-war A4 does not look old, like a museum piece, and at even today's modest speeds looks as good as ever.

The bogie and wheels are much as their A1 and A3 ancestors looked. The check plates over the middle of the bogie frame can be seen beneath the

cylinder blocks, together with the three cylinder drain pipes once clipped to the long guard irons, but now shortened and the long irons removed. Above, below the running plate on either side one can see the tube into which the operating handle for the doors is inserted, and the guides carrying the valve extensions for the conjugated valve gear. On the driver's side under the nameplate was the whistle control valve. When AWS was fitted, the cable conduit was brought out from the receiver ahead of the left-hand cylinder and was clipped to the edge of the aerofoil running board on the driver's side, back to the cab.

Some details of naming and embellishments are described earlier but are repeated here to provide a complete A4 description in this chapter. The nameplates are fitted on the outside of the smokebox casing and bolted through. Some of the nameplates are long and heavy, and were made in two sections. As mentioned earlier, in service SILVER LINK and her sisters originally had their names painted on, midway along the casing, in a lighter shade of silver with bright blue shading. When the livery changed to garter blue the nameplates were restored to the first four. Those of SILVER LINK and QUICKSILVER had rounded corners, probably having been cast before a change of mind. There appear to be four nameplates in circulation off the prototype. SILVER KING and SILVER FOX received plates with square corners, as did the rest of the class. Two, both preserved, were provided with new nameplates on which the stainless steel characters and edge strips were secured with set screws, DOMINION OF CANADA and SIR NIGEL GRESLEY.

Eleven A4s were renamed as mentioned previously, one A4 twice and two were given the same name after the 35th A4 was withdrawn, to commemorate directors and officers of the LNER. Apart from names apposite to the three streamlined services, and the name of their designer, the original naming theme was a mixture of waterfowl and birds of prey. In some cases such as GREAT SNIPE, POCHARD and GARGANEY the Assistant charged with producing suitable names had clearly plunged to the bottom of the barrel. However, none was so bad as to be replaced by a group of people who were no doubt most worthy but known only in business and the LNER boardroom. The details are included in the individual engine histories.

Several A4s carried plaques or embellishments amidships on the boiler side. SILVER FOX was the first, with her fox in full flight, together with stainless steel trim. Post-war, three of Haymarket's septet, KINGFISHER, MERLIN and UNION OF SOUTH AFRICA were fitted with plaques, the last only on one side – the driver's. MERLIN's were originally carried on the cab sides, but were later moved to the boiler sides. In 1948, MALLARD was fitted with commemorative plaques, and in preservation, SIR NIGEL GRESLEY was similarly fitted, commemorating her post-war speed record of 112 mph.

Three small inspection doors are fitted above the coupled wheels, just above the curve to running board level, to give access to oil reservoirs and to the sand boxes. Those of SILVER LINK were full depth and curved, but they proved awkward, and so those of the rest of the A4s were reduced in depth. The doors were originally fastened by a pair of bolts but for the last batch single locking handles proved a better answer, and became standard for the class. A fourth door was added to the last six A4s being built, below the nameplate and above the cylinders, to give better access to the cylinder oil boxes. This was a short door with two hinges during the 1938-45 period before it was lengthened with three hinges.

The Wakefield mechanical lubricators were located on the fireman's side between the second and third coupled axle, at running board level. The ratchet drive to the axlebox and cylinder lubricators was taken off an eccentric crank on the rear coupled axle with the Flaman drive. SILVER LINK as built had a cover to the lubricators, but this was omitted with the rest, and the prototype was altered at overhaul. Once the reservoir capacity had been increased to two gallons for some A4s it would have been more difficult. It is unclear how many one gallon lubricators survived, and on which locomotive. The streamlined valancing was formed with oval access holes, closed by sliding plates, and later a hinged panel was provided to give access to the conjugated valve gear.

The handrail was straight with SILVER LINK but with the rest, and No.2509 after the general overhaul in 1937, it was curved down roughly parallel with the running board. This was to make it a more effective handhold for staff whilst working on the locomotive. Below the handrail on the driver's side the ejector exhaust is piped to the smokebox. Beneath the running board on the driver's side the Doncaster reversing rod is tucked underneath but partly visible, and the BR speedometer is carried on an eccentric crank on the rear coupled axle, with its flexible electrical conduit connected to a junction box under the running board. On the fireman's side, as well as the mechanical lubricator there was, and still is on MALLARD, the drive to the Flaman speed recorder located in the cab under the fireman's seat. Above the Cortazzi axleboxes on the fireman's side is the linkage operating the drop grate.

The A4s were unusual at Doncaster in only having one pattern of boiler, Diagram 107, throughout their life, and so the number and location of inspection plugs remained constant. The cab was similar to that of the A3s but with angled forward faces as with the Mikados. The first four A4s had slightly shorter vertical handrails that were never replaced. The cabs tended to become hot, and an additional ventilator was fitted. Also a rubber fairing was originally provided between tender and cab, but this split with age – and the odd overheated fireman's shovel – and disappeared post-war.

The tenders were of three types, ex-A3 corridor, new corridor, and new non-corridor. The second and third were built in two batches each with a slight variation in weight, making five an all. In addition three, one in 1935 and two in 1937, were fitted with roller bearings; no revised figures were quoted, but eight roller bearing axleboxes would have involved some additional weight. SILVER LINK's No.5590 received Timken roller bearings in October 1938, DOMINION OF NEW

SIR NIGEL GRESLEY New England in July 1963; Top Shed had closed at the end of steam south of Peterborough. The A4 had worked a special to commemorate the 25th anniversary of MALLARD's record run, achieving 103 mph down Stoke Bank. She had just been transferred away from Kings Cross, where, apart from six years, she had been allocated since building. The A3 corridor tender is No.5324, and the boiler is No.27966, which I assume she still has. (B. Richardson, The Transport Treasury)

EMPIRE OF INDIA's cabside, with the panel carrying the coat of arms. (P.J. Coster)

faced with one that wouldn't couple, or worse, wouldn't uncouple. There was a proposal to fit the non-corridor tenders with buckeyes, but the normal screw coupling worked perfectly well and no doubt it was felt to be unnecessary.

Curiously, none of the A4 corridor tenders have survived: on the preserved engines there are two 1928 tenders on SIR NIGEL GRESLEY (5324) and DOMINION OF CANADA (5326). The 1930 'Hush-hush' one is on UNION OF SOUTH AFRICA (5484), and there are three non-corridor tenders on MALLARD, (5670 renumbered 5642), BITTERN (5638), and DWIGHT D. EISENHOWER (5671). Perhaps even more curiously, when SIR NIGEL was first preserved, MILES BEEVOR was cannibalised to provide a better set of coupled wheels. The preservation group thereby had the corridor tender with which 'Flying Scotsman' achieved 100 mph for the first time, and the non-corridor tender with which MALLARD reached 126 mph, a fascinating if obscure thought.

The footplate of an A4 is very similar to the A3 and the A1 before it. The A4 has of course left-hand drive, which means that the regulator, vertical reverser and brake valves are all grouped on the left-hand side ahead of the driver's bucket seat, together (later) with the speedometer and AWS indicator with its cancellation handle. The regulator is the normal Doncaster pull-out type located in a quadrant. I remember one on which the regulator persisted in closing down with the vibration, until the driver, with a oath, whacked a piece of a permanent way key into the quadrant with the coal hammer to keep the regulator wide open, its normal position with a clear road! Below the AWS indicator, on the backplate is the cut-off indicator. Originally the A4 reverser operated in the opposite way to the A1 and A3 reverser. This was due to the need to angle the reversing shaft under the running board. It was simply asking for trouble since the Pacifics were widely used and many drivers were familiar with them, and it was only a matter of time before one set off in the opposite direction to that intended. All that was required was to alter the linkage of the A4 so that when the driver lengthened the cut-off, the indicator pointer dropped rather than rose. There have been enough horror stories on the railway concerning locomotives apparently deciding for themselves where they will go – especially on turntables – rather than the driver.

The main brake valve is right in front of the driver, and in the large casting there is the ejector control. The blower valve is to right of the brake valve casting. By the driver's

ZEALAND's No.5647 received Hoffman in March of that year, and WOODCOCK's No.5648 received Skefco in September 1939. The first two remained with the engines, but the Skefco tender moved to MALLARD and FALCON, and at least one axle reverted to plain bearings late in its life. Curiously, I have travelled on all three.

The corridor tenders built for the A4s had curved rear ends to reflect the coaching stock design, and were slightly wider than the 1928 design. The later batch of seven, Nos.5646-5652 built for Nos.4491-4497, were significantly heavier than the four built in 1935 as the Appendix shows. The vertical handrails of the first batch were 4ft 3ins long but this was altered to 4ft 6ins for the second batch. Three of the 'silvers' kept their 1935 tenders, and that of SILVER KING was exchanged with UNION OF SOUTH AFRICA in 1948 to ensure that the Haymarket septet all had corridor tenders for Non-stop duty.

The 1928 tenders, plus that of the 'Hush-hush' built in 1930, were modified to attach to Nos.4482-4490 and 4498 and 10000 as rebuilt. Although they were widened and fitted with disc wheels, they retained the beading at the top of the side

sheets enabling the observer to identify them. They were fitted with the shorter handrails, except for those on the 'Coronation' duties. All of the latter had the stainless steel trim carried by the locomotives as well. Post-war, the three A4s selected for the 1948 Exchanges had their non-corridor tenders swopped for 1928 corridor tenders, and the rear plates of the tenders had to be reduced in order to accommodate the lower water cranes, notably at Euston on the LMR.

The third batch, of 14 engines, was built with streamlined non-corridor tenders similar to those built for Mikados Nos.2003-2006 in the previous year. They were similar to the design used on the 1930 and 1934/5 batch of A3s. With the withdrawal of the Raven Pacifics, their tenders were attached to A1s and A3s, and the displaced A4 pattern high sided tenders were reconditioned and attached to five A4s – Nos.4464, 4468 and 4901-4903. Several of the class kept their original tender throughout their working life, indeed several retrieved their original tender. As mentioned before, the corridor tenders were fitted with buckeye couplers which, with their safety record, in my view was well worthwhile. But then I haven't been

FALCON at New England in the later part of 1963, after its transfer there from Kings Cross. (B. Richardson, The Transport Treasury)

leg is the sanding lever, which means that the cylinder drain cock control must be operated by the fireman on his side. High on the backplate are the boiler and steam chest pressure gauges, the former duplicated on the fireman's side. The injectors and gauge glasses are in their normal places, and the train heating steam pressure gauge is again on the fireman's side. Above the gauges are the various cocks for serving the steam heating, sanding, etc. On the fireman's side, under his seat, are the handles to the injector water supply, and pre-war, the speed recorder.

Behind the driver on the tender front is a vertical pipe drilled with small holes, if I remember correctly, at 500 gallon intervals. When it is rotated 90° it opens a valve at the base and fills with water from the tender tank and the approximate water level is indicated by the number of weeping holes! Simple but effective, and I recall seeing the number increase as we took water over the troughs. Indeed taking water was a skilled business. The scoop operating handle, rotated horizontally as with the reverser, with a locking handle beneath, was on the tender front behind the driver. One needed to assess how much was needed, what the speed was, and most importantly, where the troughs started and finished. It wasn't difficult to damage the scoop or even knock it off, and one had to pull it up quickly at the end of the troughs, for there were many such things as farm crossings or crossovers to foul the

scoop. If it was dropped too early, the water would pull it down and the handle of the operating mechanism would spin out of control, and water would be everywhere. For the fireman a bad bruise or even a broken forearm beckoned. The scoop could not be pulled out against the speed of the train. Bill Hoole was one of a number who wound the tender handbrake on whilst taking water, so that with the engine pulling, the scoop would drop another fraction of an inch or so and the lift would be a few hundred gallons more.

As the engine passes a signal the sound of the AWS can be heard, a bell indicating clear signals, or a horn indicating a caution aspect and hence a need to reduce speed. The AWS indicator changes from yellow/black spokes to black with the caution, and the driver has to cancel the warning on the indicator and take over the braking. If he leaves it too long, the equipment takes over and makes a heavy brake application. If the signals clear, the driver can blow the brake off and resume speed, but once the AWS takes over the train will reduce to a crawl or stop altogether. The bell is fixed to the cab roof above the driver's head. The one weakness with AWS that has emerged in recent years is the possibility, incredibly, that the driver would cancel the signal but fail to make the necessary brake application properly. It is more common now with electric and diesel traction, but there were some instances where steam engines were running on yellow or caution

(semaphore) aspects, and a driver could cancel the AWS indication mechanically and then mishandle the brake when the next signal was not another caution but 'stop'. With ATP the equipment will make the appropriate brake application regardless. The other change which has recently been implemented in preservation is the change to air braking, which requires the concealment of a Westinghouse air pump about the locomotive, and a change of brake controls. With diesel traction the change from vacuum to air braking, in service, brought a greater degree of reliability and a reduced braking distance.

There were of course smaller detail changes visible externally, and various changes to the interior workings of the locomotive. New ideas, new equipment with better performance continually displaces older methods and older equipment. I have written much of the above in the present tense, because through the generosity and kindness of some special people, supported by many other like-minded people, there are six A4s still in existence, at least one currently working, for which these words are still true, and God willing, will be true for many more years. I will finish once again by saying that I have written this history and captioned the photographs illustrating it using the records and wisdom of many good folk, and such as I can add of my own knowledge. There may well be errors of fact or recognition in the captioning as my knowledge of the East Coast main line is not exhaustive, nor is my recall as reliable as I would wish. All authors of such works must be haunted by the thought that they have made a misjudgement that, after publishing and in retrospect, is both obvious and ridiculous. If I have, I apologise.

Below. MERLIN at the western end of Haymarket, being prepared for a turn farther north or west. With the cod's mouth open one can see the family likeness with the first two P2s and A3 HUMORIST. The date is given as April 1960 but as she was in the Works until mid-May, it will be later. Clean as she is, she was on the Non-stop in the summer and would have been specially turned out. The tender was A4 corridor No.5652. Look at the old six-planker over the ashpits – at one time they were in their tens of thousands on the system, and yet now they are long gone. (The Transport Treasury)

Above. The cabside coat of arms of COMMONWEALTH OF AUSTRALIA. Haymarket firemen had the habit of hanging the slacker pipe out of the cab window (at least during the 1950s) with unfortunate results for the paintwork. 60012 is on the down 'Elizabethan' at Kings cross, with the driver testing the brake.

Two A4s stand at Darlington Works, having run their last miles in service. EMPIRE OF INDIA and GUILLEMOT were withdrawn in 1964, and were cut up on site. (Paul Chancellor Collection)

A final polish for QUICKSILVER. It must be later than August 1957, and could well be in connection with the Royal specials on June 8th 1961.

SIR RONALD MATTHEWS at York shed on August 6th 1939, taking water. She has her usual tender, non-corridor No.5674. (R.J. Buckley, Initial Photographics)

A view of two A4s in Doncaster Works. The nearer one is MERLIN, and one can just see the 'breeches pipe', the double blastpipe under the double chimney. Another A4 is at the back, with a B1 4-6-0, a Britannia and (I think) a V2 2-6-2. Not a photo to be commended to Health & Safety Inspectors. (B. Richardson, The Transport Treasury)

Top right. The Chairman of the LNER Board's Locomotive Committee and one closely involved with the great days of the 1930s. An excellent detailed shot for modellers showing fine detail, even the joint between the two halves of Andrew's nameplate. (The Transport Treasury)

Middle and bottom right. The first one. SILVER LINK in the last year or two of her existence. The nameplates of SILVER LINK that were originally fitted on construction had rounded corners, but they were removed before the locomotive went into traffic. The four 'silvers' ran with their names painted at the mid-point of the boiler barrel, but when the garter blue livery was applied the nameplates were refitted. Those on QUICKSILVER were also rounded, presumably having been cast for the new locomotive before the naming policy switch. The remainder of the class had nameplates with rectangular corners from the outset, and SILVER KING and SILVER FOX received similar plates, new, at the change of livery. The cabside view shows the familiar Doncaster works plate.

SILVER LINK backs down to old platform 8. Kings Cross usually turned its Pacifics out well cleaned, often superbly so, and the A4 is a good example of the high standard that was set. This view gives an excellent view of SILVER LINK's A4 corridor tender No.5590, which was fitted with Timken roller bearings in October 1938. The A4 has paused in order that the shunter could swing the buckeye coupler up and lock it in the horizontal position. The corridor door is open showing how the passage turns sharply right and steps up. With the vacuum brake there was one connection, the right-hand pipe (or in railway vernacular, 'bag') being for train steam heating. A memory of steam and early diesel days is the piles of vestibule end boards on the platforms. The driver, I would imagine, is watching the shunter's hand signals, bringing SILVER LINK back on to her train, with his hand on the brake ready to stop and hold her until the coupling has been checked. (The Transport Treasury)

The 12.55 Kings Cross-York parcels at Grantham with SEAGULL, August 15th 1962. (J. Hodgkinson)

DOMINION OF CANADA, now a Ferryhill engine, at Eastfield on May 17th 1964. She retained her nameplate with the stainless steel characters and edging. (Peter Groom)

Left. That Bell Again. And our friend from page 74. DOMINION OF CANADA receives the final touches to the presentation bell at Kings Cross shed.

Below. The later BR totem as carried by UNION OF SOUTH AFRICA. The earlier ferret and dartboard totem is discernable beneath. Haymarket, April 20th 1957. (The Transport Treasury)

The A4 Portfolio

Date applied or Ex-overhaul	GARGANEY/SIR RONALD MATTHEWS Doncaster Works No 1873
26 Apr 38	LNER No 4500, tender No 5674, painted garter blue livery, named GARGANEY and allocated to Gateshead
11 Mar 39	Renamed SIR RONALD MATTHEWS
7 Dec 41	Side valancing removed and wartime black livery
29 Oct 43	Max cut-off changed to 75%
16 Nov 46	New number LNER No 1 and garter blue livery restored
14 Jul 48	New number BR No 60001
10 Feb 50	BR blue livery
2 Aug 51	BR dark green livery
5 Feb 54	Long guard irons removed
11 Apr 58	Double chimney fitted
9 Jan 59	AWS fitted
5 Oct 61	BR speedometer fitted
12 Oct 64	Withdrawn from service
Life Mileage	1,504,409

Date applied or Ex-overhaul	POCHARD/SIR MURROUGH WILSON Doncaster Works No 1872
12 Apr 38	LNER No 4499, tender No 5673, painted garter blue livery, named POCHARD and allocated to Gateshead
8 Apr 39	Renamed SIR MURROUGH WILSON
7 Feb 42	Side valancing removed and wartime black livery
11 Oct 46	New number LNER No 2 and garter blue livery restored
11 Mar 43	Max cut-off changed to 75%
14 May 48	New number BR No 60002
18 Jul 57	Double chimney fitted
2 Feb 50	BR blue livery
14 Aug 51	BR dark green livery
26 Mar 59	AWS fitted
13 Feb 53	Long guard irons removed
26 Jan 61	BR speedometer fitted
4 May 64	Withdrawn from service
Life Mileage	1,270,010

Date applied or Ex-overhaul	OSPREY/ANDREW K McCOSH Doncaster Works No 1859
12 Aug 37	LNER No 4494, tender No 5649, painted LNER apple green livery with black front and valancing and allocated to Heaton
26 Jan 38	Tender coal space modified
20 Oct 38	Garter blue livery
21 Aug 42	Side valancing removed and wartime black livery
30 Oct 43	Max cut-off changed to 75%
29 Oct 45	Coupled to A3 tender No 5584 for two weeks
11 Sep 46	New number LNER No 3
21 Jun 47	Garter blue livery restored and middle cylinder lined to 17ins dia
04 Mar 49	New number BR No 60003
19 Apr 50	Exptl ATC fitted and BR blue livery
10 Oct 51	BR dark green livery
29 Jan 53	Long guard irons removed
18 Jun 54	Middle cylinder liner removed
05 Jul 57	Double chimney fitted
02 Feb 61	BR speedometer fitted
29 Dec 62	Withdrawn from service
Life Mileage	1,348,732

Date applied or Ex-overhaul	GREAT SNIPE/WILLIAM WHITELAW Doncaster Works No 1864
10 Dec 37	LNER No 4462, tender No 5667, painted garter blue livery and allocated to Kings Cross
23 Jul 41	Side valancing removed and renamed WILLIAM WHITELAW
03 Sep 41	Hudd ATC fitted
31 Oct 42	Wartime black livery
19 Apr 44	Max cut-off changed to 75%
25 Aug 46	New number LNER No 4
14 Nov 46	Garter blue livery restored
20 Jan 48	New number BR No E4
25 May 48	New number BR No 60004
10 Aug 50	BR blue livery
29 Feb 52	BR dark green livery
22 May 53	Long guard irons removed
05 Dec 57	Double chimney fitted
13 Nov 58	AWS fitted
25 Jan 61	BR speedometer fitted
17 Jul 66	Withdrawn from service
Life Mileage	1,463,692

Date applied or Ex-overhaul	CAPERCAILLIE/CHARLES H NEWTON/SIR CHARLES NEWTON Doncaster Works No 1875
8 Jun 38	LNER No 4901, tender No 5641, painted garter blue livery. Double Kylchap chimney and allocated to Gateshead
22 Aug 42	Side valancing removed and wartime black livery
19 Aug 42	Renamed CHARLES H NEWTON
4 Jun 43	Renamed SIR CHARLES NEWTON
2 Feb 45	Repaired after middle cylinder fractured
3 Aug 46	Garter blue livery restored and new No LNER No 5
23 Nov 49	BR blue livery
4 May 57	Max cut-off changed to 75%
9 Jul 48	New number BR No 60005
10 Dec 58	AWS fitted
11 Nov 52	Long guard irons removed, BR dark green livery
14 Jul 60	BR speedometer fitted
12 Mar 64	Withdrawn from service
Life Mileage	1,330,582

Date applied or Ex-overhaul	HERRING GULL/ SIR RALPH WEDGWOOD Doncaster Works No 1868
26 Jan 38	LNER No 4466, tender No 5670, painted garter blue livery and allocated to Kings Cross
13 Feb 42	Side valancing removed and wartime black livery
6 Jan 44	Max cut-off changed to 75% and renamed SIR RALPH WEDGWOOD
26 Jan 46	
27 May 46	New number LNER No 605
2 Apr 47	New number LNER No 6
2 Dec 48	Garter blue livery restored
31 May 50	New number BR No 60006
1 Nov 50	BR blue livery
17 Oct 51	Exptl ATC fitted
15 May 53	BR dark green livery
25 Sep 57	Long guard irons removed
29 Dec 60	Double chimney fitted
3 Sep 65	BR speedometer fitted Withdrawn from service
Life mileage	1,295,453

Date applied or Ex-overhaul	SIR NIGEL GRESLEY Doncaster Works No 1863
30 Oct 37	LNER No 4498, tender No 5329, painted garter blue livery and allocated to Kings Cross
25 Feb 38	Tender coal space modified
16 Jan 39	Stainless steel relief nos and letters fitted
21 Feb 42	Side valancing removed and wartime black livery
12 Jan 47	New number LNER No 7
06 Mar 47	Restored to Garter blue livery
24 Mar 48	New number BR No 60007
08 Oct 48	Employed at Opening of Rugby Test Station
27 Sep 50	Exptl ATC fitted and BR blue livery
17 Apr 52	BR dark green livery
19 Oct 53	Long guard irons removed
12 Mar 55	Max cut-off changed to 75%
13 Dec 57	Double chimney fitted
16 Apr 59	BR speedometer fitted
01 Feb 66	Withdrawn from service for preservation Subsequently fitted with plaques denoting 112mph postwar record
Life Mileage	1,328,734

Date applied or Ex-overhaul	GOLDEN SHUTTLE/DWIGHT D EISENHOWER Doncaster Works No 1861
4 Sep 37	LNER No 4496, tender No 5651, painted garter blue livery and allocated to Doncaster
10 Dec 37	Tender coal space modified
30 Jan 42	Side valancing removed and wartime black livery
3 Jun 44	Max cut-off changed to 75%
25 Sep 45	Renamed DWIGHT D EISENHOWER and restored to Garter blue livery
23 Nov 46	New number LNER No 8
29 Oct 48	New number BR No 60008
23 Jun 50	Exptl ATC fitted
23 Jun 50	BR blue livery
9 Nov 51	BR dark green livery
18 Jun 54	Long guard irons removed
20 Aug 58	Double chimney fitted
30 Jun 60	BR speedometer fitted
20 Jul 63	Withdrawn from service for preservation
Life Mileage	1,409,000

Date applied or Ex-overhaul	UNION OF SOUTH AFRICA Doncaster Works No 1853
17 Apr 37	Painted LNER garter blue livery and named OSPREY in Doncaster Works LNER No 4488, tender No 5325. Fitted with South African Railways whistle
29 Jun 37	Renamed UNION OF SOUTH AFRICA, allocated and delivered to Haymarket
18 Jun 38	Tender coal space modified
29 Jul 39	Hudd ATC fitted
21 Mar 42	Side valancing removed and wartime black livery
12 Feb 47	New number LNER No 9 and garter blue livery restored
5 May 48	New number BR No 60009
4 Aug 49	BR blue livery and max cut-off changed to 75%
2 Oct 52	BR dark green livery and long guard irons removed
12 Apr 54	Springbox plaque fitted to driver's side
2 Nov 57	Double chimney fitted
18 Apr 61	BR speedometer fitted
1 Jun 66	Withdrawn from service for preservation. Temporarily renamed OSPREY
Life Mileage	1,582,593

Date applied or Ex-overhaul	WOODCOCK/DOMINION OF CANADA Doncaster Works No 1854
4 May 37	Painted LNER lined works grey livery and named WOODCOCK. LNER No 4489, tender No 5326
15 Jun 37	Renamed DOMINION OF CANADA, garter blue livery with cabside crests and Canadian Pacific Railways whistle, allocated to Kings Cross
6 Dec 37	Tender coal space modified
16 Mar 38	CPR bell fitted to front
21 Feb 42	Side valancing removed and wartime black livery
10 May 46	New number LNER No 10
20 Nov 47	Garter blue livery restored
27 Oct 48	New number BR No 60010
29 Sep 50	Exptl ATC fitted
29 Sep 50	BR blue livery
8 May 52	BR dark green livery
27 Aug 53	Long guard irons removed
1 Jun 56	Max cut-off changed to 75%
27 Dec 57	Double chimney fitted and CPR bell removed
15 Oct 60	BR speedometer fitted
29 May 65	Withdrawn from service for preservation in Canada
Life Mileage	1,366,378

Date applied or Ex-overhaul	EMPIRE OF INDIA Doncaster Works No 1855
25/06/37	LNER No 4490, tender No 5328, painted LNER garter blue livery with cabside crests, allocated to Kings Cross
11/01/38	Tender coal space modified
20/09/40	Hudd ATC fitted
01/11/41	Side valancing removed
22/10/42	Wartime black livery
23/11/46	New number LNER No 11 and garter blue livery restored
30/11/46	Max cut-off changed to 75%
16/03/49	New number BR No 60011
08/06/50	BR blue livery
10/04/52	BR dark green livery
30/07/53	Long guard irons removed
11/01/58	Double chimney fitted
22/10/58	AWS fitted
28/10/60	BR speedometer fitted
11/05/64	Withdrawn from service
Life Mileage	1,538,829

Date applied or Ex-overhaul	COMMONWEALTH OF AUSTRALIA Doncaster Works No 1856
22/06/37	LNER No 4491, tender No 5646, painted LNER garter blue livery with cabside crests, allocated to Haymarket
09/02/38	Tender coal space modified
30/09/39	Hudd ATC fitted
12/09/42	Side valancing removed and wartime black livery
12/01/47	New number LNER No 12
09/08/47	Max cut-off changed to 75%, inside cylinder lined to 17ins and garter blue livery restored
26/05/48	New number BR No 60012
24/08/49	BR blue livery
21/11/52	BR dark green livery
25/03/54	Long guard irons removed
18/07/58	Double chimney fitted
12/03/59	AWS fitted
01/06/60	Fitted with Western Australia Railways whistle
27/10/61	BR speedometer fitted
20/08/64	Withdrawn from service
Life Mileage	1,534,607

Date applied or Ex-overhaul	DOMINION OF NEW ZEALAND Doncaster Works No 1857
27/06/37	LNER No 4492, tender no 5647, painted LNER garter blue livery with cabside crests, allocated to Kings Cross
13/12/37	Tender coal space modified
16/03/38	Tender No 5647 fitted with Hoffman roller bearings
25/05/39	Fitted with a New Zealand Government Railways whistle
21/11/41	Side valancing removed and wartime black livery
17/08/46	New number LNER No 13 and garter blue livery restored
20/05/49	New number BR No 60013 and BR blue livery
08/10/52	BR dark green livery
06/11/52	Exptl ATC fitted
18/03/54	Long guard irons removed
29/03/57	Max cut-off changed to 75%
04/07/58	Double chimney fitted
29/06/61	BR speedometer fitted
18/04/63	Withdrawn from service
Life Mileage	1,459,904

Date applied or Ex-overhaul	SILVER LINK Doncaster Works No 1818
7 Sep 35	Painted name SILVER LINK on boilerside, Silver Jubilee livery (three greys). Numbered LNER 2509, tender No 5589
13 Sep 35	Allocated and delivered to Kings Cross
16 Nov 35	Probable date of fitting Flaman recorder
30 Jan 36	Coupled to tender No 5590
26 Jul 36	Longer buffers fitted
6 Dec 37	Nameplates fitted, Garter blue livery and tender coal space modified
22 Oct 38	Tender No 5590 fitted with Timken roller bearings
6 Dec 41	Side valancing removed and finished in wartime unlined black livery
14 Jun 46	New number LNER No 14, Garter blue livery restored
22 Aug 47	Inside cyl lined to 17ins, cut-off lengthened to 75%
22 Jun 49	New number BR No 60014, BR blue livery, inside cyl liner removed
28 Sep 50	ATC fitted
4 Jan 52	BR dark green livery
24 Jul 53	Long guard irons removed
1 Dec 54	Max cut off changed to 75%
1 Oct 57	Double chimney fitted
12 Apr 61	BR speedometer fitted
29 Dec 62	Withdrawn from service
Life Mileage	1,527,412

Date applied or Ex-overhaul	QUICKSILVER Doncaster Works No 1819
21 Sep 35	Painted name QUICKSILVER on boiler side. Silver Jubilee livery (three greys). LNER No 2510. Tender No 5590. Allocated and delivered to Kings Cross
21 Jan 36	Coupled to tender No 5589
11 Jul 36	Longer buffers fitted and number added at front
10 Dec 37	Tender cladding reduced
28 May 38	Nameplates added, garter blue livery
7 Nov 41	Side valancing removed
5 Oct 43	Finished in wartime unlined black livery
13 Apr 46	Cut-off lengthened to 75%
1 Sep 46	Renumbered to LNER No 15
4 Oct 47	Restored to garter blue livery
17 Dec 48	Renumbered to BR No 60015
25 Nov 49	BR blue livery
22 Nov 51	BR dark green livery
11 Feb 53	ATC fitted
1 May 53	Long guard irons removed
9 Aug 57	Double chimney fitted
13 Jan 61	BR speedometer fitted
25 Apr 63	Withdrawn from service
Life Mileage	1,529,463

Date applied or Ex-overhaul	SILVER KING Doncaster Works No 1281
5 Nov 35	Painted name SILVER KING on boiler side. LNER No 2511, tender No 5591 Silver Jubilee livery (three greys)
18 Nov 35	Allocated to Kings Cross, then transferred to Gateshead
31 Jul 36	Longer buffers fitted and number added at front
21 Jan 38	Tender cladding reduced
9 Aug 38	Nameplates added, garter blue livery
10 Apr 43	Finished in wartime unlined black livery and side valancing removed
15 Jul 44	Cut-off lengthened to 75%
24 Nov 46	Renumbered to LNER No 16
10 May 47	Restored to garter blue livery
11 Jun 48	Renumbered to BR No 60016 and coupled to non-corridor tender No 5636
21 Oct 49	BR blue livery
10 Jul 52	BR dark green livery
14 Jan 54	Long guard irons removed
13 Jun 57	Double chimney fitted
19 Aug 59	AWS fitted
8 Jul 60	BR Speedometer fitted
19 Mar 65	Withdrawn from service
Life Mileage	1,490,852

Date applied or Ex-overhaul	SILVER FOX Doncaster Works No 1823
18 Dec 35	Painted name SILVER FOX on boilerside, Silver Jubilee livery (three greys) LNER No 2512, tender No 5592. Allocated and delivered to Kings Cross
2 Oct 36	Longer buffers fitted
6 Nov 37	Nameplates fitted, Garter blue livery and tender coal space modified
23 Nov 41	Side valancing removed and finished in wartime unlined black livery
1 Sep 46	New number LNER No 17
25 Sep 47	Garter blue livery restored
27 Apr 49	New number BR No 60017
21 Sep 50	ATC fitted
21 Sep 50	BR blue livery
1 Dec 51	BR dark green livery
19 Jun 53	Long guard irons removed
31 Dec 55	Max cut off changed to 75%
18 May 57	Double chimney fitted
26 Oct 60	BR speedometer fitted
20 Oct 63	Withdrawn from service
Life Mileage	1,596,459

Date applied or Ex-overhaul	SPARROW HAWK Doncaster Works No 1865
27 Nov 37	LNER No 4463, tender No 5668, painted garter blue livery and allocated to Gateshead
01 Nov 41	Side valancing removed
22 Aug 43	Wartime black livery
15 Sep 46	New number LNER No 18
28 Dec 46	Restored to Garter blue livery
16 Oct 48	New number BR No 60018
05 Apr 50	BR blue livery
04 Oct 51	BR dark green livery
01 May 53	Long guard irons removed
17 Apr 56	Max cut-off changed to 75%
05 Oct 57	Double chimney fitted
19 Nov 58	AWS fitted
17 Feb 61	BR speedometer fitted
19 Jun 63	Withdrawn from service
Life Mileage	1,288,947

Date applied or Ex-overhaul	BITTERN Doncaster Works No 1866
18 Dec 37	LNER No 4464, tender No 5638, painted garter blue livery and allocated to Kings Cross
14 Nov 41	Side valancing removed and wartime black livery
06 Aug 46	New number LNER No 19
07 Mar 47	Garter blue livery restored
14 Oct 48	New number BR No 60019
28 Jul 50	Max cut-off changed to 75% and BR blue livery
12 Feb 52	BR dark green livery
12 Jun 53	Long guard irons removed
06 Sep 57	Double chimney fitted
13 Dec 58	AWS fitted
16 Mar 60	BR speedometer fitted
05 Sep 66	Withdrawn from service for preservation
Life mileage	1,260,870

Date applied or Ex-overhaul	GUILLEMOT Doncaster Works No 1867
03 Jan 38	LNER No 4465, tender No 5669, painted garter blue livery and allocated to Gateshead
23 Oct 41	Side valancing removed
07 Aug 43	Wartime black livery
15 Sep 46	New number LNER No 20
26 Oct 46	Restored to Garter blue livery
10 Oct 47	inside cylinder lined to 17ins dia
01 Oct 48	New number BR No 60020
28 Apr 50	BR blue livery
30 Nov 51	BR dark green livery
22 Apr 53	Long guard irons removed
18 May 56	Max cut-off changed to 75%
07 Nov 57	Double chimney fitted
06 Nov 58	AWS fitted
19 May 61	BR speedometer fitted
20 Mar 64	Withdrawn from service
Life Mileage	1,311,352

Date applied or Ex-overhaul	WILD SWAN Doncaster Works No 1869
19 Feb 38	LNER No 4467, tender No 5671, painted garter blue livery and allocated to Kings Cross
11 Apr 42	Side valancing removed and wartime black livery
25 May 46	New number LNER No 21
30 Apr 47	Restored to Garter blue livery
5 Feb 48	New number BR No E21
21 Sep 48	New number BR No 60021
31 Mar 50	BR blue livery and exptl ATC fitted
8 Aug 51	BR dark green livery
10 Mar 54	Long guard irons removed
11 Jun 55	Max cut-off changed to 75%
30 Apr 58	Double chimney fitted
17 Nov 61	BR speedometer fitted
20 Oct 63	Withdrawn from service
Life Mileage	1,361,527

Date applied or Ex-overhaul	MALLARD Doncaster Works No 1870
3 Mar 38	LNER No 4468, tender No 5642, painted garter blue livery. Double Kylchap chimney and allocated to Doncaster
13 Jun 42	Side valancing removed and wartime black livery
29 Sep 46	New number LNER No 22
5 Mar 48	Max cut-off changed to 75%, garter blue livery restored and new no BR E22
16 Sep 49	New number BR No 60022 and BR blue livery
4 Jul 52	BR dark green livery
10 Feb 53	ATC fitted
8 May 53	Long guard irons removed
29 Mar 60	BR speedometer fitted
25 Apr 63	Withdrawn from service for preservation
Life mileage	1,422,000

Date applied or Ex-overhaul	GOLDEN EAGLE Doncaster Works No 1847
22 Dec 36	Painted LNER apple green with black front and valancing LNER No 4482, tender No 5323. Allocated and delivered to Kings Cross
29 Jan 38	Tender coal space modified and painted garter blue
25 Apr 40	Hudd ATC fitted
5 Jun 41	Corridor tender replaced with non-corridor No 5667
26 Jul 41	Hudd ATC and side valancing removed
10 Sep 43	Wartime black livery
28 Sep 46	Garter blue livery restored
22 Nov 46	New number LNER No 23
25 Mar 48	New number BR No 60023
31 Aug 49	Max cut off changed to 75%, BR blue livery
4 Sep 52	BR dark green livery
1 Mar 54	Long guard irons removed
18 Sep 58	Double chimney fitted
23 Mar 59	AWS fitted
10 Jun 60	BR speedometer fitted
30 Oct 64	Withdrawn from service
Life Mileage	Approx 1,450,000. Official figure of 1,902,372 clearly wrong

Date applied or Ex-overhaul	KINGFISHER Doncaster Works No 1848
26 Dec 36	Painted LNER apple green with black smokebox, front and valancing LNER No 4483, tender no 5331. Allocated and delivered to Haymarket
7 Jan 38	Tender coal space modified and painted garter blue
7 Jun 40	Hudd ATC fitted
6 Nov 41	Hudd ATC and side valancing removed
4 Feb 43	Wartime black livery
30 Mar 46	New number LNER No 585
5 May 46	New number LNER No 24
31 Aug 46	Max cut off changed to 75%, Garter blue livery restored
18 Jun 48	New number BR No 60024, exptl BR purple livery
24 Aug 50	BR blue livery
12 Mar 52	BR dark green livery
30 Jan 54	Long guard irons removed
19 Jul 55	KINGFISHER plaques fitted
20 Aug 58	Double chimney fitted
15 Dec 60	AWS fitted
15 Jun 61	BR speedometer fitted
5 Sep 66	Withdrawn from service
Life Mileage	1,566,961

Date applied or Ex-overhaul	FALCON Doncaster Works No 1849
23 Jan 37	Painted LNER apple green with black smokebox, front and valancing LNER No 4484, tender No 5327. Allocated and delivered to Haymarket
18 Dec 37	Tender coal space modified and garter blue livery
30 Nov 41	Side valancing removed and wartime black livery
31 Mar 46	New number LNER No 586 allocated but not applied
5 May 46	New number LNER No 25
31 Dec 47	Garter blue livery restored
27 Jan 50	New number BR No 60025, BR blue livery, exptl ATC fitted and max cut off changed to 75%
6 Dec 52	BR dark green livery and long guard irons removed
27 Jan 55	ATC fitted
4 Sep 58	Double chimney fitted
16 Jun 60	BR speedometer fitted
20 Oct 63	Withdrawn from service
Life Mileage	1,548,928

Date applied or Ex-overhaul	KESTREL/MILES BEEVOR Doncaster Works No 1850
20 Feb 37	Painted LNER apple green with black smokebox, front and valancing LNER No 4485, tender No 5324. Allocated and delivered to Haymarket
8 Dec 37	Tender coal space modified and garter blue livery
18 Jan 42	Side valancing removed and wartime black livery
18 Apr 46	New number LNER No 587
26 May 46	New number LNER No 26
1 Nov 47	Garter blue livery restored, renamed MILES BEEVOR
23 Sep 49	New number BR No 60026, BR blue livery and max cut off changed to 75%
30 Oct 50	Exptl ATC fitted
20 Feb 53	BR dark green livery and long guard irons removed
12 May 55	ATC fitted
15 Aug 57	Double chimney fitted
21 Oct 60	BR speedometer fitted
21 Dec 65	Withdrawn from service
Life Mileage	1,349,578

Date applied or Ex-overhaul	MERLIN Doncaster Works No 1851
13 Mar 37	Painted LNER apple green with black smokebox, front and valancing LNER No 4486, tender No 5332. Allocated and delivered to Haymarket
18 Dec 37	Tender coal space modified and garter blue livery
27 Dec 41	Side valancing removed and wartime black livery
10 Aug 44	Temporary renaming in Works
31 Mar 46	New number LNER No 588
5 May 46	New number LNER No 27
26 May 46	MERLIN plaques fitted
25 Jan 47	Garter blue livery restored
11 Mar 48	New temporary BR No E27
2 Jun 48	New number BR No 60027, BR purple livery
7 Jul 50	BR blue livery, max cut-off changed to 75%
6 Jun 52	BR dark green livery
20 Aug 53	Long guard irons removed
12 Feb 58	Double chimney fitted
19 May 60	AWS and BR speedometers fitted
3 Sep 65	Withdrawn from service
Life Mileage	1,556,803

Date applied or Ex-overhaul	SEA EAGLE/WALTER K WHIGHAM Doncaster Works No 1852
20 Mar 37	Painted LNER apple green with black smokebox, front and valancing Numbered LNER 4487, tender No 5330. Allocated and delivered to Haymarket
12 Feb 38	Tender coal space modified and garter blue livery
5 Jul 41	Side valancing removed
22 Nov 41	Wartime black livery
30 Jan 44	Max cut-off changed to 75%
20 Nov 46	New number LNER No 28
1 Oct 47	Garter blue livery restored and renamed WALTER K WHIGHAM
7 Jun 48	New number BR No 60028, BR purple livery
13 Oct 50	Exptl ATC fitted and BR blue livery
22 Feb 52	BR dark green livery
10 Jun 53	Long guard irons removed
2 Nov 57	Double chimney fitted
18 Apr 61	BR speedometer fitted
29 Dec 62	Withdrawn from service
Life Mileage	1,471,623

Date applied or Ex-overhaul	WOODCOCK Doncaster Works No 1858
26/07/37	LNER No 4492, tender No 5648, painted LNER apple green livery with black front and valancing and allocated to Gateshead
21/01/38	Tender coal space modified
25/07/38	Garter blue livery
25/09/39	Tender No 5648 fitted with Skefco roller bearings
11/09/42	Side valancing removed and wartime black livery
26/05/46	New number LNER No 29
04/06/47	Garter blue livery restored
16/07/48	New number BR No 60029 and BR purple livery
16/07/48	Max cut-off changed to 75%
13/01/50	BR blue livery
17/10/50	Exptl ATC fitted
30/10/52	BR dark green livery
22/04/54	Long guard irons removed
03/10/58	Double chimney fitted
08/04/60	BR speedometer fitted
20/10/63	Withdrawn from service
Life Mileage	1,489,772

Date applied or Ex-overhaul	GREAT SNIPE/GOLDEN FLEECE Doncaster Works No 1860
30 Aug 37	LNER No 4495, tender No 5650, painted LNER apple green livery with black front and valancing and allocated to Doncaster
7 Dec 37	Tender coal space modified
25 Sep 37	Renamed GOLDEN FLEECE and repainted in garter blue livery
20 Dec 41	Side valancing removed and wartime black livery
23 Nov 46	New number LNER No 30
7 Dec 46	Garter blue livery restored
30 Jul 48	New number BR No 60030
23 Jan 57	Max cut-off changed to 75%
10 Nov 49	BR blue livery
15 Jan 53	Exptl ATC fitted
24 Sep 52	BR dark green livery
28 Apr 54	Long guard irons removed
15 May 58	Double chimney fitted
28 Jul 61	BR speedometer fitted
29 Dec 62	Withdrawn from service
Life mileage	1,419,855

Date applied or Ex-overhaul	GOLDEN PLOVER Doncaster Works No 1862
2 Oct 37	LNER No 4497, tender No 5652, painted garter blue livery and allocated to Haymarket
15 Dec 39	Hudd ATC fitted
16 May 42	Side valancing removed and wartime black livery
30 May 46	New number LNER No 31
01 Aug 47	Max cut-off changed to 75%, inside cylinder lined to 17ins dia and garter blue livery restored
04 Jun 48	New number BR No 60031
05 Jul 49	BR blue livery
23 Jul 52	BR dark green livery
20 Jan 54	Long guard irons removed
11 Mar 58	Double chimney fitted
06 Feb 59	Inside cylinder liner removed
13 May 60	AWS fitted
15 Mar 61	BR speedometer fitted
29 Oct 65	Withdrawn from service
Life Mileage	1,523,805

Date applied or Ex-overhaul	GANNET Doncaster Works No 1874
17 May 38	LNER No 4900, tender No 5675, painted garter blue livery and allocated to Doncaster
4 Sep 42	Side valancing removed and wartime black livery
26 Nov 46	New number LNER No 32
3 May 47	Restored to Garter blue livery
10 Jun 49	New number BR No 60032 and BR blue livery
20 Feb 53	ATC fitted
24 Oct 52	BR dark green livery
30 Mar 54	Long guard irons removed
26 Jan 46	Max cut-off changed to 75%
27 Nov 58	Double chimney fitted
29 Apr 60	BR speedometer fitted
20 Oct 63	Withdrawn from service
Life Mileage	1,351,887

Date applied or Ex-overhaul	SEAGULL Doncaster Works No 1876
28 Jun 38	LNER No 4902, tender No 5636, painted garter blue livery. Double Kylchap chimney and allocated to Kings Cross
27 May 42	Side valancing removed and wartime black livery
31 Oct 46	New LNER No 33
5 Dec 47	Garter blue livery restored
10 Apr 48	New number BR No 60033
16 Apr 48	Max cut-off changed to 75%
10 Nov 50	BR blue livery
13 Jun 52	BR dark green livery
25 Feb 53	ATC fitted
2 Dec 53	Long guard irons removed
8 Jun 61	BR speedometer fitted
29 Dec 62	Withdrawn from service
Life Mileage	1,384,729

Date applied or Ex-overhaul	PEREGRINE/LORD FARINGDON Doncaster Works No 1877
1 Jul 38	LNER No 4903, tender No 5639, painted garter blue livery. Double Kylchap chimney and allocated to Doncaster
14 Sep 42	Side valancing removed and wartime black livery
3 Nov 46	New LNER No 34
10 Dec 47	Garter blue livery restored
25 Feb 48	Max cut-off changed to 75%
24 Mar 48	Renamed LORD FARINGDON
24 Mar 48	New number BR No 60034
4 Dec 50	BR blue livery
7 Aug 52	BR dark green livery
11 Nov 52	ATC fitted
7 Feb 53	Long guard irons removed
2 Nov 60	BR speedometer fitted
24 Aug 66	Withdrawn from service
Life Mileage	1,246,748

Date applied or Ex-overhaul	GADWALL/SIR RALPH WEDGWOOD Doncaster Works No 1871
30 Mar 38	LNER No 4469, tender No 5672, painted garter blue livery and allocated to Gateshead
1 Mar 39	Renamed SIR RALPH WEDGWOOD
25 Oct 41	Side valancing removed and wartime black livery
20 Jun 42	Damaged by enemy action and withdrawn from service. Tender No 5672 stored, renumbered 703 and reused on BR No 60507
Life Mileage	Estimated mileage approx 250,000

Date applied or Ex-overhaul	(Unnamed: 'The Hush-hush' unofficially) No Darlington or Doncaster Works number
4 Nov 29	Experimental locomotive with water-tube boiler completed at Yarrows and sent to Darlington Works. Temporary tender No 763.
21 Jun 30	LNER No 10000, tender No 5484, painted grey livery and allocated to Gateshead
10 May 35	Double chimney fitted
1 Jul 35	Transferred to Neville Hill
10 Jul 35	Hood fitted at front end
21 Aug 35	Placed in store
6 Nov 37	Rebuilt as 4-6-2-2-3 cyl simple expansion locomotive, painted in garter blue livery and allocated to Kings Cross. Boiler 18193 was returned to Darlington Works for use as a stationary boiler
19 Jan 38	Tender coal space modified
4 Apr 42	Side valancing removed
12 Oct 42	Wartime black livery
14 Dec 46	Garter blue livery restored, number remained at 10000
18 Jun 48	New number BR No 60700
11 Jan 52	BR blue livery
27 May 52	BR dark green livery
18 Aug 53	Long guard irons removed
1 Sep 55	Derailed due to bogie frame fracture
13 Dec 56	Cylinder diameter reduced to 19ins and tractive effort to 37,397lbs
1 Aug 57	Max cut-off changed to 75%
5 Dec 58	AWS fitted
1 Jun 59	Withdrawn from service
Life mileage	Approx 875000

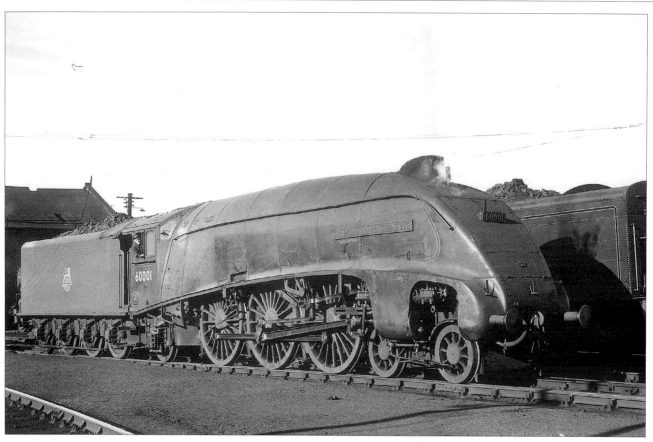

SIR RONALD MATTHEWS, née GARGANEY, at Haymarket waiting to work back to Newcastle on October 30th 1955. The A4 is some two months from its last general overhaul and is already in typical Gateshead condition. She still has a single chimney, and the autumn light shows the detail of the front end well, conjugated gear and the keyway for opening the 'cod's mouth' below it. The drain from the middle cylinder can be seen emerging from beneath the cylinder to be fixed with other two. She was only coupled to one non-corridor tender, No.5674. (J. Robertson, The Transport Treasury)

SIR RONALD MATTHEWS coasts into Newcastle Central with an up express. No date is given but it must be after 1960. The A4 has now been rebuilt with a double chimney, and she seems to have a rather bruised look, with her casing dented and whistle awry. The habit of painting the buffers of an otherwise scruffy A4 silver was an unfortunate fashion which was presumably intended to make the engine seem clean. It didn't work. Tender non-corridor No.5674. (The Transport Treasury)

The A4 had an unfortunately amorphous appearance when dirty and neglected, as most were in the war years. Gateshead's A4s were often in much the same state, as one can see with SIR RONALD MATTHEWS, at York on a relief with LMR stock. The A4 is single blast and without AWS. Date, September 10th 1957, non-corridor tender No.5674. (J.F. Aylard)

SIR RONALD in better health, now with double chimney and AWS, backing out of Kings Cross platform one on May 24th 1960. This platform was usually used for parcels trains, and the morning commuters usually encountered a sort of ad hoc 100 yard hurdles over their contents, en route from York Road platform to the Underground! Tender No.5674. (J.F. Aylard)

SIR MURROUGH WILSON, née POCHARD, at Haymarket in 1951 alongside her Tyneside sister FAIRWAY. The condition of the A4 is uncommonly good which leads me to suspect that she was weeks and not months from Doncaster Paint Shop, wearing her new dark green livery. She retains the long guard irons that were to be removed at the next overhaul in early 1953. As No.4499 she worked the last 'Silver Jubilee' on August 31st 1939. Another A4 to remain united with the same tender, non-corridor No.5673. (J. Robertson, The Transport Treasury)

SIR MURROUGH WILSON was another rare bird down south, caught here on the 15.00 Kings Cross-Newcastle emerging from the north portal of the new down Potters Bar Tunnel. This was at a time when the widening project was virtually finished, and the train is on the new down slow here. The date is April 22nd 1959, and the engine is only a month from General overhaul. Tender non-corridor No.5673. (J.F. Aylard)

The driver has the expression of one doomed, for time being, to relieving top link crews, a mixture of boredom and curiosity, awaiting the pleasure of the signalmen, and ferrying locomotives in and out of the terminus. SIR MURROUGH WILSON, just out of shops, looks in good fettle for a pleasant change and no doubt has the younger platform-enders marking her capture in their notebooks! There is a surprising amount of coal in the tender after a Newcastle-Kings Cross trip. Date August 2nd 1957, regular non-corridor tender No.5673. (J.F. Aylard)

SIR MURROUGH WILSON, fresh from Doncaster Works with a double chimney, is luxury indeed for the crew of No.266 down, the famous 'Scotch Goods'. The train is at speed on the down main at Cadwell, just north of Hitchin, in August 1957. 'No.2' was a Gateshead engine for almost her entire life, apart from a couple of months in 1943 when, probably covering for a severe shortage, she was at Top Shed. Tender non-corridor No.5673. (P.J. Coster)

ANDREW K McCOSH heads the down 'Yorkshire Pullman' with the new Metro-Cammell Pullmans through New Southgate in 1961 – A4 non-corridor tender No.5670. (P.J. Coster)

ANDREW K McCOSH standing at Kings Cross in 1960. The A4 has the smokebox door casing open as the crew make a last-minute check. Non-corridor tender No.5670. (The Transport Treasury)

ANDREW K McCOSH heads the 9.40 Kings Cross-Newcastle through Sandy. The date is August 7th 1961 and the A4 has non-corridor tender No.5670. The A4 was unusual in that it was the only one to have had an A3 non-corridor tender, albeit for a very short period, possibly due to wartime shortages or victory euphoria! (M. Mensing)

June 8th 1961 and a memorable day for the guests travelling to the Wedding of the Duke and Duchess of Kent. Top Shed turned out four A4s, one for the Royal train, two for VIP specials and a pilot. The engines were in magnificent condition, and here one of the VIP specials, the 8.40, accelerates north of New Barnet behind ANDREW K McCOSH. Tender No.5670. (J.F. Aylard)

The 10.24 departs from Edinburgh Waverley behind WILLIAM WHITELAW. The A4 is blowing on the right-hand side, but once under way the engine would warm through and the leak hopefully would lessen. The A4 is in BR blue livery and, interestingly, has the Flaman drive in place, although that is no guarantee that an instrument is fitted. Although it is over seven months since she left Doncaster, the condition of the A4 is a tribute to the staff at Haymarket. The date is March 24th 1951. The engine is coupled to the A3 type corridor tender built for the W1, No.5484. (J. Robertson, The Transport Treasury)

A superb portrait of WILLIAM WHITELAW at Haymarket, now in BR dark green livery. The date is given as May 10th 1952, but as the A4 was at Doncaster Works at the time it must be wrong. The month must be July, and I would guess from the polished buffers that the engine is on the Non-stop. Tender W1 corridor No.5484. (W. Hermiston, The Transport Treasury).

WILLIAM WHITELAW, now with double chimney, and the later BR emblem, on Haymarket turntable, with fireman either attaching or detaching the turntable vacuum motor connection. The date must be 1958 since the presence of a double chimney and lack of AWS define the date. W1 corridor tender No.5484. (W. Hermiston, The Transport Treasury).

WILLIAM WHITELAW, with double chimney, AWS, and in final condition but for the BR speedometer still to be fitted on the driver's side. The view is at Haymarket, taken on June 21st 1959. Tender W1 corridor No.5484. (W. Hermiston, The Transport Treasury).

The southbound start from Stonehaven is the hard climb to Carmont, as the line rises from the valley sharpening to 1 in 102 near the top. WILLIAM WHITELAW heads south with a troop train, not appearing to make hard work of it with a clearish chimney and the safety valves showing the 'white feather'. The date is July 11th 1964, and by now the A4 has been despatched to Ferryhill shed. Tender W1 corridor No.5484. (M. Mensing)

WILLIAM WHITELAW in old platform 5 at Kings Cross, about to couple on to the 'Capitals Limited' in its last summer. The date is August 22nd 1952, the tender W1 corridor No.5484. (J.F. Aylard)

To many of those in the south, the Gateshead A4s were creatures of the night – if at all – for a long while, and photographs of them on the early morning overnight expresses were not easy. So it is a pleasure to see a good photograph of SIR CHARLES NEWTON climbing past Grantshouse with a down express. The engine is not terribly clean considering her last general overhaul was only a month or so ago. The distinctive underbridges installed after the 1948 floods have now lost their reinforced concrete handrails (!) in favour of metal. The Gateshead A4s rarely if ever changed tenders, and SIR CHARLES was always coupled to A4 non-corridor tender No.5641. The date is June 20th 1957. (J. Robertson, The Transport Treasury)

An engine fresh from the paint shops was always a joy to behold, and I can imagine John Aylard's delight at being able to photograph SIR CHARLES NEWTON in such a condition. The A4 is in BR blue livery, which was not as good as garter blue, but many times better than the Swindonian khaki that they wore later. The date is June 10th 1951, and the A4 has tender No.5641. (J.F. Aylard)

An up express bursts out of Penmanshiel Tunnel headed by Gateshead's SIR CHARLES NEWTON on May 31st 1952. The tunnel, short and curved, has been sealed after the tragic accident when the tunnel headroom was being increased, and now the main line swings west of the high ground making the site impossible to see as in the photograph. The tender is non-corridor No.5641. (W. Hermiston, The Transport Treasury)

The Widening Project has just been completed, and SIR RALPH WEDGWOOD is heading an up Fred Olsen Line boat express from Tyneside south of the Hadley Wood South Tunnel. The date is given as May 18th 1959, and from the condition of the engine, one might think she had just been overhauled. In fact she was shortly to become due for general overhaul. The A4 is coupled to non-corridor tender No.5675. (The Transport Treasury)

Near the end of her career at the southern end of the East Coast line, SIR RALPH WEDGWOOD accelerates past Finsbury Park No.3 signalbox with the 9.00 Newcastle, not a very heavy train but tightly timed. The locomotive is well turned out as usual, but there seems to be some leakage underneath and from the right-hand gland. The double chimney was so effective that it tended to mask minor problems that in earlier days would have required it to be taken out of service. The date is May 30th 1962; the A4 is coupled to non-corridor tender No.5675. (J.F. Aylard)

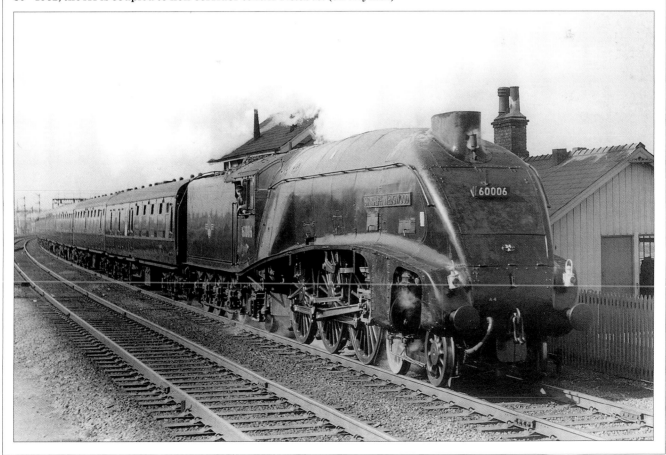

Formerly HERRING GULL, now honoured as SIR RALPH WEDGWOOD, draws into Peterborough North with an up express, watched by a pair of drivers and a wheel tapper (Ahem – a Carriage and Wagon Examiner). The A4 has a double chimney and AWS fitted. The date is August 6th 1960, the A4 is coupled to non-corridor tender No.5675. (Frank Hornby)

A famous occasion in East Coast history, May 23rd 1959. To celebrate the 50th Jubilee of the Stephenson Locomotive Society a special train was run to Doncaster and back behind SIR NIGEL GRESLEY with Driver Bill Hoole, who was within a month or two of retirement. The A4 is descending at speed from Potters Bar towards Kings Cross, near the site of the old Greenwood signalbox. The leading inspection door has shaken open and the main steam pipe can be seen. The A3 corridor tender is No.5324, first used on FLYING SCOTSMAN. (J.F. Aylard)

SIR NIGEL GRESLEY stands at the head of a southbound express at York. The A4 was a Grantham engine at the time, in garter blue livery with a single chimney. The date must lay between March 1948 and June 1950 when the garter blue was replaced by BR blue. The tender is A3 corridor No.5324. (W. Hermiston, The Transport Treasury)

This page. SIR NIGEL GRESLEY at New England. The engine is well cleaned and the excellent views show the detail of the AWS conduit and the BR speedometer. The A3 corridor tender is No.5324. (B. Richardson, The Transport Treasury)

SIR NIGEL GRESLEY at New England shed. The A4 is well cleaned and the marvellous view reveals considerable detail. The A3 corridor is, as usual, No.5324. (B. Richardson, The Transport Treasury)

There are no notes to suggest where and when this view of SIR NIGEL GRESLEY was taken. With signs of overhead electrification in the distance, I would plump for Crewe South depot after the A4 was withdrawn and before she was restored at Crewe Works. The builder's plate has been removed for safe keeping, and the engine has that 'dead' look that became so depressingly familiar. She still has A3 corridor tender No.5324. (The Transport Treasury)

The down 'Elizabethan' getting into its stride at Welwyn Garden City with SIR NIGEL GRESLEY at the head. This duty was only worked by SIR NIGEL as a single chimney engine in summer 1956 for a few days, and can be dated quite easily. The carmine and cream livery lasted little longer, weathering badly, and was replaced by maroon. The freight on the up slow seems to have no engine, and is sheeted very reminiscently of the 'Ashburton Pullman', the local name for the trains of refuse from Ashburton Grove. However, a few trains started or picked up here, and with all of the sidings on the up side, it may well be a northbound departure. The refuse wagons were usually taken down the Welwyn-Hertford branch (now long closed) to Holwell tip, and the connection was on the up side. The A4 has A3 corridor tender No.5324.

Two of the most famous engines of the steam age on the East Coast Route, SIR NIGEL GRESLEY and SILVER FOX, stand at New England with, I suspect, little to do. The former went to St. Margarets and on to Ferryhill, and very sadly the latter went initially to Scotland but returned and was withdrawn. A fine engine, she might just have survived into preservation as one of the original four, some compensation for the loss of SILVER LINK. The tender of No.60007 is A3 corridor No.5324; the other is A4 corridor No.5592. (B. Richardson, The Transport Treasury)

SIR NIGEL GRESLEY at Stirling with one of the three hour expresses between Glasgow and Aberdeen. The date is May 15th, 1965. Tender: A3 corridor No.5324. (A Scarsbrook, Initial Photographics)

The down 'Tees-Tyne Pullman' accelerating north from Wood Green Tunnel behind SIR NIGEL GRESLEY with Bill Hoole and Albert Leech in charge. Date, mid-1956, tender A3 corridor No.5324. (P.J. Coster)

SIR NIGEL GRESLEY passes Cambridge Junction at Hitchin with the 15.10 Scots Goods in late 1959. The much-maligned signalbox was widely known as 'Sabotage Junction' to the footplate fraternity because of the occasional habit of cautioning southbound expresses while a down Cambridge branch service crossed the junction. Tender: A3 corridor No.5324. (P.J. Coster)

DWIGHT D EISENHOWER was again the engine on the down 'White Rose' on September 22nd, 1962, and here she is getting up speed past Finsbury Park No.3 at the south end of the station. She is in typical Top Shed condition, well cleaned, front coupling properly hung, no leaks, and the exhaust thrown well clear of the cab. The exhaust was not easy to photograph with the double chimney engines and in hot weather it was invisible. Tender: non-corridor No.5671. (J.F. Aylard)

Although it was a southern area engine, and a London one for many years, DWIGHT D EISENHOWER was not photographed so frequently as the others, so good illustrations are less common. With all due respects to 'Ike' it was a hell of a name for an A4. 'No.8' was not one of the most popular London engines while single blast, and spent most of her time as a pool engine, working such as the down 'White Rose', a heavy train seen here north of Doncaster. The A4 would be returning with the heavy 17.15 back from Leeds later in the day. The date and location are not given, but with double chimney, speedometer and electrification flashes, clearly it is 1961 or later. Tender: non-corridor No.5671. (The Transport Treasury)

As C.J. Allen might have said 'The glory hath departed'. A scruffy DWIGHT D EISENHOWER stands at Kings Cross, old number 7 platform, ready to take out the 14.00 to Edinburgh on May 13th 1958. It looks as though the A4 has been stopped for repairs and the cleaning gang have not got their hands on her yet, and she will shortly be going to Doncaster Works for general overhaul and a double chimney. Tender: A4 non-corridor No.5671. (J.F. Aylard)

Haymarket's UNION OF SOUTH AFRICA stands at the head of the non-stop 'Capitals Limited' in old platform 5 at Kings Cross on June 21st 1950, early in the summer season. The A4 was one of two, both at Haymarket, where the supply of 'ferret and dartboard' totems had been exhausted. As a result they appeared in BR blue with no evidence of ownership. Here is another Haymarket A4 with the Flaman recorder drive still in place. The man on the extreme right has the cut of a senior locomotive inspector of the day, while two of the District Engineer's Works Department enjoy the sunshine up on the roof. The A4 has A4 corridor tender No.5591, off SILVER KING. (J.F. Aylard)

UNION OF SOUTH AFRICA, her springbok plaque in view, starts the 'Elizabethan' from old platform 6 in its last year. The date is August 18th 1961; the engine still has the same A4 corridor tender, No.5591. (J.F. Aylard)

UNION OF SOUTH AFRICA at Edinburgh Waverley, her driver waiting for the 'right away', on September 22nd 1961. Photographs taken on the north side of the Waverley train shed are comparatively unusual, and photographers usually waited until the train had started away and was in better light. In this case the A4 is well cleaned and shows up well. It has A4 corridor tender No.5591. (Dr. A.H. Roscoe, The Transport Treasury)

UNION OF SOUTH AFRICA, with a single chimney, on Eastfield turntable, May 9th 1953. Originally she was OSPREY before the 'Coronation' theme was adopted. The profile of the single chimney is very clear here, and again the Flaman drive can be seen. A4 corridor tender No.5591. (W. Hermiston, The Transport Treasury)

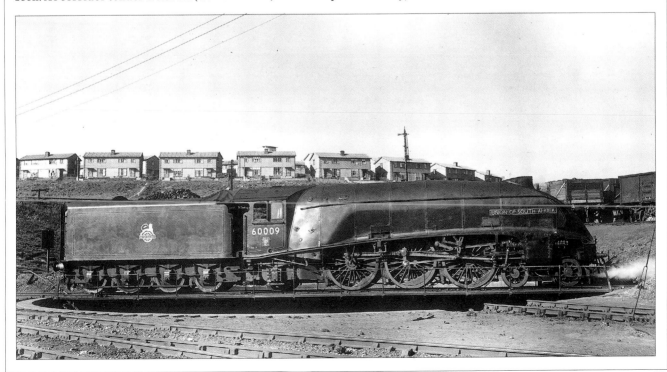

UNION OF SOUTH AFRICA with single chimney, Flaman drive and BR green livery, Haymarket, January 30th 1956. The return crank rod and expansion link foot are disconnected as the shed staff attend to a minor problem. A4 corridor tender No.5591. (The Transport Treasury)

UNION OF SOUTH AFRICA with a single chimney, Flaman drive, and BR blue livery but now with the totem on the tender. The engine has just been released as the ECS of the 'Capitals Limited' was drawn out. No details are given but it is clearly Kings Cross, and the date would be 1951. The A4 corridor tender is No.5591. (The Transport Treasury)

By 1964 the remainder of the class were working in Scotland, and UNION OF SOUTH AFRICA is seen here at Perth on a three hour service to Glasgow from Aberdeen. By now she has lost her A4 corridor tender and acquired an A3 version, No.5332. (The Transport Treasury)

UNION OF SOUTH AFRICA was still hard at work in Scotland in 1965, and here she is starting away with the 'Bon Accord' on April 6th of that year. The tender is A3 corridor No.5332. (The Transport Treasury)

The northbound 'Elizabethan' going hard up the 1 in 200 at New Southgate behind UNION OF SOUTH AFRICA. The A4 had a single chimney at this time, and was raising the echoes. Tender A4 corridor No.5591. (P.J. Coster)

DOMINION OF CANADA was considered by many to be the black sheep at Kings Cross in her single chimney days. Four A4s were transferred out to Grantham in April of that year, including 'No.10', which explains why she is on a Grantham duty. The 35B plate on an A4 is unusual in the 1950s. She is on the 9.35 Newcastle, standing in the celebrated old platform 10, with single chimney and the bell. The date is July 19th 1957, but the A4 is within a few months of her general overhaul when she was fitted with the double exhaust that transformed her. As one can see here, with the larger chimney, there was insufficient space for chime whistle and bell between that and the 'cod's mouth', and it would not have been practical to mount it on the door! The tender is A3 corridor No.5328. (J.F. Aylard)

The transformed DOMINION OF CANADA races south of New Southgate with the 12.30 from Leeds on March 11th, 1961. It now has A3 corridor No.5326. (J.F. Aylard)

DOMINION OF CANADA, now with a double chimney, makes light work of the 17.00 Peterborough and Cambridge semifast as she emerges from Wood Green Tunnel in the summer of 1958. The tender is A3 corridor No.5328. (P.J. Coster)

The 9.50 Newcastle-Kings Cross races down from Welwyn South Tunnel with DOMINION OF CANADA on June 17th 1961; the tender is A3 corridor No.5326. (P.J. Coster)

Above. DOMINION OF CANADA pulls spectacularly out of old platform 6 at Kings Cross. No information is given, but it must be late 1961 or later. The tender is A3 corridor No.5326.

Left. The start out of Forfar was heavily curved in either direction, and DOMINION OF CANADA is about to leave for Aberdeen on March 30th 1964. If she was about to take water, as the characters by the water crane seem to suggest, the driver needed to pull forward. The tender is A3 corridor No.5326. (The Transport Treasury)

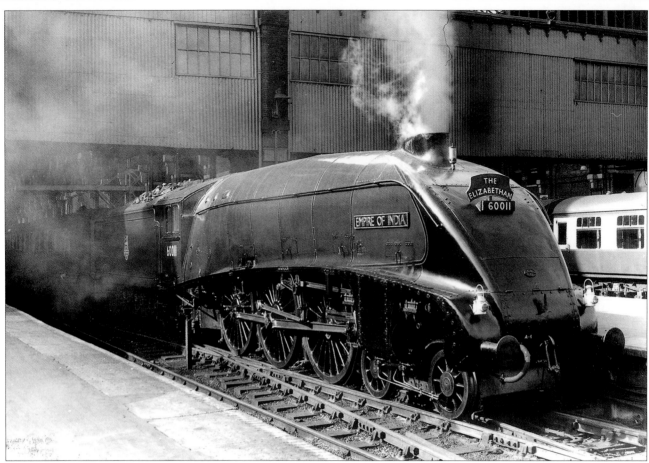

A Summer Haymarket visitor, EMPIRE OF INDIA reverses on to her train on September 4th 1953. It is of course the 'Elizabethan', and the A4 is in the normal gleaming condition for this most prestigious duty. This was the first season for the renamed Non-stop. The A4 always had an A3 corridor tender, in this case No.5326. (J.F. Aylard)

Five years later EMPIRE OF INDIA, now with a double chimney and AWS, backs down to the 'Elizabethan' again, August 8th 1958. The external condition of EMPIRE OF INDIA can only be described as truly spotless, and it is salutary to recall that it was seven months beforehand when she was repainted, not seven days! The tender was A3 corridor No.5326. (J.F. Aylard)

The 'Heart of Midlothian' bursts out of Penmanshiel Tunnel behind EMPIRE OF INDIA making a superb photograph. The date is August 12th 1951 and, although it is not clear, the A4 is in BR blue livery. The tender is an A3 corridor tender No.5326. (J. Robertson, The Transport Treasury)

The down Sunday 'Flying Scotsman', turned in to the down slow for engineering work, eases through the platforms at New Southgate in summer 1955. At that time there was a heavy PSR, which is why EMPIRE OF INDIA's driver was taking things gently. A3 corridor tender No.5326. (P.J. Coster)

The up 'Elizabethan' races through New Southgate behind EMPIRE OF INDIA in the summer of 1958. The tender was A3 corridor No.5326. (P.J. Coster)

COMMONWEALTH OF AUSTRALIA standing at Glasgow Queen Street in August 1949, waiting for the road to Eastfield shed. The A4 is in garter blue livery, but is about to go for general overhaul, when it will emerge in the darker BR blue livery. Always a Scottish engine, she has the first of the second build of A4 corridor tenders attached, No.5646, which was the only one used. By this time the middle cylinder had been lined down to 17ins dia. From the shadow it looks as through the cod's mouth was not quite fully closed. A D30 'Scott' No.62427 DUMBIEDYKES is in the background. (The Transport Treasury)

COMMONWEALTH OF AUSTRALIA worked the 'Elizabethan' in 1957, and she is seen here preparing to depart old platform 6 at Kings Cross. The A4 has the Haymarket headboard with its pale blue background, the Scottish Regional colour. The tender is piled high, and the coat of arms on the cab side is nicely visible. I am not sure that a spirit level was used to set out the tender lining, but occasionally the Doncaster painters did slip from their normally high standards. A4 corridor tender No.5646. (J.F. Aylard)

COMMONWEALTH OF AUSTRALIA, on the up main with the Saturday 'Elizabethan', speeds through Hitchin station. It is summer 1958, and the A4 has recently been converted to double blast. A4 corridor tender No.5646. (P.J. Coster)

In the 1956 season, COMMONWEALTH OF AUSTRALIA worked the 'Elizabethan' from Haymarket, still single blast and the middle cylinder lined to 17ins. On this occasion the well-known drivers Ted Hailstone and Bill Stevenson were working the train. On this run she touched 101mph at Arlesey. A4 corridor tender No.5646. (P.J. Coster)

Another A4 with a long name and a distinguished record of service was DOMINION OF NEW ZEALAND. On April 17th 1954, just a few weeks after general overhaul, she is heading north to Newcastle with the 9.40 express north of Welwyn South Tunnel. The chipping bin has recently been topped up, something rarely seen in railway modelling. The A4 was usually coupled to a corridor tender, but here she has non-corridor No.5670. (R. Wilson, The Transport Treasury)

By September 26th 1956, DOMINION OF NEW ZEALAND had retrieved her corridor tender No.5647, which was equipped with Hoffman roller bearings. She is hauling the 'Talisman', and will be getting into her stride on the descent from Potters Bar down to Hatfield. It is only the second week of the service, and it is also a good illustration of the effectiveness of the streamlined shape in smoke deflection. A4 corridor tender No.5647. (J.F. Aylard)

View of the 'Morning Talisman' pulling out of Kings Cross behind DOMINION OF NEW ZEALAND. The New Zealand Government Railways chime whistle is noticeable here. It had a distinctively low note, and one could note the passage of DOMINION OF NEW ZEALAND a few miles or so from the East Coast main line. A4 corridor tender No.5647.

DOMINION OF NEW ZEALAND hauling the 9.45 SO to Kings Cross, the Saturday balancing turn of the 'Elizabethan', on September 6th 1958 at Welham Green. This is the site of the new station, close to Marshmoor signalbox. A4 corridor tender No.5647. (J.F. Aylard)

Top Shed's DOMINION OF NEW ZEALAND at New England depot. The view is at low level showing the detail on the driver's side. A sister A4 stands on shed and some of the New England V2s are in the background, plus one of the Top Shed Kylchap V2s, No.60903, untypically dirty. A4 (Hoffman bearings) corridor tender No.5647. (B. Richardson, The Transport Treasury)

The down 'Elizabethan', headed by DOMINION OF NEW ZEALAND, rolls round the sharp curve off the King Edward VII bridge into Newcastle Central. In July 1955 the Newcastle Resignalling had not yet removed the magnificent if perplexing semaphore gantry at the west end. The A4 has A4 corridor tender No.5647. (P.J. Coster)

The down 'Tees-Tyne Pullman' could be relied on for a much faster exit from the capital, and here DOMINION OF NEW ZEALAND's driver is in a hurry! The train is on the 1 in 200 north of New Southgate, and it's summer 1960. She has A4 corridor tender No.5647. (P.J. Coster)

The up 'Northumbrian' speeds through New Southgate behind 60013 DOMINION OF NEW ZEALAND in summer 1958. The A4 has a double chimney, and is on the return leg of No.266 down, the 'Scotch Goods' of the previous day. A4 corridor tender No.5647. (P.J. Coster)

The up 'Elizabethan' at the north Junction at York, behind DOMINION OF NEW ZEALAND, in summer 1958. It was one of the few trains to use the middle roads through the station, now removed. The A4 was converted to double blast earlier in the year. A4 corridor tender No.5647. (P.J. Coster)

The doyen – or should it be doyenne? – of the class, SILVER LINK racing through Huntingdon North with the up 'Tees-Tyne Pullman'. No other information is given, but the single chimney, long guard irons and the probability of dark green livery tie the period down to summer 1952. Although the A4 was fitted with ATC two years previously, the equipment seems to be missing and only the mounting plate is visible on the bogie frame. She was coupled to the Timken roller-bearing A4 corridor tender No.5590 for most of her life. Just out of view on the right is the old LMSR line to Kettering from Huntingdon East, while a WD 2-8-0 trundles along the up slow in the distance.

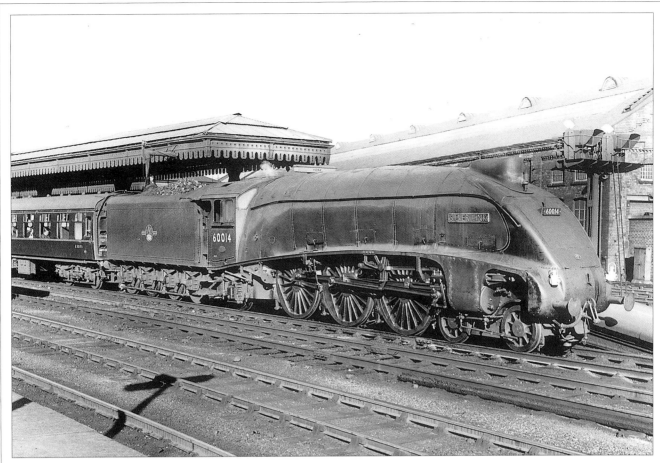

SILVER LINK, now with a double chimney, on the 16.05 Newcastle-Kings Cross at York, August 17th 1958. Tender A4 corridor No.5590. (B.K.B. Green, Initial Photographics)

SILVER LINK, in the unusual surroundings of Haymarket. She was a popular choice for special occasions, although not so much as MALLARD of course. Here she has been specially turned out for one of Alan Pegler's Northern Rubber Specials, after previously working an Ian Allan special over the GC Section. Quite how she was prised from Mr Hailstone's grip I cannot say! It would not surprise me if he had been given a ticket to travel on the train. The crew looks like a shed crew, not the usual top link crews. The date is June 26th 1956; tender A4 corridor No.5590. (J. Robertson, The Transport Treasury)

A magnificent study of SILVER LINK. It is difficult to be certain, but if the cab roof is white then the date must be June 1961, when she was prepared as pilot for the Royal Train. This is not Top Shed as one might assume, but New England, where an engine in such magnificent condition would have existed only in the realms of fantasy for most of the time. The tender is A4 corridor No.5590. (J. Robertson, The Transport Treasury)

SILVER LINK gets her train away from Wakefield Westgate in October 1961. It is not clear but I assume it is an up train, and it would be the 9.50 Leeds-Kings Cross – although it was usually an A3 at that time. Otherwise it would be the down 'White Rose'. The tender is A4 corridor No.5590. (J.A.C. Kirke, The Transport Treasury)

The down 'Heart of Midlothian' with SILVER LINK at the head stands in old platform 10 at Kings Cross waiting the 'Right Away', about 1961. As the BR speedometer is not yet fitted, it would be early in the year. The condition of the paintwork is good, which suggests even the year earlier. One has to be careful about Top Shed; they had a very fine painter on the strength! The tender is A4 corridor No.5590. (J. Robertson, The Transport Treasury)

In winter 1957 SILVER LINK emerged from Doncaster with a double chimney, and here is passing New Southgate with the 10.40 semifast to Grantham. The tender is A4 corridor No.5590. (P.J. Coster)

The return leg of the Leeds lodging turn was the 9.50 from Leeds Central, and SILVER LINK is bringing the train into Kings Cross. It is summer 1956, and the tender is A4 corridor No.5590. (P.J. Coster)

SILVER LINK standing at Kings Cross, old platform 5, with the down 'Yorkshire Pullman'. The date is July 1956, and the engine has a single chimney. By the cab Ted Hailstone is without doubt extolling the virtues of SILVER LINK to an interested passenger. Fireman Jack Law brings the lamp off the tender back to set the express headcode. The A4 had been overhauled a few months before, and was in immaculate condition. Her tender is the Timken A4 corridor No.5590. (P.J. Coster)

SILVER LINK at speed through Hitchin, past Cambridge Junction, with the 15.00 Kings Cross-Newcastle in late 1959. Her tender was the Timken A4 corridor No.5590. (P.J. Coster)

The up 'Flying Scotsman' at speed through New Southgate in summer 1961 with SILVER LINK at the head. Timken A4 corridor tender No.5590. (P.J. Coster)

There were times when the condition of the A4 on the 'Elizabethan' defied superlatives. It was always exceptionally clean, but at times words failed. On June 15th 1959 such an occasion arose. The down 'Elizabethan' started away behind QUICKSILVER, the engine almost cleaner than it would have been in Doncaster Paint Shop! Such a sight, to anyone who loved the steam locomotive, was priceless. At her first visit to Doncaster QUICKSILVER exchanged tenders with SILVER LINK, and she kept the first A4 corridor tender, No.5589, for the rest of her existence. (J.F. Aylard)

A close up view of the nameplate of QUICKSILVER showing the rounded corners, which was only so for the first two A4s. There are no details as to the date, but clearly it is post-1961. The access doors can be clearly seen, giving access to lubrication points, also the small sand filler just below the left-hand edge of the nameplate. The detail of the casing can be clearly seen, such as the plate giving access to the superheater header, and the louvres alongside the anti-vacuum valve at the rear of the chimney. (The Transport Treasury)

QUICKSILVER at Haymarket having brought the down 'Elizabethan' from London. The crew are removing the headboard while among the watchers, I suspect, is Willie Hermiston. The photographer is probably his compatriot John Robertson. The A4 has had the long guard irons removed, and ATC fitted. A B1 passes in the background on the up line from Fife, and the adjacent NBR tender has an affinity to those of the GNR. The tender is A4 corridor No.5589. The date is given as June 13th 1955, but the Non-stop did not start for another week or two and (I may be wrong) but I do not recall her on the duty in 1955. In 1953, however, she ran three consecutive turns from August 18th and I suggest that she is on one of these here. (The Transport Treasury)

The 'Norseman' was a fairly light and relatively fast train, run in the summer season to connect with boat services from Tyne Commission Quay. Kings Cross men worked to York with their own engine, but the return leg was rather more ad hoc. Here QUICKSILVER has the train approaching New Southgate in June 1955. The tender is A4 corridor No.5589. On the horizon is Alexandra Palace ('Ally Pally') where you can see Irwell Press every year at the London Festival of Railway Modelling. (P.J. Coster)

SILVER KING, sadly, was one of the most elusive A4s where photographers were concerned. In the south, on the rare occasions when she appeared, it was on the overnight lodging turn when photography was difficult at best and usually impossible. With the lightening of loads and more through working she was a less rare sight, and here the A4 is heading back north at New Barnet with the 15.00 to Newcastle. As usual with a Kylchap A4, there is little visible exhaust to suggest movement. The date is July 24th 1960, the A4 is only a few weeks out of Doncaster Works. She lost her corridor tender to UNION OF SOUTH AFRICA in 1948, and kept her non-corridor tender No.5636 (the first of the batch) for the rest of her life. (J.F. Aylard)

The down 'Norseman' gets away from Kings Cross behind a dirty 60016 SILVER KING. The photograph was taken in late 1952 when the A4 was in dark green livery, although it looks more like unlined matt black. A clean Thompson Pacific (!) sits in the background with a stovepipe chimney. The tender is non-corridor No.5636. (The Transport Treasury)

SILVER KING at Neville Hill depot, Leeds. The A4s were uncommon on the Leeds Northern line and so she is a rare visitor. The date is September 4th 1954, tender No.5636. (Eric Webb, The Transport Treasury)

In late 1963, SILVER KING left Tyneside after 28 years for Scotland. She was sent on to Ferryhill, where she frequently worked the heavy 15.30 'Postal' to Perth and on to Carstairs with the postal or Glasgow with the passenger portion. She is seen here pulling away from Forfar, on the now closed and lifted section from Kinnaber to Stanley Junction. The heavily curved approaches were good locations for telephoto or film shots of the engine and train, from the train. By July 4th, 1964, cleaning locomotives seemed to have become a matter of history and the A4 is a sorry sight. The tender is non-corridor No.5636. (M. Mensing)

SILVER KING stands at Tay Bridge depot at Dundee, looking rather good for the period, on November 7th 1964. The tender is Timken A4 corridor tender No.5636. (Les Elsey)

SILVER FOX was a Kings Cross engine until the depot shut in June 1963. Always a favourite, and often in the top link, regularly manned, she brings the up 'Flying Scotsman' under Caledonian Road overbridge and down Holloway Bank towards Copenhagen Tunnel. Actually she had been displaced from the top link by LORD FARINGDON, and had replaced ANDREW K McCOSH on this turn, and therefore either Driver Willers or Frost was in charge. The old up goods flyover is far right and the down goods in the foreground, and a trolleybus is behind the gantry. The date is May 11th 1954, the tender is her original A4 corridor No.5592. (R. Wilson, The Transport Treasury)

Temporarily rebuilt as an Atlantic, SILVER FOX is 'Not to be moved' outside Doncaster depot, 'Carr Loco' on September 5th 1954. The copper cladding has either corroded or been damaged. Tractive effort enthusiasts will notice that the figure for the A4 is unaltered despite bits missing! The tender is A4 corridor No.5592. (Frank Hornby)

SILVER FOX was the first A4 to be converted to double blast, and here she is bringing an up express through Welwyn Garden City two years on. The trip on the down main has a B1 4-6-0 at its head, while the young chap on the up platform is probably wishing the number was one more or one less! The tender is A4 corridor No.5592. (A.E. Bennett, The Transport Treasury)

Doncaster shed once more, SILVER FOX now with all wheels restored and a double chimney. Kings Cross A4s were not common visitors to Doncaster post-war, other than for routine inspections and maintenance. They normally turned at Gateshead, Copley Hill, Grantham and Peterborough – indeed, anywhere but Doncaster. The curved rear to the tender and the porthole to illuminate (somewhat) the corridor can be seen. The date is January 14th 1962, the tender is A4 corridor No.5592. (The Transport Treasury)

A super shot of a fast and heavy up freight at New England, hauled by SILVER FOX. The LM Region line to Stamford and Leicester is on the left, and New England yard is to the right. The date must be 1961 or later. The tender is A4 corridor No.5592. (B. Richardson, The Transport Treasury)

The 14.00 to Newcastle and Edinburgh leaves Kings Cross behind SILVER FOX on September 19th 1957. Just below the cylinder cover one can see the check plate bolted to the bogie frame to curb the rolling of the engine at speed – or on poor track! The tender is A4 corridor No.5592. (J.F. Aylard)

SPARROW HAWK was not a frequent visitor down south, and when she did, the cameramen were notably absent. This is a fine study of the A4 at Haymarket, in remarkably clean condition considering it is six months since repainting in dark green livery. The date is March 22nd 1952, and the A4 is coupled to its original non-corridor tender No.5668. (W. Hermiston, The Transport Treasury)

Looking much more like a Geordie A4, a travel-stained SPARROW HAWK stands at Newcastle while her driver creates the brake. It is June 22nd 1962 and the A4 is about to leave for Edinburgh. The tender is non-corridor No.5668. (J.F. Aylard)

The 'Scotch Goods' approaching New Barnet with SPARROW HAWK instead of the usual Top Shed Pacific. It was taken in summer 1961; the tender is non-corridor No.5668. (P.J. Coster)

The up 'Flying Scotsman' between Newcastle and Grantham was diagrammed for a Gateshead A4, and here is a superb photograph of BITTERN at Grantham on July 31st 1953. Curiously, on the many occasions when I saw the train it was usually an A1 and sometimes an A3, but only once an A4. The process of changing engines required the Gateshead engine to run forward and back through a crossover on to the down main, where it would stand clear of the 15.40 Lincoln, in the left background, while the London engine backed on and coupled up. Even more curiously, I have notes of that day, and the A4 which relieved BITTERN for the final section was MALLARD. A week earlier the train had arrived at Kings Cross behind N2 No.69537! This was also the memorable day when GOLDEN PLOVER failed at Doncaster with the up 'Elizabethan'. Bill Hoole took the pilot, MERRY HAMPTON, and arrived a minute early! The train's headboard is particularly well illustrated. The non-corridor tender is No.5638. (M.N. Bland, The Transport Treasury)

Now worth an unthinkable amount of money, the nameplate of BR No.60019. The A4 has been converted to double blast, but there is no further intimation as to time or place. Hopefully it is among the heap of components currently being repaired and reassembled on the Mid-Hants Railway, and we shall see her in her glory before long. The tender is No.5638 and the boiler at withdrawal was No.29332. (The Transport Treasury)

BITTERN, now double blast, arriving at Kings Cross. It looks very much like a lunchtime or early afternoon arrival, probably from Newcastle. The date would be 1959-60, tender non-corridor No.5638. (The Transport Treasury)

BITTERN coupling on at Newcastle, on June 22nd 1962. The non-corridor tender is No.5638. (J.F. Aylard)

The third of an elusive triumvirate, GUILLEMOT is at Haymarket in March 1955. The A4 is in clean condition with single chimney, before the days of AWS, and the tender is piled high, suggesting that she is about to depart for Waverley and a southbound service. Most of the Gateshead A4s remained coupled to the same tender, and GUILLEMOT kept a non-corridor tender No.5669 till withdrawal. (W. Hermiston, The Transport Treasury)

At the other end of the East Coast route, GUILLEMOT waits release from platform one at Kings Cross after working the 17.05 arrival from Newcastle on June 9th 1960. The A4 now has a double chimney and AWS. The engine has her non-corridor tender No.5669. (J.F. Aylard)

WILD SWAN hauling what was, strictly speaking, the up 'Norseman', although on Saturdays with additional reliefs, the name was not often carried. The A4 is at Corby Glen, no doubt gathering speed down the bank, on August 5th 1957. WILD SWAN has only recently lost her non-corridor tender 5671 in favour of A4 corridor No.5651, off DWIGHT D EISENHOWER. (M. Mensing)

WILD SWAN at New England shed at some time after April 1958, before electrification flashes were fitted. She has worked the 14.00 'Heart of Midlothian' from London, and will return with the up Glasgow-Kings Cross service. Chime whistles sometimes suffered under the coalers or from the impact of a short-sighted bird, and this one will require some delicate rectification on shed. The shining A4 is a shattering contrast to the state of the New England resident on the right. The engine has her A4 corridor tender No.5651. (B. Richardson, The Transport Treasury)

WILD SWAN hauling what appears to be a down evening service, perhaps the 17.00 Peterborough, somewhere down the main line. The full tender suggests that the A4 is not so very far north. The two white posts of the post and rail fence tease the mind as to their function. She has her A4 corridor tender No.5651, and her whistle is at the more correct angle! (The Transport Treasury)

WILD SWAN pulls away from Sandy to the 10.40 semifast on June 3rd 1961. At this point the down line was restored to two tracks, but the convergence of the two up lines was further north. The late lamented Bedford-Cambridge line is in the background. The tender is No.5651. (The Transport Treasury)

Another temporary Atlantic, WILD SWAN is at the side of Kings Cross shed waiting for repairs to the driving axle and axleboxes. The date is September 9th 1959, the tender is No.5651. (R.F. Smith, The Transport Treasury)

In her last year or so, MALLARD starts the down 'Flying Scotsman' from old platform 8 at Kings Cross, post-1961. When small boys were fascinated not by computer games but by real steam engines... Did they become railway engineers, I wonder, or accountants and lawyers? The world's fastest steam locomotive is a compelling sight for them as she pulls away. The boiler is no doubt the one currently on the A4, No.27965, but the exhaust steam masks the identity of the corridor tender, either A4 type 5651, or A3 type 5330. The tenders were changed as late as May 1962 so it may be either. (The Transport Treasury)

MALLARD leaves Kings Cross with a down express. The route is set on indicator A to down main one. The BR speedometer and the A3 type corridor tender, No.5330, date it between April 1960 and May 1962. The ganger trudges away, no doubt concentrating on keeping his footing on wet sleepers rather than the magnificence behind him. (C. Martin, The Transport Treasury)

The Centenaries Exhibition was held in late 1952 to celebrate the centenary of the terminus and of the direct GN main line north from Peterborough. The locomotives and rolling stock were stood on the westernmost siding of the Milk Dock in rather murky surroundings that would never do today. MALLARD, together with GNR Nos.251 and 1, attracted much attention. The date is October 17th 1952, when the A4 was coupled to the prototype A3 corridor tender No.5323. (A.R. Carpenter, The Transport Treasury)

On May 13th 1959 the famous two-track 'bottleneck' at Hadley Wood was no more. MALLARD is hauling an evening express, possibly the 17.00 Peterborough or a summer extra. The A3 corridor tender is No.5330. (J. Robertson, The Transport Treasury)

The 10.10 Edinburgh on Sundays was the balancing turn for the up 'Elizabethan', and a driver might expect to be diverted for engineering work somewhere down the line. Here MALLARD climbs the sharp bank up to Wood Green flyover as she takes the New Line to Langley Junction with her heavy train. The date is May 3rd 1959, and no doubt the engineers are putting the final touches to the Potters Bar modernisation. The line to the right is the down goods, locally known as the 'Khyber Pass'. It was in fact quite steeply graded to avoid extensive earthworks, and a long down freight starting from a signal stop at Wood Green could have quite a struggle. The A3 corridor tender is No.5330. (J.F. Aylard)

MALLARD, only a month from overhaul, heads the 14.00 from Kings Cross on September 26th 1958. The engine had been exhibited at Noel Park with other GN line engines earlier in the year, and was always well cleaned. The A4 has just been coupled to A3 corridor tender No.5330. (J.F. Aylard)

The first 'Elizabethan' of the 1957 summer season starts from old platform 6 at Kings Cross. Two loco inspectors, one of whom was Jack Goodhand, watch the A4 get away. The A4 was coupled to the Skefco A4 corridor tender No.5648. (P.J. Coster)

That first 1957 'Elizabethan' again. Statements about cleanliness of the engines of the Non-stop tend to wear a bit thin, but I clearly remember that MALLARD, a few weeks out of Doncaster, was not only spotless, but her varnish shone as if prepared to exhibition standard. Even the upper chimney gleamed, the deep gloss not dimmed by heat and time. (P.J. Coster)

As railtours became more common, MALLARD assumed celebrity status, and was used on a trip from Waterloo to Exeter and back in early 1962. The outward journey was diverted via East Putney, and here the A4 is approaching Clapham Junction on the 'Windsor lines', coming under the infamous Clapham 'A' signalbox. Five years later the steelwork of the supporting bridge structure came out with its hands up as it were, and the box sank slowly to ground level, causing widespread operational chaos and delay. The boiler is no doubt the one currently on the A4, No.27965, and the corridor tender is A3 type 5330. (P.J. Coster)

GOLDEN EAGLE was the fifth A4 and the first of the class intended for general service. For an engine that had a splendid name its work post-war seemed a disappointment, and it was rarely seen on express work down south. As with several of the class, when a double chimney was fitted, the performance changed out of all recognition. GOLDEN EAGLE is backing off Haymarket shed, which suggests that the Shedmaster was borrowing the Gateshead A4 for a little extra mileage! The date is 1959, the non-corridor tender is No.5667. (The Transport Treasury)

GOLDEN EAGLE freshly repainted, no doubt on its way back to Gateshead. No information is given, but the presence of D49 No.62744 THE HOLDERNESS suggests the York area. The A4 is in BR blue and it is September 1949. Orthochromatic emulsion, which was used at that time, tended to show the livery somewhat lighter than the later panchromatic type, and this may be the reason for the A4 looking as though it had been painted garter blue. The non-corridor tender is No.5667. (The Transport Treasury)

It is July 31st 1960, and GOLDEN EAGLE has just been turned on the Haymarket turntable. She lost her A3 type corridor tender to WILLIAM WHITELAW in 1941, and kept her non-corridor tender, No.5667, for the rest of the time. (W. Hermiston, The Transport Treasury)

A different view of the 11.00 Kings Cross-Glasgow, passing New Southgate behind GOLDEN EAGLE. The A4 non-corridor tender is No.5667. (P.J. Coster)

The evening York parcels was always a train worth watching, as the sight of a freshly painted locomotive running-in was always a treat. By 1963 (as at New Southgate here, heading north) it had become less of a running-in turn since fewer engines were being overhauled, and one could see such as GOLDEN EAGLE employed on it. The A4 non-corridor tender is No.5667. (P.J. Coster)

GOLDEN EAGLE at St. Margarets shed on June 21st 1962, next to a J38 or J39 0-6-0. It was still a Gateshead engine at the time, although she was later allocated there. The non-corridor tender is No.5667. (J.F. Aylard)

GOLDEN EAGLE, north of New Barnet with the 10.10 Glasgow express. This was the balancing turn for the up 'Talisman', which is the headboard reversed on the front of the engine. The date was April 6th 1957, the A4 was still single blast, the non-corridor tender No.5667. (J.F. Aylard)

KINGFISHER was, after the pre-war skirmishing, a long term Haymarket resident. Here she is standing at the head of a long line of locomotives outside the shed to tantalise any passing youngster armed with an ABC. The A4 is single blast, with the earlier BR totem and her 'Kingfisher' plaques, which dates the picture between July 1955 and August 1958. Notice the cleanliness of all of the engines. KINGFISHER's tender seems to be overloaded and at a distance the quality doesn't seem calculated to inspire the fireman on the next duty! The tender is A3 type corridor No.5331. (W. Hermiston, The Transport Treasury)

KINGFISHER was one of the A4s to be painted in the experimental blue-purple livery, but here it has reverted to the BR dark blue livery. The A4 is at Dundee Tay Bridge waiting to back down to the shed, on September 11th 1951; the tender is A3 type corridor No.5331. (R.H. Fullagar, The Transport Treasury)

60024 KINGFISHER in sylvan scenery as she rolls on to the turntable. Those acquainted with the Victorian depot at St. Margarets may be astonished both to learn that it is the location for this photograph, and that such a clean locomotive visited there once at least. Although she was allocated there in 1963-64, there is little doubt in my mind that the date is later, indeed during the last two weeks of the existence of A4s on BR, in late August/early September 1966. The tender is A4 non-corridor No.5640 from FLYING SCOTSMAN via LORD FARINGDON. (The Transport Treasury)

Gleneagles was near the summit of the long 12 mile climb from the Tay valley, gentle at first but steepening to 1 in 100 to the summit. KINGFISHER stands in the up platform with one of the three hour expresses from Aberdeen to Glasgow. Ferryhill kept her clean, and this would be 1965-66. The tender is A3 type corridor No.5329.

The down 'Flying Scotsman', headed by KINGFISHER, makes a magnificent sight as it climbs through Grantshouse to Penmanshiel Tunnel. It was the second day of the operation of the ' Elizabethan', June 30ᵗʰ 1953, and I would guess from her immaculate condition that KINGFISHER was the reserve engine for the Non-stop A4, UNION OF SOUTH AFRICA. The reserve A4 worked the 8.35 Glasgow - Kings Cross from Edinburgh to Newcastle, and returned with the 'Scotsman'. Most of the Newton stock would have formed the Non-stop, and BR1 coaches have replaced them, except the leading BG, still in teak livery. The driver, probably McLeod, is looking at the injector overflow, or rather lack of overflow! The A3 corridor tender is No.5331. (J. Robertson, The Transport Treasury)

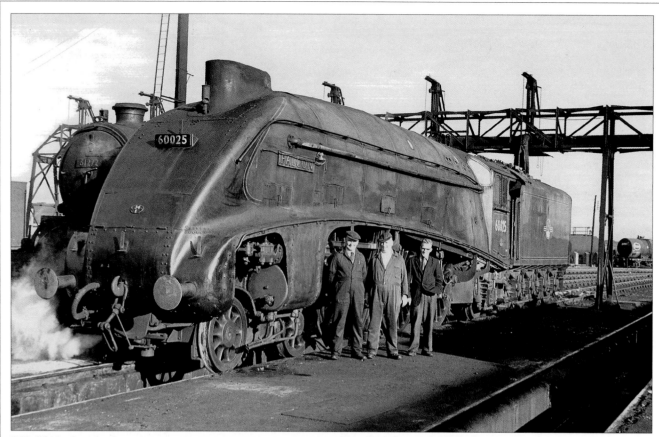

FALCON, after the first two years at Haymarket, was always at the southern end of the line. For much of the time post-war, she was a top link engine, and was not often missing from the principal expresses. As steam was prohibited south of Peterborough, she was moved to New England where this photograph was taken, but only lasted another four months before withdrawal. The staff seem very pleased with their illustrious new arrival. Date - the second half of 1963, and the A4 has the Skefco roller bearing tender No.5648. (B. Richardson, The Transport Treasury)

The Sunday balancing turn for the Non-stop is probably the reason for FALCON being at Joppa. It was not impossible, of course, for the A4 to be borrowed for a little extra mileage by Gateshead or Heaton, but unlikely. The A4 is gathering speed, and would have a good load behind the tender. The date is given as 'circa 1960', and FALCON did work the Non-stop that year, in September. By that time the A4 would have had a double chimney. However, the presence of A3 corridor tender No.5330 limits the date to before July 1958 when the A4 was single blast, and the chimney looks a little slim for a double. The BR totem is indecipherable, but I would plump for the second version. This evidence plus the preponderance of red and cream liveried stock suggests that it might well be 1956-1957. (The Transport Treasury)

FALCON about to leave old platform 5 at Kings Cross with the 'Yorkshire Pullman'. The A4s allocated to the two Pullmans that left in the evening were always well cleaned and made a fine picture. In the background N2 No.69529 waits for the road with empty stock. The date is July 6th 1953, the A4 has her A3 corridor tender No.5330. (B.K.B. Green, Initial Photographics)

After the successful introduction of the 'Talisman' in the winter 1956/57 timetable, a 'Morning Talisman' was introduced on June 17th 1957. FALCON was the A4 on both inaugural services, and here she is starting away from old platform 6 on June 20th. Adjacent is one of the excellent sleeping car versions of the 'Newton' stock, introduced by the LNER just after the 1939-45 war. The A4 has A3 corridor tender No.5330. (H.D. Ramsey, Initial Photographics).

A less-than-flattering view of an A4 over the pits at New England. It an unusual view that will be of interest to modellers. FALCON had just been transferred there from Kings Cross when the modernisers ordered the line south of Peterborough to be steam-free. Date - the second half of 1963, and the A4 has the Skefco roller bearing tender No.5648. One pair of the tender wheels had the roller bearing axleboxes replaced with plain axleboxes during overhaul when attached to MALLARD in August 1958. The overhauled tender was then attached to FALCON. (B. Richardson, The Transport Treasury)

FALCON at speed through Hitchin with the 15.00 Newcastle express in the summer of 1958. The A4 has A3 corridor tender No.5330. (P.J. Coster)

FALCON hauling the Scotch Goods, running over the new down slow line north of Potters Bar new tunnel. The down main was not yet operational. The date is April 22nd 1959 and the A4 has A4 corridor tender No.5648. (J.F. Aylard)

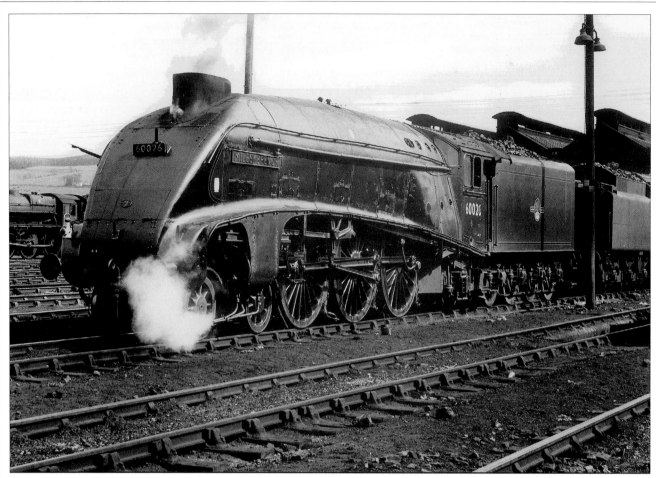

An excellent study of one of the less famous and less photographed A4s. MILES BEEVOR, née KESTREL, is standing at Perth shed on May 16th 1965. For the latter half of her service, she had a non-corridor tender, and here is coupled to No.5642, originally attached to MALLARD during the record run. Her coupled wheels are today under SIR NIGEL GRESLEY, along with other parts. The engineers at Crewe working on the preserved A4 were surprised to find that parts of one A4 would not necessarily fit the other, notably the ashpan, and had to be adapted to fit. (A. Scarsbrook, Initial Photographics)

Top Shed, just before Christmas 1957 and MILES BEEVOR is prepared for her next duty. It was never a top link engine but several drivers were happy to run her while their regular engine was not available. Once converted to double blast there was little to choose between them. She was unique in that she was the one A4 at Kings Cross that never worked the post-war Non-stop. That is not necessarily the same as never having worked into Edinburgh of course! The tender is non-corridor No.5642. The A4 left with the exodus of steam in 1963, and moved to Ferryhill by way of New England and St. Margarets. (A.G. Ellis, The Transport Treasury)

MILES BEEVOR slows for the permanent speed restriction through Selby station and over the swing bridge, a route which has disappeared off the main line long ago. It is August 16th 1952, and presumably the train is the summer 9.40 Kings Cross-Newcastle, the only train that normally brought a London engine north of Doncaster in those days. The A4 has her A3 corridor tender No.5329. (W. Hermiston, The Transport Treasury)

MILES BEEVOR at New England. The date is given as 1954, but Willie Yeadon's date for the removal of the long guard irons is February 1953. One of the dates must be wrong. The A4 had a non-corridor tender from October 1952 to June 1953 and from January 1954 onwards. She had received experimental ATC by this time. The lighting and the length of the shadows lead me to surmise that this is an evening shot in summer, possibly in 1953 but more likely in 1954. In which case I would guess that the ATC was fitted in October 1952 or February 1953, and the long irons were removed in September 1954. She might have worked in on the 'Heart of Midlothian', or more likely the 17.00 from Kings Cross, which reached Peterborough just after 19.00. The tender is non-corridor No.5642. (The Transport Treasury)

The 9.50 from Leeds leans to the curve round past Cambridge Junction, with MILES BEEVOR going well. The date was late 1959, the tender is non-corridor No.5642 . (P.J. Coster)

An unusually filthy MILES BEEVOR heads one of the evening services from Kings Cross in 1961. It may be that she had failed and been repaired, and Dick Ball and his cleaners had not yet got their hands on her. The tender looks to be dangerously overcoaled but perhaps the fireman will attend to that before starting. The inhabitants of old platform 10 have grown older and more respectable, but there is still a goodly throng. The tender is non-corridor No.5642. (The Transport Treasury)

MERLIN working hard on an express. The date lays between March 1952 and June 1953 as determined by the livery and the long guard irons. The location is impossible to tell, but it may well be on the four track section west of Haymarket, on a Glasgow express. The A4 was the regular engine of one of the senior top link men, Bill Stevenson. The tender was A4 corridor No.5652. (The Transport Treasury)

Haymarket's MERLIN stand in the yard of Carr Loco (Doncaster), resplendent in the experimental BR purple livery in June 1948. It is readily distinguished by the lining extended down to the buffer level. The livery, as I recall it (dimly) was not as attractive as the LNER garter blue, nor the later Caledonian dark blue, but it suited the A4 far better than the dark green used from 1951 onwards. MERLIN had a non-corridor tender for four months, originally with MALLARD, No.5642. (The Transport Treasury)

This photograph has the feel of a summer Sunday evening about it. Saturday would have been busier, and oh yes, there was a Pullman on Sunday, the wonderfully named 'Harrogate Sunday Pullman', and that is in old platform 5. MERLIN has arrived in old platform 6 with the summer 10.50 Edinburgh-London service, with the reversed headboard for tomorrow's Non-stop. I would incline towards the 'Elizabethan' rather than the 'Capitals Limited' simply because the ubiquitous BR Mk1 had not displaced so much ex-LNER stock in 1952. The tender was A4 corridor No.5652. (George Heiron, courtesy Mrs Shirley Heiron, The Transport Treasury)

MERLIN gets under way from the Perth stop with a Glasgow express on August 11th 1963. The express appears to have started from the Dundee platforms rather than the direct route from Aberdeen via Forfar, and will cross to the main line before Hilton Tunnel. The tender was A4 corridor No.5652. (The Transport Treasury)

On Sunday July 17th 1955, MERLIN was a very unexpected engine on the 12.05 Newcastle express, making an energetic departure from London. She had worked the up 'Elizabethan' in place of LORD FARINGDON the evening before, and appeared on the 'Northumbrian' and 'White Rose' before making her way back north in the following week. The tender was A4 corridor No.5652. New Southgate goods shed is in the background. (P.J. Coster)

The up 'Elizabethan' headed by MERLIN racing into London in summer 1958. She was one of the most prolific performers on the train, and many summer seasons saw 'Magnificent MERLIN' working the Haymarket end. The tender was A4 corridor No.5652. (P.J. Coster)

'Magnificent MERLIN' with the 'Elizabethan' at speed sweeps through the old Hatfield station in summer 1960. The old footbridge linking the two staggered platforms was a superb vantage point, the impression being heightened by the structure shaking vigorously as an express flew past! The tender was A4 corridor No.5652. (P.J. Coster)

Magnificently turned out, the first 'Elizabethan' stands in old platform 5 at Kings Cross, an immaculate WALTER K WHIGHAM at its head. Even a 'Newton' BCK, of which there were not too many, has been found for the Aberdeen portion. Meanwhile a Locomotive Inspector, distinguished by the obligatory trilby, leans out of the cab. (The Transport Treasury)

Left, above and below. Magnificently turned out, the first 'Elizabethan' stands in old platform 5 at Kings Cross, an immaculate WALTER K WHIGHAM at its head. Even a 'Newton' BCK, of which there were not too many, has been found for the Aberdeen portion. She reached Waverley 5 minutes BT. The A4 was one of the most reliable single blast engines on the Non-stop over the years. Joe Howard was the Kings Cross driver, with Fireman Ivor Brooks. The A4 has just received ATC equipment, and still has the Flaman drive visible. Meanwhile a Locomotive Inspector, distinguished by the trilby, leans out of the cab. On the platform side a throng of Public Relations representatives and cameramen are with the crew. The tender was A4 corridor No.5649. (The Transport Treasury)

September 3rd 1962 at Grantham and WALTER K WHIGHAM waits in the down platform with her express. The onlooker has the air of a retired driver who has spent much of his life waiting for platform staff to sort things out and give the Right Away. It is difficult to appreciate that in four months time, this fine machine would be discarded and withdrawn. The tender was A4 corridor No.5649. (The Transport Treasury)

The down Scotch Goods gathers speed through Wood Green on May 14th 1960, headed by WALTER K WHIGHAM. It looks as though the fireman has just started a round of firing. One of the difficulties with fast freight was that the wagon sheets used to sheet loads had to be securely roped to avoid the slipstream lifting them and causing mayhem. Sometimes the East Coast's fast freights were very fast indeed especially when the crew was on the return leg of a diagram. The sheets were not really intended for protecting the cargo from a leaky roof as appears to be the case on the second wagon here, and the sheet is already billowing. The tender was A4 corridor No.5649. (Frank Hornby)

Top Shed, near the end. Apart from a gleaming WALTER K WHIGHAM, it looks more like a freight shed with two 9Fs and a WD. The 9Fs had started to replace the V2s on freight by then, slightly inferior machines at speed, but easier and cheaper to maintain. The date must be 1961-62. The tender was A4 corridor No.5649. (C. Martin, The Transport Treasury)

The up 'Tees-Tyne Pullman' headed by WALTER K WHIGHAM threads its way through the temporary track layout at Hadley Wood. The old down line is now the up main, and the formation is being prepared for the new down main. Greenwood signalbox of happy memories has become marooned in its last hours. How curious the workforce looks now in the days of high-visibility clothing! The date must be April-May 1959, and the tender was A4 corridor No.5649. (The Transport Treasury)

Surely an A4 has never been cleaner? The Royal Wedding on June 8th 1961 involved three trains, the last one of which was the Royal Train itself. WALTER K WHIGHAM was selected for the Royal Train – 'The Grove' in railway telegraphspeak – and was specially prepared. Although the A4 was only two months from overhaul, Dick Ball and his cleaners, even by their own exacting standards, achieved a high-water mark. The tender was A4 corridor No.5649.

The Newcastle express leaving at 12.05 was the first part of the 'Flying Scotsman', and it is seen here running through the suburbs (New Southgate) behind WALTER K WHIGHAM in 1961. Tender: A4 corridor No.5649. (P.J. Coster)

WOODCOCK's work on the Non-stop was often qualified by unreliability but, fortified by conversion to double blast, any such difficulties were disposed of. On June 17th 1960, she sets off northwards with the 'Elizabethan'. She is coupled to the prototype A3 corridor tender, No.5323. (J.F. Aylard)

A close up of the name and front of an A4. The date must lie between late 1952 and late 1958, dark green with a single chimney. It is salutary to think that the fetching price for the nameplate would have paid for at least eight A4s at 1935 prices! (The Transport Treasury)

WOODCOCK at Carr Loco, in 1961 or later, with a typical Doncastrian medley of locomotives. It is still, as for most of its life, a Kings Cross engine, which dates the shot as before June 1963. The tender was A3 corridor No.5323. (The Transport Treasury)

WOODCOCK emerges from the Stygian gloom of Kings Cross train shed. Taken contre-jour, the drifting smoke adds to the 'feel' of the shot. A3 tender No.5323 was one of three removed, coincidentally, from three Haymarket A4s, and attached to the three double chimney A4s representing the old LNER in the 1948 Exchanges. The transfer involved reducing the back plate so as to accommodate the water cranes of the other Regions, notably the old LMSR, as can be seen here. The others were Nos.5325/5332. The view illustrates the size of these large tenders, the A4 version being the heaviest to run in the UK. (George Heiron, courtesy Mrs Shirley Heiron, The Transport Treasury)

WOODCOCK, no doubt at speed, brings a relief up under the old LNWR line from Bedford to Cambridge at Sandy. The intersection bridge has not long been renewed. One might comment, cynically perhaps, that it was just in time to be closed. Often, however, these things were dragged out, and the patience of the CCE in keeping a life-expired structure going became exhausted. The date is August 7th 1961 and the A4 has her usual A3 corridor tender, No.5323. (M. Mensing)

The 12.05 from Newcastle speeds past New Southgate in the summer of 1960, hauled by WOODCOCK. The A4 appears to be linked up almost to mid-gear; a notice plate in the cab required drivers to run at 25% cut-off when the regulator was shut. Old hands preferred to leave the regulator cracked open with a short cut-off, to avoid cold air being drawn into the hot cylinders. Tender: A3 corridor No.5323. (P.J. Coster)

GOLDEN FLEECE, the first of the two A4s allocated to the 'West Riding Limited' in 1937, 21 years later heads the down 'Elizabethan' out of Kings Cross. She was very highly regarded at Grantham, working consistently well on the principal turns. A pool engine at Kings Cross much of the time, she was often on the down 'White Rose' and the heavy return 17.15 from Leeds. An interesting point about this photograph is that one can see clearly the use of sand under the leading coupled wheels. The driver has already linked up to about 50% having only just started. The date is June 25th 1958, and the A4 has A3 corridor tender No.5327. (J.F. Aylard)

GOLDEN FLEECE on June 10th 1950, still in BR dark blue, working an up semifast south of Potters Bar. It had been transferred a week earlier to Kings Cross. At this time she had a non-corridor tender, which was, inevitably, one feels, No.5642, MALLARD's original tender. (A.G. Forsyth, Initial Photographics)

GOLDEN FLEECE at Top Shed on September 9th 1959. There is little to suggest what turn she is intended for, but I would assume it to be one of the principal expresses. The A4 has her usual A3 corridor tender, No.5327. (R.F. Smith, The Transport Treasury)

In 1954, Kings Cross used two pool engines for the Non-stop, and they ran well. They were obviously single blast, the double blast engines being regularly manned, and the latter came into the operation later in the season. Although no headboard is carried, it is the Saturday 'Elizabethan' of July 10th 1954. GOLDEN FLEECE has ascended the sharp climb out of Berwick past Marshall Meadows signalbox on to the cliffs at Ayton, and it is a nice touch by John Robertson to include one of the lineside signs erected by the LNER. The tender is A3 corridor No.5327. (J. Robertson, The Transport Treasury)

Views at Top Shed are usually of the front of the main shed, and an A4 using the turntable is rather a change. GOLDEN FLEECE is the A4, and she would be turning to face north for the next turn. The tender is A3 corridor No.5327. (J.A.C. Kirke, The Transport Treasury)

This is a superb shot of the down 'Elizabethan', near Thirsk. The Haymarket crew will have taken over by now, preparing for the crucial lift at Wiske Moor troughs ten miles ahead. The speed will be about 70-75 mph. At some angles the chimneys can be confused, but I think that she is still single blast, making the year 1954. From the condition of the A4, it could well be the first down train of the season. The tender is A3 corridor No.5327. (J.W. Hague, The Transport Treasury)

GOLDEN PLOVER was a Scottish A4, and a Haymarket one for most of the time. She was turned out in BR blue in July 1949, by which time Doncaster had run out of the 'Ferret and Dartboard' transfers that were to be used with the new livery. As a result both GOLDEN PLOVER and UNION OF SOUTH AFRICA were outshopped with blank tender sides. She was about to start away with the down 'Capitals Limited' on August 6th 1949. The tender was A4 corridor No.5650. (J.F. Aylard)

GOLDEN PLOVER stands at Waverley with a southbound departure. The date must be after April 1954 when the long guard irons were removed, and before the later totem was used. The tender was A4 corridor No.5650. (The Transport Treasury)

In a superb shot, 60031 GOLDEN PLOVER pulls out of Waverley. The burnished buffers, the immaculate engine – all point to this being the Non-stop. It wasn't; for the BR Mk.1 standard stock is not that of the Non-stop and looks very much like the 'Heart of Midlothian' or the 8.35 Glasgow to Kings Cross, both of which were Haymarket turns. Further proof is that the 'Flying Scotsman' and the 10.5 to St Pancras are missing, and a solitary ex-LMSR 2-6-4T is in the former's place. The date lays somewhere between October 1952 (dark green) and March 1954 (removal of long guard irons). I would plump for summer 1953, as the A4 was on the Non-stop then. It is a magnificent shot and it has all the signs of John Robertson's skill. She has A4 corridor tender No.5650. (The Transport Treasury)

GOLDEN PLOVER stands in old platform 6 at Kings Cross with the 'Elizabethan' in the summer of 1958 or later. The tender is A4 corridor No.5650, demonstrating in this view the curved backplate and the porthole for the corridor. One was grateful for this, especially when the corridor had been used to stow fireirons the ends of which were just below red heat! (The Transport Treasury)

Nearly there! The up 'Elizabethan' has less than three miles to go, as GOLDEN PLOVER passes No.6 signalbox at Finsbury Park. The tender is the usual A4 corridor, No.5650. (P.M. Alexander, The Transport Treasury)

Now in strange hands at St. Rollox, GOLDEN PLOVER stands on a northbound special at Carlisle. This was no ordinary special, but a railtour that started and finished in Glasgow. GOLDEN PLOVER took the train from Glasgow to Edinburgh, then on to the Waverley route (complete with wrong line working from Hawick to Riccarton) through to Carlisle. There she turned and completed the run over Beattock to Glasgow. By this time both GOLDEN PLOVER and MERLIN had been given a yellow diagonal stripe to indicate that they should not be used under overhead wires south of Weaver Junction. The tender is the usual A4 corridor, No.5650. (The Transport Treasury)

Well, it can only be the A4 for the 'Elizabethan'. GANNET was first used post-war in 1954, and became one of the regular choices for the duty. Only six weeks from overhaul, the A4 is wonderfully clean, and ran well. It is June 13th 1960, and although the A4 had a number of different tenders, the A3 corridor No.5331 is the one shown, which she kept to the end. (J.F. Aylard)

This must be the Scottish counterpart to John Aylard's portrait. GANNET, also magnificently turned out, moves off Haymarket shed to Waverley to couple on to her train. The tender is her A3 corridor, No.5331. (The Transport Treasury)

The down 'Yorkshire Pullman', hauled by GANNET, nears the summit at Potters Bar. It was a heavy pull, 12 Pullmans, and although the gradient was quoted as 1 in 200, it was actually measured as 1 in 165, which explains why the last mile or so dragged the speed back more than somewhat. The A4 is still in BR dark blue livery, and still has her original non-corridor tender No.5675. (A.G. Forsyth, Initial Photographics)

GANNET speeds over Southgate's long crossover with the up 'Elizabethan'. The date is 1960, the tender A3 corridor No.5331. (P.J. Coster)

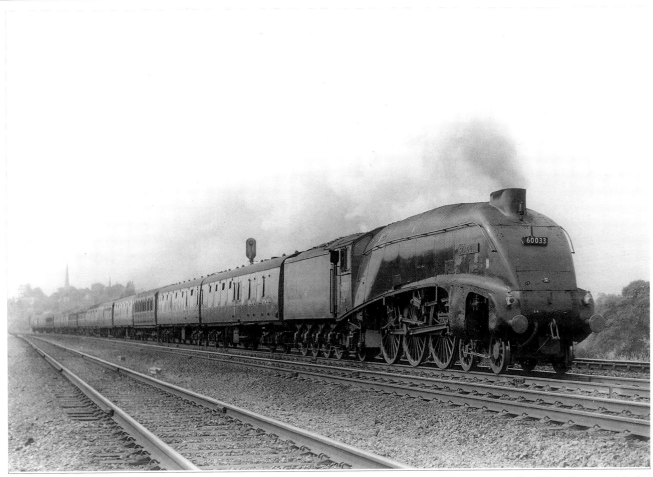

One of the finest of the class, with many feats of speed and power to her credit, SEAGULL is north of New Barnet with the 10.28 to Hull, the second portion of the morning Leeds service. The date is July 22nd 1961, by which time many express loads had been reduced, but the 10.28 is still some 460-470 tons. SEAGULL was one of the Kylchap triumvirate at Kings Cross until 1957, all three of which had simple prosaic bird names, less romantic than their sisters – at least until PEREGRINE was unfortunately renamed. The tender is A3 corridor No.5332. (J.F. Aylard)

A very filthy and no doubt run down SEAGULL waits at the outlet from Kings Cross Station Loco. She was a Grantham engine at the time, otherwise no doubt she would be up at Top Shed. Her condition is very untypical of Grantham's engines, but this is soon after the end of the 1939-45 war. I think that the A4 is painted black, making the date late 1946 or 1947. She would have been attached to her original non-corridor tender, No.5636 at the time. This tender was originally attached to Gresley A1 ST. GATIEN. (The Transport Treasury)

The 1948 Exchanges were the reason for SEAGULL appearing in 3rd rail territory with Bulleid coaching stock. As this is a familiarisation trip and not a test run with the dynamometer car, the date must be June 1st 1948, and the driver Bob Marrable of Kings Cross. The train is the 10.50, the 'ACE' to Southern men, the 'Atlantic Coast Express' of immortal memory. Sadly, SEAGULL's middle big end overheated before she reached Exeter, and MALLARD took her place only to go down later with the same failure. The adapted tender backsheet on A3 corridor No.5325 can be clearly seen. (The Transport Treasury)

SEAGULL at Grantham with the 15.25 Leeds-Kings Cross 'White Rose' on Saturday July 16th 1955. She had worked the train all week, running in 11 early on the Monday. The balancing turn was the down 12.18 'Northumbrian' as far as Grantham, and the A4 will probably have taken over from a Grantham Pacific. The A3 corridor tender is No.5332. (B.K.B. Green, Initial Photographics)

SEAGULL at Top Shed with A3 MELTON in the background. The date must be 1961 or later. The operation of the A4s had been greatly improved with conversion of the single chimney engines to double blast, improved middle big ends and lubrication and rigorous periodic examinations, and as a result some of the class were achieving high mileages. SEAGULL was one such, and I believe was still on the principal expresses having run well over 130,000 miles since her last general overhaul. I could not help noticing the track on which the A4 is standing. One wonders how, for there seems to be very little railhead left! (Compare with the foreground tracks.) The A3 corridor tender is No.5332. (E.A. Elias, The Transport Treasury)

SEAGULL stands in the down slow platform at Grantham with a parcels train on August 15th 1962. Just over four months later, with another five of the most famous and capable A4s, she was withdrawn and scrapped. The A3 corridor tender is No.5332. (J. Hodgkinson)

SEAGULL leans to the curve north of Hitchin, at speed with the 14.00 Kings Cross-Newcastle 'Tees-Thames'. The date is 1959, and the A4 has her usual tender No.5332. To the left is the Cambridge branch and sidings; the Midland branch from Bedford is on the right with its yard and depot, the latter now used by the CCE. (P.J. Coster)

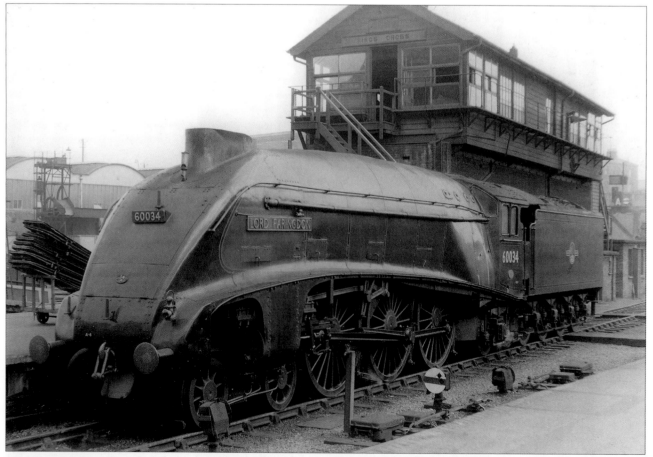

The third member of the Kylchap trio, LORD FARINGDON, formerly PEREGRINE, waits for the road up to Top Shed in old platform 5 at Kings Cross. The period is May 25th 1959, and the A4 has her A3 corridor tender No.5325. (J.F. Aylard)

LORD FARINGDON at Top Shed on September 9th 1959 standing alongside SIR RALPH WEDGWOOD. She has her A3 corridor tender No.5325. (R.F. Smith, The Transport Treasury)

It is July 1955 when the Non-stop was mainly powered by two of the Kylchap 'club' from Kings Cross. LORD FARINGDON is about to leave Haymarket for Waverley, but not before trimming that huge tender load of coal to fit the tunnels into Waverley, I hope. There is almost enough there to come back without recoaling! GUILLEMOT lurks behind in rather more grubby condition than her London sister, which is beautifully clean. The tender is A3 corridor No.5325. (The Transport Treasury)

LORD FARINGDON comes into the old Peterborough North with a down express, underneath the distinctive bowstring girder bridge at Crescent Junction. It is August 20th 1962 and the Deltics are beginning to take over, but the A4's train looks like one of the principal trains. There were only two lines through the station, a critical bottleneck, and the signalling was reputed to be more than somewhat primitive. Quite how that platform barrow got where it is, I cannot guess. The A4 has her A3 corridor tender No 5325. (The Transport Treasury)

The 'Yorkshire Pullman' blasts up Holloway Bank behind LORD FARINGDON with, if I am not mistaken, Driver George Graham in charge. It is a very fine photograph, taken on May 11th 1954. It is unusual for the fact that the leading Pullman brake has had to be replaced, probably at short notice since a rather better replacement ought to have been used. Driver Graham was not far from retirement, and on the return run the following day the 9.50 from Leeds ran in 15 minutes BT! The A4 has a different A3 corridor tender, No.5332 from the 1948 Exchanges. (The Transport Treasury)

LORD FARINGDON drifts past Westwood Junction into Peterborough with an up express. In those days whether one stopped at Peterborough or ran through, the speeds were much the same on the approach due to the heavy PSR through the awkwardly curved station. In the right-hand background are two wonderfully archaic vehicles, possibly the District Engineer's Tunnel Inspection train – although I don't think the Peterborough man had any tunnels! It is difficult to date the photograph, but from the livery of the stock I would guess at 1957-59. The tender is A3 corridor No.5325. (B. Richardson, The Transport Treasury)

LORD FARINGDON pauses at Gleneagles with the up 'Grampian' on August 16th 1966. The tender is A4 non-corridor No.5640. (Paul Cotterell)

APPENDICES

The W1 at Carr Loco, Doncaster, on September 5th 1954. By now she was coupled to A4 non-corridor tender No.5639, which started with A3 SINGAPORE, was reconditioned and passed to PEREGRINE and then MALLARD before reaching the W1. (A.R. Carpenter, The Transport Treasury)

There have been a myriad number of changes of livery, equipment, numbers and names to the 35 A4s and the W1, and therefore I have compiled a series of simulated records for each engine with its own history. These should not be confused with the real record cards, which are held in the Public Records Office at Kew, but are now difficult to reproduce. I have decided that there would be no purpose in repeating the detailed list of overhauls in the Registers, with boiler changes, especially since the class were equipped only with Diagram 107 boilers, or in the case of the W1, a Diagram 103 up to 1937 and Diagram 111 from there on. The dates for conversion to double Kylchap are quoted by both the RCTS Survey and Yeadon's Registers, but some engines were converted whilst undergoing inspection at the home shed or Doncaster Works.

The mileages quoted in the individual locomotive tables, as in the case of the A1s and A3s, need to be placed in context. Recording of steam locomotive mileages was carried out by the Works Accountants from information on driver's tickets. The latter was completed by the driver as a record of the duties performed and distances travelled. Nationalisation split this work by Regions, and three separate Regional Works Accountants became involved. Recording ceased for steam traction at the end of 1962, and obviously those engines which continued in service acquired a higher but unrecorded mileage by withdrawal. Those Eastern Region A4s that were not withdrawn until later obviously increased their mileages until steam haulage was banned south of Peterborough in 1963. Then they were stored at Peterborough before some went north and some were scrapped. The North Eastern engines also increased their mileages before withdrawal and I am not aware of their A4s being stored before withdrawal. The Scottish Region used its A4s until they were finished, unlike many other Pacifics that were stored for a lengthy period before withdrawal. The figures seem low, but as I have described, the war and immediate post-war years were not their best years for reasons that their designer could not have foreseen. The estimated mileage for LNER No.4469 GADWALL would have been in the region of 220-250,000 assuming a rate of 55,000 miles per annum. The figures seem largely credible, although one might wonder why FALCON and KESTREL, built adjacently at Doncaster, differ substantially in

their life mileages. However, the case of GOLDEN EAGLE, Gateshead's *bête noire* as I recall her, strains credulity. A total little short of two million miles seemed highly unlikely, and eventually I found a copy of an official letter giving 1,441,000 as the figure for March 1961. Somehow another 400,000 miles had been acquired, possibly by the Works Accountant's typist!

In Appendix A I have listed the dimensions of the A4 Pacifics as they are quoted and have been corrected from time to time in the various books and papers covering the subject. The principal sources of information are the RCTS LNER Locomotive Survey (Parts 2A and 6C) and the Register of LNER Locomotives, which derive from the same remarkable source, the late W.B. Yeadon. A number of us charted the detailed history of these locomotives, but we were completely outstripped by Willie Yeadon!

I maintain the civil engineer's healthy scepticism regarding the CMEE's stated dimensions, especially weight, and these figures need to carry the usual health warning. As I have observed before, steam engines, like the rest of us, tended to put on weight with maturity, but in the former case through development and modification. They are the published figures and while generally correct, they were not updated to reflect for example, the subsequent removal of streamlined cladding on the tender to facilitate coaling or the conversion to double Kylchap, both of which would have modified the quoted weight. Similarly the addition of roller bearings must have affected the tender weight marginally. One can understand the reluctance of the CMEE to advertise increased axle loading. One of the more important values is the ratio of free gas area in the grate, and Gresley's design provided a good figure of 56%. Over the years the design and procurement of firebars changed, and the ratio was therefore affected. The areas quoted for the single blastpipe orifice do not take account of the various experiments carried out in the 1950s, and the value for the Kylchap double blastpipe is the one relating to the cast 'clover-leaf' orifice.

Appendix B sets out the annual Regional mileage statements. It will be noted that the annual mileages were higher in the Scottish Region, which is probably a reflection of the fewer numbers of A4s and the high level of attention given – necessarily – to each locomotive.

Appendix C deals with the unique performance of SILVER LINK on September 27th 1935 with an assessment of her performance and a theoretical extension of an uninterrupted run to Grantham.

Appendix D lists the published details of running on the three pre-war streamliners together with details of operational incidents, and the post-war 'Elizabethan' and 'Talisman' services.

Appendix E gives a selection of times recorded to the nearest minute or fraction thereof in Guard's Journal or Control Records for a number of runs. These are provided by the kindness of my good friend Gordon Pettitt from his days at Knebworth. They are far less accurate than normal enthusiasts' timings and cannot be argued to support specific achievements, but indicate clearly that a special effort was being made. They comprise a number of runs with the 'Elizabethan', 'Flying Scotsman' and 'Talisman'. The 'Tees-Tyne Pullman' runs refer to the controversial '117 mph' and comprise the Control record of November 16th 1955, and the speeds listed believed to be for the same train two days later. I have assumed that the speeds in the latter case were taken from the Hallade trace, and have worked them up into passing times, but I accept that it is an exercise in mere speculation. The two runs on the 'Talisman' are those of the amazing week of Monday November 5th 1956, when Bill Hoole gave his own

inimitable firework display – twice. The run on the 'Morning Talisman' is curious, timed to the nearest ¼ minute, but is annotated with speeds from elsewhere, showing that it is the famous 107½ mph run. Unfortunately I have no main line Working Time Table for winter 1957, so I have used the timings of the very similar 16.00 'Talisman' beyond Hitchin. The record is endorsed 'Not to be published until later'!

It is worth pointing out that the guard booked time lost against a particular cause by calculating the difference in punctuality between timing points. This system failed to take into account any time regained by the crew intermediately, and produced some estimates of delay which were quite inadequate. A 20mph TSR for example would cost at least 4 minutes or more depending on its length and certainly not 2 minutes as often booked. This can easily be demonstrated by calculating the running time at typical speeds over the section and then comparing it with the actual time. It also depended very much on the weight of the train, and one would expect the 500 tons 'Flying Scotsman' to recover speed more slowly than one of the streamliners. Therefore I have inflated the amounts of 'Lost' time where it seems necessary and appropriate. Of course it can be argued that had the train not been delayed the effort would not have been made, but the net time shows the extent to which the crew and engine had attempted to ensure punctuality. In the particular case of FALCON on November 9th 1956, I think the allowances for the various delays are inadequate. In Appendix D I have shown a lesser net time than was published, as shown in Appendix F. I think it may very well have been the fastest run between London and Newcastle with steam traction.

Appendix F is a list of published A4 runs taken from the Railway Magazine, Trains Illustrated, and the books of C.J. Allen and O.S. Nock. Although it is not exhaustive, it gives a representative picture of the work of the class. One might argue that the fact that a run was published was in itself recognition of an exceptional effort, and less than wholly representative of the work of the class. And of course we all had those runs that for one reason or another, were best forgotten. All classes were prey to injector malfunction, bad coal or whatever, and spent some time cold and lifeless waiting for repair or inspection, but here, we are remembering the class and its great achievements.

Appendix G gives the principal high speed performances on Stoke Bank in both directions. In all the appendices dealing with

performance, I emphasise once again that the contents, although comprehensive, are not exhaustive. Many years ago, a friend gave me some notes when clearing his files, of which Appendix H is a sample. The dates were chosen for the simple reason that that was the information that I had, and not because it was particularly good. The East Coast main line pre-war had a well-organised team of enthusiasts monitoring the daily events. The late Eric Neve and Leslie Burley were two such. Bryce Greenfield, who lived at or near Newcastle was part of the team, and I have reproduced his notes for part of the first half of 1939 to show how the railway was running in those far-off days. Readers will see that the astonishing punctuality of the 'Coronation' was indeed no Doncastrian myth. Nearly half a century later such running would be the stuff of dreams for some of today's operations managers. It is accompanied by a similar record for the 'Flying Scotsman'. This is interesting if only for the somewhat bizarre piloting on occasions north of Newcastle.

Finally, there are a number of railway acronyms or expressions used for the sake of brevity in the book, and a glossary is given below.
BR: British Railways (British Rail)
BRB: British Railways Board
BTC: British Transport Commission
CME: Chief Mechanical Engineer
CMEE: Chief Mechanical & Electrical Engineer
CCE: Chief Civil Engineer
CGM: Chief General Manager
DMPS: Divisional/District Motive Power Superintendent
TSR: Temporary Speed Restriction
PSR: Permanent Speed Restriction
CWR: Continuous welded rail
S&C: Switches and Crossings - pointwork in lay terms.
WTT: Working timetable
ECS: Empty Coaching Stock
BT: Before time - early
RT: Right time
SOS: Short of steam
ATC: Automatic Train Control
AWS: Automatic Warning System
MBE: Middle big end
LNER: London & North Eastern Railway
NER: North Eastern Railway
GER: Great Eastern Railway
GCR: Great Central Railway
NBR: North British Railway
RCTS: Railway Correspondence & Travel Society

APPENDIX A
THE PRINCIPAL DIMENSIONS OF THE CLASS A4 PACIFICS

	Class A4	Class A4	Class A4	Class A4	Class A4
Introduced	1935	1938	1943	1947	1957
Boiler:					
Boiler Diagram no	107	107	107	107	107
Boiler Pressure	250	250	250	250	250
Grate Area	41.25	41.25	41.25	41.25	41.25
Max Outside Diameter	6ft 5ins	6ft 5ins	6ft 5ins	6ft 5ins	6ft 5ins
Min Outside Diameter	5ft 9ins	5ft 9ins	5ft 9ins	5ft 9ins	5ft 9ins
Tube length	17ft 11.75ins	17ft 11.75ins	17ft 11.75ins	17ft 11.75ins	17ft 11.75ins
No tubes	121	121	111.105	121	121
No superheater flues	43	43	43	43	43
Boiler Heating Surface Area:-					
Firebox	231.2	231.2	231.2	231.2	231.2
Tubes	1281.4	1281.4	1175/1112	1281.4	1281.4
Flues	1063.7	1063.7	1063.7	1063.7	1063.7
Subtotal (Evaporative)	2576.3	2576.3	2470/2407	2576.3	2576.3
Superheater	748.9	748.9	706.0	748.9	748.9
Total	3325.2	3325.2	3176/3113	3325.2	3325.2
Wheel Diameter:-					
Bogie	3ft 2ins	3ft 2ins	3ft 2ins	3ft 2ins	3ft 2ins
Coupled	6ft 8ins	6ft 8ins	6ft 8ins	6ft 8ins	6ft 8ins
Trailing	3ft 8ins	3ft 8ins	3ft 8ins	3ft 8ins	3ft 8ins
Cylinders (3)	18.5 x 26ins	18.5 x 26ins	18.5 x 26ins	(2) 18.5 x 26ins (1) 17 x 26ins	18.5 x 26ins
Valves:-					
Piston Valve Diameter (all variations)	9ins	9ins	9ins	9ins	9ins
Travel (ins)	5.75	5.75	6.625 (75%)	6.625 (75%)	6.625 (75%)
Lap (ins), Steam/Exhaust	1.625/0	1.625/0	1.625/0	1.625/0	1.625/0
Lead (ins)	0.125	0.125	0.125	0.125	0.125
Clearance volume as % swept volume	7.7%	7.7%	7.7%	7.7%	7.7%
Tractive Effort (85% boiler pressure) (Five engines)	35.455	35.455	35.455	33.616	35.455
Single Blastpipe orifice (ins) Double Blastpipe orifice (ins)	21.14	39.27	21.14 or 39.27	21.14	39.27
Total length, with NC tender	71.26ft	71.26ft	71.26ft	71.26ft	71.26ft
Locomotive Weight (tons)	102.95	102.95	102.95	102.95	102.95

TENDER DETAILS

Type	Corridor	Corridor	Corridor	Corridor	Non-corr	Non-corr
Built	1928	1930	1935	1937	1937	1938
Coal	9 tons	9 tons	9 tons	9 tons	9 tons	9 tons
Water	5000 galls	5000 galls	5000 galls	5000 galls	5000 galls	5000 galls
Weight	62.40	62.40	63.05	65.60	60.60	60.50
Weight as fitted to A4 Pacifics/W1	65.60	65.60				

APPENDIX B
MILEAGE AND AVAILABILITY : CLASSES A4 AND W1

Year	Owning Region	No of Locos	Average annual Mileage	Average Repairs	Average Not Used	Average Used	Average % Availability
Eastern and North Eastern Regions							
1937	E&NE	27	82,166				90*
1950	E&NE	27	56,641	93	3	214	69.0
1951	E&NE	27	52,841	99	3	207	67.0
1952	E&NE	27	58,387	93	2	214	69.3
1953	E&NE	27	60,868	94	1	220	69.9
1954	E&NE	27	62,841	92	1	216	69.9
1955	E&NE	27	60,521	88	13	208	67.3
1956	E&NE	27	65,575	85	3	221	71.5
1958	E	19	61,237	96	3	210	68.0
1959	E	19	60,982				
1959	NE	1(A4/1)	52,224				
1959	NE	7	64,022				
1960	E	19	61,289				
1960	NE	7	49,961				
1960	NE	1(A4/1)	57,201				
Scottish Region							
1950	Sc	7	63,714	93	0	217	70.0
1951	Sc	7	67,069	66	0	244	78.7
1952	Sc	7	63,427	79	0	231	74.5
1953	Sc	7	61,736	87	0	227	72.3
1954	Sc	7	63,492	78	0	233	74.9
1955	Sc	7	62,783	74	3	234	75.2
1956	Sc	2(A4/1)	72,917	51	0	259	83.6
1956	Sc	5	62,844	89	0	221	71.3
1957	Sc	2(A4/1)	76,328	59	0	251	81.0
1957	Sc	5	63,301	80	0	230	74.2
1958	Sc	2(A4/1)	71,899	97	0	213	68.7
1958	Sc	5	70,418	80	1	229	73.9
1959	Sc	2(A4/1)	77,029				
1959	Sc	5	77,459				
1960	Sc	5	67,771				
1960	Sc	2(A4/1)	60,594				
CLASS W1							
1950	E&NE	W1	19,354	212	0	98	31.6
1951	E&NE	W1	39,969	114	2	193	62.5
1952	E&NE	W1	31,602	180	1	128	41.4
1953	E&NE	W1	23,448	175	4	136	43.2
1954	E&NE	W1	14,841	189	0	120	38.8
1955	E&NE	W1	30,290	165	21	163	46.7
1956	E&NE	W1	60,352	64	5	240	77.7
1958	E&NE	W1	42,959	133	0	176	57.0

*estimated

APPENDIX C
THE SILVERJUBILEE PRESS TRIP

Locomotive No 2509 SILVER LINK
Load: 230 tons gross
Date: September 27th 1935

Miles	Location	Mins	Secs	Speed Mph	Av Sp Mph	Est'd DBHP	Est'd EDBHP	Est'd IHP	Remarks
0.00	KINGS CROSS	0	0	0.0	30.0	0	0	0	
1.50	Holloway Nth	3	0	35.0	35.6	592	942	1151	
2.51	Finsbury Park	4	42	50.0	59.4	798	1088	1429	
4.97	Wood Green	7	11	70.0	69.7	1002	1242	1830	
6.50	New Southgate	8	30	71.5	71.7	1017	1401	2010	
9.15	New Barnet	10	43	72.0	74.3	972	1335	1951	
12.72	PottersBar	13	36	75.0	84.6	1087	1482	2142	
17.68	HATFIELD	17	7	94.5	95.6	973	895	1928	98 at MP19
20.31	Welwyn Gar City	18	46	92.0	91.1	977	1140	2113	
23.50	Woolmer Green	20	52	88.0	87.4	908	1085	1972	
25.03	Knebworth	21	55	92.0	92.3	950	947	1915	No water 93.5 at Langley
28.57	Stevenage Old	24	13	96.0	99.7	1002	1028	2081	
31.92	HITCHIN	26	14	107.0	108.0	972	666	1989	
35.70	Three Counties	28	20	111.5	112.0	965	671	2114	
37.04	Arlesey	29	3	112.5	108.3	1047	814	2284	105 at Langford
41.16	Biggleswade	31	20	109.0	108.0	879	694	2057	112.5 at MP43
44.13	Sandy	32	59	110.0	109.6	1200	1151	2536	
47.51	Tempsford	34	50	109.5	106.2	974	806	2172	
51.73	St Neots	37	13	104.5	102.6	1038	1062	2288	109.5 at MP54 PSR
55.95	Offord	39	41	85.0	87.6	-186	-579	216	
58.87	HUNTINGDON	41	41	88.0	85.4	954	1070	1919	
62.00	MP 62	43	53	83.5	84.2	1004	1296	2058	
63.52	Abbotts Ripton	44	58	84.0	90.8	388	198	967	93.5 at MP67.5
69.37	Holme	48	50	90.0	82.7	507	292	1168	
75.00	Fletton Jct	52	55	70.0	38.6	189	121	660	
76.36	PETERBOROUGH NTH	55	2	20.0	46.1	-349	-480	-381	PSR
79.50	Werrington Jct	59	7	62.0	76.9	919	1141	1602	Water
82.00	Helpston	61	4	75.0	79.3	1015	1224	1865	
84.84	Tallington	63	13	85.0	87.1	1137	1346	2157	
	ACTUAL								
88.64	Essendine	65	58		46.5				Signals
92.22	Little Bytham	70	35		40.5				Signals
97.10	Corby Glen	77	49		59.5				Signals
100.11	Stoke	80	51		77.9				
102.10	Gt Ponton	82	23		34.4				Signals
105.46	GRANTHAM	88	15	0.0					
	ESTIMATED								
88.64	Essendine	65	50	90.0	89.5	1225	1492	2397	Est time/speed
92.22	Little Bytham	68	14	90.0	87.8	1042	1232	2132	Est time/speed
97.10	Corby Glen	71	34	85.0	82.7	960	1193	1992	Est time/speed
100.11	Stoke	73	45	80.0	82.3	1027	1382	2090	Est time/speed
102.10	Gt Ponton	75	12	85.0	48.8	403	136	930	Est time/speed
105.46	GRANTHAM	79	20	0.0	83.2	0	0	0	Est time

APPENDIX D
1. THE SILVER JUBILEE: KINGS CROSS- DARLINGTON-NEWCASTLE

Engine BR No	Load	Time Actual	Time Net	Av Speed Actual	Av Speed Net	Dn/Up
60014	235	194.67	187.25	71.58	74.42	D
60005	270	198.00	188.00	70.38	74.12	D
60016	235	191.17	188.00	72.89	74.12	D
60014	230	195.25	191.00	71.37	72.96	D
60014	230	201.03	191.00	69.32	72.96	D
60016	230	196.20	192.00	71.02	72.58	D
60015	230	195.87	192.50	71.15	72.39	D
60017	230	198.07	193.75	70.36	71.92	D
60014	270	194.83	194.83	71.52	71.52	D
60014	235	196.35	195.50	70.97	71.28	D
60014	230	196.80	196.80	70.81	70.81	D
60014	230	196.95	197.00	70.75	70.74	D
60017	230	197.45	197.50	70.57	70.56	D
60015	230	196.13	190.00	71.05	73.34	U
60014	230	199.67	192.00	69.79	72.58	U
60025	278	195.97	193.00	71.11	72.20	U
60014	225	199.03	193.00	70.01	72.20	U
60014	230	196.27	193.50	71.00	72.02	U
60017	230	196.77	193.75	70.82	71.92	U
60017	270	205.00	194.00	67.98	71.83	U
60015	230	196.65	194.50	70.86	71.65	U
60014	230	195.13	195.00	71.41	71.46	U
60015	235	195.38	195.38	71.32	71.32	U
60017	230	198.87	196.00	70.07	71.10	U

APPENDIX D
2. THE SILVER JUBILEE: LOG OF OPERATIONAL INCIDENTS

Date		
1935		NIL
1936		
4 Aug	U	A4 2510 failed at York, C7 732 to Doncaster, C1 4452 to Kings Cross in 139 mins
14 Oct	D	A4 2510 off Doncaster, A1 4477 on. Replacement following day was A4 2511
1937		
11 Jan	D	A4 2509 off at York, A1 2576 to Newcastle. Replacement following day was A4 2510
14 Apr	D	A4 2512 off at Durham, G5 1752 to Newcastle. Replacement following day was A4 2511
27 May	D	A4 2510 off at Corby Glen, A1 2551 to Newcastle. Replacement following day was A4 2511
17 Aug	D	A4 2510 off at Newark, A3 2596 to Newcastle. Replacement following day was A4 2512
22 Sep	D	A4 2509 off at Grantham, A1 4470 to Newcastle. Replacement following day was A4 4483
1938		
14 Jan	D	A4 2510 off York (?), A3 2501 on. No replacement since 14th was a Friday
2 May	U	A4 2510 off at Peterborough. D2 4379 + C1 3293 forward to Kings Cross
13 Jun	U	A4 2509 off at Peterborough. C1s 4403/4400 forward to Kings Cross
2 Aug	U	A4 2510 off at Doncaster (?). A1 4471 forward to Kings Cross
15 Aug	U	A4 2510 off at Hitchin. C1 4437 forward to Kings Cross
28 Dec	U	A4 2510 off at Peterborough. C1 4446 forward to Kings Cross
1939		
3 May	D	A4 2509 off at Peterborough. A1 4476 to Newcastle. Replacement following day was A4 4492.
6 Jul	U	A4 4495 off near Peterborough. C1 3290 forward to Kings Cross
24 Aug	D	A4 2509 off at York, A1 2575 to Newcastle. Replacement following day was A4 4499

APPENDIX D
3. THE CORONATION: KINGS CROSS–EDINBURGH

Engine BR No	Load	Time Actual	Time Net	Av Speed Actual	Av Speed Net	Dn/Up
KINGS CROSS – YORK (188.15 miles)						
60009	325		154.00		73.31	D
60012	325	155.60	154.00	72.55	73.31	D
60008	325	154.58	154.58	73.03	73.03	D
60011	325	157.12	156.00	71.85	72.37	D
NEWCASTLE – KINGS CROSS (268.35 miles)						
60042*	295	227.50	222.50	70.8	72.4	U
60031	295	235.30	224.00	68.4	71.9	U
60084*	295	229.00	225.00	70.3	71.6	U
60005	270	237.50	226.00	67.8	71.2	U
60013	325	230.50	230.50	69.9	69.9	U
60012	330	240.00	237.00	67.1	67.9	U
NEWCASTLE – EDINBURGH (124.45 miles)						
60084*	295	113.10	113.10	66.0	66.0	D
60012	325	117.93	117.93	63.3	63.3	D
60016	252	118.00	118.00	63.3	63.3	D
60012	325	119.23	119.23	62.6	62.6	D
60016	252	114.00	114.00	65.5	65.5	U
60031	295	120.35	114.00	62.0	65.5	U
60013	325	115.33	115.33	64.7	64.7	U
60012	325	118.82	118.00	62.8	63.3	U
*-A3						

APPENDIX D
4. THE CORONATION: LOG OF OPERATIONAL INCIDENTS

1937			
Aug 25th	D	13 late	A4 4491 failed; assisted from Waverley East.
Sept 16th	U	4 late	A4 4490 replaced by A3 2597 at Newcastle.
Sept 24th	D	12 late	A4 4490 replaced at York: 5 mins regained.
Sept 24th	U		A4 4491 replaced at Newcastle by A1 2577.
Oct 4th	U	59 late	A4 4489 burst steam pipe, replaced by A1 2568 which lost 26 mins.
Oct 15th	U	35 late	A4 4490 out of coal at Potters Bar and replaced by unidentified loco.
Oct 29th	U	129 late	A4 4496 badly delayed by sigs and derailment. Replaced at Doncaster by A3 2743 via Lincoln.
Nov 16th	U	83 late	A4 4488 failed at Potters Bar with hot MBE, replaced by N2 4582.
Dec 2nd	U	19 late	A4 4490 out of coal and assisted by C1 3272 from Hitchin. 6 mins gained previously.
Dec 10th	U	14 late	A4 4492 SOS and assisted by C1 4427 from Peterborough. 6 mins gained previously.
Dec 13th	U	5 late	A4 4490 SOS, replaced by A3 2597 at Newcastle. 11 mins regained.
Dec 14th	U	24 late	A4 4489 SOS, replaced by A3 2505 at Newcastle. Fog and TSRs caused further delay.
Dec 30th	D	9 late	A4 4497, defective cylinders, replaced at Newcastle by unidentified engine.
1938			
Jan 10th	U	28 late	A4 4486 SOS Tweedmouth, assisted by C7 2165. Replaced by A3 2505 at Newcastle.
Jan 19th	U	11 late	A4 4490 SOS, replaced by A3 2507 at Newcastle.
Jan 21st	U	17 late	A4 4496 SOS, replaced by A1 2546 at Grantham. Fog delay N London.
Jan 28th	D	12 late	A4 4488 with defective brakes, replaced at York by V2 No 4782.
Mar 8th	D	10 late	A4 2512 replaced at Newcastle by A3 2746. TSRs 7 mins, 2 regained.
Mar 9th	D	1 BT	A4 4497 failed with broken injector pipe at York. Replaced by V2 No 4782. 12 mins recovered.
Mar 10th	D	13 late	A4 4488 failed with defective brakes at York. Replaced by A1 2577 to N/C. A1 2575 to ED.
May 13th	D	11 late	A4 4488 replaced at Newcastle by A3 2507. 12 mins regained.
May 17th	D	55 late	A4 2512 with hot MBE replaced at Grantham or Doncaster by A1 4473.
May 18th	U	16 late	A1 4473 used throughout.
June 13th	D	41 late	A4 4483 replaced at York by A1 2570.
June 17th	D	45 late	A4 4482 replaced at York by A1 2575 and at Tweedmouth by unidentified loco.
June 21st	D	38 late	A4 4467 with hot MBE replaced at Hitchin by K3 2428, then at Grantham by A3 2744.
June 23rd	D	1 late	A4 4485 with broken little end pipe replaced at Newcastle by A4 4490.
June 23rd	U	1.5 late	A4 4497 replaced at Newcastle by A3 2598. 12 mins regained.
June 24th	D	RT	A4 4485 with defective oil feed pipe replaced at Newcastle. 5 mins regained.
July 7th	D	6 late	A4 2510 with defective brakes replaced at Newcastle by A1 2571.
July 20th	U	29 late	A4 4487 with hot MBE replaced at Newark by V2 4773
Sept 27th	D	RT	A4 4464 replaced at Newcastle by A4 4463.
Oct 24th	D	48 late	A4 4487 replaced at Newcastle by A3 2746. 45 mins lost due to signals and wrong line working.
Dec 9th	D	61 late	A4 4483 failed at Abbotts Ripton, replaced by C1 4413 to York, replaced again by A1 2577.
Dec 20th	U	48 late	A4 4487 with hot axlebox at Crow Park, replaced by A3 4480.
1939			
Jan 4th	D	57 late	A4 4482 replaced at Grantham by W1 10000 which ran hot at Durham. G5 1837 replaced to Newcastle and A1 2575 was the third replacement.
Jan 9th	D	6 late	A4 4486 SOS. Replaced at Newcastle by unidentified loco.
Jan 12th	U	72 late	A4 4467 with hot MBE replaced at Claypole by J6 3580, then at Grantham by A1 2546.
Jan 13th	D	RT	A4 4464 with failed injectors replaced at Newcastle by A4 2511.
Feb 2nd	U	15late	A4 4485 with defective brick arch, replaced by A1 4476.
Mar 13th	U	5 late	A4 4902 with hot axlebox, replaced at Doncaster by A3 2747.
Mar 22nd	U	RT	A4 4491 with hot bearing replaced at Newcastle by A3 2595. 19 mins regained.
Mar 24th	U	23 late	A4 4493 with hot axlebox, replaced at Tweedmouth by C7 2205, then at Newcastle by A3 2507. 14 mins regained.
June 7th	D	18 late	A4 4483 with hot MBE replaced at Newcastle by A1 2571.
June 16th	D	17 late	A4 4497 with hot axlebox at York, replaced by unidentified loco, and again at Newcastle by unidentified loco.
Aug 1st	D	1 late	A4 4496 replaced at Newcastle by unidentified loco.
Aug 21st	U	28 late	A44465 failed and replaced at Alnmouth by A1 2582, and again by A4 4499 to Kings Cross.

APPENDIX D
5. THE WEST RIDING LIMITED: KINGS CROSS-LEEDS

Engine BR No	Load	Time Actual	Time Net	Av Speed Actual	Av Speed Net	Dn/Up
60029	295		155.00		71.88	D
60007	295	156.75	156.75	71.08	71.08	D
60007	295	158.33	156.75	70.37	71.08	D
60007	295	158.00	158.00	70.52	70.52	D
60008	295	161.43	158.50	69.02	70.30	D
60029	290	168.63	161.00	66.07	69.20	D
60012	290	169.07	162.25	65.90	68.67	D
60029	295	162.33	155.50	68.64	71.65	U
60007	295	158.00	157.25	70.52	70.86	U
60013	295	160.42	158.00	69.46	70.52	U
60030	295	161.92	161.50	68.81	68.99	U
60005	295	166.17	161.75	67.05	68.88	U
60010	295	162.68	162.75	68.49	68.46	U

APPENDIX D
6. THE WEST RIDING LIMITED: LOG OF OPERATIONAL INCIDENTS

Date			
1938			
Jan 14th	D		A4 2512 failed at Kings Cross, replaced by V2 4789.
Mar 29th	D		A4 4489 failed at Carcroft, replaced by K3 1166.
Mar 30th	U		A4 4468 borrowed from Doncaster for up service.
July 7th	U	10 late	A1 2553 substituted for rostered A4 4492. A4 4496 took return leg of diagram.
July 12th	U	4 late	A3 2750 substituted for rostered A4 4496. A4 4500 took return leg of diagram.
July 22nd	U		A1 2555 substituted for rostered A4 4492. A4 4901 took return leg of diagram.
Aug 11st	U	11 late	A1 2555 substituted for rostered A4 2512. A4 4467 took return leg of diagram.
Aug 31st	U	1 BT	A1 2555 substituted for rostered A4 4467. A4 2512 took return leg of diagram.
Nov 25th	U	10 late	A1 2547 substituted for rostered A4 4489. A4 4467 took return leg of diagram.
1939			
Mar 14th	U	6 late	A1 4473 substituted for rostered A4 4467. A4 4496 took return leg of diagram.
May 5th	D		A4 4495 failed at Kings Cross, replaced by A1 4472.
June 6th	U	2 late	A1 4470 substituted for rostered A4 4494. A4 4902 took return leg of diagram.

APPENDIX D
7: THE ELIZABETHAN: KINGS CROSS-EDINBURGH

LOCO (BR No)	LOAD Tons	TIME Net	TIME Actual	MPH Net	MPH Actual	D/U
60027	390	362.00	396.75	65.10	59.40	D
60033	425	365.00	388.77	64.57	60.62	D
60032	425	370.00	387.80	63.70	60.77	D
60032	425	370.00	387.75	63.70	60.78	D
60012	425	371.00	389.32	63.53	60.54	D
60027	385	371.00	392.00	63.53	60.12	D
60027	390	371.00	392.00	63.53	60.12	D
60033	425	371.00	389.08	63.53	60.57	D
60013	425	372.00	387.18	63.35	60.87	D
60032	425	372.00	397.82	63.35	59.24	D
60009	420	374.00	386.72	63.02	60.94	D
60017	425	380.00	405.62	62.02	58.10	D
60011	425	381.00	389.30	61.86	60.54	D
60028	425	386.00	398.67	61.06	59.12	D
60033	420	397.00	425.30	59.37	55.42	D
60029	465	402.00	431.25	58.63	54.65	D
60029	460	402.00	431.33	58.63	54.64	D
60033	425	357.00	390.00	66.02	60.43	U
60027	385	362.00	380.00	65.10	62.02	U
60027	385	363.00	399.25	64.93	59.03	U
60033	430	365.00	383.02	64.57	61.53	U
60027	385	366.00	395.35	64.39	59.61	U
60027	385	366.00	398.92	64.39	59.08	U
60033	425	366.00	392.00	64.39	60.12	U
60033	425	366.00	378.00	64.39	62.35	U
60013	425	367.00	382.08	64.22	61.68	U
60024	385	367.00	396.75	64.22	59.40	U
60012	425	368.00	382.17	64.04	61.67	U
60030	425	369.00	385.17	63.87	61.19	U
60011	425	370.00	386.12	63.70	61.04	U
60033	425	370.00	396.48	63.70	59.44	U
60009	425	372.00	385.50	63.35	61.14	U
60032	425	372.00	387.67	63.35	60.79	U
60032	425	373.00	403.65	63.18	58.39	U
60009	425	373.00	384.47	63.10	61.30	U
60022	425	374.00	393.88	63.02	59.83	U
60032	425	375.00	387.63	62.85	60.80	U
60032	425	380.00	397.47	62.02	59.30	U
60008	430	382.00	422.50	61.70	55.78	U
60032	425	384.00	389.33	61.38	60.53	U
60011	425	389.50	400.23	60.51	58.89	U
60017	415	392.00	402.42	60.12	58.57	U
60017	430	401.00	436.00	58.77	54.06	U
60006	425	412.00	425.48	57.20	55.39	U

APPENDIX D
8. THE TALISMAN: KINGS CROSS-EDINBURGH

Engine BR No	Load	Time Actual	Time Net	Av Speed Actual	Av Speed Net	Dn/Up
KINGS CROSS - NEWCASTLE						
60025	290	281.50	228.00	57.20	70.62	D
60026	290	263.00	240.00	61.22	67.09	D
60025	300	274.13	247.00	58.73	65.19	D
60025	290	271.25	248.00	59.36	64.92	D
60017	300	266.18		60.49		D
60015	325	267.00		60.30		D
60019	290	260.5		61.81		U
60018	285	260.90	236.00	61.71	68.22	U
60066*	295	261.15	240.00	61.65	67.09	U
60021	325	242.00				U
NEWCASTLE-EDINBURGH						
60004	285	120.93	109.25	61.74	68.35	D
60043*	325	122.07	112.50	61.17	66.37	D
60027	285	117.65	113.75	63.47	65.64	D
60087*	320	118.83	116.25	62.84	64.23	D
60031	290	123.28	119.00	60.57	62.75	D
60009	320	128.48	119.00	58.12	62.75	D
60027	325	121.78	121.78	61.31	61.31	D
60009	300	125.47		59.51		D
60057*	285	128.55	124.50	58.09	59.98	D
60009	295	122.85		60.78		U
60009	295	122.85	119.00	60.78	62.75	U
60031	285	126.08	119.00	59.22	62.75	U
60031	325	137.92	119.50	54.14	62.49	U
60009	295	124.58	124.58	59.94	59.94	U

*A3

APPENDIX E
PASSENGER TRAIN JOURNAL TIMES: THE ELIZABETHAN

Driver	Howard: Kings Cross-Tollerton
Driver	T. Smith Tollerton-Edinburgh
Load 403/425 tons	Date: July 25th 1955
Locomotive	No 60033

STATIONS	SCHEDULE	ACTUAL	LATE	LOST	NOTES
KINGS CROSS	9:30:30	9:30			
Hatfield	9:53:00	9:53:00			
Hitchin	10:06:00	10:06:00		4	TSR Sandy
Huntingdon	10:28:00	10:31:00	3		
Peterborough	10:44:30	10:45:00	0.5		
Grantham	11:13:30	11:13:00	0.5BT		
Newark	11:26:00	11:25:00	1BT	2	TSR MP132
Retford	11:43:00	11:42:00	1BT		
Doncaster	12:00:00	11.58.00	2BT		
Shaftholme Jct	12:05:00	12.03.00	2BT		
York	12:33:00	12:31:00	2BT		
Northallerton	13:01:30	12:58:00	3.5BT		
Darlington	13:13:00	13.09.00	4BT		
Ferryhill	13:25:30	13:21:00	4.5BT	6	Sigs Hett Mill
Durham	13:34:30	13.35.30	1		
Newcastle	13:51:30	13.49.00	2.5BT		
Berwick	14:59:00	14:49:00	10BT		
Marshall Meadows	15:01:00	14:51:00	10BT		
Dunbar	15:29:00	15:20:00	9BT		
Drem	15:39:00	15:30:00	9BT		
EDINBURGH	16.00:00	15.48:00	12BT		
RUNNING TIME	390	378.0			
NET RUNNING TIME		366.0		12	

APPENDIX E
PASSENGER TRAIN JOURNAL TIMES: THE ELIZABETHAN

Driver	Gemmell: Edinburgh-Tollerton
Driver	Green: Tollerton-Kings Cross
Load 363/385 tons	Date: August 25th 1955
Locomotive	No 60033

STATIONS	SCHEDULE	ACTUAL	LATE	LOST	NOTES
EDINBURGH	9.45	9.45	0		
Drem	10.06	10.06	RT		
Dunbar	10.16	10.30	14	14	7 bells Dn Main goods
Marshall Meadows	10.44	10.56	12		
Berwick	10.46	10.57	11	3.5	TSR 20 Alnmouth
Newcastle	11.51	12.03	12		
Durham	12.07	12.18	11		
Darlington	12.29	12.39	10	4.5	TSR 20 Northallerton
Northallerton	12.41				
York	13.07	13.15	8		
Shaftholme Jct	13.38	13.42	4		
Doncaster	13.43	13.46	3		
Retford	14.00	14.02	1.5	2.5	TSR 40 Lincoln Rd
Newark	14:17	14:18	1		
Grantham	14:30	14:30	RT	4.5	TSR 20 L Bytham
Peterborough	14:55	14:57	2		TSR 20 Abbotts Ripton
Huntingdon	15:13	15:15	2		
Hitchin	15:36	15:38	2	4	Sigs Stevenage
Hatfield	15:50	15:55	5		
Kings Cross	16:15	16:15	RT		
TOTALS	390 Sch	357 net		33	

APPENDIX E
PASSENGER TRAIN JOURNAL TIMES: THE ELIZABETHAN

Driver	Redpath: Edinburgh-Tollerton
Driver	Cull: Tollerton-Kings Cross
Load 363/385 tons	Date: July 16th 1956
Locomotive	No 60033

STATIONS	SCHEDULE	ACTUAL	LATE	LOST	NOTES
EDINBURGH	9:45:00	9:45:00	0		
Drem	10:06:00	10:06:00	RT		
Dunbar	10:16:00	10:16:00	RT		
Marshall Meadows	10:44:00	10:43:00	1BT		
Berwick	10:46:00	10:45:00	1BT	4	Sigs Manors & N'cle
Newcastle	11:51:00	11:52:00	1	6	TSR Chester-le-St
Durham	12:07:00	12:14:00	7		
Darlington	12:29:30	12:35:30	6		
Northallerton	12:41:30	12:46:30	5		
York	13:07:30	13:11:30	4		
Shaftholme Jct	13:38:30	13:42:30	4		
Doncaster	13:43:00	13:47:00	4	2	Sigs Canal
Retford	14:00:30	14:06:00	5.5	3 / 6	Sigs Lincoln Rd / TSR Br 291/5
Newark	14:17:00	14:31:00	14		
Grantham	14:30:30	14:44:00	13.5	3	TSR Walton
Peterborough	14:55:30	15:09:30	14		TSR 20 Abbotts Ripton
Huntingdon	15:13:00	15:25:00	12		
Hitchin	15:36:30	15:47:00	10.5		
Hatfield	15:51:00	15:59:00	8		
Kings Cross	16:15:00	16:17:00	2		
TOTALS	390 Sch	366 net		24	

Note: no notes given on second run

APPENDIX E
PASSENGER TRAIN JOURNAL TIMES: THE FLYING SCOTSMAN

Driver W Hoole	Newcastle-Kings Cross				Newcastle-Kings Cross			
Load 435/460 tons	Date: July 5th 1955				Date: August 10th 1955			
Locomotive	No 60007				No 60025			
STATIONS	SCHEDULE	ACTUAL	LATE	NOTES	ACTUAL	LATE	LOST	NOTES
Doncaster	14:21:30	14:39:30	18.0					
Retford	14:39:00	14:54:30	15.5					
Newark	14:56:30	15:09:30	13.0					
Barkston Sth Jct	15:07:30	15:19:00	11.5		15:29:30			
Grantham	15:11:30	15:22:30	11.0		15:33:30	22.0		
					15:38:00			Stoke
Peterborough	15:38:00	15:43:00	5.0		15:54:00	16.0		
Huntingdon	15:56:00	15:58:30	2.5		16:09:30	13.5		
Hitchin	16:20:00	16:18:00	2BT		16:29:00	9.0		
Knebworth	16:27:30	16:24:30	3BT		16:35:00	7.5		
Hatfield	16:35:00	16:30:30	4.5BT		16:41:30	5.0		
Potters Bar	16:42:00							
Finsbury Park	16:55:00	16:46:00	9BT	Sigs	16:54:30	0.5BT		
Kings Cross	17:00:00	16:55:00	5BT		16:58:00	2BT		
RUNNING TIME	158.5/112.5	135.5			88.5			
NET RUNNING TIME		131.0			88.5			
ANALYSIS	SCHEDULE	ACTUAL	MILES	AV	ACTUAL	MILES	AV	
Doncaster-Grantham	50.0	43.0	50.50	70				
Grantham-Peterborough	26.5	20.5	29.10	85	20.5	29.10	85	
Peterborough-Huntingdon	18.0	15.0	17.49	70	15.5	17.49	68	
Huntingdon-Hitchin	24.0	19.5	26.95	83	19.5	26.95	83	
Hitchin-Hatfield	15.0	12.5	14.24	68	12.5	14.24	68	
Hatfield-Finsbury Park	20.0	15.5	15.17	59	13.0	15.17	70	

APPENDIX E
PASSENGER TRAIN JOURNAL TIMES: THE TEES-TYNE PULLMAN

Driver Hoole	Newcastle-Kings Cross			
Date	November 16th 1955			
Locomotive	No 60007			
Load	380/400 tons			
STATIONS	SCHEDULE	ACTUAL	LATE	NOTES
Newcastle	9:25:00	9:25:00	RT	
Barkston Sth Jct	12:11:30	12:14:00	2.5	
Grantham	12:15:30	12:17:00	1.5	
Peterborough	12:45:00	12:40:00	5BT	*
Huntingdon	13:02:30	12:57:00	5.5BT	*
Hitchin	13:26:00	13:17:00	9BT	
Hatfield	13:40:00	13:30:00	2BT	
Finsbury Park		13:38:00		
Kings Cross	14:04:00	13:46:00	18BT	
* Delay unspecified				

Driver W Hoole	Newcastle-Kings Cross				
Date	November 18th 1955				
Locomotive	No 60007				
Load	304/325				
Location	Speed mph	Distance	Calc'd Time	Running Total	Mileage
Grantham	72	0.00	4.59		105.46
Stoke	68	5.35	2.31	4.59	100.11
Corby Glen	88	8.36	1.98	6.90	97.10
MP 94	100	11.46	1.02	8.88	94.00
Little Bytham	108	13.24	1.57	9.91	92.23
MP89.5	100	15.96	0.52	11.48	89.50
Essendine	98	16.82	2.35	12.00	88.64
Tallington	96	20.62	1.96	14.35	84.84
Helpston	78	23.46	2.04	16.31	82.00
Werrington Jct	69	25.96	3.59	18.35	79.50
Peterborough	36	29.10	4.46	21.93	76.36
Yaxley	65	32.85	2.72	26.40	72.61
Holme	78	36.09	1.56	29.12	69.37
Connington	76	38.09	3.14	30.67	67.37
Abbotts Ripton	71	41.94	3.55	33.81	63.52
Huntingdon	86	46.59	2.12	37.37	58.87
Offord	79	49.51	3.19	39.49	55.95
St Neots	80	53.73	4.55	42.68	51.73
TSR20	25	57.71	0.55	47.22	47.75
Tempsford	27	57.95	4.83	47.77	47.51
Sandy	57	61.33	2.81	52.61	44.13
Biggleswade	70	64.30	3.41	55.42	41.16
Arlesey	75	68.42	1.04	58.82	37.04
Three Counties	80	69.76	2.96	59.86	35.70
Hitchin	73	73.54	2.85	62.82	31.92
Stevenage	68	76.89	1.28	65.67	28.57
Langley Jct	75	78.41	1.64	66.95	27.05
Knebworth	72	80.43	2.38	68.60	25.03
Welwyn North	81	83.47	1.26	70.98	21.99
Welwyn G. City	79	85.15	2.09	72.24	20.31
Hatfield	72	87.78	4.05	74.33	17.68
Potters Bar	75	92.74	1.66	78.38	12.72
Hadley Wood	80	94.88	1.08	80.04	10.58
New Barnet	78	96.31	3.21	81.13	9.15
Wood Green	78	100.49	0.74	84.34	4.97
Hornsey	72	101.41	1.43	85.08	4.05
Finsbury Park	57	102.95	5.28	86.51	2.51
Kings Cross	0	105.46	4.00	91.79	0.00
Calculated running time 91.8 mins					
Net of TSR 86 mins					
(The mileages are taken from the distances in the WTT)					

APPENDIX E
THE TALISMAN

	Kings Cross – Newcastle					Kings Cross – Newcastle				
Driver W Hoole Driver T Smith Load 274/295 tons Locomotive	Newcastle – Edinburgh Date: November 5th 1956 No 60026					Date: November 9th 1956 No 60025				
STATIONS	BOOKED	ACTUAL	Late	Lost	Notes	BOOKED	ACTUAL	Late	Lost	Notes
Kings Cross	16:00:00	16:23:00	23	23	ECS late sigs	16:00:00	0:00:00 16.13/39	28	32	Stop 26.5 min at N Barnet
Hatfield	16:22:30	16:43:30	21			16:22:30	16:52:00	29.5	0.5	Sigs
Hitchin	16:35:30	16:55:30	20	2	Sigs Sandy	16:35:30	17:02:30	27	2	TSR40
Huntingdon	16:56:30	17:16:30	20			16:56:30	17:22:30	26		
Peterborough	17:18:00	17:32:00	14	3	PSR20 TSR Essdn	17:18:00	17:36:00	18	3	PSR20 TSR30
Grantham	17:45:30	18:00:30	15			17:45:30	18:03:30	18	3	
Newark	17:58:00	18:12:00	14			17:58:00	18:15:00	17		
Retford	18:15:00	18:27:00	12	2	TSR Bawtry	18:15:00	18:32:00	17	16	Sig stop
Doncaster	18:37:30	18:42:30	5			18:37:30	19:01:00	23.5		
Shaftholme Jct	18:42:00	18:47:00	5			18:42:00	19:06:00	24		
York	19:09:00	19:12:00	3			19:09:00	19:31:00	22	1.5 3	Sigs TSR40
Thirsk	19:29:00	19:31:00	2			19:29:00	19:53:00	24		
Northallerton	19:35:00	19:37:00	2			19:35:00	19:58:30	23.5		
Darlington	19:47:00	19:48:00	1			19:47:00	20:09:00	22		
Ferryhill	19:59:00					19:59:00	20:20:00	21		
Durham	20:09:00	20:08:00	1BT			20:09:00	20:28:00	19		
Newcastle arr	20:28:00	20:22:00	6BT			20:28:00	20:41:30	13.7		
dep	20:34:00	20:34:00	RT							
EDINBURGH	22:40:00	22:39:00	1BT							
TIME, K+-NC	268.0	239.0				268.0	281.5			
NET TIME		232.0					220.5		61.0	

APPENDIX E
THE FAIR MAID

	Kings Cross – Newcastle					
Driver W Hoole Load 309/325 tons Locomotive	Date: November 5th 1957 No 60003					
STATIONS	BOOKED	ACTUAL	Late	Lost	Notes	Speeds annotated
Kings Cross	7:50:00	8:01:00	11	11 0.5	Sigs	
Greenwood	8:04:00	8:13:45	9.75	0.5	Sigs	69 66
Hatfield	8:12:00	8:20:15	8.25	2.5	TSR40	80.86
Hitchin	8:24:30	8:32:30	8			92 107.5
Sandy	8:33:30	8:39:30	6		PSR70	100 70
Huntingdon	8:44:30	8:49:00	4.5			80.5 75.94
Peterborough	9:08:00	9:02:00	6BT		PSR20	85
Essendine	9:20:00	9:12:30	7.5BT			75 (Not min)
Stoke	9:31:30	9:22:30	10BT	4	TSR20/Sigs	
Grantham	9:35:30	9:31:00	4.5BT			60 91
Newark	9:48:00	9:41:15	6.75BT	5	Sig stop	
Retford	10:05:00	10:03:45	1.25BT			
Doncaster	10:27:30	10:18:00	9.5BT	0.5	Sigs	
Shaftholme Jct	10:32:00	10:24:00 10:33:00		11.5	Sig stop 9 mins	90
York	10:59:00	11:00:00	1	1	Sigs	
Darlington	11:37:00	11:34:15	2.75BT			
RUNNING TIME, K+-DAR	227.00	213.75		25.50		
NET RUNNING TIME		188.25				

APPENDIX F
A SUMMARY OF PUBLISHED RUNS BY A4 PACIFICS (in mileage order)

LOCO (BR No)	LOAD Tons	TIME Net	TIME Actual	MPH Net	MPH Actual	SOURCE	DATE
PETERBOROUGH-GRANTHAM 29.1 miles							
60007	320	26.10	26.10	66.90	66.90	RM	February 63
60033	315	27.20	27.20	64.19	64.19	RM	February 63
YORK-DARLINGTON 44.15 miles							
60030	325	34.68	34.68	76.38	76.38	TI	May 59
60033	235	35.00	35.00	75.69	75.69	RW	May 59
60003	325	35.95	35.95	73.69	73.69	TI	July 58
60007	340	36.55	36.55	72.48	72.48	TI	September 54
60029	335	37.50	39.60	70.64	66.89	RM	February 63
60026	395	37.75	43.25	70.17	61.25	RM	March 61
60026	330	38.63	37.00	68.57	71.59	RW	November 59
60029	335	39.58	39.58	66.92	66.92	RM	October 60
60002	275	39.58	39.58	66.92	66.92	RW	May 59
60034	480	43.25	51.23	61.25	51.70	RW	May 59
KINGS CROSS-PETERBOROUGH 76.35 miles							
60014	230	55.03	55.03	83.24	83.24	RM	November 35
60014	505	70.75	73.67	64.75	62.18	RM	Junr 57
60007	480	72.00	76.68	63.63	59.74	RW	May 59
60007	435	72.00	79.53	63.63	57.60	RW	August 59
60003	500	73.73	73.73	62.13	62.13	CJA	Book
60034	505	74.25	76.37	61.70	59.99	CJA	Book
60014	470	75.00	80.30	61.08	57.05	RM	June 57
60034	550	80.00	91.37	57.26	50.14	RM	July 53
60032	540	80.00	83.33	57.26	54.97	RM	July 53
KINGS CROSS-GRANTHAM 105.45 miles							
60010	325	86.05	86.05	73.53	73.53	CJA	Book
60010	325	87.57	87.57	72.25	72.25	CJA	Book
60033	425	90.50	97.62	69.91	64.81	TI	October 56
60033	330	90.50	97.17	69.91	65.11	TI	October 61
60028	330	90.50	104.13	69.91	60.76	TI	February 58
60014	460	91.00	92.58	69.53	68.34	RM	April 57
60033	425	91.00	92.93	69.53	68.08	TI	October 56
60014	500	92.50	101.68	68.40	62.22	RM	January 62
60009	380	93.00	96.72	68.03	65.42	TI	April 62
60021	320	94.50	97.27	66.95	65.05	RM	July 59
60028	325	96.00	109.62	65.91	57.72	TI	February 58
60022	415	96.50	110.65	65.56	57.18	RM	October 64
60014	410	96.83	96.83	65.34	65.34	TI	November 53
60015	515	97.00	97.00	65.23	65.23	RM	April 57
60007	495	97.00	101.90	65.23	62.09	RM	March 55
60007	295	97.05	97.05	65.19	65.19	RW	August 59
60017	300	98.60	98.60	64.17	64.17	TI	August 57
60014	510	101.50	105.38	62.33	60.04	TI	October 56
60021	510	102.00	116.17	62.03	54.46	RMW	May 59
60003	440	102.00	109.10	62.03	57.99	TI	October 56
60006	510	102.65	102.65	61.64	61.64	TI	August 58
60015	505	103	114.92	61.13	55.06	BCB	
60006	505	104	118.55	60.55	53.37	BCB	
60005	545	105	118.22	60.26	53.52	BCB	
60019	510	105	110.27	60.26	57.38	RM	July 59
60015	505	105	113.25	60.26	55.87	BCB	
60033	480	105	111.67	60.26	56.66	OSN	Book
60032	505	106	137.75	59.69	45.93	BCB	
4469	580	108	108.25	58.45	58.45	TI	August 58
60013	510	110	118.50	57.26	53.39	TI	July 53
60021	420	110	119.73	57.26	52.84	TI	February 56
60025	545	113	132.48	55.74	47.76	BCB	
60033	590	114	129.77	55.50	48.76	OSN	Book
60017	615	119	123.17	52.95	51.37	OSN	Book
60015	615	119	123.17	52.95	51.37	OSN	Book
60015	680	123	123.65	51.17	51.17	OSN	Book
60006	740	127	127.42	49.66	49.66	OSN	Book
60033	660	128	137.17	49.43	46.13	OSN	Book

(CONT)

NEWCASTLE-EDINBURGH 124.45 miles						
60004	285	109.25	120.93	68.35	61.74	TI	June 61
60034	420	111.00	113.03	67.27	66.06	RM	October 55
60034	425	111.50	113.03	66.97	66.06	TI	September 55
60031	295	114.00	120.35	65.50	62.04	TI	June 53
60016	252	114.00	114.00	65.50	65.50	CJA	Book
60013	325	115.33	115.33	64.74	64.74	TI	June 53
60012	325	117.93	117.93	63.32	63.32	TI	October 52
60012	325	118.00	118.82	63.28	62.84	OSN	Book
60016	252	118.00	118.00	63.28	63.28	CJA	Book
60009	320	119.00	128.48	62.75	58.12	RM	October 60
60009	320	119.00	128.48	62.75	58.12	RM	October 60
60009	295	119.00	122.85	62.75	60.78	RM	September 57
60031	290	119.00	123.28	62.75	60.57	RM	November 56
60031	285	119.00	126.08	62.75	59.22	RM	November 56
60012	325	119.23	119.23	62.63	62.63	TI	October 52
60031	325	119.50	137.92	62.49	54.14	TI	April 59
60009	300	120.00	125.47	62.23	59.51	RM	September 57
60027	325	121.78	121.78	61.31	61.31	RM	June 58
60023	370	124.00	132.00	60.22	56.57	OSN	Book
60011	370	124.00	138.75	60.22	53.82	OSN	Book
60009	295	124.58	124.58	59.94	59.94	RM	June 58
60020	475	137.00	169.53	54.50	44.04	CJA	Book
60005	475	145.00	149.83	51.50	49.84	CJA	Book
KINGS CROSS – DONCASTER 155.95 miles						
60007	295	131.00	137.70	71.43	67.95	RM	August 59
60022	330	141.00	149.20	66.36	62.71	TI	July 62
60014	425	142.00	147.12	65.89	63.60	TI	November 53
60006	245	145.00	165.93	64.53	56.39	TI	July 53
60022	460	160.00	170.25	58.48	54.96	OSN	Book
KINGS CROSS – LEEDS CENTRAL 185.7 miles						
60029	295	155.00		71.88		GO	September 75
60029	295	155.50	162.33	71.65	68.64	RM	November 40
60007	295	156.75	156.75	71.08	71.08	GO	September 75
60007	295	156.75	158.33	71.08	70.37	RM	November 40
60007	295	157.25	158.00	70.86	70.52	RM	November 40
60013	295	158.00	160.42	70.52	69.46	RM	November 40
60007	295	158.00	158.00	70.52	70.52	GO	September 75
60008	295	158.50	161.43	70.30	69.02	RM	November 40
60029	290	16.00	168.63	69.20	66.07	RM	November 40
60030	295	16.50	161.92	68.99	68.81	RM	November 40
60005	295	16.75	166.17	68.88	67.05	RM	November 40
60012	290	162.25	169.07	68.67	65.90	RM	November 40
60010	295	162.75	162.68	68.46	68.49	RM	November 40

(CONT)

KINGS CROSS – YORK 188.15 miles							
60014	235	148.00	155.03	76.28	72.82	CJA	Book
60012	325	154.00	155.60	73.31	72.55	TI	June 53
60009	325	154.00		73.31		GO	September 75
60008	325	154.58	154.58	73.03	73.03	TI	June 53
60008	325	154.58	154.58	73.03	73.03	GO	September 75
60014	270	154.63	154.63	73.00	73.00	CJA	Book
60011	325	156.00	157.12	72.37	71.85	OSN	Book
60007	370	163.00	185.85	69.26	60.74	RM	April 64
60024	430	164.00	180.20	68.84	62.65	TI	November 54
60024	425	165.00	180.20	68.42	62.65	RM	March 55
60007	375	165.00	185.62	68.42	60.82	TI	November 63
60033	420	167.00	167.00	67.60	67.60	TI	August 57
60011	420	169.00	169.00	66.80	66.80	TI	August 57
60021	340	172.00	191.75	65.63	58.87	TI	March 57
60013	425	173.00	175.20	65.25	64.43	RM	January 62
60034	405	174.00	186.80	64.88	60.43	RM	May 59
60026	330	174.00	183.67	64.88	61.46	TI	October 56
60026	435	176.00	190.50	64.14	59.26	RM	November 59
60014	360	180.00	188.20	62.72	59.98	TI	October 56
60022	490	186.00	205.02	60.69	55.06	RM	January 62
KINGS CROSS – DARLINGTON 232.25 miles							
60014	235	187.25	194.67	74.42	71.58	GO	December 35
60005	270	188.00	197.50	74.12	70.56	SLS	December 38
60016	235	188.00	191.17	74.12	72.89	RM	December 36
60015	230	190.00	196.13	73.34	71.05	RM	August 36
60014	254	191.00	195.25	72.96	71.37	RM	November 35
60014	230	191.00	201.03	72.96	69.32	RM	August 36
60014	230	192.00	199.67	72.58	69.79	RM	August 36
60015	230	192.50	195.87	72.39	71.15	RM	August 36
60014	230	193.50	196.27	72.02	71.00	RM	August 36
60017	230	193.75	196.77	71.92	70.82	RM	August 36
60017	230	193.75	198.07	71.92	70.36	RM	August 36
60017	270	194.00	205.00	71.83	67.98	CJA	Book
60015	230	194.50	196.65	71.65	70.86	RM	August 36
60014	235	194.83	194.83	71.52	71.52	GO	August 36
60003	325	195.00	222.00	71.46	62.77	TI	July 58
60014	230	195.00	195.13	71.46	71.41	RM	August 36
60015	235	195.38	195.38	71.32	71.32	GO	September 75
60014	235	195.50	196.35	71.28	70.97	GO	September 36
60017	230	196.00	198.87	71.10	70.07	RM	August 36
60014	230	197.00	193.95	70.74	71.85	RM	August 36
60017	230	197.50	197.45	70.56	70.57	RM	August 36
60022	435	208.25	241.35	66.91	57.74	RM	October 60
60015	330	210.00	223.00	66.36	62.49	RM	September 53
60015	330	210.00	223.00	66.36	62.49	RM	September 53
60017	335	212.50	235.63	65.58	59.14	TI	June 56
KINGS CROSS – NEWCASTLE 268.35 miles							
60005	270	226.00	237.50	71.24	67.79	SLS	December 38
60007	405	256.00	271.08	62.89	59.40	RM	June 67
60007	410	262.00	272.33	61.45	59.12	RM	August 59
60011	635	278.83	278.83	57.74	57.74	RM	September 62
60012	325	237.00	240.00	67.94	67.09	OSN	Book
60013	325	230.50	230.50	69.85	69.85	TI	June 53
60014	230	233.30	233.30	69.01	69.01	RM	December 35
60014	230	235.10	234.10	68.49	68.78	RM	December 35
60017	300	256.00	266.18	62.89	60.49	RM	September 57
60018	285	236.00	260.90	68.22	61.71	RM	November 56
60021	325	242.00		66.53		CJA	Book
60025	290	248.00	271.25	64.92	59.36	RM	November 56
60025	290	228.00	281.50	70.62	57.20	TI	August 57
60025	300	258.00	274.13	62.41	58.73	RM	September 57
60026	290	240.00	263.00	67.09	61.22	TI	August 57
60042*	295	227.50	222.50	72.36	70.77	RM	1939
60084*	295	229.00	225.00	71.56	70.31	RM	1939

(CONT)

KINGS CROSS – EDINBURGH 392.8 miles								
60027	390	362.00	396.75	65.10	59.40	BCB		D
60033	425	365.00	388.77	64.57	60.62	TI	December 55	D
60027	395	369.50	392.10	63.78	60.11	G Vuillet		D
60032	425	370.00	387.80	63.70	60.77	RM	March 55	D
60032	425	370.00	387.75	63.70	60.78	TI	April 55	D
60033	425	371.00	389.08	63.53	60.57	PJC		D
60012	425	371.00	389.32	63.53	60.54	PJC		D
60027	390	371.00	392.00	63.53	60.12	RM	October 60	D
60027	385	371.00	392.00	63.53	60.12	RM	October 60	D
60032	425	372.00	397.82	63.35	59.24	BCB		D
60013	425	372.00	387.18	63.35	60.87	TI	December 55	D
60009	420	374.00	386.72	63.02	60.94	TI	April 55	D
60017	425	380.00	405.62	62.02	58.10	BCB		D
60011	425	381.00	389.30	61.86	60.54	BCB		D
60028	425	386.00	398.67	61.06	59.12	TI	September 53	D
60033	420	397.00	425.30	59.37	55.42	TI	November 52	D
60029	465	402.00	431.25	58.63	54.65	TI	October 51	D
60029	460	402.00	431.33	58.63	54.64	OSN	Book	D
60033	425	357.00	390.00	66.02	60.43	PTJ		U
60027	390	361.50	400.13	65.20	58.90	G Vuillet		U
60027	385	362.00	380.00	65.10	62.02	RM	October 60	U
60027	385	363.00	399.25	64.93	59.03	PJC		U
60033	430	365.00	383.02	64.57	61.53	TI	December 55	U
60033	425	366.00	392.00	64.39	60.12	PTJ		U
60033	425	366.00	378.00	64.39	62.35	PTJ		U
60027	385	366.00	395.35	64.39	59.61	RW	November 59	U
60027	385	366.00	398.92	64.39	59.08	BCB		U
60013	425	367.00	382.08	64.22	61.68	PJC		U
60024	385	367.00	396.75	64.22	59.40	TI	April 62	U
60012	425	368.00	382.17	64.04	61.67	PJC		U
60030	425	369.00	385.17	63.87	61.19	OSN	Book	U
60033	425	370.00	396.48	63.70	59.44	PJC		U
60011	425	370.00	386.12	63.70	61.04	BCB		U
60032	425	372.00	387.67	63.35	60.79	TI	April 55	U
60009	425	372.00	385.50	63.35	61.14	TI	March 55	U
60032	425	373.00	403.65	63.18	58.39	PJC		U
60009	425	373.50	384.47	63.10	61.30	TI	April 55	U
60022	425	374.00	393.88	63.02	59.83	BCB		U
60032	425	375.00	387.63	62.85	60.80	PJC		U
60032	425	380.00	397.47	62.02	59.30	BCB		U
60008	430	382.00	422.50	61.70	55.78	TI	November 54	U
60032	425	384.00	389.33	61.38	60.53	PJC		U
60011	425	389.50	400.23	60.51	58.89	TI	September 53	U
60017	425	392.00	402.42	60.12	58.57	OSN	Book	U
60017	425	401.00	436.00	58.77	54.06	TI	November 52	U
60006	425	412.00	425.48	57.20	55.39	TI	November 52	U
60017	207	363.00	363.00	64.93	64.93	TI	November 51	U
60017	207	365.00	365.00	64.57	64.57	TI	November 51	D

KEY:
RM – Railway Magazine
TI – Trains Illustrated
CJA – Publications by C J Allen
OSN – Publications by O S Nock
PTJ – Passenger Train Journal
PJC – Recorded by the Author
BCB – Recorded by Canon B C Bailey
*A3

APPENDIX G
STOKE BANK; THE BEST PUBLISHED PERFORMANCES
Down: Tallington-Stoke

(In ascending order over 15.27 miles) / (In ascending order over last 3 miles)

Engine (BR No)	Load (Tons)	Time (Mins)	Average speed	Speed Last 3 miles	Train	Engine (BR No)	Load (Tons)	Speed Last 3 miles	Train
60014	235	10.82	84.70	78.26	SJ	60007	295	82.44	Spl
60017	290	10.90	84.06	78.83	Tal	60103	147	81.82	Spl**
60014	230	11.10	82.54	78.26	SJ	60028	330	81.20	Ord
60014	270	11.10	82.54	76.06	SJ	60008	295	80.00	WRL
60103	147	11.12	82.42	81.82	Spl**	60022	290	80.00	Spl
60014	230	11.20	81.80	76.06	SJ	60017	290	78.83	Tal
60017	230	11.20	81.80	77.14	SJ	60012	290	78.83	WRL
60015	230	11.23	81.56	77.70	SJ	60022	415	78.83	Ord
60014	235	11.23	81.56	77.00	SJ	60014	235	78.26	SJ
60011	325	11.32	80.96	75.52	C	60014	230	78.26	SJ
60008	295	11.34	80.79	80.00	WRL	60015	230	77.70	SJ
60012	290	11.36	80.65	78.83	WRL	60017	230	77.14	SJ
60012	325	11.42	80.25	73.47	C	60014	235	77.00	SJ
60017	230	11.47	79.90	76.06	SJ	60014	270	76.06	SJ
60007	295	11.48	79.79	82.44	Spl	60014	230	76.06	SJ
60029	290	11.67	78.51	73.97	WRL	60017	230	76.06	SJ
60022	415	11.67	78.51	78.83	Ord	60011	325	75.52	C
60028	330	11.83	77.45	81.20	Ord	60096	217	75.52	Spl*
60014	230	11.83	77.43	73.47	SJ	60029	290	73.97	WRL
60016	235	11.95	76.67	72.00	SJ	60012	325	73.47	C
60096	217	12.03	76.14	75.52	Spl*	60014	230	73.47	SJ
60014	410	12.35	74.19	71.05	Spl	60033	425	73.47	ELIZ
60033	425	12.45	73.59	73.47	ELIZ	60016	235	72.00	SJ
60007	295	12.82	71.47	66.67	WRL	60014	410	71.05	Spl
60028	325	13.38	68.46	66.26	Ord	60007	295	66.67	WRL
60022	490	13.60	67.37	62.43	Ord	60028	325	66.26	Ord
60104	395	14.15	64.75	61.02	Ord**	60022	490	62.43	Ord
60033	425	14.17	64.66	57.14	ELIZ	60104	395	61.02	Ord**
60012	425	14.45	63.40	58.06	ELIZ	60012	425	58.06	ELIZ
60022	290	14.73	62.19	80.00	Spl	60033	425	57.14	ELIZ
60013	425	15.23	60.14	54.55	ELIZ	60013	425	54.55	ELIZ
60033	590	15.40	59.49	48.21	Ord	60033	660	54.05	Ord
60033	660	15.63	58.61	54.05	Ord	60007	510	54.05	Spl
60007	510	15.88	57.68	54.05	Spl	60033	590	48.21	Ord
60015	680	18.85	48.60	43.90	Ord	60015	680	43.90	Ord

APPENDIX G
STOKE BANK; THE BEST PUBLISHED PERFORMANCES
UP: Stoke – Werrington Jct

Engine (BR No)	Load (Tons)	Time (Mins)	Average speed	Maximum Speed	Train
60007	310	12.55	98.53	112	Spl (net)
60012	330	12.98	95.25	106	C
60096	217	13.17	93.92	108	Spl*
60017	270	13.17	93.92	113	SJ
60010	325	13.58	91.04	109.5	C
60013	295	13.68	90.37	101	WRL
60030	295	13.78	89.72	94	WRL
60033	425	13.92	88.86	100	Eliz'n
60103	207	14.10	87.70	100	Spl**
60014	230	14.12	87.60	95	SJ
60014	425	14.22	86.98	97.5	Spl
60017	230	14.30	86.48	95.5	SJ
60027	380	14.33	86.29	98	#Eliz
60017	230	14.37	86.07	98	SJ
60033	315	14.50	85.28	100	Spl
60007	310	14.55	84.99	103.5	Spl
60015	230	14.58	84.80	X	SJ
60014	230	14.60	84.70	90	SJ
60015	235	14.60	84.70	90	SJ
60015	230	14.62	84.60	90	SJ
6005	270	14.67	84.31	90	WRL
60015	230	14.78	83.65	93.5	SJ
60014	230	14.95	82.72	90	SJ

SJ The Silver Jubilee
C The Coronation
WRL The West Riding Limited
ELIZ The Elizabethan
Spl Special or test run
Ord Ordinary service train
*A3
** A1
# Net time
X None given

APPENDIX H
TYPICAL EXAMPLES OF DAILY RUNNING: ARRIVAL TIMES AT NEWCASTLE
1. CORONATION
ARRIVAL TIMES AT NEWCASTLE FOR FEBRUARY TO APRIL 1939

DATE 1939 Schedule	ENGINE No	Up 19.57	ENGINE No	Down 18.30	
Feb 1st	4485	19.57	4490	18.30	Dr Beach K + up, Dr Coates GHD down
2	4490	19.55	4485	18.29	4476 on up at Grantham, arr 11 late
3	4902	19.55	4490	18.28	
6	4485	19.57	[4902]	18.29	Dr Beach K+ up, Dr Ferguson GHD down
7	4900	19.56	4485	18.29	
8	4485	19.56	4900	18.29	
9	4900	19.55	4485	18.28	
10	4485	19.56	4900	18.29	
13	4485	19.57	[4900]	18.26	Dr Samwells K+ down, Dr Hannah GHD down
14	[4900]	19.55	4485	18.28	
15	4485	19.56	4900	18.27	
16	[4900]	19.55	[4485]	18.27	
17	[4485]	19.56	[4900]	18.27	
20	4497	20.03	4493	18.26	Dr Peachey K+ up, Dr Moreton GHD down
21	4493	19.55	4497	18.29	
22	4497	20.03	4493	18.27	
23	4493	20.01	4497	18.27	
24	4497	20.00	4493	18.27	
27	4485	20.02	4498	18.30	Dr Ovenden K+ up, Dr Hutchinson GHD down
28	4498	19.54	4485	18.27	
March 1st	4485	20.01	4498	18.30	
2	4498	19.57	4485	18.29	
3	4485	19.55	4498	18.28	
6	4497	19.55	4493	18.26	Dr Taylor K+ up, Dr Nicholson GHD down
7	4493	20.11	4497	18.27	
8	4497	19.57	4493	18.26	
9	4493	19.55	4497	18.26	
10	4497	19.52	4493	18.26	
13	4497	19.57	4902	18.29	2747 on up at Doncaster
14	2509	19.57	4497	18.29	Dr Burfoot K+ down, Dr Silson GHD up
15	4497	19.57	2509	18.28	
16	3509	19.59	4497	18.27	
17	4497	20.01	2509	18.27	
20	4497	20.07	4488	18.30	Dr Nash K+ up, Dr Coates GHD down
21	4488	19.57	4497	18.27	
22	4497	19.55	4491	18.27	2595 on up at Newcastle
23	4493	19.56	4497	18.28	
24	4497	19.55	2205	18.54	4493 off up at Berwick, 2507 on up at Newcastle
27	4497	19.56	4484	18.28	Dr Hardiman K+ up, Dr Ferguson GHD down
28	4484	19.58	4497	18.29	
29	4497	19.58	4484	18.27	
30	4484	19.54	4497	18.27	
31	4497	19.55	4484	18.24	
April 3rd	4497	19.56	4492	18.26	Dr Auger K+ up, Dr Hannah GHD down
4	4492	19.55	4497	18.25	
5	4497	19.56	4492	18.26	[Easter]
11	4497	19.54	4489	18.25	Dr Sheen K+up, Dr Moreton GHD down
12	4489	19.57	4497	18.25	
13	4497	19.57	4489	18.26	
14	4489	19.58	4497	18.28	
17	4498	19.54	4497	18.25	Dr Ellis K+ up, Dr Hutchinson GHD down
18	4497	19.54	4498	18.25	
19	4498	19.54	4497	18.26	
20	4497	19.55	4467	18.28	
21	4467	19.54	4497	18.25	
24	4497	19.54	4485	18.28	Dr Giddens K+ up, Dr Nicholson GHD down
25	4485	19.54	4497	18.28	
26	4497	19.54	4485	18.29	
27	4485	19.55	4497	18.28	
28	4497	19.54	4485	18.28	[37th consecutive run by 4497]

2. FLYING SCOTSMAN
ARRIVAL TIMES AT NEWCASTLE FOR APRIL/MAY 1939

DATE 1939	Up train ENGINE off No	Up train ENGINE on No	Arrival	Down train ENGINE off No	Down train ENGINE on No	Arrival
Schedule			12.22			14.49
April 1st	2200:2507	1792:2167	12.19:12.40	2511	2598	14.48
3	4490	4901	12.21	4463	4490:211	14.48
4	4466	1792:4484	12.14	2511	2747	15.00
5	2200:734	4901	12.24	4463	4490	14.51
6	2576	4484	12.31	2511	729:736	15.07
8*	2512	2512	12.25	2507	4488	14.56
10	9416:4497	2554	12.41	2509	4497	14.52
11		Unknown	12.20	2581	4490	14.50
12	4463	4902	12.17	4465		14.52
13	4469	2512	12.19	2511		14.53
14	2505	4900	12.24	4465		14.50
15*	4495:211	4495		2511	4487	14.54
17		4465	12.23	4462		14.51
18	4484	10000	12.18		4488	14.53
19		4484	12.20	4462		14.49
20		10000	12.20	4463	4488	14.47
21	4466	4469	12.21			14.55
22	2575	4492	12.21	4463	4488	14.49
24	4491	4902	12.19	4469	4491:232	14.54
25	2576	10000	12.22		4491	14.49
26	2596	2509	12.23	4469	4491	14.50
27			12.20		4491	14.45
28	4901		12.19		4491	14.58
29	4903	4489	12.20	4463	4491	14.52
Nonstop wkg starts Schedule	Up train ENGINE		Arrival 12.19	Down train ENGINE		Arrival 14.36
May 1st	4487		12.14	4498		14.34
2	4498		12.15	4487		14.34
3	4487		12.18	4498		14.34
4	4498		12.17	4487		14.33
5	4487		12.16	4498		14.33
6*	4498		12.15	4487		14.32
8	4487		12.18	4497		14.44
9	4497		12.19	4483		14.34
10	4483		12.18	4497		14.33
11	4465		12.17	4492		14.35
12	4492		12.17	4465		14.55
13*	4465		12.17	4492		14.34
15	4482		12.18	4484		14.34
16	4484		12.16	4482		14.33
17	4482		12.18	4484		14.36
18	4484		12.16	4482	2576 on	14.48
19	4482		12.18	4484		14.33
20*	4484		12.17	4482		14.38
22	4484		12.17	4482		14.35
23	4482		12.23	4484		14.40
24	4484		12.22	4482		14.35
25	4482		12.17	4484		14.34
26	4484		12.17	4482		14.38
27*	4482		12.18	4484		14.38
29	4482		12.15	4489		14.32
30	4489		12.18	4482		14.44
31	4482		12.15	4489		14.34